The Aryeh Kaplan Anthology II.

The
Aryeh Kaplan

Published by

ncsy

ORTHODOX UNION · תורה · ומצוות · U

Anthology II.

*Illuminating expositions
on Jewish thought and practice
by a revered teacher*

THE ARYEH KAPLAN ANTHOLOGY VOL. II

© *Copyright 1974, 1975, 1976, 1982, 1984, 1986, 1991, 1994, 1995, 1997, 1998, 2012*
by National Conference of Synagogue Youth /
Union of Orthodox Jewish Congregations of America
333 Seventh Avenue / New York, N.Y. 10001 / (212) 563-4000

Published and Distributed by
MESORAH PUBLICATIONS, Ltd.
313 Regina Avenue / Rahway, N.J. 07065

Distributed in Europe by
LEHMANNS
Unit E, Viking Business Park
Rolling Mill Road
Jarrow, Tyne & Wear NE32 3DP
England

Distributed in Australia & New Zealand by
GOLDS WORLD OF JUDAICA
3-13 William Street
Balaclava, Melbourne 3183
Victoria Australia

Distributed in Israel by
SIFRIATI / A. GITLER _ BOOKS
POB 2351
Bnei Brak 51122

Distributed in South Africa by
KOLLEL BOOKSHOP
Northfield Centre 17 Northfield Avenue
Glenhazel 2192, Johannesburg, South Africa

ITEM CODE: KA2H
ISBN 10: 0-89906-868-5
ISBN 13: 978-0-89906-868-8

Printed In The United States Of America
Custom bound by Sefercraft, Inc., Rahway, NJ

Contents

JERUSALEM THE EYE OF THE UNIVERSE

ARYEH KAPLAN

Abba Issi said in the name of Samuel the Lesser:
The world is like a human eyeball.
The white of the eye
  is the ocean surrounding the world,
 The iris is this continent,
The pupil is Jerusalem,
And the image in the pupil is the Holy Temple.

Derech Eretz Zuta 9.

"Jerusalem: Eye of the Universe"

Preface

Rabbi Nachman said, "Wherever I go, I go to Jerusalem." And so it is for every Jew. The eternal message of Jerusalem accompanies the Jew every day of his life. He longs for Jerusalem the 'city of peace' to find its complete fulfillment. He mourns for its Temple temporarily removed from its people.

Daily we pray for Jerusalem "the mother of Israel." She is brought to mind when we thank God for our food, in our Sabbath and holy-day observances, and in our prayers. Even when we paint and plaster our homes we leave an empty space to recall Jerusalem.

Under the bridal canopy ashes are placed upon the head of the bridegroom and a glass is broken in solemn remembrance of Jerusalem. When a Jew dies, earth of Jerusalem is placed inside the coffin.

The entire Jewish people concludes the Passover seder and the Yom Kippur service with a unified insistence that the end of our longing for her comfort is nigh by proclaiming "Next year in Jerusalem."

We are in love with Jerusalem. It is this love which causes us to call upon her at every opportunity. We cannot remove her from our thoughts. As the Talmud relates: "Ten measures of beauty descended to this world. Nine were given to Jerusalem and one to the rest of the world."

Clearly, in the Jewish experience, Jerusalem is everywhere. More than a city, Jerusalem is a basic Jewish concept which affects the heart of Jewish life in every age.

The events of 28 Iyar 5727 (June 7, 1967) which marks the reunification of Jerusalem under Jewish rule were historic for Jews all over the world. Jerusalem, the capital of Israel, is a great modern day occurrence.

It is the purpose of this book, however, to go beyond the geography, inhabitants, history and capital that is Jerusalem. The primary goal of this work is to explain why Jerusalem has preoccupied the Jewish conscience through every period of Jewish history; to define Jerusalem the religious concept rather than Jerusalem the city.

Bearing this in mind, it would be unfair to conclude that omissions were made in this treatment of Jerusalem. 'Jerusalem: Eye of the Universe' is a thorough and exhaustive study of a major tenet of our Torah.

Once again we are grateful to the noted scholar, Rabbi Aryeh Kaplan, for gracing the NCSY library of publications with another masterful presentation.

Ramban (Nachmanides) stated in 1268: "The glory of the world is Eretz Yisroel; the glory of Eretz Yisroel is Jerusalem; the glory of Jerusalem is the Holy Temple."

May the glory of the Shechina be restored to the rebuilt Temple speedily, in our day.

"Leshana Haba B'yerushalayim;" Next Year in Jerusalem!

Baruch Taub

Introduction

Two holy days are observed by virtually every Jew: Yom Kippur and Passover, two of the most significant days of the Jewish calendar.

The most dramatic part of the Yom Kippur service occurs at the close of the day, just as the service is about to end. To announce to conclusion of this most sacred day, a long clear blast is sounded on the *Shofar*. The congregation responds, "Next year in Jerusalem!"

At the conclusion of every Jewish wedding ceremony, it is customary for the groom to break a glass.[1] Among Ashkenazic (Northern European) Jews, the custom is to shout *Mazel Tov* at this point. But Sefardic (Southern European) Jews recite the verse, "If I forget you O Jerusalem, let my right hand forget its cunning" (*Psalms* 137:5).

The glass is broken so that even at the happiest moment of their lives, the bride and groom should recall the destruction of Jerusalem. This is in keeping with the next verse, "Let my tongue stick to my palate if I remember you not, if I set not Jerusalem above my greatest joy" (Ibid. 137:6).

Every synagogue in the world is built facing Jerusalem. Since both Europe and the United States are west of Jerusalem, their synagogues, were traditionally built facing east. But in any part of the world, when a synagogue is built, it always faces Jerusalem. Thus, whenever a Jew prays, he faces this Holy City.

But what is the significance of Jerusalem? Why should this one city be so all-important to the Jewish people? What makes it unique?

In the following pages, we shall explore some of these questions and attempt to understand just what Jerusalem is.

A song of steps by David:

I rejoiced when they said,
  "Let us go up to God's House."
Our feet would stand
  Within your gates, O Jerusalem.
Jerusalem is built
  Like a city that is bound together.
For it is there that the tribes ascend
  The tribes of God
    A testimony to Israel
  To praise the name of God.
For it is there that thrones of justice are set,
  Thrones of the house of David.
Seek peace for Jerusalem
  May those who love you prosper.
Peace be within you ramparts,
  Prosperity in your palaces.
For the sake of my brothers and friends
  I say, "Peace be within you."
For the sake of the House of the Lord our God,
  I will seek your good.

Psalm 122.

1. Focus of A People

Imagine yourself in Jerusalem two thousand years ago. It is the festival of Passover, and Jews from all over the world are coming to celebrate the holy season. They come from every direction, first by hundreds, then by thousands, and finally by hundreds of thousands. When the festival arrives, a good portion of the entire Jewish population is concentrated in this one city. As far as the eye can see, the mountain slopes are covered with tents, where people will roast their Pascal Lamb, which in the time of the Temple was the focal point of the Passover service.

As the Torah prescribes, the Pascal Lamb can be prepared only in one place: "You shall sacrifice the Passover offering to the Lord your God . . . in the place that God shall choose to make His Name dwell there" (Deuteronomy 16:2). The Torah states that God would choose a place, and that it would be the only place in the world where such an offering could be made. And what was true of the Passover offering was true of many other important aspects of Jewish life. According to the rule set down by the Torah, these rituals could be observed only in "the place that God would choose."[1] This "place" was Jerusalem.

For almost a thousand years, from the time that it was dedicated by King David until it was destroyed by the Romans, Jerusalem was the focal point of the Jewish people.[2] There were certain things that could only be accomplished in Jerusalem; no matter where a Jew lived, he would have to go to this holy city to do these things. Since there were so many rituals that could be performed only in Jerusalem, our sages teach us that "Jerusalem is more holy than the rest of the Land of Israel."[3]

Among the most dramatic of these observances were the three annual pilgrimages. There are three festivals, Succot, Passover, and Shavuot, during which, in the days of the Temple, the Torah required every Jew who was able to make a pilgrimage to "the place chosen by God." The Torah thus states, "Three times a year shall all your males appear before the Lord your God in the place which He shall choose, on the feast of *Matzot* (Passover), on the feast of Shavuot, and on the feast of Succot" (Deuteronomy 16:16).

During these pilgrimages, Jews poured into Jerusalem from all over the world. they renewed friendships and exchanged news. As a result, the Jews were united and molded into a single people.[4] But most important, all this was done within a context of holiness and serving God. The fact that so many people were gathering in worship would reinforce all of them religiously and morally, so much so that in the course of these pilgrimages, no Jew would be suspected of harming another in any way.[5] Thus, Jerusalem united the Jewish people in a context that directed *this* unity toward the unity of God.

This helps us to understand why the "place chosen by God" had to be a city. What is a city? Besides a mere concentration of people, it is a place where civilization grows and develops. The very concentration of people in a city results in an exchange and growth of ideas. It is therefore not coincidence that the growth of civilization in general has historically emanated from its cities. While the farmlands provided food for the body, the cities provided food for the mind and soul. As Rabbi Samson Raphael Hirsch points out the Hebrew word for city, *Ir* (עיר), comes from the same base as the word *Ur* (עור), meaning "to awaken."[6] It is the city that awakens mankind, bringing out his best creative instincts. Indeed, in the Torah we find that the building of cities led to many of the most important developments in civilization.[7]

The focal point of Jewish civilization was to develop a relationship with God; and this too required a city. Jerusalem became the place where Jews from all over the world would gather to exchange ideas and develop a civilization enhancing this relationship. Vital to this process were the Temple and the many teachers of Torah who lived in Jerusalem, which will be discussed in a further chapter. But in general, it was Jerusalem that was *the* city — the "awakener" — arousing and motivating the Jew toward his mission. It is not very surprising that our sages teach that Jerusalem is the highest realization of the concept of the City.[8]

This is seen very explicitly also with respect to the "Second Tithe" (*Maaser Sheni*). There were a number of tithes from all crops grown in the Holy Land, that had to be given as a kind of income tax to support the Priests (*Cohanim*) and Levites, who served as religious leaders and teachers. One-tenth of all produce grown in the Holy Land was the tithe given to the Levites, while a smaller portion, known as *Terumah*, was given to the Cohen-Priest.

In addition, there was the Second Tithe.[9] This was not given away; instead, the owner himself had either to eat it in Jerusalem, or redeem it and spend the money for food in Jerusalem. Here, the Torah itself provides a reason: "You shall eat before the Lord your God in the place that He shall choose for His Name to dwell, the tithe of your corn, wine and oil . . . that you may learn always to fear the Lord your God" (Deuteronomy 14:23).

Instead of giving this tithe to the Priest and Levite, the owner himself would become a "Priest and Levite" while living off this tithe in Jerusalem.[10] He would have to take time off from his usual occupation, purify himself in the prescribed manner, and remain in Jerusalem until the tithe was consumed. If he could not go himself, he would send his children to Jerusalem to live off the tithe. In this manner, either he or his children would be exposed to the atmosphere of Jerusalem, to the worship and intellectual ferment that filled the air; and they would be able to grow and develop in the ways of the Torah. In this manner the ideal would be fulfilled, wherein the entire Jewish people would become "a kingdom of priests and a holy nation" (Exodus 19:6). The system of the "Second Tithe" insured that every Jew would spend at least a part of the year as a resident of Jerusalem, and this would be a period of spiritual regeneration for all members of the Jewish people."[11]

There were many other observances that could be kept only in the "place chosen by God," that is, in Jerusalem. There was a tithe of all livestock that had to be eaten in the Holy City.[12] The First Fruits had to be brought to the "place that God will choose," involving a meaningful ceremony.[13] These practices served the important purpose of causing each and every Jew to make regular visits to Jerusalem, thus experiencing the spiritual renewal and unifying influence associated with this city.

Most of these practices affected only Jews living in the Holy Land. There were other commandments, however, that affected Jews wherever they lived. These involved the system of sacrifices. In the Torah, particularly at the beginning of Leviticus, a number of sacrifices are prescribed. Some can be brought as a free will offering, but the most common reason for the offering of a sacrifice was the atonement of a sin.

According to the Ramban (Nachmanides), the primary purpose of the sacrifice was that by being involved in the slaughter of an animal, the person bringing it would also experience vicarious death. When the Cohen-priest slaughtered the animal and burned it on the altar, the person bringing it would feel as though he himself had been killed and burned for having gone against the word of God.[14] Furthermore, God gave man the power of intellect so that he would be able to perfect himself. When a person sins, it is as if he has rejected his God-given intellect. Since the main thing distinguishing man from the animals is his intellect, when a person sins he is actually identifying with the animals. For this reason, an animal must be sacrificed.[15]

On a deeper level, man consists of two elements, the animal and the divine; and these two elements are in constant conflict with each other.[16] While the divine in man pulls him toward the spiritual, the animal in him draws him toward the physical and the mundane. When a person sins, he must therefore bring an animal as a sacrifice. By being an offering to God, the animal itself is elevated; at the same time, the animal in man, which can identify with this animal being sacrificed, is also elevated. The animal in man, which caused him to sin, is then brought back under the subjugation of the divine.[17]

All of these reasons merely touch the surface of the concept of sacrifices, which involves some of the deepest ideas of Judaism. It is obvious that the entire sacrificial system would appear brutal and barbaric unless administered in an almost perfect religious atmosphere. Only a nation of the highest moral and spiritual caliber could be worthy of it. Therefore, because of the moral laxity and spiritual degeneration of the Jewish people, the sacrificial system was eventually abolished.[18]

Sacrifice could be offered only in one place, the Holy Temple (*Bet HaMikdosh*) in Jerusalem. This is explicitly prescribed in the Torah: "God shall choose a place for His Name to dwell; there shall you bring your offerings and sacrifices, your tithes and gifts" (Deuteronomy 12:11). Ever since the Temple was built in Jerusalem, in no other place in the world can sacrifices be offered.

It is considered a most serious sin to offer a sacrifice outside the Jerusalem Temple.[19] Here again, the reason is that it must be done in a place of the utmost holiness, so that the sacrificial system will not degenerate into something barbaric and brutal. The author of the *Sefer HaChinuch* writes that killing an animal wantonly, if not done for food or in the proper worship of God in the proper place, is an act of murder.[20] In this manner, the sacrificial system actually taught us to respect all life, even that of an animal. The severest penalties were invoked against a person who killed an animal as a sacrifice, not in a place of holiness and according to the prescribed law.

There was therefore a commandment that a person bringing a sacrifice must be actively involved in bringing it to the Temple in Jerusalem, as the Torah states, "You shall take the holy things that you have and your vow-offerings, and go to the place that God will choose" (Deuteronomy 12:26).[21] Beyond this, it was important that every individual be physically present to place his hands on his sacrifice before it was offered. One could send his sacrifice to Jerusalem through an agent or messenger, but the latter could not perform the ritual of laying the hands on the offering. The sacrifice might be valid without this laying of hands, but the atonement was not complete.[22]

The actual offering of the sacrifice, of course, could be done only by a Cohen-Priest.

Thus, whenever a person committed a sin requiring a sacrifice, he was virtually compelled to make a pilgrimage to Jerusalem to seek atonement. There was a particular significance in the fact that one had to make this pilgrimage. In sinning, the person demonstrated that his relationship to God was not perfect and complete; therefore, he would have to visit Jerusalem to strengthen this relationship. Only in Jerusalem could he once again become spiritually whole, renewing his commitment so as to avoid future sin.

The Temple was destroyed by the Romans in the year 68 C.E. and since then, sacrifices are no longer offered. People sin so often today that if they had to bring a sacrifice for each offense, everyone would be bringing an offering daily. In the *Neillah* service on Yom Kippur, we say, "there is no end of the offerings required of us, countless would be our guilt sacrifices." As mentioned earlier, this is actually one reason why the sacrificial system had to be abolished. Today we make up for the lack of sacrifices with prayer and Torah study, as the prophet said, "We shall render for bullocks the offerings of our lips" (Hosea 14:3).[23]

From all this we learn a most important lesson. The fact that a single city was central to Judaism is not an accident. In many places, the Torah mentions such a central city — the "place that God will choose" — and mandates many practices that will obligate the Jew to make periodic pilgrimages to this place. God knew that if the Jewish people were to be molded into a people worthy of fulfilling their mission, they would have to have such a center as its focus.

Although most of these practices are no longer observed, Jerusalem still retains its status as a focal point of Judaism. God Himself determined that Jerusalem would be the holy city; and something so prescribed by God cannot be retracted. Thus, the status of Jerusalem as a holy city exists even to this day.[24] God considers it necessary that such a focal point exist even today. Jerusalem still serves as a focus of the Jewish people, as well as a central point of their mission.

2. The Temple

If Jerusalem was the focal point of the Land of Israel, it was the Temple (*Bet HaMikdash*) that was the focal point of Jerusalem. The first Temple was built by King Solomon. It stood for 410 years until it was destroyed by Nebuchadnezzar and the Babylonians. Seventy years later, the second Temple was built by Ezra. According to tradition, it stood for 420 years, until it was razed by the Roman legions under Titus.[1]

Many people think of the Jerusalem Temple as being some kind of synagogue, but it was actually a unique structure. Shortly after the Exodus from Egypt, God commanded the Israelites to build a Tabernacle (*Mishkan*) in the desert.[2] God said, "They shall make for Me a sanctuary, and I will dwell inside them" (Exodus 25:8). The commentaries note that the verse does not say, "I will dwell inside it," but rather, "inside them." Through this Tabernacle God's presence would dwell in the heart of each and every Jew.[3]

One can obtain an idea of the importance of the Tabernacle from the fact that almost the entire second half of the Book of Exodus is devoted to its description and building. To some extent, we can understand its significance from the teaching that this Tabernacle was meant to be a microcosm of all creation.[4] As such it was meant to teach man that he has a responsibility to elevate and sanctify all creation. The Tabernacle represented man's partnership with God in bringing the world toward its final goal; thus, in a sense, the building of the Tabernacle paralleled God's own act of Creation.

The Tabernacle was a most remarkable building, all the more so since it was probably the world's first prefabricated structure. Although it was rather large, some 20 feet high, 24

24 □ *Jerusalem*

feet wide, and 64 feet long, the entire structure could be taken apart and transported from place to place. The Tabernacle thus accompanied the Israelites throughout their period of wandering in the desert. Even after they entered the Holy Land, it was occasionally moved from place to place. According to Biblical tradition, it stood in Gilgal for 14 years, in Shiloh for 369 years, and eventually in Nob and then in Gibeon for a total of 57 years.[6]

Besides the general commandment to build a sanctuary, there was also a commandment that a permanent Temple be built, as the Torah states, "You shall seek [God's] habitation" (Deuteronomy 12:5).[7] This could not be accomplished until after the Israelites had occupied the Promised Land, appointed a king, and attained a state of peace with the neighboring lands. The Torah thus continues, "When you cross the Jordan, dwelling in the land which the Lord your God gives you to inherit, and He gives you rest from all your enemies round about so that you dwell in safety; then there shall be the place which the Lord your God will choose to make His Name dwell there" (Deuteronomy 12:10, 11). Such peace was not attained until the time of David and Solomon; therefore, only then could the place be chosen and the Temple built.[8]

One of the important features of the Temple was the Great Altar (*Mizbeach*) upon which all sacrifices were offered. As discussed earlier, this Altar was the only place in the world where a sacrifice could be offered to God.

It is interesting to note that to this very day, a central platform, called a *Bimah* or *Almemar*, is built in the synagogue. On this platform the Torah is read. This platform parallels the Great Altar, which was located in the center of the Jerusalem Temple. On the festival of Succot, we march around this platform, just as people once marched around the Great Altar of the Temple.[9]

The Temple also had an inner chamber called the *Hechal*, containing three main features. The best known of these was the golden Menorah, a huge seven branched candelabrum, taller than a man. Six of the seven lamps on this Menorah were kindled each evening, while the middle lamp burned constantly as the Eternal Light.[10] This was the Menorah that played a key role in the miracle of Chanukah during the time of the Second Temple.

Besides the Menorah, this inner chamber contained a golden altar for incense and a special table upon which the show-bread was placed.[11]

Past this chamber was the Holy of Holies, the innermost chamber and the focal point of the Temple. So great was the holiness of this chamber that no person was ever allowed to enter it, other than the High Priest (*Cohen Gadol*) and only on Yom Kippur. This was part of a most impressive service. Jews from all over the world would gather in Jerusalem to see the High Priest emerge in peace after having worshiped in this inner sanctuary.[12] Even today, one of the most dramatic portions of the Yom Kippur service is the portion in the Mussaf which recounts how the High Priest would enter the Holy of Holies.

In the center of the Holy of Holies stood the Ark of the Covenant, which was made of wood covered with gold. On this Ark was a cover of pure gold, and attached to this cover were the two gold Cherubim. The entire structure of the Ark, its cover and the Cherubim are described in detail in the Torah, and they were made under the personal supervision of Moses.[13]

But even more important was the Ark's contents. For in it were the objects that were most sacred to Judaism: the two Tablets inscribed with the Ten Commandments, which God had given to Moses; and the original Torah that Moses himself had written as dictated by God.[14]

When King Solomon built the Temple, he constructed a deep labyrinth going under the Temple Mount, where the holy vessels could be hidden in case of danger. Foreseeing that Jerusalem would be threatened, King Josiah commanded that the Ark be concealed in this labyrinth, sealing it off so that it would not be discovered by the enemy. Thus, even to this day, the Ark is hidden somewhere under the Temple Mount in Jerusalem.[15]

This is a most important point. The single most significant event in Jewish history was the revelation at Sinai, when God

Himself proclaimed the Ten Commandments. It was at this time that God made the covenant establishing His unique relationship with His people Israel. In some places, these Tablets are known as "the Tablets of the covenant," indicating that they contain the words of the covenant made at Sinai.[16] Elsewhere, they are called "the Tablets of testimony," since they are a permanent, tangible testimony to the existence of this covenant.[17] The Tablets represent the physical reality of the covenant, the special relationship between God and the Jewish people.

No less central to Judaism is the Torah as a whole. In general, a scroll of the Torah is the most sacred object of the Jew. If this is true of *any* Torah scroll, how much more so is it true of the original Torah, written by Moses at the expressed word of God! This unique Torah was written by Moses shortly before he died, and he commanded that it be placed in the Ark, next to the Tablets: "Take this book of the Torah, and put it in the side of the Ark of the covenant of the Lord your God, that it may be there as a witness for you (Deuteronomy 31:24). Moses' Torah was thus placed in the Ark, right next to the Tablets of the covenant. As Rambam (Maimonides) writes, this is the "witness" to all mankind of the special relationship and responsibility that we have to God.[18]

Even though the Ark, the Tablets and the original Torah were not on display, every Jew coming to Jerusalem knew that he was in close proximity to these most sacred objects.[19] He might meditate on the covenant, mentally going back to the revelation at Sinai, contemplating all the miracles that accompanied the giving of the Torah.

Even today, it is possible to experience this feeling of proximity. These most sacred objects still remain hidden in Jerusalem, buried deep in a vault under the Temple Mount. Here they will remain until the time when we are worthy to uncover them once again. And even though we may not actually be aware of these sacred objects, the very fact of their proximity is sure to make a most profound impression on our souls.

One remnant of the Temple still stands today. This is the Western Wall of the Temple Mount, the *Kotel Maaravi*. To this day, it is considered one of the most sacred spots in the world; it is the focus of pilgrimage for Jews from all over. Our sages teach us that even though the Temple was destroyed, the Divine Presence never left the Western Wall.[20] The Western Wall is special, since it was the wall that was closest to the Holy of Holies.

3. The Sanhedrin

"Out of Zion shall go forth the Torah, and the Word of God from Jerusalem" (Isaiah 2:3). Jerusalem was more than a place where people gathered; it was also a place from which teaching emanated. As the prophet so aptly puts it, Zion and Jerusalem were the main places where the Torah was taught, guiding Jews wherever they might live. It is the Torah that makes the Jew what he is; it directs the life of the entire Jewish nation. Jerusalem was the center of the interpretation and teaching of the Torah.[1]

Built into the outer north wall of the Temple, not far from the Great Altar, was a room known as the Chamber of Cut Stone. In this chamber the great Sanhedrin sat, teaching and judging all Israel.[2]

The establishment of this Sanhedrin as well as other judicial bodies, to interpret and decide questions of Torah law, was decreed by the Torah: "Judges and officers shall you appoint in all your gates, that God will give you" (Deuteronomy 16:18). The primary obligation implied by this commandment was to set up and support such a duly ordained Sanhedrin.[3] This Sanhedrin consisted of seventy one men, chosen from the greatest sages of Israel. This is learned from God's commandment to Moses, "Gather to Me seventy elders of Israel. . . and bring them to the Tent of Meeting, that they may stand there with you" (Numbers 11:16). According to tradition, this was the first Sanhedrin, and since Moses himself must be counted as its head, it is obvious that it consisted of seventy-one members.[4]

The "Tent of Meeting" *(Ohel Moed)* in this verse refers to the Tabernacle in the desert, which, as discussed in the previous

chapter, had its counterpart in the Holy Temple in Jerusalem.[5] Thus, when God told Moses to "bring them to the Tent of Meeting," this is an allusion that the Sanhedrin must convene in close proximity to the Temple. There are numerous other allusions teaching that the Sanhedrin must be near the Great Altar.[6]

Every member of the Sanhedrin had to be distinguished in wisdom, humility, fear of God, disdain for monetary gain, a passion for truth, and love for his fellow man, as well as outstanding expertise in all areas of Torah scholarship. Regarding their selection, the Torah thus states, "You shall search from among all the people, able men, who fear God, men of truth, disdaining unjust gain, and you shall place [these men] over [the people]" (Exodus 18:21). Moses, too, told the people, "Take from each of your tribes men who are wise, understanding and full of knowledge, and I will make them leaders over you" (Deuteronomy 1:13).[7]

The Sanhedrin was in existence from the time of Moses until it was disbanded after the destruction of Jerusalem by the Romans.[8] As long as the Sanhedrin convened, it functioned as both the supreme court and the central legislative body for all Israel. As a supreme court, it was the final authority in all matters of Torah law; any case that could not be judged adequately by a lower court was brought to it.[9] As a legislature, the Sanhedrin had the authority to enact religious laws that would be binding on all Israel. This authority was given to it by the Torah itself, as it is written, "According to the law that they teach you . . . you shall do" (Deuteronomy 17:11). Any legislation enacted by the Sanhedrin is called a Rabbinical Law, as distinguished from a Torah Law.[10]

The most important function of the Sanhedrin, however, was the preservation, interpretation, and teaching of the Oral Torah.[11]

The Torah that God gave Moses actually consisted of two parts, the written and the oral. The Written Torah was the original Torah scroll written by Moses, which was copied and recopied with the greatest accuracy, insuring that the Torah we read today is identical with that transmitted by God. The Oral Torah consisted of all the explanations and interpretations surrounding the Written Torah, as well as many laws given to Moses by God which were never written down. Since the Written Torah is sometimes ambiguous, and often omits important details, it can be kept adequately only through the Oral Tradition.

There are numerous cases where the Torah refers to details not included in the written text, implying that there was an oral tradition. For example, when the Torah speaks of kosher ritual slaughter, it states, "You shall slaughter your cattle . . . as I have commanded you" (Deuteronomy 12:21), alluding to an oral commandment.[12] Similarly, the Torah speaks of such commandments as the Sabbath, Tefillin, and Tzitzith, and since no details are supplied, it must be assumed that they are included in the Oral Torah.[13]

The need for such an Oral Torah should be obvious. The Torah was not meant to be merely a book, lying on the shelf. It was intended to be the main motivating force in the daily lives of an entire people. As such it could only be transmitted by word of mouth, entrusted to a body of elders who would interpret it according to the needs of the time. This Oral Torah was handed down from teacher to disciple for almost fifteen hundred years, from the time of Moses until after the Romans destroyed Jerusalem. During this entire period, the tradition was preserved by the Sanhedrin. Only after the Sanhedrin was exiled and finally disbanded was the Oral Torah written down to form the Talmud and Midrash.

In many respects, the Oral Law is seen as being even more important than its written counterpart. In one place, the Talmud teaches that the Oral Torah is more dear to God than the Written Torah.[14] It is, furthermore, taught that the main covenant God made with Israel was based on the Oral, not the Written Torah.[15] While the Tablets and the written scroll testified to the existence of the covenant, it was the Oral Torah that taught how to live by it.

Jerusalem was the center of both parts of the Torah, the Written and the Oral. As discussed earlier, both the Tablets and the original Torah scroll written by Moses were kept in the Ark, in the Holy of Holies. And the Oral Torah was entrusted to the Sanhedrin, only a short distance away.[16]

As in the case of the Temple itself, the Torah prescribes that the Sanhedrin be located in "the place chosen by God." The Torah states, "When there arises a matter too hard for you to judge . . . within your gates, you shall rise and go up to the place that the Lord your God shall choose. And you shall go to the priests, the Levites, and the Judge who shall exist in those days, and you shall inquire, and they shall declare to you the word of judgment" (Deuteronomy 17:8, 9). Just as the Temple had to be in the place chosen by God, so did the Sanhedrin.

It is important to note that only from the commandment regarding the Sanhedrin have we an allusion as to where this chosen place would be. In speaking of the Sanhedrin, the Torah states, "you shall. . . go up to the place," indicating that the chosen place would be in one of the highest elevations in the Promised Land.[17] As mentioned earlier, the Sanhedrin had to be in close proximity to the Altar, so this also defined the place of the Temple. Indeed, we find that King David and the Prophet Samuel used this verse when they attempted to determine the place chosen by God.[18]

The fact that the chosen place is determined by the location of the Sanhedrin appears to indicate the primary reason such a place had to exist was for the sake of this body. As discussed earlier, one of the main functions of the Temple was educational — "That you may *learn* always to fear the Lord your God" (Deuteronomy 14:23). But if such education was the goal, the main source of such education indeed was the Sanhedrin, who taught the Torah to all Israel. If unification of the Jewish nation was the goal, then again the Sanhedrin was of central importance. The main unifying force among the Jewish people was the Torah; since a single body — the Sanhedrin — would interpret and teach it, all Jews, no matter where they lived, would keep it in the same manner. Nothing united the Jews more than this, so the Torah says, "There shall be one Torah for you" (Numbers 15:16).[19] Furthermore, even today, over nineteen hundred years after the destruction of the Temple, the influence of the Sanhedrin still plays a dominant role in the religious life of the Jew, no matter where he lives.

The room in which the Sanhedrin convened was called the *Lishkat HaGazit,* the Chamber of Cut Stones. This was a chamber built in the wall of the Temple, half inside the sanctuary and half outside, with doors providing access both to the Temple and to the outside. The place where the Sanhedrin actually convened was outside of the sanctuary area, since the members sat while in judgment, and it is forbidden to sit inside the sanctuary area.[20] If there were no entrance from the outside, people would have to go through the Temple in order to come to the Sanhedrin; and it is forbidden to make use of the Temple to go to someplace outside the sanctuary area.[21]

On the other hand, part of this chamber had to be inside the sanctuary area, since the Sanhedrin judged many things involving the priests and the Temple service, which had to be done within the Temple grounds.[22] Furthermore, questions would often arise in the midst of the divine service, and at such times, it was forbidden for a priest to leave the sanctuary area.[23] Also the requirement that the Sanhedrin be near the Altar meant that there had to be direct access from the Altar to the Sanhedrin.[24]

The reason why this chamber was built into the north wall is not defined, but several points come to mind. The members of the Sanhedrin could not sit with their backs to the Temple, so, when they sat facing the Temple, they faced toward the south. The Talmud teaches that facing in this direction has the potential to inspire wisdom.[25] In a mystical sense, the north is associated with judgment, which is the main task of the Sanhedrin.[26]

The reason why this chamber in particular is said to be built of cut stone is also not clear. Here, however, there is a clear contrast to the Altar, of which the Torah states, "You shall *not* build it of cut stones" (Exodus 20:22). For this reason the stones for the Altar had to be dug up from deep in the ground, or taken from the depths of the sea, where they could not possibly have come in contact with human tools.[27]

The reason for this is that the cutting and shaping of stones is a human activity, based on man's intellectual ability, as distinguished from his animal nature. The Altar, as discussed earlier, was meant to rectify man's animal nature, and therefore had to be built entirely of natural stones.

Furthermore, the introduction of man's intellectual nature into the formation of these stones might sully them with his animal nature as well. If the Altar itself were defiled by man's animal nature, it would not be able to rectify this element in man. In forbidding cut stones, the Torah therefore says, "for your sword has been lifted against it to desecrate it" *(Ibid.)*. The sword represents the subjugation of man's intellect to his animal nature, because in war man makes use of his intellect to satisfy his animal instincts. This is the precise opposite of the function of the Altar, which was meant to subjugate the animal in man to his Divine element. If man's animal nature were allowed to interject, the entire sacrificial system represented by the Altar would become brutal and barbaric. Therefore, the Altar had to be made of stones as created by God, and not as modified by man.[28]

The Sanhedrin, on the other hand, was meant to teach the Torah, thus rectifying man's Divine nature. The stones of the chamber of the Sanhedrin were especially cut so that they would be the product of man's intellect. Here it was specifically demonstrated that there was no fear that man's animal nature, represented by the sword, would interject, because the Torah taught by the Sanhedrin was precisely that which had the power to subjugate man's animal nature. Therefore, unlike the Altar, the hall of the Sanhedrin was made particularly of cut stone.[29]

Since the hall of the Sanhedrin was built of cut stone, we see a sharp contrast between its concept and that of the Altar. While the Altar was directed toward man's animal nature, the Sanhedrin was directed toward his Divine, intellectual nature. While the Altar was meant to rectify the evil in man, the Sanhedrin would enhance the Torah, which was his ultimate good. While the Altar would burn the sacrifice and return it to its natural elements, the Sanhedrin would teach man how to take the world that God created and use it in fulfilling God's purpose.

Still, as mentioned earlier, there had to be direct access from the Altar to the Sanhedrin. Man is a complex being; only between these two ideals could he be totally rectified and elevated. This entire process was centered in one place — Jerusalem.

Another important point is that the Sanhedrin was invested with its full powers only when it sat in this Chamber of Cut Stone. The Torah thus says, "You shall follow the decision that they tell you from the place which God shall choose, and you shall be careful to do like all that they teach you" (Deuteronomy 17:10). The Sanhedrin legally could be convened in any place in the Holy Land; but if it were not in the Chamber of Cut Stone, its authority and powers were severely limited.[30]

It is also important to note that the hall of the Sanhedrin also served as the synagogue on the Temple grounds, where the daily prayer service was held.[31] The commentaries state that this is because worship is most acceptable before God when conducted in a place where the Torah is taught and studied. For this reason, even today, a Yeshiva where people study the Torah is considered a preferred place for worship.[32]

The counterpoint between the Temple and the Sanhedrin may also explain an interesting discussion in the Midrash. The mountain upon which the Temple is built is called Mount Moriah, and there are numerous opinions as to the reason for this name. In the Midrash, two opinions are noted. One states that it indicates awe and fear (*Yirah*); and the other, that it indicates decision and teaching *(Horah).* [33] Fear and awe of God are the main concepts of the Temple itself, as the Torah states, "You shall fear My sanctuary" (Leviticus 19:30, 26:2). Thus, according to one opinion, the main point of Jerusalem was the Temple itself. According to the other opinion, however, the main purpose of this mountain was the teachings and decisions rendered by the Sanhedrin.

The fact that the Sanhedrin was centered in Jerusalem had very important implications for the city itself. It must be remembered that the members of the Sanhedrin were the greatest minds and foremost teachers in the Jewish world. Besides their judicial responsibilities, many members of the Sanhedrin headed important academies, where the Oral Torah was taught and expounded. Disciples by the tens of thousands would flock to Jerusalem to study in its numerous academies, which were the best and most prestigious in the Jewish world. All of this had the effect of making Jerusalem the uncontested intellectual capital of the Jewish people.[34]

A pilgrim coming to Jerusalem would thus be engulfed in a sea of intellectual activity. He could not help but come in contact with the thousands of disciples who filled the streets of Jerusalem; and on occasion, he might even catch a glimpse of the great masters of Torah, the members of the Sanhedrin themselves. A person living in Jerusalem while consuming his Second Tithe would be in such an atmosphere for weeks at a time, and he might even enroll in one of the academies himself. The teachings of the Torah were thus spread throughout the entire Jewish nation, making the Jews a truly holy people, dedicated to God and His teachings.

4. Kings and Prophets

Among other things, Jerusalem was the seat of government of the Jewish nation. In Jerusalem, David established his kingdom; as long as there was a central government in Israel, this was its center.

Obviously, if the nation were to be unified, some sort of central government would be necessary. The head of this government was called a king *(Melech),* even though his powers were severely limited by the Torah. Once the promised land was occupied and inhabited, the Torah commanded the Jews to appoint a king. "When you come to the land that the Lord your God gives you, possessing it and dwelling in it . . . you shall appoint a king over you, whom the Lord your God shall choose" (Deuteronomy 17:14,15). The fact that the Torah says that God must choose the king indicates that he must be chosen with the concurrence of both a prophet and the Sanhedrin.[1]

The power of a Jewish king was far from absolute. Like every other Jew, he was bound by the law of the Torah; in the case of a king, this was emphasized all the more, since the king was required to write his own scroll of the Torah and keep it on his person at all times.[2] In this respect, the government was a constitutional monarchy, with the Torah being its God-given constitution. Similarly, like every other Jew, the king was bound to obey the dictates of the Sanhedrin, so for all practical purposes, he was little more than the chief administrator of the government.[3]

The permanent place "chosen by God" could not be revealed until after a king had been appointed. Furthermore, the site of the Temple, as well as the Holy City surrounding it, had to be dedicated in a special manner, with an involved ceremony. This dedication could only be accomplished when a king, a prophet, and the Sanhedrin were present.[4] Thus, Jerusalem was not chosen to be the Holy City until after David was appointed as king over all Israel. Although it is not explicitly stated, it appears that dedicating this city is the main function of a king; it is actually the only place where the Torah requires the presence of a king.

There was also a tradition that whoever occupied this "place that God would choose," would be the one to initiate the royal line in Israel.[5] In performing the one act where the Torah actually requires a king, this person would define himself as the king mentioned in the Torah. The law then states that this king's children would inherit the kingdom forever, as it is written, "he will prolong the days of his kingdom, him and his children" (Deuteronomy 17:20). The one who becomes king as defined in the Torah therefore sets the royal line for all time. Thus, when David's son Solomon dedicated Jerusalem as the "Chosen Place," the royal line became fixed with the descendants of David forever.[6]

There is a tradition in the Oral Torah that David's royal line would have its seat of government in Jerusalem. It is thus written regarding Jerusalem, "It is there that thrones of justice are set, thrones of the house of David" (Psalms 122:5). The "thrones of justice" refer to the seats of the Sanhedrin, while the "thrones of the house of David" refer to those of the royal line.[7] Besides this, King David himself served as the head of the Sanhedrin in his time; therefore, its headquarters had to be in the same vicinity.[8]

Among the most important leaders and teachers of Israel during the period of the First Temple were the prophets. This was still a formative period for the Jewish people. It was through these prophets that God revealed His will, guiding His people along the path that He had chosen for them. Indeed, the Bible consists of three portions, the Torah, the Prophets, and the Writings, and the last two were composed chiefly by the Prophets of Israel.

The Talmud teaches that most of the prophets lived and taught in Jerusalem.[9] According to a number of traditions, most of their prophecies were pronounced in the Hall of the Sanhedrin.[10]

There were a number of important reasons for this. First, not everyone could be recognized as a prophet. Among other things, for a person to be chosen by God as His prophet, an individual would have to be outstanding in piety and knowledge of the Torah.[11] Such an individual would most likely be found among the members of the Sanhedrin, since these were the greatest saints and sages of Israel. Looking at the record, we find that in many cases, the great prophets themselves served as the heads of the Sanhedrin.[12]

Another reason why the prophets had to be in Jerusalem was that a prophet could be accredited and recognized only by the Sanhedrin.[13] No one could simply declare himself a prophet and have himself accepted as a spokesman of God, since to permit this would open the door to any charlatan or demagogue. Before a person could be accepted as a prophet, he would have to provide some unequivocal sign, the most common being an accurate prediction of the future. The Torah thus prescribes, "Should you ask yourselves, 'How can we know that the word was not spoken by God?' If the prophet speaks in the name of God and his word does not come true, then that word was not granted by God, but the prophet spoke it presumptuously" (Deuteronomy 18:21,22).

From this, we also learn the converse, that the way of testing the authenticity of a prophet is to see if he can accurately predict the future. If a person otherwise deemed worthy of prophecy makes an accurate prediction of the future three times in the presence of the Sanhedrin, then his prophecy is assumed to be true, and he is universally accepted as a prophet.[14] If, however, even the most minor aspect of his prophecy fails to come true, then his prophecy is judged to be completely false.[15] In the case of a false prophet, only the Sanhedrin has the authority to render judgment.[16]

Whenever a prophecy involved all Israel, it was pronounced before the Sanhedrin, since they were the only body that had the power to disseminate a message to the entire nation. Thus, for example, when Moses was sent by God with a message for the Jewish people, he was first sent to the elders of the people, who convened a Sanhedrin to publicize his words.[17]

Apparently, the Sanhedrin kept a record of all prophecy that was meant for posterity. We thus find that the prophet Isaiah was killed before he was able to put his prophecies into writing; this was subsequently accomplished by the Sanhedrin under the leadership of King Hezekiah. Similarly, a number of the smaller prophetic books were written in their final form by the Sanhedrin led by Ezra the Scribe.[18]

The source of all prophetic inspiration was the Temple in Jerusalem, particularly the two Cherubim on the Ark of the Covenant that stood in the Holy of Holies.[19] In describing the Ark, God told Moses, "I will commune with you, and I will speak with you from above the ark-cover from between the two Cherubim, which are on the Ark of testimony" (Exodus 25:22).[20] What was true of Moses was also true of the other prophets, and the main influence of prophecy came through these two Cherubim in the Holy of Holies. There is some evidence that the prophetic experience actually came about through intense meditation on these two Cherubim.[21]

Each of the Cherubim had the form of a child with wings.[22] Although God had generally forbidden the construction of such images He Himself had commanded that these two forms be placed over the Ark.[23] Rather than facing the people, the Cherubim faced each other. This clearly showed that they were not meant to be worshiped, but rather, that they indicated a place where spiritual force was concentrated.[24] The fact that the Cherubim stood on the Ark containing the Tablets and the original Torah scroll proves that these were the source of this spiritual power.

The fact that the Cherubim had the form of winged human beings means that man has the ability to transcend his earthly bonds. Although man is bound to the earth by his mortal body, he can fly with the wings of his soul, soaring through the highest spiritual universes. This concept was embodied in the very shape of the Cherubim, and by meditating on them, a person could indeed fly with his own spiritual wings.

In order to explore this on a somewhat deeper level, we must look at the other important places where the Cherubim are mentioned in the Bible. After Adam and Eve were expelled from the Garden of Eden, the Torah states, "[God] expelled the man, and He placed the Cherubim at the east of the Garden of Eden . . . to guard the way of the Tree of Life" (Genesis 3:24). The "Tree of Life" refers to the most profound spiritual experience; therefore, before one can enter into this experience, he must first encounter the Cherubim.[25] These Cherubim, of course, are a type of angel.

We then find the Cherubim in the vision of Ezekiel, which, according to the commentaries, is a paradigm of the prophetic experience in general.[26] The first thing that Ezekiel sees are the "Living Creatures" *(Chayot)*, which are later identified as being the Cherubim.[27] The prophet reaches the highest levels of the mystical experience, actually transcending the bonds that tie his mind and soul to the physical world. In doing so, he is actually approaching the "Tree of Life," and the first thing that he encounters are its guardians, which are the Cherubim.

The Cherubim on the Ark were meant to parallel the Cherubim on high. Thus, in a sense, the space between these two forms was seen as an opening into the spiritual dimension.[28] In concentrating his thoughts between the Cherubim on the Ark, the prophet was able to pass between the angelic Cherubim, and ascend on the path of the Tree of Life. Conversely, when God's message was sent to the prophet, it followed this same path, first passing through the spiritual Cherubim, and then through those on the Ark. Hence, the space between the Cherubim was the source of all prophetic inspiration.[29]

Jerusalem was therefore the source of both Torah interpretation through the Sanhedrin and revelation through the prophets. It is thus written, "Out of Zion shall come forth the Torah, and the word of God from Jerusalem" (Isaiah 2:3, Micah 4:2). "Out of Zion shall come forth the Torah," refers primarily to the teachings of the Sanhedrin; since the name Zion is specific to the Hall of the Sanhedrin, "the gates marked *(zion)* by Law."[30] "The word of God from Jerusalem," on the other hand, refers to prophetic revelation.

The fact that the prophets and Sanhedrin worked hand in hand was very significant. In many religious societies, there is a strong conflict between the mystic and the teacher of religious law. There is always a danger that the mystic might consider himself above the law, or seek to change and modify it according to his own spiritual experiences. The prophets of Israel, however, were the greatest mystics that the world has ever seen, and yet, they clearly realized that the Torah was the very root of their power. The concept of mysticism and prophecy is included in the framework of the Torah law, and hence there could be no conflict. Furthermore, the prophets always worked very closely with the Sanhedrin; thus, they themselves were interpreters of the Law rather than its antagonists.

5. The Gate of Prayer

All the things we have discussed until now have been historical. The pilgrimages, the Temple, the Sanhedrin, kings and prophets, no longer exist in Jerusalem, although, of course, their influence is strongly felt. But in many ways, Jerusalem is still considered a most important spiritual center for the Jew.

One area where Jerusalem still plays a most important role is that of prayer. All over the world, whenever a Jew stands in prayer, he faces Jerusalem. Every synagogue in the world is built with its ark on the side toward Jerusalem, so that all worshipers pray in that direction. Since both the United States and Europe are west of the Land of Israel, people in these countries always pray facing east.

The fact that prayer should be directed toward Jerusalem was indicated by King Solomon when he built the Temple. Upon dedicating the Temple, he prayed, "May You hearken to the prayer of Your servant, and of Your people Israel, when they pray toward this place" (I Kings 8:30). Over and over in his dedication prayer, King Solomon stressed that prayers should be directed toward Jerusalem so that they would be accepted by God.[1] Later, when the Jews were exiled in Babylon, we find that Daniel faced Jerusalem in his three daily prayers.[2]

One reason for this is that Jacob called Jerusalem, "The gate of heaven" (Genesis 28:17). On a simple level, this means that it is the gate through which prayer ascends on high.[3] In a deeper sense, this also means that it is a gate through which one enters heaven by means of a mystical or prophetic experience, as discussed in the previous chapter. Regarding this it is also written, "This is the gate to God. Let the righteous enter into it" (Psalms 118:20).[4]

Jerusalem was only generally a focus of prayer; more specifically, it was the Holy Temple, and the place of the Ark in the Holy of Holies. A person standing in Jerusalem would face the Temple grounds, no matter where he was located. An individual praying in the Temple itself would face the Holy of Holies, while a person actually praying in the Holy of Holies, would face the Ark, directing himself to the point between the Cherubim.[5]

Here we begin to see a close parallel between prayer and prophecy. Just as the space between the Cherubim was the focus from which prophecy emanated, so it was the focus to which prayer was directed. To some degree, this can be understood in light of what Rabbi Jacob ben Asher writes in his *Tur,* that prayer itself is meant to be a highly mystical experience, where one can attain a level close to that of prophecy.[6] When a person stands in prayer, his mind ascends to the spiritual realm, and he can completely divorce himself from the physical. According to Rabbenu Yonah (Gerondi), this is the meaning of the teaching, "In prayer, one's eyes should be cast downward, while his heart is directed on high."[7]

Although this is a very high level of prayer, it is cited as being realizable in the *Shulchan* Aruch, the accepted Code of Jewish Law.[8] Therefore, when a person stands in prayer, he should attempt to direct his concentration toward the place of the Cherubim in the Holy of Holies, as the prophets did, because this is the path of spiritual ascent. Our sages thus teach us that when a person prays, he should focus his mind on the Holy of Holies.[9] Of course, this does not mean that one's prayers should be directed to the Cherubim, or for that matter, anything else; all prayer must be directed only to God.[10]

Another reason we pray toward Jerusalem involves the close relationship between prayer and sacrifice. The prophet alluded to this relationship when he said, "We will make up for our bullocks with the offering of our lips" (*Hoseah* 14:3).[11] It is thus established that the daily prayer services were ordained to take the place of the regular daily sacrifices.[12] Even today, in many ways, the laws involving prayer are derived from its relationship to the sacrifice, including the rule that it must be recited standing, with the feet together, and with one's head covered, just like a priest offering a sacrifice.[13] For the same reason, when standing in prayer, one must face Jerusalem, the place of sacrifice.[14]

In light of a number of concepts already discussed, it is easy to understand the relationship between prayer and sacrifice. The slaughtering and burning of the animal sacrifice symbolized the subjugation and destruction of the animal in man. When the animal was burned on the altar, it returned to its elements and ascended on high. When a person brought a sacrifice, he was able to meditate on this, nullifying his animal self, and liberating his spirit so that it could commune with God. The soul then returned to its own element, which is the spiritual. Therefore, the bringing of a sacrifice was a highly mystical experience. The Hebrew word for sacrifice, *Korban*, comes from the root *Karav*, meaning "close," since it brought man close to God.[15]

The concept of prayer is very similar to this. When a person stands before God, he becomes a total spiritual being, totally divorced from his animal self. The only difference is that instead of experiencing this through sacrifice, the individual does so through uttering words of prayer.

The final reason we pray toward Jerusalem is that it was the place of the Sanhedrin, and as such, it was the chief location of schools where the Torah was taught. Thus, when we focus our prayers toward Jerusalem, we are also combining them with the merit of the Torah, through which they become more acceptable before God.[16] As mentioned earlier, even when worship services were held in the Temple itself, they were held in the Hall of the Sanhedrin.

Looking through the prayer book, one readily sees that virtually every major part of the service contains some mention of Jerusalem.[17] Besides the fact that we must physically face Jerusalem, it appears that there must also be a mention of Jerusalem in every prayer, whereby the prayer is bound to the Holy City. By mentioning Jerusalem in prayer, we actually help focus the prayer through the "Gate of Heaven."

Even though the Altar, the Cherubim, and the Sanhedrin no

longer stand in Jerusalem, the place retains its special holiness. The holiness of Jerusalem pertains to God's presence, which can never be nullified.[18] For this reason, even today, it is forbidden to enter the place where the Temple originally stood.[19] But in a positive sense, because of its unique history and significance, Jerusalem is still the focal point of all our prayers.

The fact that Jerusalem is the "Gate of Heaven" has another important implication. Just as things can go in through a gate, so can they emerge. Thus, all spiritual sustenance and blessing come only through Jerusalem, as it is written, "God will bless you from Zion" (Psalms 128:5).[20] It is taught that God first sends a blessing to Jerusalem, and from there it flows to the entire world.[21] Today, when the Temple no longer stands, the source of this blessing is the Western Wall.[22]

6. Beginnings

It is significant to note that Jerusalem is never actually mentioned in the Torah, although there are many allusions to it. When the Torah speaks of Jerusalem, it always uses such terms as "the place that God will choose," or "the place that God will choose to make His Name dwell there."[1]

Rambam (Maimonides) states that there are three reasons why the Torah does not explicitly name the place that would be chosen by God. First, if the nations had learned that this place was destined to be the center of the highest religious ideals, they would have occupied it and prevented the Jews from ever controlling it, even as many nations attempt to do today. Second, the tribes in possession of Jerusalem might have destroyed it; or, knowing of its spiritual importance, might have made it a center of idolatry. Third, and possibly most important, each one of the twelve tribes of Israel would have desired to have this city within its borders and under its control, leading to divisiveness and discord. Thus, the Holy City could not be designated until a king was chosen, since a strong central authority could avert these problems.[2]

The actual choosing of Jerusalem also involved its consecration, which, as mentioned earlier, required a king. Until Jerusalem was dedicated in this manner, it could not be considered to have been chosen, so the Torah speaks of its choosing as an event that would occur in the future. The location could not be revealed, since locating, occupying and dedicating the Holy City was a special function of the king, through which the royal line would be chosen for all time. Once David and Solomon had accomplished all this, they became worthy of fathering the royal line, and from then on, a king of Israel could be chosen only from their line.[3]

Actually, this place was chosen long before the time of David and Solomon, and it played a most important role in the lives of all the patriarchs, from Adam to Moses. For the above mentioned reasons, as well as others of a deeper nature, this fact could not be stated explicitly in the Torah. Furthermore, as we shall see, there is evidence that the city was not actually called Jerusalem until after the death of Moses.

The earliest tradition regarding Jerusalem states that Adam was created from the same place where the Great Altar later stood in the Temple, "so that he should be created from the place of his atonement."[4] This is more than a mere legend; Maimonides states that the place of the altar was later selected partially on the basis of this tradition.[5]

If Adam were created out of "dust from the ground," it was very special dust, that of the Altar. As discussed earlier, the concept of the Altar was to allow man to nullify his physical nature and rise above it. Thus, the very physical nature of man — the "dust from the ground" from which he was formed — was taken from the place that would allow him to overcome it and elevate it.

God then brought Adam to the Garden of Eden, but Adam sinned and was ejected. He returned to the place where he had been created, and, attempting to atone for his sin, built an altar on the Temple Mount and offered a sacrifice to God.[6] This altar remained as a permanent shrine where all people could worship God, until it was destroyed by the flood in the time of Noah.[7] Adam remained in Jerusalem, immersing in a spring called Gichon as a further atonement for his sin.[8] There is evidence from tradition that Adam lived in Jerusalem all of his life.

When Cain and Abel brought their offerings to God, they did so on this altar built by Adam.[9] Abel had brought his best sheep, while Cain begrudgingly brought some wilted flax. For this reason, God accepted Abel's offering, but not that of Cain. Cain was so angry at being rejected that he eventually murdered his brother.

Adam's altar in Jerusalem was destroyed by the flood, but after the deluge, Noah returned there and rebuilt it.[10] Noah himself had been wounded in the Ark, so his son Shem offered the first sacrifices there. [11] As a result of this offering, God made his first covenant with mankind, that He would never again bring a flood that would destroy the world. The altar in Jerusalem thus became the symbol of man's protection, guaranteeing that humanity would never again be destroyed by God.[12]

Shortly after this, Noah's youngest son Ham displayed gross disrespect toward his father, and Shem protected his father's honor. Noah then gave Shem a blessing, 'May [God] dwell in the tents of Shem" (Genesis 9:27). This indicated that Shem's inheritance would include Jerusalem, which was where the altar of God stood, and where the Temple would eventually be built.[13] Shem became the priest on this altar, bringing offerings and worshiping God. Thus, even at this early period, Jerusalem was an important place of worship; regarding this period the Psalmist said, "In Salem was set His tabernacle, and His dwelling place in Zion" (Psalms 76:3).[14]

Shem and his children occupied Jerusalem, and soon, together with his grandson Eber, Shem set up an academy where the word of God was taught.[15] Even at this early stage, Jerusalem had become a place of teaching, anticipating the important role that it would play after the establishment of the Sanhedrin.

When the city became large enough to require a government, Shem was crowned king and given the title of Malchizedek.[16] This title actually means "king of Tzedek," tzedek meaning righteousness. Tzedek was a name frequently given to Jerusalem, because it was a place where righteousness was taught.[17]

Geographically, Jerusalem is divided into two parts, a "Lower City" to the east, and an "Upper City" on a higher elevation to the west.[18] These two parts are separated by a ridge running from north to south, which divides the city into these eastern and western sections. This division has existed since ancient times, with the boundary passing right through the area where the Temple would eventually be built.

The Lower City, which included the eastern slope of the Temple Mount, was known as Salem (Shalem) in ancient times. The Upper City, which included the western part of the Mount and the place of the Altar, was known as the Land of Moriah.[19]

It was 340 years after the Flood that the Tower of Babel was built. Its builders were subsequently scattered over the face of the earth. The Canaanite tribes began to invade the Holy Land, and the Amorites occupied the western Upper City of Jerusalem, including the place of the Altar. As a sign of their disdain for Shem and his blessing, they destroyed the altar that he and Noah had built.[20] Shem and his people, however, retained control of Salem, the Lower City, and continued to maintain the academy there.

According to some legends, Abraham went to Jerusalem as a young child to study the traditions with Noah and Shem.[21] He might have learned then that a holy place existed, where Adam had been created and where the original Altar had been built, but he was not yet worthy of having the place revealed to him. As Abraham grew in his devotion to God, more and more he sought to ascertain the location of this most perfect place of worship. For many years he lived in Mesopotamia (presently Iraq), but when God told him to return to the Promised Land, Abraham directed his wanderings so that they brought him closer and closer to Jerusalem.[22]

Abraham soon became caught up in a war that was raging in the Holy Land, and his efforts were largely responsible for the outcome of this war. Although this war was fought on a physical plane, it was also symbolic of Abraham's battle against evil, and Abraham's victory thus had a twofold significance. After the decisive battle Shem came out to greet Abraham: "And Malchi-zedek, king of Salem, brought out bread and wine, and he was a priest to the highest God" (Genesis 14:18). He gave Abraham a blessing, declaring, "Blessed be Abram to God most high, maker of heaven and earth" (Ibid. 14:19). In conferring this blessing, Shem was making Abraham the bearer of many of the traditions that had been handed down from the times of Adam and Noah.[23]

Shortly after this, God destroyed Sodom and Gemorrah, radically altering the balance of power in the Holy Land. One result was that eastern Jerusalem — Salem — the place of

Shem's academy, increasingly began to come under the domination of the Philistines, who were occupying the area. In order to negotiate with them, Abraham went to the city of Gerar, where Abimelech, king of the Philistines, had his capital. Abraham had presented Sarah as his sister rather than his wife, and Abimelech had come close to adding her to his harem. After a serious epidemic and a disturbing dream, Abimelech finally gave Abraham free access to Jerusalem, saying, "Behold my land is before you, dwell wherever you please" (Genesis 20:15). The safety of Shem's academy was thus assured.

Abraham then finally had the son of his old age, Isaac. Abimelech realized that Jerusalem was important to Abraham, and now that he had an heir, there might eventually be a dispute regarding the city. Abimelech therefore approached Abraham and asked that he make a covenant, to which Abraham agreed. The two made a treaty that as long as a descendant of Abimelech dwelt on the land, no descendant of Abraham would wage war against them. This covenant was later to be the reason why the Israelites could not capture the eastern part of Jerusalem.[24]

One tradition had not yet been given to Abraham, the location of the Altar. Before this could be revealed to him, Abraham had to be tested ten times by God.[25] The tenth and most difficult of these tests occurred when God told Abraham to sacrifice his only beloved son, Isaac. God told Abraham, "Take your son, your only son, Isaac whom you love, and go to the land of Moriah, and bring him up for a sacrifice on one of the mountains that I will reveal to you" (Genesis 22:2). Even at this point, God did not tell Abraham the location of the holy Altar; it was not revealed to him until he had actually taken his son, embarked on the journey, and made all the preparations for the sacrifice. The only thing that Abraham knew was that he was going to Moriah, the western section of Jerusalem.

As Abraham and Isaac approached Jerusalem, they saw a ring of clouds over the Temple Mount, and they realized that this was the mountain where the Altar stood.[26] As they came closer, a pillar of fire pointed out the precise location of the Altar.[27] These clouds drove away the Amorites, and concealed

Abraham's activities on the mountain. Abraham rebuilt the Altar of Adam and Noah, and prepared to sacrifice Isaac on it, binding him as an offering. At the very last minute, God reprieved Isaac and substituted a ram for Abraham to sacrifice. With this, Abraham had the entire tradition, and he took Shem's place as the priest at the Altar on Mount Moriah.[28]

Abraham called the place of the Altar Yirah or Yiru (Jeru).[29] When this was united with the eastern part of the city, which was called Salem, the city got its present name, Jeru-Salem.[30] To this very day, the merit of Abraham and Isaac is concentrated there on the place of the Altar.[31]

Directly after this, Abraham purchased his first permanent plot in the Promised Land. Near Hebron, Abraham had discovered the cave of Machpelah, where Adam and Eve were buried, and when Sarah died, he wished to bury her in this sacred cave. The land, however, belonged to Ephron the Hittite, who lived on a mountain just to the west of Jerusalem.[32] Ephron realized that Abraham's descendants would someday occupy the Holy Land; therefore, before he would sell Abraham the cave, he demanded that Abraham make an everlasting treaty that they would never take his city away by force. After the sale, Ephron made a huge monument, inscribed with the words of this treaty. As a result, the western part of Jerusalem was never taken by force, but was eventually purchased from Ephron's descendants.[33]

There appears to be a special providence involved in this, since this part of Jerusalem would contain the Great Altar. With regard to this Altar, the Torah states, "You shall not build it out of cut stones, for if you lift your sword against it, you have profaned it' (Exodus 20:22). The reason for this has been discussed earlier. However, if lifting a sword or iron tool against an inanimate stone can profane the Altar, how much more so can lifting a sword against a fellow human being! For this reason, of all places in the Holy Land, the place of the Altar was not taken by force, but was purchased.

Meanwhile, Isaac had not returned with Abraham, but remained in Jerusalem for three years while he studied in the Academy of Shem.[34] Isaac would frequently go to the place of the Altar to worship God, and there he ordained the daily afternoon service.[35] Although a number of tribes lived around Jerusalem at the time, the Temple Mount was uninhabited, since the people had been frightened away by the clouds and pillar of fire that had appeared on the mountain when Isaac was brought there for an offering.

While Isaac was in Jerusalem, Abraham sent his servant Eliezer to his cousins in the north to seek a wife for his son. Eliezer returned with Rebecca, and on this mountain she first met Isaac, who introduced her to the Academy of Shem in Jerusalem. Later, when it was discovered that Rebecca could not have children, Isaac returned to Jerusalem to the place of the Altar, and there he prayed for a child.[36]

Rebecca eventually conceived, but as her pregnancy progressed, she became disturbed by the unusual activity in her womb. Not knowing its meaning, she went to Jerusalem, where she prayed in the Academy of Shem, which was also a house of worship.[37] There she was informed that there were twins in her womb, and that Jacob, the younger son, would inherit the traditions from Abraham and Isaac. Isaac, however, was not aware of this, and he wished to give the tradition and blessing to Esau, the older son. It was because of Rebecca's knowledge that she connived to have the blessing given to Jacob instead of Esau.[38]

As a young boy, Jacob was drawn to Jerusalem, and he eventually became a student in Shem's academy. Shem's grandson, Eber, had set up a separate academy, and Jacob delved into his studies there as well.[39] Abraham died when Jacob was fifteen years old, and at that time Jacob bought the birthright from Esau for a bowl of pottage.[40]

When Isaac grew old, the time came for him to give the blessing and the traditions to his children. He naturally wished to give the blessing and leadership to Esau, who was the older of the twins. Rebecca, however, knew the true nature of the two boys, and she went so far as to disguise Jacob as Esau so that he would receive the blessing. When Jacob came in for the blessing, Isaac became aware of his identity, and also saw prophetically that Jacob's descendants were destined to build the Temple in Jerusalem.[41] Isaac then blessed him with the "dew of the heaven" (Genesis 27:28), alluding to the fact that he would be worthy of having revealed to him the place of the Holy of Holies, the door of all blessing.[42]

When Esau heard that Jacob had "stolen" his blessing, he was furious, and threatened to kill his brother. Jacob escaped to Jerusalem, to the Academy of Eber, where he remained for fourteen years.[43] He then visited Beersheba, and prepared to go north to find a wife among his cousins there. On the way, he passed through Jerusalem, and coming to the Altar of Abraham in the evening, he prayed there, thus initiating the evening service.[44]

It is significant to note that Isaac had initiated the afternoon service in precisely the same place. The very fact that at least two of the three daily prayers were initiated by the Patriarchs in Jerusalem clearly indicates that it is a focus of prayer. Indeed, this is yet another reason why all Jews face Jerusalem when they pray.

In the Holy of Holies, the Ark of the Covenant stood on a rock known as the *Evven Shetiyah,* the Foundation Stone. As discussed earlier, this spot was the "gate of heaven," the focus of prayer, and the place from which all prophecy emanated. Until this time, no man had known the location of this precise spot, even though the Patriarchs must have known that it was somewhere on the Temple Mount. Providence now guided Jacob so that he fell asleep precisely at this place.[45]

While sleeping on this rock, Jacob had his spectacular dream, where he saw the ladder standing on the ground, with its top reaching the heavens. This indicated that this place was the focus of spiritual elevation, through which a person could climb to the highest spiritual levels. When Jacob awoke from this prophetic dream, he realized the significance of the place and said, "How awesome is this place! It is none other than the house of God, it is the gate of heaven" (Genesis 28:17). On the place of the Ark, Jacob set up a stone as a monument and poured oil on it. Anticipating the Temple, he said, "This stone that I have set up as a monument shall be God's house" *(Ibid.* 28:22).

It was in this manner that the three most important features of the Temple were dedicated. The Chamber of the Sanhedrin was first dedicated by Shem, who built both an academy and a house of worship on this spot. The Altar was originally dedicated by Adam, and was rededicated by Abraham when he offered the ram in place of his son. Finally, the place of the Ark in the Holy of Holies was dedicated by Jacob, when he poured oil on the stone upon which he had slept.

Jacob then went to the north, to the land of Aram Naharayim, where he married his two cousins, Leah and Rachel. There he had eleven of his twelve sons, who would become the twelve Tribes of Israel. He then returned to the Holy Land.[46]

At this time, Jacob met with Esau for the first time since leaving home, and he and the eleven children who had been born bowed down to Esau.[47] Jacob then wrestled with the angel of Esau, who represented all the forces of evil, and when this angel could not overcome him, it was finally decided that Jacob would be the one to father the chosen people. The angel then gave him the name Israel (Yisrael), which means "a prince of God."[48]

Soon after this, God told Jacob to return to "the house of God," the place of the Holy of Holies in Jerusalem, where he had seen the vision of the ladder. Here God Himself confirmed what the angel had told Jacob, that he would father the chosen people and that his name would indeed be Israel. Jacob remained in Jerusalem for six months, worshiping and serving God in the place of the Holy of Holies.[49]

Right after this, Rachel gave birth to Jacob's twelfth child, Benjamin. Providence had chosen Benjamin for a special task. It was in his portion of the Holy Land that the Altar and the Holy of Holies would be situated. There are several reasons for this. Benjamin was the only child born in the Holy Land, and he was the only one born after Jacob had been designated as Israel. Since he had not yet been born when Jacob's other children bowed down to Esau, he had never subjugated himself to Jacob's evil brother. Furthermore, as Jacob's youngest son, he was closest to his father, learning all good traits from him.[50]

Eight years passed, and Joseph was seventeen years old, while his oldest brothers were in their early twenties. At this time, an event occurred that would have a powerful influence on the tribes of Israel, to a large extent designating their status for all times. This was the selling of Joseph by his brothers.

Of all the brothers, one had been particularly devoted to the study of the traditions that had been handed down from Abraham and the Academy of Shem. This was Judah; he had developed well, both in leadership and in a judicious nature. When the older brothers, Simon and Levi, wanted to kill Joseph, it was Judah who said, "What gain do we have if we slay our brother?" (Genesis 37:26). As a result of this, we find that Judah was already destined to be a leader among his brothers.[51] Benjamin, of course, remained innocent, since he was too young to take part in this episode.[52]

In the very next account, the Torah speaks of the birth of Peretz to Judah and Tamar. As known from the genealogy, King David was a direct descendant of Peretz, and as we shall see, it was David who was destined to reveal Jerusalem as the city chosen by God.[53] This juxtaposition is deliberate, since it was due to Judah's role in saving Joseph that he became worthy to father the hereditary royal house of Israel.

It is known that Noah and his sons were given seven commandments by God. The first six of these forbid idolatry, adultery and incest, murder, robbery, cursing God, and eating flesh from a living animal. The seventh commandment requires the establishment of courts of law to uphold the first six.[54] Among other things, the Academy of Shem functioned as such a court of law, and we indeed find that when Esau threatened to murder Jacob, the latter replied that if he did, he would be judged by the judiciary of Shem.[55]

After the death of Shem and his grandson Eber, this judiciary was taken over by Isaac and Jacob. Of all the twelve sons of Jacob, we find none joining this judiciary other than Judah. Thus, when Tamar was suspected of adultery and so judged, we find that, as the youngest member of this judiciary, Judah was its spokesman. This is the common practice in capital cases.[56] Judah had thus proven himself in two fields, in leadership and in judgment.

From this point on, we find that Judah always took a leadership role among his brothers. When the brothers were to go back to Egypt for provisions, Judah took responsibility for the safety of Benjamin and convinced Jacob to let him go along with them. Later, when Joseph, who as viceroy of Egypt was still not recognized by his brothers, wished to imprison Benjamin for stealing his cup, it was Judah who defended him. Finally, when Jacob was about to emigrate to Egypt to join Joseph, he sent Judah ahead to establish an academy so that the traditions would not be forgotten in Egypt.[57]

After Joseph revealed himself to his brothers, the Torah states that "he fell on Benjamin's neck and wept" (Genesis 45:14). According to tradition, at this moment Joseph saw the Altar and Holy of Holies built in Benjamin's portion, and he foresaw that they would eventually be destroyed.[58]

When Jacob blessed his sons, the destinies of these two tribes, Benjamin and Judah, were revealed. To Judah he said, "The scepter shall not depart from Judah, nor the staff of judgment from between his feet" (Genesis 49:10). "The scepter" refers to the royal line, which would go to King David, a descendant of Judah, and remain in his family forever. "The staff of judgment between his feet," indicates that the Hall of the Sanhedrin would be in the portion of Judah.[59] Judah was thus worthy of both leadership and judgment.

In Benjamin's blessing, Jacob said, "Benjamin is a tearing wolf, in the morning he devours his prey, and in the evening he divides the spoil" (Genesis 49:27). This alludes to fact that the Great Altar would be in the portion of Benjamin, taking the sacrifices as its "prey," especially the daily offerings, morning and evening.[60] The Great Altar could therefore not be built in any other place than in the portion of Benjamin.[61]

The Promised Land would later be divided among the Twelve Tribes by Joshua. The Temple Mount would be divided in half, so that the eastern part, where the Chamber of the Sanhedrin stood, would be in the portion of Judah, while the western half, with the Great Altar, would be in Benjamin's portion. This later helped locate the chosen city, because there was a firm tradition that the Altar would be in Benjamin's portion, and the Sanhedrin in that of Judah.[62]

It is significant to note the differences between these two brothers and their destinies. Judah was the fourth son of Leah, while Benjamin was the younger son of Rachel. While Judah was the symbol of leadership and judgment, Benjamin was the symbol of innocence and purity, never acting, but instead, allowing himself to be acted upon by God's providence. The royal line and the Sanhedrin were thus Judah's heritage, since these required boldness and leadership. The Altar, on the other hand, was in Benjamin's portion, since this is indicative of total submission to God — the Altar had to be built out of uncut stones, just as they had been created by God. Just as Judah protected Benjamin, so the royal house and the Sanhedrin would protect the sanctity of the Altar.

As time passed, Jacob and his sons died in Egypt. The last of the twelve brothers to die was Levi, who outlived Judah by seven years.[63] For these last seven years, Levi was the bearer and teacher of the traditions, and after he died, these were given to his grandson, Amram, who became the principal teacher and leader of the Israelites.[64] Very soon after Levi died the Israelites were enslaved, a condition that they would endure for over a century.

As leaders and bearers of the traditions, the tribe of Levi alone was able to avoid being enslaved. They had scrolls containing the traditions, and these they studied and taught to the other Jews. Alone of all the tribes, the Levites never worshiped idols in Egypt, and they also kept the covenant of circumcision.[65] It was thus no coincidence that Amram's two sons, Moses and Aaron, as well as his daughter Miriam, became the most important leaders of the Israelites in the generation of the Exodus.

The most spectacular event of the Exodus was the splitting of the Red Sea, and here again we find Judah and Benjamin in counterpoint. Before the sea could be split, the Israelites had to show an act of faith, demonstrating that they believed in the imminent miracle. Judah assumed the leadership role. The head of the tribe, Nachshon ben Aminadav, jumped into the Red Sea, anticipating that it would open; at the same time, the rest of the tribe attempted to repel the Egyptians with force. At the same time, the entire tribe of Benjamin entered the sea, submitting themselves totally to God's providence. It was at this time that Benjamin became worthy of having the Holy of

Holies in his portion, in addition to the Altar, of which he was already worthy.[66]

In the desert, the Israelites frequently rebelled against God, questioning His providence over them — with the exception of the tribe of Levi. When the Israelites worshiped the Golden Calf, the only entire tribe which refrained from doing so was Levi. Thus, after the episode of the Golden Calf, the Torah tells us that "Moses said, 'Who is for God, to me!' and the sons of Levi gathered to him" (Exodus 33:28). Of all the tribes, only Levi kept the covenant of circumcision during the years in the desert. While serving God was something new for many people in the other tribes, the Levites had never ceased doing so, even during the darkest days in Egypt. Thus, the Levites, and among them, the sons of Aaron as Cohen-priests, were chosen to serve, first in the Tabernacle and later in the Temple.[67]

The ultimate status of these special tribes is most evident in Moses' final blessing to all Israel. Since the man Judah had attained his status through his own efforts in the time of Jacob, Moses did not add anything significant in his blessing. In Levi's blessing, Moses gave the tribe permanent status as the guardians and officiants of the Temple: "They shall put incense before You, and a whole burnt offering on Your Altar" (Deuteronomy 33:10). Benjamin's blessing immediately follows that of Levi, indicating that the Altar on which the Levites and Cohen-priests would serve would be in Benjamin's portion.[68] Of Benjamin, Moses said, "Between his shoulders [God] shall dwell" (ibid. 33:13). This indicates the final part of Benjamin's inheritance, indicating that the Holy of Holies would also be in his portion.[69]

When Moses sent spies to reconnoiter the Promised Land, one of the places that he wanted them to investigate apparently was Jerusalem. He thus told them, "Ascend to the mountain" (Numbers 13:17); and when the Torah speaks of a mountain in the Holy Land, it usually refers to Jerusalem.[70] We are later informed that "the Hittite, the Jebusite, and the Amorite dwell on the Mountain" (Ibid. 13:29), all these being closely related tribes. Regarding the Hittite, we already know that the family of Ephron the Hittite had a settlement in the western part of Jerusalem, and from the fact that they are mentioned first, it appears that they were predominant. The Amorites are mentioned last, which might indicate that their influence had declined, at least at that time. The Jebusites were a very small Canaanite tribe, centered around Jerusalem. Even after the Jebusites left the area and were replaced by Philistines, the place was called Jebus, and its inhabitants, Jebusites.[71] The original Jebusites may have been among the tribes that left the Holy Land and settled in Africa before it was occupied by the Israelites.[72]

One of the main reasons why Moses wished to enter the Promised Land was to see Jerusalem, and possibly to build the Temple. He thus prayed to God, "O let me cross over, and let me see the good land across the Jordan, this good Mountain and the Lebanon" (Deuteronomy 3:28). According to tradition, the "good Mountain" refers to the Temple Mount in Jerusalem, while the — "Lebanon" refers to the Temple itself. Jerusalem is the keystone of the Lebanon range, and the entire range derives its name from the fact that the Temple is built on one of its peaks. The Temple was called Lebanon, from the root *Laban* meaning white, since it 'whitens the sins of Israel.'"[73]

Since Moses was not permitted to enter the Promised Land, God told him to reveal to Joshua the secret of where the chosen place would be. God told Moses, "Command Joshua and strengthen and fortify him, for he will cross over before these people, and bring them to inherit the land that you shall see" (Deuteronomy 3:28). Only Joshua knew this secret, and later, when David and Samuel wished to locate the chosen city, they had to consult the Book of Joshua.[74]

7. Dedication

Moses did not live to enter the Promised Land; his disciple Joshua led the Israelites in the occupation. Even though Joshua knew that Jerusalem would be the chosen city, he did not reveal this to any of the tribes. This would have to wait until the permanent royal line was chosen, which did not occur until the time of David.

The first city in the Promised Land that the Israelites conquered was Jericho. Almost as soon as they entered the land, Joshua put aside the choicest fields near Jericho, later to be traded to the tribes in whose territory the chosen city would fall. This choice field was selected before the land was divided among the tribes; as territory common to them all, it was given over to the children of Moses' father-in-law Jethro for safe-keeping.[1]

The Torah itself prescribes this as the method through which Jerusalem should be chosen. In one place it states that the chosen place will be "from all your tribes" (Deuteronomy 12:5). Elsewhere, however, the Torah states that it will be "in one of your tribes" (Ibid. 12:13). The Torah is speaking of the place of sacrifice — the Altar — and initially, when the land was first divided, it would be in the portion of just one of the tribes, Benjamin. Then, however, it would be exchanged for the fields of Jericho, so that ultimately it would belong to all the tribes. Thus, when Jerusalem was eventually chosen and consecrated, it became the common property of all the tribes of Israel. As one place common to all, it had a strong effect in uniting the tribes.[2]

It is in the Book of Joshua that the first actual mention of Jerusalem occurs in the Bible. Here we see that Adoni-tzedek, king of Jerusalem, was involved in a battle with Joshua's forces and is defeated.[3] It is significant to note the resemblance of the name Adoni-tzedek to Malchi-tzedek, the title given to Shem when he became king of Jerusalem. This is because Jerusalem itself was called Tzedek — Righteousness — as discussed earlier, and Adoni-tzedek means "the lord of Tzedek." It was during the battle with Adoni-tzedek and his confederates that the Bible tells us the sun stood still for Joshua, aiding him in winning this battle.[4]

The Book of Joshua describes Adoni-tzedek as an Amorite king, so it appears that it was under the Amorites that the two parts of Jerusalem were united.[5] As discussed earlier, the western part of Jerusalem was called Jeru (Yeru), while the eastern part was known as Salem (Shalem). When the Amorite kings consolidated the two parts of the city, they also combined the names, calling the place Jeru-salem.

From certain traditions, it appears that the Jebusites, who had made Jerusalem their capital, had left some fifteen years before Joshua's conquest, and were replaced by the Philistine descendants of Abimelech.[6] The Philistines lived in Salem, the eastern district of Jerusalem, while the Hittite descendants of Ephron lived in the western half. By the time of Joshua's conquest, Jerusalem had already been united by the Amorite kings, and had been fortified and surrounded by a single wall.[7] After Joshua defeated the Amorites, it appears that Jerusalem again became divided into two districts.

Although Joshua defeated the king of Jerusalem, he did not make any attempt to conquer the city itself.[8] This was because it was still protected by two covenants made by Abraham, one to Abimelech and the Philistines, and the other to Ephron and the Hittites. These ancient tribes were to have an important effect in giving Jerusalem special status.

Joshua then divided the land among the twelve tribes, according to a lottery and by the Urim and Thumim.[9] Looking at the border of Judah's portion, we see that it runs right through Jerusalem: "The border went up by the valley of Ben-Hinnom, to the shoulder of the Jebusite from the south — this is Jerusalem — and the boundary went up to the top of the mountain which overlooks the valley of Hinnom to the west" (Joshua 15:8). The mountain mentioned here is the Temple

Mount, so we see that the boundary cuts right through the Temple area in Jerusalem. In describing the boundary of Benjamin, where the border runs from west to east, the scripture states, "The boundary descended to the edge of the mountain that overlooks the valley of BenHinnom, to the shoulder of the Jebusite to the south" *(Ibid.* 18:16).[10]

For the most part, the portion of the tribe of Benjamin was north of that of Judah. In Jerusalem, however, the boundary took a sharp turn southward, cutting the Temple area in half, with the western side in Benjamin's portion, and the eastern side in that of Judah. When the Temple was later built, the Hall of the Sanhedrin was in the portion of Judah, while the Altar and Holy of Holies were in that of Benjamin.[11]

The eastern part of Jerusalem, occupied by the Philistines, thus fell into the portion of Judah. Because of Abraham's treaty with Abimelech and the Philistines, the tribe of Judah could not drive them out, and the scripture thus states, "The sons of Judah could not drive out the Jebusites, the inhabitants of Jerusalem" (Joshua 15:63).[12] It was not until after the last descendants of Abimelech died after the time of Joshua that the tribe of Judah was able to conquer its portion of the city: "The children of Judah fought against Jerusalem and took it, smiting it with the sword and setting the city on fire" (Judges 1:8).

The western part of Jerusalem, which belonged to Benjamin, was inhabited by the Hittite descendants of Ephron, who had made a covenant with Abraham when the cave of Machpelah was purchased. Just as the sale of Machpelah had been permanent, so was this covenant, so the Benjaminites could not drive the Hittites out of their portion of Jerusalem. It is thus written, "The children of Benjamin did not drive out the Jebusites who inhabited Jerusalem" (Judges 1:21).[13] As mentioned earlier, whatever people lived in Jerusalem at the time were called Jebusites, whether they were Philistines or Hittites. Somewhat later, we still find that Jerusalem was not inhabited by Jews, since a Levite said of it, "We will not turn aside into a city of a foreigner, which is not of the children of Israel" (Judges 19:12).[14]

We thus see that of the original tribes who had lived in

Jerusalem, the only ones who remained at the time of its conquest were the Hittite and the Amorite, the Philistines having arrived later. This is what the prophet Ezekiel meant when he said of Jerusalem, "Your father was an Amorite, and your mother was a Hittite" (Ezekiel 16:3,45).[15]

No further mention of Jerusalem is found until after David's famous battle, where he defeated the Philistine warrior Goliath. Here the scripture states, "David took the head of the Philistine and brought it to Jerusalem" (I Samuel 17:54). No reason is given; it is certain that David did not yet know that Jerusalem would be the chosen city. It appears, however, that the verse stresses that Goliath was "the Philistine" to teach that David brought his head to Jerusalem to indicate that Abraham's covenant with the Philistines was no longer in force, since the Philistines had been the ones to initiate the war against the Israelites. Although the treaty had been breached in the time of Judah's conquest of Jerusalem, and had been dishonored by the Philistines during their battles with Samson, the bringing of Goliath's head to Jerusalem was a concrete symbol that the covenant was no longer in force.[16]

Even though the place of the Temple ultimately had to be revealed prophetically, there was still an obligation for the one designated to found the royal line to attempt to find it logically.[17] All his life, David sought this most sacred place, and we thus find (Psalms 132:2-5):

> [David] swore to God,
>> made a vow to the Mighty One of Jacob:
> I will not come in a tent as my house
>> I will not climb into my made up bed
> I will not allow my eyes to sleep
>> I will not let my eyelids rest
> Until I find the place of God
>> the dwelling of the Mighty One of Jacob. [18]

David called God "the Mighty One of Jacob" in this psalm. This alludes to the fact that the place he sought was that of the Holy of Holies, which had been revealed to Jacob.[19]

Saul was still king over Israel at this time, and being jealous of David, he sought to kill him. David escaped to Ramah, where he stayed with the prophet Samuel. Earlier, Samuel had already anointed David as the future king, but there was still the requirement that the king find the place of the Altar. David and Samuel carefully went over all the traditions in order to ascertain logically the precise spot. Although Samuel was the greatest prophet of the time, he did not make use of his paranormal powers, but guided David so that the latter would find the promised place.[20]

They knew the tradition that the Sanhedrin would have to be in the portion of Judah, near the Altar and Holy of Holies, which was to be in the portion of Benjamin.[21] It was therefore obvious that they would have to search along the border between Judah and Benjamin. They also knew that it would have to be the highest place on this border, since with regard to the Sanhedrin the Torah states, "You shall rise and go up to the place that the Lord your God shall choose" (Deuteronomy 17:8). Samuel also knew that the secret of the chosen place had been revealed to Joshua, so they carefully looked at the description of the border between Judah and Benjamin as described in the Book of Joshua. Here they saw that the border "went upward" as far as the "mountain overlooking the valley of Ben-Hinnom" (Joshua 15:8), which was the highest place on the border. It was thus ascertained that the mountain upon which the Temple would be built was in Jerusalem, and all that was needed now was to determine the precise place of the Altar.

Saul was later killed in battle, and at the age of thirty, David was crowned king of his tribe Judah in Hebron. There he remained for seven years until the time became ripe for him to take Jerusalem. There was a tradition that the one who would conquer the chosen city would inherit the royal house of Israel for all time. David had already determined the place, and before he went forth to Jerusalem, he was anointed by all Israel as king.[22]

By force, David occupied the eastern half of Jerusalem, where the Philistines originally lived, and which had earlier been captured and destroyed by the tribe of Judah. Since the place of the Altar could not be tainted by blood, he did not attack the western half in the portion of Benjamin, but he did remove the monuments containing Abraham's treaty, which had been erected by the Hittite sons of Ephron.[23] This was enough to indicate that David was in control of the city and thus had established himself in the hereditary role of king. David also reunited the two parts of the city and built a wall around it.[24]

There was no state of war between David and the Hittites; we later find that the Israelites dwelt together with them in peace.[25] David's conquest of the Philistine portion of Jerusalem, however, was seen as an act of war, and soon after this we find that they began to wage war against David in the Valley of Raphaim, which was to the south of Jerusalem.[26]

After all these wars, David finally brought the Ark of God to Jerusalem, knowing that it was the chosen city. He set aside a special place for the Ark, as we find, "They brought the Ark of God and set it in its place, in the midst of the tent that David had made for it" (2 Samuel 6:17).[27] A place for the Altar had not yet been determined, however, and they still sacrificed in Gibeon, outside of Jerusalem.[28] Whenever David acquired gold or other precious things in his conquests, he brought them to Jerusalem to be dedicated to the House of God that would be built there.[29]

The commandment to build the Temple became an obligation as soon as peace was attained by the king. Such peace was achieved in the time of David.[30] David very much wanted to build the House of God, and the scripture states, "When the king dwelt in his palace and God gave him rest from all his enemies round about, the king said to Nathan the prophet, 'See now, I live in a house of cedar, but God's Ark dwells in a curtain tent' " (2 Samuel 7:2).[31] David was informed that he could not be the one to build the Temple since his hands were sullied with blood, as he later told his son Solomon, "God's word came to me saying, 'You have shed much blood and have made great wars, you shall not build a house to My name, because you have shed much blood in My sight' " (I Chronicles 22:8). If even lifting iron against a stone renders it unfit for the Altar, how much more so was a king who had shed human blood unfit to build the Temple of God.[32] Still, because David had been the one to occupy the chosen city, he was the one to earn the hereditary royal house of Israel for all time, as God told him through the prophet Nathan, "Your throne shall be established forever" (2 Samuel 7:16).

The final step was the revelation of the place of the Altar, and the Bible describes this most graphically.[33] God became angry at David and tempted him to count the Israelites, bringing on them a terrible plague. David then prayed to God for forgiveness. He saw an angel standing on the threshing floor of Arnon the Jebusite. The Prophet Gad then told David, "Go raise an altar to God on the threshing floor of Arnon the Jebusite" (I Samuel 24:18), and David did so, bringing offerings to God as an atonement.

The place of the Altar was thus revealed to David. This was the same place where Adam was created, and where he had offered the first sacrifice. There Cain and Abel as well as Noah had brought offerings to God. On that very spot Abraham had bound his son Isaac when he was so commanded by God.[34] When this was revealed to David, he said, "This is the house of the Lord, God, and this is the Altar of sacrifice for Israel" (I Chronicles 22:1).

One thing that still must be clarified is the reason for the manner in which the place of the Altar was revealed. Why did it have to be revealed through a sin, and only after David's subsequent repentance? Furthermore, the scripture states that "God became angry at Israel" (I Samuel 24:1), but does not give any reason for it.

If one looks at the verse immediately before this, however, one will find a mention of Uriah the Hittite, one of David's generals. The Midrash states that God became angry at David and Israel because David had caused the death of Uriah.[35] This Uriah was the husband of Bathsheba, and when David wished to take Bathsheba for a wife, he sent Uriah to the front where he was killed. The fact that David had sent a man to certain death in order to marry his wife was considered a great wrong, and David was severely rebuked by the prophet Nathan.[36]

The Talmud teaches that King David never actually became involved with Bathsheba out of lust, since he had long since perfected himself spiritually. The only reason for this entire episode was to teach the ways of repentance, since it is clearly evident that God eventually forgave David.[37] The lesson is that no matter how great a sin a person commits, if he is truly contrite in asking God to forgive him, the sin is wiped away. Nothing can stand before repentance.[38]

The main idea of the Altar was that of forgiveness and atonement. Therefore, the episode involving Bathsheba, which was meant to teach the ways of repentance, was ultimately also the means through which the location of the Altar was revealed.[39] It was almost as if the power of repentance revealed by David would be built into the Altar. In a similar vein, it should be noted that it was the son born to David and Bathsheba — Solomon — who eventually built the Temple.

But it is also important to note exactly how God brought this about. As a result of David's misdeed with Bathsheba and her husband Uriah, God enticed him to take a census of the Israelites. God caused David to forget the injunction, "When you take the sum of the children of Israel, according to their number, then each man shall give a ransom for his soul to God when you number them, that there be no plague among them when you number them" (Exodus 30:12).[40] The atonement in the time of Moses consisted of a half-shekel given toward the building of the Tabernacle. The census was taken by counting the total number of half-shekels, and Moses used this silver to build the foundations of the Tabernacle.[41] As a result, every Israelite had a part in the foundation of the Tabernacle. Furthermore, it is evident that the idea of properly counting the Israelites was very closely related to the building of the Tabernacle and the Temple.

Thus, when God was ready to reveal the place of the Altar, he did so by tempting David to commit a wrong very closely related to the sanctuary, namely, counting the Israelites without the atonements of the half-shekel. The sin itself thus was bound to the very foundation of the Temple. When David subsequently repented and was forgiven, his repentance also became a part of the Altar's foundation.

David had thus done everything necessary to find the Altar according to Torah law. First, he had sought it himself. Finally he had been worthy of having the place revealed to him by Gad the prophet.[42] David then bought the place of the Altar from

Arnon the Jebusite for fifty silver shekels. He also collected fifty shekels from each of the twelve tribes of Israel, buying the entire city of Jerusalem from Arnon for 600 gold shekels. The entire city of Jerusalem thus became the common property of all Israel.[43]

Although David could not build the Temple himself, he prepared for its construction, assembling all the necessary materials.[44] David dug the foundations of the Temple, particularly in the place of the Altar.[45] He also gave Solomon a complete written plan of how the Temple should be built, as he had received the tradition from the prophet Samuel and from Ahitofel.[46] David gave the pattern to Solomon, saying, "All is in writing, as God has given me wisdom by His hand on me, all the works of this plan" (I Chronicles 28:19).[47]

Before David died, he made sure that his son Solomon was anointed as king. This was done on the spring of Gichon in Jerusalem.[48] Solomon took his father's place as king over all Israel, and one of his first acts was to complete the wall of the Holy City.[49] But Solomon's greatest accomplishment was building the Temple of God, in the exact spot that had been designated by God from the beginning of creation.[50]

The Bible thus says, "Then Solomon built the house of God in Jerusalem, on Mount Moriah, where there had been a vision to his father, which he prepared in the place of David on the threshing floor of Arnon the Jebusite" (2 Chronicles 3:1). Mount Moriah, of course, was the place where Abraham had bound his son Isaac as a sacrifice, and this was the place revealed to David to be the Altar of God.[51]

The Temple built by Solomon stood for 410 years, and during this time, Jerusalem was the spiritual center for all Israel. Finally, due to the many sins of the people, God allowed both Jerusalem and the Temple to be destroyed by the Babylonians, led by King Nebuchadnezzar. After a seventy year exile, the Temple was rebuilt under the leadership of Ezra and Nehemiah, with the exact place of the Altar once again revealed by one of the last remaining prophets.[52] This second Temple stood for 420 years, and Jerusalem was once again a center of worship and Torah for the entire Jewish people.[53]

Jerusalem and the second Temple were finally destroyed by the Romans in the year 70 C.E.

On the same day of the year both the first and second Temples were destroyed, and Jerusalem was laid waste. This was the ninth day of the Hebrew month of Ab, better known as Tisha b'Av.[54] This day has been one of national mourning and fasting ever since.

Even though the Temple has been destroyed, the area upon which it stood still retains its special sanctity. Today, since the modes of ritual cleansing no longer exist and we are therefore all ritually unclean, it is forbidden to enter the area of the Temple Mount.[55] The Western Wall of the Temple Mount — the *Kotel* — *is* still a shrine to Jews all over the world.

There are many things that the Jew does to recall the destruction of Jerusalem. It is a custom in some circles to leave a small square of one's house unplastered to commemorate this tragedy.[56] As mentioned earlier, this is the reason why the grooms breaks a glass at the wedding ceremony. One who sees Jerusalem in its state of destruction must rend his clothing, just as one who is in mourning.[57]

Our sages teach us that there is no joy before God since the time that Jerusalem and the Temple were destroyed.[58] Whoever mourns for Jerusalem will be worthy to witness its redemption.[59]

8. Rebirth

When a Jew says, "Next year in Jerusalem," it is more than just a prayer that he may visit the Holy City, or even that he should settle there. It is a prayer for the entire future of the Jewish people, and for the world in general. So closely is Jerusalem tied with the ultimate future and coming of the Messiah, that saying "Next year in Jerusalem" is nothing less than a prayer for the inception of the Messianic age.

The belief in the coming of the Messiah led the Jew to be optimistic about the future. Even in the darkest exile, under the worst persecutions, the Jew knew that he would survive, and that if not he, his descendants would be worthy of seeing the Messiah, when both the Jew and the world in general would be brought to a state of perfection. The Messiah would eventually bring the Jew out of his long exile, end the persecutions, and bring him back to the Holy Land where he could live in peace and pursue the Torah to its fullest extent.

This does not mean that the Messiah will necessarily be a superhuman being, or even a superman. He will be an outstanding saint, with extraordinary leadership abilities, and will be able to bring about the redemption of Israel without suspending any laws of nature. Of course, if the Jews are worthy, this redemption can come through miracles, but if not, it will still come, but without miracles in an orderly series of events.[1]

It was this messianic optimism that led to the rise of Zionism, as a movement of national liberation — the first such movement in the world. The Jew knew that things would eventually have to improve and that the redemption would have to come — God Himself had promised this — and if it did

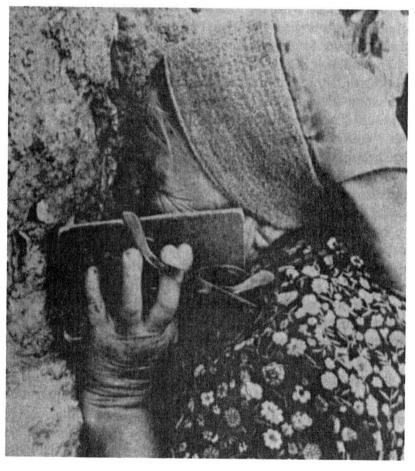

74 □ *Jerusalem*

not come through miracles, it would have to come about through human effort. Maybe some did not realize it, but the people who led the rebirth of the Holy Land were taking part in the first stages of the Messianic drama, which includes the rebuilding of the land. As the time of the redemption drew near, God sent a spirit of enthusiasm to the Jewish people, impelling them to return and recultivate the Land of Israel.

Thus, there is a tradition that the Land of Israel would have a measure of political freedom before the coming of the Messiah.[2] According to some, this will occur with the permission of the other nations.[3] There is also a tradition that the land will be cultivated before the Messiah reveals himself, based on the prophecy, "O mountains of Israel, let your branches sprout forth, and let you yield your fruit to My people of Israel, for their time has almost come" (Ezekiel 36:8).[4]

As the most holy place in the Land of Israel, Jerusalem is the most important city that must be rebuilt there.[5] There is a tradition that the ingathering of the exile and the rebuilding of Jerusalem will go hand in hand, as the two most important preludes to the coming of the Messiah. According to this tradition, first a small percentage of the exile will return to the Holy Land, and then Jerusalem will come under Jewish control and be rebuilt. Only then will the majority of Jews in the world return to their homeland. It is thus written, "God is rebuilding Jerusalem, He will gather the dispersed of Israel" (Psalms 147:2).[6]

There are many other prophecies that link the ingathering of the exile with Jerusalem. Thus, the redemption of Jerusalem and its return to Jewish hands is seen as the first definite sign of the redemption. As the prophet Isaiah said, "Break forth in joy, sing together, O you ruins of Jerusalem, for God has comforted His people, He has redeemed Jerusalem" (Isaiah 52:9). The prophet Zechariah sees the return to Jerusalem as the beginning of the total renaissance of the Jewish people: "I will bring them, and they will dwell in the midst of Jerusalem; and they will be My people, and I will be their God in truth and in righteousness" (Zechariah 8:8). Thus, the relationship between the regaining of the original (old) city of Jerusalem and the fact that many thousands of young people are now finding their way back to Judaism is more than mere coincidence.

There is also another important reason why the ingathering of the exile must precede the coming of the Messiah. There is a tradition that before the Messiah comes, the concept of prophecy will once again flourish among the Jewish people.[7] Furthermore, according to the final words ever spoken by a prophet, Elijah will return as a prophet and announce the coming of the Messiah: "Behold I will send you Elijah the prophet before the coming of the great and terrible day of God" (Malachi 3:23).[8] This is necessary because the Messiah will be a king, and a king can be anointed only by a prophet.[9] Besides this, the Messiah himself will be a prophet, the greatest of them all, second only to Moses.[10]

Thus, the re-establishment of the concept of prophecy is very important in the unfolding of the Messianic drama. This, however, requires a number of conditions. First of all, prophecy can usually take place only in the Land of Israel, and not in any other land.[11] The Land of Israel, however, is not conducive to prophecy at all times. Before prophecy can exist in the Land of Israel, it must be inhabited by the majority of Jews in the world.[12]

This is actually evident in the Torah's words regarding prophecy. The Torah states that, "The Lord your God will raise up a prophet from your midst" (Deuteronomy 18:15); and from this verse the sages derive the teaching that prophecy can only exist in the Holy Land.[13] However, the Land of Israel is only called "your midst" when it is populated by all, or at least the majority, of the Jewish people. It is through the concentrated spiritual energy of the entire Jewish people that prophecy exists, and such concentration is only effective in the Land of Israel.[14]

One of the most important events in the Messianic era will be the rebuilding of the Holy Temple. Indeed, according to Rambam (Maimonides), it is the act of building the Temple that will establish the identity of the Messiah beyond all shadow of a doubt.[15] There are, however, many things involving the Temple that can only be ascertained prophetically, such as, for example, the precise location of the Altar.

When Ezra rebuilt the Temple after the Babylonian exile, the place of the Altar had to be revealed prophetically, and the same will apparently be true when the Temple is rebuilt in the Messianic age.

Rambam (Maimonides) states that the Sanhedrin will also be re-established before the coming of the Messiah.[16] There are a number of arguments for this. Firstly, the Messiah will be preceded by a prophet, who will be identified as Elijah. As discussed earlier, however, a prophet can only be accredited by the Sanhedrin. This is logical, since the message of a prophet affects all Israel; and unless there was a formal means of accreditation, any person could claim to be a prophet, whether he truly had this gift or not. Indeed, there is a tradition that Elijah will initially appear before the great Sanhedrin in Jerusalem in order to be recognized by this body.[17]

Another argument for this is that the Messiah will be a king over Israel, and a king can only be crowned by the Sanhedrin. Thus, before the Messiah can be recognized as king, there must be a Sanhedrin in existence. Establishing a Sanhedrin would require total agreement on the part of every religious leader in the Holy Land, and such agreement itself would help make us worthy of the Messiah.

According to the prophecies, the Messiah will begin his career in Jerusalem. The prophet Zechariah thus said, "Rejoice greatly, O daughter of Zion, sound the trumpet, O daughter of Jerusalem, behold your king is coming, he is righteous and triumphant — a poor man riding on a donkey" (Zechariah 9:9)[18] One reason he might come to Jerusalem first is to be recognized by the Sanhedrin.

There are prophecies that there will be a "War of Gog and Magog" around Jerusalem.[19] According to this tradition, when the nations hear of the successes of the Jews, they will gather to do battle against them near Jerusalem, led by "Gog, the king of Magog." This battle will symbolize the final war between good and evil, where in Jerusalem all evil will ultimately be vanquished.[20]

According to tradition, there will be two Messiahs, the "Messiah son of David," of the Davidic line, and the "Messiah son of Joseph," from the tribe of Ephraim. These again represent Jacob's two wives, David from Judah and Leah, and Joseph from Rachel. The Messiah son of Joseph will be the one who will lead the Israelites to victory in the war of Gog and Magog; he will die in battle. Since the Messiah son of David will be the one to rebuild the Temple, like Solomon, his hands must be unsullied by war and bloodshed.[21]

The main idea of the Messiah includes two concepts. First, the Messiah will redeem and perfect the Jewish people, creating of them a perfect society and bringing them back to an optimal spiritual status. All Jews will return to the teachings of the Torah and rise to a very high spiritual level, which will even include universal prophecy. On this level, the Jews will be able, in turn, to perfect the world around them, teaching all nations how to live in peace under the law of God. The society of mankind will thus be rectified and perfected for all time.

All this will be centered in Jerusalem. The main purpose of the ingathering of the exile will be to worship God in Jerusalem, as the prophet Isaiah foretold, "It will be on that day, that a great Shofar will be sounded, and those lost in the land of Assyria will come, and those dispersed in the land of Egypt, and they will worship God on the holy mountain in Jerusalem" (Isaiah 27:13). There is a tradition that the Shofar (ram's horn) that will be sounded to gather the exile will be from the ram that was offered by Abraham in place of Isaac. This took place on the Great Altar in Jerusalem, and it is there that the people will be assembled.[22]

Then Jerusalem will become the great center of worship and instruction for all mankind. God thus told His prophet, "I will return to Zion, and I will dwell in the midst of Jerusalem, and Jerusalem will be called the City of Truth and the Mountain of the Lord of Hosts, the Holy Mountain" (Zechariah 8:3). This will begin the period when the teachings of God will be supreme over all mankind: "For the Lord of Hosts will be king in Mount Zion and in Jerusalem, and before His elders there will be glory" (Isaiah 24:23).

All peoples will then come to Jerusalem to seek God. The prophet Zechariah describes this graphically: "Many people and mighty nations will come and seek the Lord of Hosts in Jerusalem. . . . In those days, ten men out of all the nations shall take hold of the corner of the garment of every Jew and say, 'We will go with you, for we have heard that God is with you' " (Zechariah 8:22,23). In Jerusalem, the Jewish people will thus become established as the spiritual and moral teachers of all mankind.

At that time, Jerusalem will become the spiritual capital of all mankind.[23] This is dramatically described in the prophecy of Isaiah (Isaiah 2:2-4):

> *And it shall come to pass in the end of days*
> > *that the mountain of God's house*
> > *shall be set over all other mountains*
> > *and lifted high above the hills*
> > *and all the nations shall come streaming to it.*
> *And many peoples shall come and say:*
> > *Come, let us go up to the Mountain of God*
> > *to the house of the God of Jacob*
> > *and He will teach us His ways*
> > *and we will walk in His paths.*
> *For out of Zion shall go forth the Torah*
> > *and God's word from Jerusalem.*
> *And He will judge between nations*
> > *and decide between peoples.*
> *And they will beat their swords into plowshares*
> > *and their spears into pruning hooks,*
> *Nation shall not lift up sword against nation*
> > *neither will they practice war any more.*

9. Eye of the Universe

The last question we must discuss is why God chose the Land of Israel as the chosen land; and in particular, why He chose Jerusalem as its spiritual focus. Of course, we have seen how the Altar in Jerusalem played an important role from the time of Adam, but still, why was it this spot in particular that was chosen, and none other?

If you look at a map, you will see that the geographical location of the Land of Israel virtually guaranteed that it would play a key role in the tides of civilization. The Old World consisted of two great land masses, Eurasia (Europe and Asia) and Africa. It was impossible to travel from Eurasia to Africa without passing through the Holy Land. Therefore, every conqueror, every civilization that passed from one continent to the other, had to pass through the Holy Land and come in contact with the Jew. The Land of Israel thus interacted with virtually every great civilization, and all of them were, to some degree, influenced by the teachings of the Torah.

Besides being a gateway between north and south, the Holy Land is part of the keystone link between east and west. There are mountains in Israel where a cup of water spilled on the western slope will eventually flow into the Atlantic Ocean, while one spilled on the eastern slope will flow into the Pacific. Today, these oceans are linked by the Suez Canal, but in the past, most caravan routes linking the Atlantic and Pacific passed directly through the Holy Land.

The Land of Israel was therefore literally the crossroads of civilization. Its capital and spiritual center, Jerusalem, was the focus of a process where the Jew would interact with all peoples, absorbing all the wisdom of the ancient world, while at the same time touching every great civilization with the wisdom of the Torah. It was thus taught that "Jerusalem is the center of the world."[1] God also told His prophet, "This is Jerusalem, I have set her in the midst of nations, and countries are around her" (Ezekiel 5:5). Considering both the centrality of its location and its spiritual influence, it is not at all surprising that Jerusalem today is a sacred city to the majority of the world's population.

Even today, when land routes are no longer as important as they were in the past, Jerusalem is still a center of human concern. One need only to think of how Providence placed the major portion of the world's supply of oil — the main source of transportation energy — within a stone's throw of Jerusalem. The world would otherwise not give the Holy City a second thought, except perhaps as an ancient sacred shrine. As it is, decisions made in Jerusalem today can influence even the greatest world powers. Jerusalem thus still occupies an important role in the councils of nations. All this is certainly more than mere coincidence.

On a much deeper level, however, we see Jerusalem not only as a center of civilization, but also as the very center of creation.

As discussed earlier, the most important single object in Jerusalem was the Ark, containing the Tablets and the Original Torah. This stood in the Holy of Holies on an outcrop of bedrock known as the *Evven Shetiyah,* literally, the Foundation Stone.[2] The Talmud states that it is called the "Foundation Stone" because it was the foundation of the universe. As the Talmud explains, this is because it was the very first point at which God began the act of creation.[3]

This is based on the teaching that creation began at a single point, and from this point, the universe unfolded until God decreed that it should stop. This is the significance of Shadai, which is one of God's names. It comes from the word *Dai,* meaning "enough," and it indicates the Attribute through which God stopped the expansion of creation at a certain stage.[4]

Here we must seek to understand why creation had to begin at a single point, and what is the significance of this point. Why could creation not have been brought into existence all at once? Why did it all have to emanate from a single point in space?

The answer to these questions involves an understanding of the entire concept of the spiritual and physical, as well as the difference between the two. There are numerous discussions regarding the difference between the physical and the spiritual, but this difference is often not spelled out precisely. Very closely related is the question why God created a physical world in the first place. God Himself is certainly spiritual, as is the ultimate purpose of creation. It is therefore somewhat difficult to understand the need for a physical world at all.

With a little insight, the difference between the spiritual and the physical is readily apparent. In the physical realm, there is a concept of physical space; while in the spiritual, this concept is totally absent. All that exists in the spiritual realm is conceptual space. Two things that are similar are said to be close, while things that are different are said to be far from one another. While in the physical world it is possible to push two different things together, this is impossible in the spiritual realm.[5]

We see a good example of this in the case of the teachings involving angels. It is taught that one angel cannot have two missions, while two angels cannot share the same mission.[6] There is no spatial concept unifying an angel. Therefore, if an angel had two missions, by definition it would become two angels. On the other hand, if two angels had the same mission, there could be no physical space separating them, and by definition they would be a single angel.[7]

We now begin to see why a physical world is needed. If only a spiritual world existed, there would be no way in which two different things could be brought together. Because they are different, by definition they are separated, and there would be no physical space in which they could be "pushed" together.

Spiritual entities, however, can be bound to physical objects, very much as the soul is bound to the body. The only way, then, in which two different spiritual entities or forces can be brought together is when they are bound to the same physical thing, or to two physical things which themselves are brought together.

A good example of this involves the impulses for good and evil in man, respectively known as the *Yetzer Tov* and the *Yetzer HaRa.* In a purely spiritual sense, good and evil are opposites, which can never be brought together. Without man's physical body, they could not be brought together in a single entity, indeed, in angels, which are purely spiritual, good and evil cannot co-exist.[8] It is only in a physical body that good and evil can be brought together, and man therefore had to be created with such a body before he could have within himself the combination of good and evil that would allow him to have free will and free choice.[9]

God created many different spiritual concepts, forces and entities with which to create and direct the universe. Spiritual concepts can consist of such opposites as good and evil, or justice and mercy; as well as the basic concepts of giving and receiving, which are the spiritual roots of masculinity and femininity. There are also countless angels and spiritual potentials, all interacting to bring about the processes through which the universe is directed and guided.

All these are different, and in some cases opposite, and there would be no way for them to come together so that they could act in concert. The only way in which all spiritual forces can be brought together is for all of them to be associated with a single physical point. This point is the *Evven Shetiyah* — the Foundation Stone of all creation.

Jerusalem's original name was Shalem (Salem), coming from the same root as *Shalom,* meaning peace. One of the main concepts of Jerusalem is peace, as it is written, "Seek Jerusalem's peace" (Psalms 122:6). But, as the *Zohar* explains, this peace is not only in the physical world; it also implies peace in the spiritual world.[10] The meaning of this is that all spiritual forces are brought together so that they can act in concert and in harmony.[11]

The act of creation involved all these spiritual forces acting in concert. Before they could do so, however, a physical point had to be created, which would serve as a focus for all these forces. This was the Foundation Stone, the first point of creation. Since it was the focus of all spiritual forces, it brought them all into play in the creation of the physical universe. It is therefore not surprising to find that the very first word in the Torah — *Bereshyt* — contains an allusion to this spot that was the focus of creation.[12]

It was in this same place that God created man. When God was about to create man, the Torah relates that He said, "Let us make man in our image" (Genesis 1:26). The meaning of this is that God was speaking to all the spiritual forces that He had created, bringing them all into the creation of man, the final goal of His creation. In order to bring all these forces to bear upon the creation of man, God created him in the very place where all these forces are focused.[13]

In a dynamic sense, all these forces are actually concentrated in man himself, and this is the meaning of the teaching that man is a microcosm.[14] But man would multiply and become many, while these forces would have to be focused on a single stationary place. Jerusalem, and particularly the Foundation Stone, is therefore a place of gathering, first only for the Jewish people, but ultimately for all mankind. As all men return to their spiritual source, they tend to strengthen the spiritual concentration in this place.[15]

The sages teach that God created man from the place of the Great Altar, the place of his atonement.[16] The meaning of this is that the sacrifices, brought on the Altar, would ultimately atone for man's sins. This, however, can also be understood in light of the above. The entire concept of sin is one of spiritual separation, where spiritual forces are separated from each other, and where man is thus separated from God.[17] The concept of sacrifice, on the other hand, is to reunite these forces. thus bringing man back to God. Indeed, for this reason, the Hebrew word for sacrifice, *Korban,* comes from the root *Karav,* meaning to "be close."[18] But sacrifice and atonement would be accomplished primarily in close proximity to this Foundation Stone, which is the one point that unifies and brings together all spiritual forces. Indeed, the primary purpose of the entire Temple Service was to rectify and strengthen the bond between these forces.

Upon this Foundation Stone stood the Ark, containing the

Two Tablets upon which God had written the Ten Commandments, as well as the Original Torah written by Moses. This was to underscore the fact that all creation is sustained by the Covenant of the Torah, as God said, "If not for My covenant day and night, I would not have appointed the decrees of heaven and earth" (Jeremiah 33:25).[19] All creation was contingent upon this covenant, which was made when Israel accepted the Torah from God.[20] The fact that the Ark stood on the Foundation Stone of creation means that all creation is infused with the power of the Torah.

Since this spot is where all spiritual forces come together to influence the physical world, this is indeed the "Gate of Heaven." It is from this spot — between the two Cherubim on the Ark — that prophecy emanates, and through there all prayers are channeled. This spot is the focus of all spiritual forces, and all communication that we have with these forces is through this location. It is thus taught that spiritual channels emanate from the Foundation Stone, bringing spiritual sustenance to all the world.[21]

This also explains the meaning of Jacob's dream, where he saw "A ladder standing on the earth, with its head reaching the heaven" (Genesis 28:12). The concept of a ladder is that of a single entity in which many steps are united. There are many steps on a ladder, but they are all connected by the body of the ladder itself. The same is true of the Foundation Stone, the place where Jacob slept. This too was a single entity to which all spiritual levels are attached.[22]

Since the Foundation Stone unites all spiritual forces, there must be a realm in the spiritual domain where all these forces come together. In the words of our sages, this realm is called "Jerusalem on High," and is said to parallel the physical Jerusalem.[23] This supernal Jerusalem is the realm where all spiritual forces are brought together to interact. In the words of some of our sages, this "Jerusalem on High" is called Shalem, from the root *Shalom,* since this is where even opposing spiritual forces exist together in harmony.[24]

As Creator of all spiritual forces, God Himself is infinitely higher than even the highest of them. The difference between God and any created entity, even the highest, is infinitely greater than the difference between even the very highest and very lowest things in creation. God is the Creator, while everything else is created, and there can be no greater fundamental difference than this.

This, however, presents some very serious difficulties. If God is utterly different from all spiritual forces, how can they have any association with Him? We know that God constantly acts upon these forces, this being the entire mechanism of Divine Providence.[25] Furthermore, like everything else, these constantly depend on God for existence itself — if God did not constantly infuse them with His creative force, they would instantly cease to exist.[26] But if both God and these forces are spiritual and different, then they are separated to the ultimate degree. It would only be through a physical entity that the two could be united.

In many places, when speaking of the Chosen City, the Torah calls it, "The place that God will choose to make His Name dwell there."[27] To the extent that we can understand it, this means that God associates Himself with this place. This is very difficult for the human mind to comprehend, and indeed, Solomon, the wisest of all men, found it impossible to understand. He thus said to God, "Behold the heavens and the heavens of heaven cannot contain You, how much less this house that I have built" (I Kings 8:27). Yet, he knew that God had somehow associated Himself with this place, as God himself had proclaimed in His Torah.[28]

But if both God and the entire array of spiritual forces are associated with this spot — the Foundation Stone — then they can indeed interact. Thus, it is by associating with the Temple and this Stone that God also associates with all the spiritual forces that He created, sustaining and directing them. As mentioned above, however, the array of spiritual forces is called "Jerusalem on High."[29]

We thus see that God does not associate with "Jerusalem on High" until He does so with the physical Jerusalem. This is the meaning of the Talmudic teaching, "God swore that He would not enter Jerusalem on High until He enters Jerusalem down below."[30]

This is also the meaning of the fact that God Himself

appeared at the top of the ladder in Jacob's dream. This is the concept of unification, not only affecting all spiritual levels, but also attaching them to God Himself.

The entire purpose of the Temple service was to strengthen this bond between God and the spiritual forces, thus enhancing them and giving them greater power to elevate the physical world. For example, on the festival of Succot, seventy sacrifices were brought, one for each of the seventy archetypal nations of the world.[31] Through this, the directing angels overseeing these nations would be elevated, and, as a result, the nations themselves would be brought to a higher spiritual level.

In a similar manner, other aspects of the Temple service served to enhance other spiritual aspects of humanity. Since the time that the Temple was destroyed, these spiritual aspects have also diminished.

This also explains why all our prayers are directed toward the Foundation Stone, the place of the Ark. We do not pray to any spiritual force or entity, even the highest, but only to God alone. The content of our prayer, however, is to rectify the various spiritual forces, bringing God's light to shine upon them.[32] Since the main connection between God and the spiritual forces is the place of the Ark, we focus our prayers toward this spot.

Through this, we can understand another very difficult Talmudic teaching:[33]

> Rabbi Yochanan said in the name of Rabbi Yosi (ben Zimra): How do we know that God prays? It is written, "I will bring them to My holy mountain, and make them rejoice in the house of My prayer, [for My house is a house of prayer for all nations]" (Isaiah 56:7). The scripture does not say "their prayer," but "My prayer." We thus see that God prays.
> And what is His prayer?
> Rav Zutra bar Tovia said in the name of Rav: It is, "May it be My will that My mercy should overcome My anger, and that My mercy dominate My Attributes. May I act toward My children with the Attribute of Mercy, and go beyond the requirements of the law."

At first thought this appears beyond all comprehension. How can we say that God prays? And if He does, to whom does He pray? And what is the precise meaning of His prayer?

But if we look carefully at the basic concept of prayer, this becomes somewhat easier to understand. When we pray, the object of our prayer is to bring God's spiritual Light to bear on the spiritual forces, so that they in turn should enhance the world in which we live. Prayer is therefore the enhancement and elevation of the spiritual forces. Of course, the One who enhances these forces is none other than God Himself, infusing them with His Light and creative force. When God acts upon these forces in this manner, He is said to be "praying."

This also explains the content of God's prayer. The concept of God's anger and His Attribute of Justice is essentially when He withdraws His Light from the spiritual forces, allowing them to function on their own. These forces then function almost automatically, dispensing justice according to a strict rule, in an almost mechanical fashion. This is the idea of God's "hiding His face."[34]

The concept of God's Mercy, on the other hand, is when God makes His Light shine on these forces, taking complete control of them, as it were. Thus, when God prays that His Mercy should dominate His Attributes, it means that He is infusing these Attributes with His Light and creative force. This is the concept of God praying.

It is important to note that God's prayer is associated with the Temple in Jerusalem — "For My house is the house of My prayer." According to what we have said earlier, however, the reason for this is obvious. God's prayer refers to His infusing all Attributes and spiritual forces with His Light, which takes place through the Foundation Stone, the focus of all prayer.

It is also very significant to note the ending of this verse, "For My house is a house of prayer to all nations." Here again, at first thought, it is difficult to see what connection this has to God's prayer. Why is the verse that teaches the concept of God's prayer associated with that of the Temple being a place of prayer for all peoples?

We must realize that the main reason there is distinction between Jew and Gentile is because of the withholding of

God's light. As a result of the sins of Adam, of the generation of the Flood, and of the builders of the Tower of Babel, God gradually withdrew His Light from the world, restricting it to one people, the Jews, who would inhabit Jerusalem and serve God there.[35] Therefore, there are directing angels over the gentile nations, but they are on a lower level than the spiritual forces associated with Israel.[36]

The concept of God's prayer, however, is that His Light should shine through all spiritual forces with its full intensity, and thus, to all mankind as well. Therefore, when God's house is the "house of His prayer," it is then also "a house of prayer for all nations."[37]

This again brings us to the location of the Foundation Stone, the focus of all spiritual forces. It was set on the crossroads of civilization, so that all peoples should interact with these forces and throughout history, be influenced by them. In this manner, all mankind is gradually elevated by these forces, paving the way for the ultimate rectification of the world. This will be realized in the Messianic Age, when Jerusalem becomes a center for God's teaching for all mankind: "Out of Zion shall come forth the Torah, and God's word from Jerusalem."

NOTES

INTRODUCTION

1. *Orach Chaim* 560:2, *Evven HaEzer* 65:3 in *Hagah*.
   See *Tosafot, Berakhot* 31a, s.v. *"Isi."*

1. FOCUS OF A PEOPLE

1. *Sefer HaChinukh* 487. See Chapter 6, note 1.
2. According to traditions, David captured Jerusalem in the year 2892 (868 B.C.E), and it was destroyed by the Romans in 3828 (69 C.E.), or 976 years later. See Chapter 7, notes 22 and 53. According to Josephus, however, Jerusalem retained this status for 1179 years, see *Wars* 6:10. Also see *Antiquities* 20:10.
3. *Kelim* 1:8. *Cf. Bava Kama* 62b, *Yad, Bet HaBechirah* 7:14. Also see *Ketubot* 13:11 (110b), Isaiah 52:1, 66:20.
4. *Yerushalmi, Chagigah* 3:6, *Bava Kama* 7:7, from Psalm 122:3. *Cf. Chagigah* 26a, Isaiah 33:20.
5. *Ibid. Cf. Metzudot David* (Radbaz) 266.
6. Hirsch on Genesis 4:17. Note that Cain was originally a farmer, and that the first city was built by Cain as an atonement for his murder of his brother. *Cf. Malbim ibid.* Their *altar* was in Jerusalem, see Chapter 6, note 9.
7. See Genesis 4:20-22.
8. *Ketubot* 111b, from 2 Kings 19:34; *Tanchuma, Ki Tavo* 4, from Lamentations 2:15. *Cf. Likutey Moharan* 280.
9. This was the tithe given annually, except for the fourth and sixth year of the seven year cycle, when the Tithe for the Poor *(Maaser Ani)* was substituted as a second tithe. See *Yad, Matnot Aniyim* 6, *Maaser Sheni* 1:1.
10. Hirsch on Deuteronomy 14:23.
11. Deuteronomy 14:23, Ibn Ezra, Rashbam, Sforno *ad loc., Tosafot, Bava Batra* 21a, s.v. *"Ki."* See *Chinukh* 360, *Metzudot David* 256.
12. *Chinukh* 360.
13. Deuteronomy 26:2. See *Bikkurim* 3:1-4.
14. Ramban on Leviticus 1:9. See *Tanchuma, VaYikra* 8.
15. *Chinukh* 95.
16. Man is thus like an angel in three ways, and like an animal in three ways, *Chagigah* 16a. Also see *Tanchuma, VaYikra* 8, *Zohar* 2:94b, 3:33b, Ramban on Genesis 1:20, Leviticus 17:24, Ralbag on Proverbs 12:10, *Shaarey Kedushah* 1:1, *Or HaChaim* on Genesis 1:21, Leviticus 17:10, *Likutey Amarim (Tanya)* 1:1 (5b).
17. *Etz Chaim, Shaar Kitzur ABYA* 2 (Aslag edition, Tel Aviv, 5720), Volume 2, page 395. *Cf.* Ramban on Genesis 2:8, 3:22.
18. *Cf. Yoma* 9b, 39b, *Tosefta, Minachot* 13:4, *Yerushalmi, Yoma* 1:1 (4b), *BaMidbar Rabbah* 7:10. Also see Isaiah 1:11, Jeremiah 7:11, Psalms 50:12.
19. *Yad, Maaseh Karbanot* 18:2.
20. *Chinukh* 186.
21. *Yad, Maaseh Karbanot* 18:1, *Chinukh* 453.

22. Leviticus 1:4, 3:2, 3:8, 3:13, 4:4, 4:24, 4:29, 4:33, 16:21; *Minachot* 93b, *Yad, Maaseh Karbanot* 3:6, 8.
23. *Yoma* 86b, *Shemot Rabbah* 38:4, *Pesikta* 6 (60b), *Yalkut* 2:479. Also see *Minachot* 110a, *Taanit* 27a, *Megillah* 31a; *Rosh, Rosh HaShanah 4:14*, *Orach Chaim* 1:5.
24. *Chinukh* 95, *Yad, Bet HaBechirah* 6:16.

2. THE TEMPLE

1. See Chapter 7, note 53.
2. Some say that the commandment to build the Tabernacle was given after the sin of the Golden Calf, see Rashi on Exodus 31:18, 33:11, *Tanchuma, Terumah* 8, *Pekudey* 11. Others, however, maintain that it was before the Golden Calf, see *Baaley Tosafot*, Ramban, Ibn Ezra, on Exodus 25:1, *Midrash Lekach Tov, Ki Tisa* 105a, *Tana DeBei Eliahu Rabbah* 17. Also see Josephus, *Antiquities* 3:5:8.
3. *Seder Olam Rabbah* 6; *Zohar* 1:129a in *Midrash Ne'elam*.
4. *Tanchuma, Pekudey* 2, *Zohar* 2: 162b.
5. *Berakhot* 55a, *Zohar* 2:152a, 3:324b, Ramban on Exodus 31:2.
6. *Yad, Bet HaBechirah* 1:2, *Seder Olam Rabbah* 11. See *Zevachim* 14:5-8, *Tosefot Yom Tov, Tiferet Yisrael, ad loc.* Regarding Gilgal, see Joshua 5:9, Shiloh, Joshua 18:1, Nob, 1 Samuel 21:2, Gibeon, 1 Kings 3:4, Chapter 7, note 28.
7. *Yad, Melachim* 1:1, *Lechem Mishnah ad loc.*
8. Rashi, *ad loc.* Note that a king is to be appointed when "you dwell in the land" (Deuteronomy 17:14), while the Temple is to be built "when you dwell in the land . . . and He gives you rest." See Chapter 7, note 32, Chapter 8, note 21.
9. *Orach Chaim* 660:1, *Teshuvot Chatam Sofer, Orach Chaim* 28. See *Succah* 51b, *Yad, Tefillah* 11:3, *Orach Chaim* 150:5 in *Hagah*.
10. Ramban on Exodus 27:20, *Sifra* on Leviticus 24:2, *Sifri* on Numbers 8:2, *Teshuvot Rashba* 1:79. See *Yad, Bet HaBechirah* 3:8.
11. Exodus 25:11-30, 30:1-10, 37:17-28, 40:22-27; *Yad, Bet HaBechirah* 3:17.
12. This is described in Leviticus 16, and the entire tract of *Yoma* is a description of this service.
13. Exodus 25:10,17, 40:18. See *Likutey Moharan* 2:6.
14. Deuteronomy 31:26, Rashi, ad loc.; *Bava Batra* 14a. See Radak, Ralbag, Abarbanel on 1 Kings 8:9.
15. *Shekalim* 6:2, *Tiferet Yisrael ad loc., Yad, Bet HaBechirah* 4: 1. See *Yoma* 52b, *Horiot* 12a, *Keritot* 5b; *Tosefta Yoma* 2:13, *Tosefta Sotah* 13:2, *Yerushalmi Shekalim* 6:1 (24b), *Seder Olam Rabbah* 24, *Yalkut* 2:247; *Kuzari* 3:39 (48b); Rashi, Radak, Ralbag, on 2 Chronicles 35:3. For a discussion whether the ark was concealed or carried off to Babylon, see *Yoma* 53b. There is a debate as to whether it was hidden under the Holy of Holies or in the Chamber of the Woodshed in *Yoma* 54a.
16. Deuteronomy 9:9 11, 15.
17. Exodus 31:18, 34:29. See Bachya on Exodus 31:18.
18. *Yad, Sefer Torah* 10:11.
19. Actually, the curtains of the Holy of Holies may have been opened during the annual pilgrimages so that the people would be able to see the Ark.

See *Yoma* 54a, *Tosafot Yeshenim ad loc, s.v.* "U'Marin." They thus actually may have seen the Ark and Cherubim of Moses, see Ritva *ibid.*

20. *Shemot Rabbah* 2:2, *Midrash Tehillim* 11:3. This seems to be disputed by the saying in *Rosh HaShanah* 31b, from Amos 7:7. The Midrash, however, apparently assumes that only seven of these steps actually occurred, and that the *Shekhinah* remained on the Western Wall. See Chapter 5, note 22.

3. THE SANHEDRIN

1. *Berakhot* 63b.
2. *Middot* 5:4, *Yoma* 19a, *Yad, Bet HaBechirah* 5:17. In *Middot*, the reading is that the *Lishkat HaGazit* was to the south, but according to most authorities, the correct reading is that it is to the north. See *Tosafot Yom Tov ad loc., Tosafot Yeshenim, Yoma, loc. cit.* Also see *Peah* 2:6, *Sanhedrin* 11:2(86b).
3. *Sanhedrin* 16b, *Yad, Sanhedrin* 1:1, *Chinukh* 491.
4. *Sanhedrin* 1:6 (2a), *Yad, Sanhedrin* 1:3. Cf. *VaYikra Rabbah* 33:2, *Eikhah Rabbah,* introduction:24.
5. The only place where *Ohel Moed* has a different meaning is in Exodus 33:7 (see Rashi *ad loc.*), but there it is rendered by the Targum as *Mishkan Bet Ulfana,* meaning "Tabernacle of teaching." Usually, however, *Ohel Moed* is rendered by the Targum as *Mishkan Zimna;* in such cases, it refers to the Tabernacle, as, for example in Exodus 27:21. The verse used here from Numbers is also rendered *Mishkan Zimna.*
6. *Yerushalmi, Makkot* 2:6, *Mekhilta* on Exodus 20:23, 21:14, Rashi on Exodus 21:1; *Tosafot, Avodah Zarah* 8b, s.v. *"Melamed."* Cf. *Sanhedrin* 7b.
7. *Yad, Sanhedrin* 2:7, *Choshen Mishpat* 7:11. Cf. *Sanhedrin* 88b, *Yerushalmi, Sanhedrin* 1:4 (8b), *Tosefta, Chagigah* 2:4, *Devarim Rabbah* 1:7.
8. During the persecutions of Constantine (337-361 C.E.), the Sanhedrin had to go into hiding, and soon after this it was disbanded. See Ramban on *Sefer HaMitzvot, Mitzvah Aseh* 153. Also see *Bava Metzia* 86a, *Bereshit Rabbah* 31:12, *Yad,* Introduction.
9. *Sanhedrin* 88b, *Tosefta Sanhedrin* 7:1, *Tosefta Chagigah* 2:4, *Yerushalmi Sanhedrin* 1:4 (8b), *Yad, Sanhedrin* 2:8, *Mamrim* 1:4.
10. *Sifri* on Deuteronomy 17:11, *Yad, Mamrim* 1:2, *Berakhot* 6:2, 11:3, *Chinukh* 496, Maharitz Chajot, *Succah* 46a; Ramban on *Sefer HaMitzvot, Shoresh* 2 (27b).
11. *Yad, Mamrim* 1:1.
12. *Sifri,* Rashi *ad loc., Chulin* 28a, *Yoma* 75b, *Yad, Shechitah* 1:4. Cf. *Tana DeBei Eliahu Rabbah* 15 (74a).
13. See Deuteronomy 6:8, Numbers 15:38; *Chagigah* 1:8 (10a), *Mekhilta* on Exodus 35:1, *Shabbat* 97b (top), *Yerushalmi, Shabbat* 7:2 (44a), *VaYikra Rabbah* 22:1, *Kohelet Rabbah* 5:7. Also see *Sanhedrin* 88b, *Kuzari* 3:35 (39a), Raavad on *Sifra,* introduction (1a); *Shabbat* 31a.
14. *Yerushalmi, Peah* 2:4 (13a), *Chagigah* 1:8 *(7b),Megillah* 4:1 (28a); *BaMidbar Rabbah* 14:12, *Shir HaShirim Rabbah* 1:18.
15. *Gittin* 61b, *Tanchuma, Noah* 3.

16. Kuzari 3:39 (46a)
17. *Sifri,* Rashi, *ad loc., Sanhedrin* 87a, Rashi on Joshua 15:3, Psalms 132:6.
18. *Zevachim* 55b, *Sifri* on Deuteronomy 33:12.
19. *Kuzari* 3:38 (42b), Rarnban on *Megillah* 2a; Rashi, *Yebamot* 13b s.v. *"Lo."*
20. *Yoma* 25a.
21. *Berakhot* 9:5 (54a).
22. *Yoma* 25a. See commentaries on Psalm 52:16. This was an important task of the Sanhedrin, see *Middot* 5:4, *Yad, Biyat HaMikdash* 6:11.
23. *Yad, Biyat HaMikdash* 2:5, *Chinukh* 151, from Leviticus 10:7, 21:2.
24. *Mekhilta* on Exodus 20:23 and 21:14. Both derivations are required; one teaches that they should be in proximity to one another, while the other teaches that there should be direct access from one to the other. See note 6.
25. *Bava Batra* 25b, *Orach Chaim* 94:2 in *Hagah.*
26. *Pardes Rimonim* 23:18, s.v. *"Tzafon."*
27. *Zevachim* 54a, *Yad, Bet HaBechirah* 1:14. Cf. I Kings 6:7.
28. *Bachya* on Exodus 20:22.
29. See Hirsch on Exodus 20:22. Cf. Ritva, *Yoma* 19a; *Arukh, s.v. "Gazit."* Others, however, define *Gazit* differently, see *Arukh loc. cit.,* from Numbers 11:31. See I Kings 5:31, 6:36, 7:9, 7:11, Isaiah 9:9, Ezekiel 40:42, Amos 5:11, Lamentations 3:9, 1 Chronicles 22:2. Note that the Tablets were also made of cut stone, see Exodus 34:1.
30. *Yerushalmi, Horiot* 1:1; *Avodah Zarah* 8b; *Sifri,* Hirsch on Deuteronomy 17:10.
31. *Tamid* 4:3 (end), Bertenoro, *Tiferet Yisrael* (63) *ad loc., Yad, Temidim U'Musafim* 6:4. Cf. *Beer Sheva, Tamid* 31b.
32. *Berakhot* 8a, *Megillah* 28a, *Yad, Tefillah* 8:3, *Orach Chaim* 90:18. While worshiping there, they also faced the south, the direction of wisdom, see note 25.
33. *Bereshit Rabbah* 55:7. See *Taanit* 16a, *Yerushalmi, Berakhot* 4:5 (35b).
34. See *Chinukh 404;* Ibn Ezra, Sforno, on Deuteronomy 14:23. Cf. *Yerushalmi Megillah* 3:1 (23a), *Ketubot* 13:1 (67b), *Shir HaShirim Rabbah* 5:10, *Eichah Rabbah,* Introduction: 12.

4. KINGS AND PROPHETS

1. *Tosefta, Sanhedrin* 3:2; *Sifri,* Ramban, on Deuteronomy 17:5; *Yad, Sanhedrin 5:1, Melakhim* 1:3.
2. Deuteronomy 17:18,19; *Sanhedrin* 21a, *Yad, Melakhim* 3:1.
3. See Maharitz Chajot, *Torat Nevi'im* 7, for discussion regarding this.
4. *Sanhedrin* 1:5 (2a), *Shavuot* 2:2 (14a), *Yad, Bet HaBechirah* 6:11 (from Exodus 25:8,9), *Sanhedrin* 5:1. See *Sifri,* Ramban, on Deuteronomy 12:5, from 2 Samuel 24:18. This is particularly true of the initial dedication of Jerusalem, see *Yerushalmi, Sanhedrin* 1:3, from 2 Chronicles 3:1, *Yad, Bet HaBechirah* 6:14. See *Bava Batra* 4a.
5. Radak on 2 Samuel 5:6, Psalms 2:6.
6. In this respect, the king was very much like a sacred vessel, which was sanctified through its prescribed use, *cf. Yad, Kli HaMikdash* 1:12. A king was anointed in a similar manner, *ibid.* 1:11. Regarding the anointing of

priests, see *Ibid.* 4:13. See Deuteronomy 17:20, *Horiot* 11b.

7. See *Tanchuma, Kedoshim 1, Zohar* 3:78a. There are other allusions in the Torah that the Royal Palace should be in Jerusalem. First, the reading describing the king follows directly after that prescribing that the Sanhedrin should be in Jerusalem. Second, the king is said to rule forever "in the midst of Israel" (Deuteronomy 17:20), and Jerusalem is said to be central to the Jewish people. Furthermore, in the entire book of Deuteronomy, the expression stating that God "will choose" (*YiBh'char*) only occurs in reference to Jerusalem, and in this one case, to the king. Also see Deuteronomy 33:5, Bachya on Deuteronomy 17:14.

8. See *Yad,* Introduction.

9. *Megillah* 15a, *Eikha Rabbah,* Introduction:24.

10. Rashi, *Taanit* 16a "*Horah,*" *Agadat Bereshit* 14:3, *Targum Sheni* on Esther 4:1, *Torah Temimah,* Genesis 22:5. Samuel thus had his first prophecy near the sanctuary, see 1 Samuel 3:3, commentaries *ad loc.* Cf. Isaiah 6:1. Abraham's vision described in Genesis 15 also occurred directly after he met with Malchi-tzedek, king of Jerusalem, and also may have been in proximity to the Holy City.

11. *Shabbat* 92a, *Nedarim* 38a, *Yad, Yesodey HaTorah* 7:1, *Moreh Nebukhim* 2:36, Ramban on *Avot* 4:1, *Shemonah Perakim* #7, *Iggeret Temon* (Warsaw 5686) p. 31, *Tshuvot Rashba* 1:548.

12. *Yad,* Introduction. See *Megillah* 17b, Ramban on *Sefer HaMitzvot, Shoresh* 2 (27b); *Shabbat* 14b, *Succah* 44a, *Bava Kama* 82a; *Tosafot, Bava Batra* 147a, s.v. "*Menayin,*" Rashash, *Megillah* 14a, *Kuzari* 3:41 (50a), Rash, Bertenoro on *Yadayim* 4:3, s.v. "*Maaseh,*" *Mishnah LaMelekh* on *Yad, Megillah* 1:11.

13. Hai Gaon, in *Tshuvot HaGaonim (Shaarey Tshuvah)* #14.

14. *Turey Aven* on *Yad, Yesodey HaTorah* 10:2, from *Yebamot* 64b. Moses was accordingly given three signs, Exodus 4:9.

15. *Yad, Yesodey HaTorah* 10:1. Cf. *Sotah* 12b.

16. *Sanhedrin* 1:5 (2a), *Yad, Sanhedrin* 5:1. See *Tshuvot HaGaonim* loc. cit.

17. Exodus 3:16, 4:29. See *Mekhilta,* Ramban, on Exodus 12:21.

18. *Bava Batra* 15a.

19. *Derashot HaRan* #8 (Jerusalem 5734) p. 128; *Avodat HaKodesh* 4:25. See *Bereshit Rabbah* 70:8. Before the Temple was built and the Ark stood in its proper place, prophecy was therefore difficult to attain, see 1 Samuel 3: 1.

20. See Numbers 7:89.

21. Abarbanel on 1 Samuel 3:3. This may be why God was said to "dwell among the Cherubim" (1 Samuel 4:4, 2 Samuel 6:2), and to "ride on a Cherub," Psalm 18:11, see *Targum ad loc.*

22. *Succah* 5b, *Chagigah* 13b; Rashi, Rashbam, Ibn Ezra, on Exodus 25: 18.

23. *Mekhilta* on Exodus 20:20.

24. *Moreh Nebukhim* 3:45, *Chazkuni* on Exodus 25:18.

25. The Cherubim are therefore seen as the angels of Gehenom, through which one must pass before he enters Paradise, see *Targum J.,* Bachya, on Genesis 3:24. The "Tree of Life" also is said to refer to the Torah (Proverbs 3:18), and the Cherubim thus "guarded" the original Torah that stood in the Ark.

26. Radak, Abarbanel, on Ezekiel 1:28; *Devarim Rabbah* 7:8, Rashi, *Chagigah* 13b *"Ra'ah."*
27. Ezekiel 1:5, 10:20; *Chagigah* 13b.
28. The Cherubim on the Ark are thus called the *Markava*, see 1 Chronicles 28:18, commentaries *ad loc.* Regarding the meaning of the *Markava* in general, see commentaries on *Chagigah 2:1*, *Hekhelot Rabatai* 1:1; R. Chananel, Hai Gaon (quoted in *HaKotev* in *Eyin Yaakov*) on *Chagigah* 14b.
29. See *Midrash HaGadol*, Ramban, Bachya, *Tzioni*, Hirsch, on Exodus 25:18, *Tanchuma VaYakhel* 7, *Moreh Nebukhim* 3:45, *Zohar* 1:32b.
30. *Berakhot* 8a, from Psalms 87:2. Zion thus refers to Jerusalem, but primarily to the place of the Sanhedrin. Also see Isaiah 33:20, *Pesikta Rabatai* 41. The Temple Mount is called Zion, 1 Kings 8:1, Isaiah 1:27. Zion is also in the portion of Judah, the part of the Temple Mount where the Sanhedrin sat, Psalms 78:67. Cf. 2 Samuel 5:7.

5. THE GATE OF PRAYER

1. See 1 Kings 8:29,30,33,35,38,42,44,48; 2 Chronicles 6:21 ff.
2. Daniel 6:11. See *Tosefta, Berakhot* 3:8.
3. Ramban *ad loc., Pirkey Rabbi Eliezer* 35 (82b). Cf. Ibn Ezra on Psalm 76:3, Radak on 2 Samuel 24:16, *Metzudot David* (Radbaz) 304. Also see *Kuzari* 2:14 (17b), *Zohar* 1:150b, 2:79a. Regarding Jacob, see below, Chapter 6, note 45.
4. See Radal on *Pirkey Rabbi Eliezer* 35:63.
5. *Berakhot* 30a, *Tosefta, Berakhot* 3:16.
6. *Tur, Orach Chaim* 98.
7. R. Yonah on *Berakhot,* Rif 22b *"Tzarikh."*
8. *Shulchan Arukh, Orach Chaim* 98:1.
9. *Berakhot* 4:5 (28b).
10. *Perishah* on *Tur, Orakh Chaim* 94:1.
11. See Chapter 1, note 23.
12. *Berakhot* 26b; *Yad, Tefillah* 1:5.
13. *Tur, Orach Chaim* 98.
14. *Noam HaMitzvot* 440. In the Temple itself, one would never turn his back to the Holy of Holies. Therefore, all sacrifices were offered with the priest facing this direction. See *Yoma* 53a, *Yad, Bet HaBechirah* 7:4, *Tosafot, Yoma* 25a, s.v. *"Hah."* Cf. Ezekiel 8:16.
15. *Bahir* (Ed. Margolies, Jerusalem 5711) #123. See *Avodat HaKodesh* 1:6, 2:14. Also see *Bahir* 109, *Zohar* 3:9a, 1:89b, Ramban on Genesis 2:8.
16. See *Berakhot* 31a, *Zohar* 1:202b, 3:8b, Radak on Psalm 135:21, *Likutey Moharan* 1:1.
17. *Berakhot* 49a, *Midrash Tehillim* 121:3, *Shir HaShirim Rabbah* 4.
18. *Yad, Bet HaBechirah* 6:16.
19. *Kaftor VaPherach* 6 (15a), Radbaz 691, *Magen Avraham* 561:2, *Tshuvot Chatam Sofer, Yoreh Deah* 233,234. Others, however, dispute this and maintain that there is no penalty today, Raavad, *Bet HaBechirah* 6:15. Cf. *Zevachim* 107b, *Tosafot, Shabbat* 14b, s.v. *"VeNe'elam."*
20. Rashi *ad loc., VaYikra Rabbah* 24:4.
21. *Zohar* 3:36, 3:74, *Likutey Torah* (R. Shneur Zalman of Liadi), *Masai* 91b.

22. *Metzudot David* (Radbaz) 418. See Chapter 2, note 20.

6. BEGINNINGS

1. Deuteronomy 12:5,11,14,18,21,26, 14:23,24,25, 15:20, 16:2,7,15,17, 17:8,10,15, 26:2, 31:11.
2. *Moreh Nebukhim* 3:45, Bachya on Deuteronomy 12:5. See Radak on 1 Kings 8:16.
3. See *Zohar* 2:198a, Abarbanel, *Kli Yakar*, on Deuteronomy 12:5.
4. *Yerushalmi, Nazir* 7:2, *Targum J.*, Rashi, on Genesis 2:7, *Bereshit Rabbah* 14:8, *Midrash Tehillim* 92:6, *Tanchuma, Pekudey* 3, *Pirkey Rabbi Eliezer* 12, 20, *Tana DeBei Eliahu Zuta* 2, Bachya on Deuteronomy 32:43. Also see *Sanhedrin* 38b (top).
5. *Yad, Bet HaBechirah* 2:2.
6. *Tosefta, Chulin* 3:7, *Shabbat* 28b, *Chulin* 60a, from Psalms 69:32. According to one tradition, this was offered on the first Sunday after Adam was created, see *Avodah Zarah* 8a, *Etz Yosef, Rif* (Pinto) *ad loc.* (in *Eyin Yaakov*), *Avot Rav Natan* 1:6, *Targum J.* to Genesis 8:20. There are some opinions that Adam was not driven out of the Garden of Eden until Saturday night, since the merit of the Sabbath protected him, see *Pirkey Rabbi Eliezer 19* (44a), *Kuzari* 2:20 (26a), *Kol Yehudah ad loc.* According to another tradition, however, he was driven out on a Friday afternoon, see *Sanhedrin* 38b, *Yalkut* (758) on Psalm 49:21. Also see *Pirkey Rabbi Eliezer* 20, *Shaar HaGamul* (in *Kitvey Ramban*) p. 296. *Cf.* Ramban on Genesis 2:8, *Bereshit Rabbah* 16:5.
7. *Targum J.* on Genesis 22:9.
8. *Pirkey Rabbi Eliezer* 20 (47b). This also took place on Sunday morning.
9. *Targum J.* on Genesis 8:30, *Pirkey Rabbi Eliezer* 31 (70b), *Yad, loc. cit.,* Rekanti on Genesis 8:20.
10. *Targum J.* on Genesis 8:20, 22:19, *Bereshit Rabbah* 34:9. This might be related to the question as to whether the flood destroyed the Land of Israel, see *Zevachim* 113b.
11. *VaYikra Rabbah* 20:1, *Tanchuma, Noah* 9. Shem was not the oldest son, but the foremost in wisdom and piety; *Sanhedrin* 69b, *Bereshit Rabbah* 26:3, Rashi on Genesis 5:32.
12. *Cf.* Isaiah 54:9.
13. See Rashi, *Midrash Agadah, Chazkuni,* on Genesis 12:6.
14. *Bereshit Rabbah* 56:10, *Midrash Tehillim* 76:3.
15. See notes 21, 34, 37, 39, 43, 55, 56.
16. Genesis 14:18, Rashi, *Targum J. ad loc.;* Psalm 110:4; Radak, Ralbag, on Joshua 10:1; *Nedarim* 32b.
17. *Bereshit Rabbah* 43:6, Ibn Ezra, Ramban, Hirsch, on Genesis 14:18. *Cf.* Isaiah 1:26.
18. See *Midrash Pinchas ben Yair (Midrash Tadshe'h)* 22, in *Bet HaMidrash* 3:192, *Otzar Midrashim* 2:474; Abarbanel on Joshua 15:63, Judges 1:21, 19:12, 2 Samuel 5:6. Cf. Josephus, *Antiquities* 7:3:1, 5:2:2. Also see *Arkhin* 32b, that there were two cities called Jerusalem.
19. This explains why God told Abraham to go to the Land of Moriah (Genesis 21:2), while Malchi-tzedek was said to be the king of Salem. See

Moreh Nebukhim 3:45. This may be related to the discussion regarding the meaning of the name Moriah. If Moriah also indicates teaching *(Horah)*, then it also includes the place of the Sanhedrin. See Chapter 3, note 33.

20. Noah's Altar was destroyed in the Generation of Separation after the building of the Tower of Babel, *Targum J.* on Genesis 22:9, Radal on *Pirkey Rabbi Eliezer* 31:33. After that, Moriah was in Amorite territory, see Rashbam, *Chizkuni,* on Genesis 22:2. Also see Ramban, end of commentary on Genesis 10:16. Regarding this conquest, see note 13. There is, however, a tradition that the builders were wiped away by a tidal wave, see *Bereshit Rahbah* 38:11.

21. *Sefer HaYashar* (Ed. Alter Bergman, Tel Aviv) p. 23. This is disputed by the tradition that Abraham had no teacher, see *Bereshit Rabbah* 61:1.

22. *Zohar* 1:78a, Rashi on Genesis 12:9; *Bereshit Rabbah* 39:16, Radak on Genesis 12:9.

23. *Nedarim* 32b, Ran *ad loc.* "U'Malchi Tzedek," *Pirkey Rabbi Eliezer* 8 (18b). Radal *ad loc.* 8:17; *Bereshit Rabbah* 43:6.

24. Genesis 21:23; Rashi on Joshua 15:63, quoting *Sifri* on Deuteronomy 12:17. (In our editions of *Sifri,* this statement regarding the oath is lacking, and Rashi there speaks of a different oath, see note 33.) Also see Rashi, Radak, on 2 Samuel 5:6, *Sifetey Chachamim* on Deuteronomy 12:17. This was besides the oath that Abraham later made with Ephron, see *Tosafot Shantz, Sotah* 10a, Maharitz Chajot *ad loc.* Also see *Bereshit Rabbah* 54:2, *Mekhilta* on Exodus 13:17.

25. See commentaries on *Avot* 5:3.

26. *Bereshit Rabbah* 56:1, *VaYikra Rabbah* 20:2, *Kohelet Rabbah* 9:2, *Tanchuma, VaYera* 23.

27. *Pirkey Rabbi Eliezer* 31, Radal *ad loc.* 31:9,28.

28. *Pesikta Rabatai* 40, *Yalkut* 2:988. See *Bereshit Rabbah* 55:7, *Nedarim* 32b.

29. Genesis 22:14, Rosh *ad loc.*

30. *Baaley Tosafot* on Genesis 22:14, *Midrash Tehillim* 76:3, *Bereshit Rabbah* 56:10; *Tosafot, Taanit* 16a, s.v. "*Har,*" *Minchat Shai* on Joshua 10:5. From the general context, it appears that Moriah or Jeru was the western half of the city, while Salem was to the east. See *Midrash Pinchas ben Yair, loc. cit.,* that David united these two parts of the city to form Jerusalem.

31. See *Berakhot* 62b, *Zevachim* 62a, *Kuzari* 2:14 (17a) Josephus, *Antiquities* 7:13:4.

32. In Joshua 15:9, there is a mention of Mount Ephron near Jerusalem. (This might be the present Mt. Zion.) Abraham lived at peace with at least some of the Amorites, see Genesis 14:13. Cf. Genesis 15:16.

33. *Pirkey Rabbi Eliezer* 36 (84b), *Midrash HaGadol* on Genesis 23:13, Rashi on Deuteronomy 12:17, Radak on 2 Samuel 5:6, *Tosafot Shantz loc. cit.* See *Mekhilta* on Exodus 13:11, Malbim (18), *Meir Eyin, ad loc.* See note 24.

34. *Bereshit Rabbah* 56:11. Isaac did not return with Abraham, Genesis 22:19, *Targum J. ad loc.* When Abraham took Isaac to Mount Moriah, he told Sarah that he was bringing him to Shem's academy, *Tanchuma, VaYera* 22, *Midrash HaGadol* on Genesis 22:3, *Sefer HaYashar* pp. 59, 60. Isaac mourned Sarah for three years before marrying Rebecca, *Pirkey*

Rabbi Eliezer 32 (73a). Also see *Yoma* 28b.

35. *Pesachim* 88a, Rashi *ad loc. s.v.* "Har," Tosafot, *Berakhot* 34b, s.v. "Chatzif." Isaac instituted the afternoon service, *Berakhot* 26b, *Yad, Melakhim* 9:1. It was called a field since it was not inhabited.

36. *Targum J.* on Genesis 25:21, *Pirkey Rabbi Eliezer* 32 (73a). Cf. *Zohar* 1:137a. Some say that Rebecca was with him when he offered this prayer, see *Bereshit Rabbah* 63:5, Rashi on Genesis 25:21.

37. *Targum J.* on Genesis 25:22, *Bereshit Rabbah* 63:6, *Pirkey Rabbi Eliezer* 32, Radal *ad loc.* 32:29. We find that Rebecca prayed on Mt. Moriah, see *Sefer HaYashar* p. 69. Also see Rashi, Ramban, on Genesis 25:22, *Moreh Nebukhim* 2:41 (end).

38. Rashbam on Genesis 25:28, Ramban on Genesis 27:4, *Zohar* 1:139a.

39. *Targum J.*, Rashi, on Genesis 25:27, *Bereshit Rabbah* 63:10, *Tanchuma B, VaYishlach* 9. Until this time, it appears that Shem and Eber shared the same academy. This is the first mention that Eber had his own school. However, the reason why they are spoken of separately may be because Jacob studied in Eber's academy after the death of Shem.

40. *Bava Batra* 16b, *Bereshit Rabbah* 63:11. Jacob was 15 years old when Abraham died, since Abraham lived to be 175 years old, Abraham was 100 when Isaac was born, and Isaac was 60 years old when Jacob was born. See *Sedar HaDorot* 2123. Regarding the sale, see *Tshuvot HaRivash* 328.

41. *Targum J.* on Genesis 27:27, *Bereshit Rabbah* 65:23, *Tanchuma B, Toldot* 10, *Agadat Bereshit* 42, *Sifri* on Deuteronomy 33:12.

42. *Bereshit Rabbah* 66:3, *Tanchuma B, Toldot* 16.

43. *Megillah* 17a, Rashi on Genesis 25:17, 28:9.

44. *Pesachim* 88a, *Targum*, Rashi, Ramban, on Genesis 28:11, *Targum* on 2 Chronicles 3:1, 21:15, *Pirkey Rabbi Eliezer* 35, *Bereshit Rabbah* 69:7, *Kuzari* 2:14 (f7a). Even though the Torah states that this "House of God" was originally called Luz, (Genesis 28:19), this might have been a name for the point in Jerusalem where creation began, see Bachya, *Tzioni, ad loc.*, *Bereshit Rabbah* 69:8, Radak, HaGra, on Joshua 16:1, Rashi on Joshua 18:13, Judges 1:23,26. God saw the merit of Jacob in this place, *Berakhot* 62b. Jacob initiated the evening service, *Berakhot* 26b, *Yad, Melakhim* 9:1.

45. *Pirkey Rabbi Eliezer* 35, *Midrash Tehillim* 91:7, *Zohar* 1:131a, 1:72a. Some say that he slept in Beer Sheva, Bachya on Genesis 28:18. Also see Bachya on Genesis 28:10, *Bereshit Rabbah* 68:5, Radal (3,4), Maharzav, *ad loc.*, Radak on Psalm 132:2.

46. According to some authorities, the verse, "Jacob came to Salem, a city of Shechem" (Genesis 33:18), is to be interpreted to mean that he actually returned to Jerusalem at this time. See *Maaseh HaShem*, Rashbam, *ad loc.*, *Zohar* 1:172b, Bachya on Deuteronomy 21:9. Another opinion is that it was a different Salem in the territory of Shechem, Abarbanel *ad loc.* Others write that the city called Shechem was in the land of Salem, *Sefer HaYashar*, p. 87. This position is supported by the fact that every place in the Bible where the word *Shalem* appears meaning "perfect," it is in conjunction with the word "heart," indicating a "perfect heart." The only exception is 2 Chronicles 8:18, but there

Shalem can also be interpreted to be a place name. Others, however, maintain that in the short verse, *Shalem* means "complete," so that the verse reads, "Jacob came complete to the city of Shechem." See Rashi, *Midrash Lekach Tov, Chizkuni,* Ibn Ezra, *Targum, ad loc., Shabbat* 33b. We find (Genesis 33:19) that Jacob bought a parcel of a field in this area, and in Joshua 24:32 we see that this parcel is actually in the city of Shechem, this being the place where Joseph is buried. There are firm traditions that Joseph is buried in Shechem and not in Jerusalem.

47. Genesis 33:7. See *Torah Temimah,* Genesis 32:9, Deuteronomy 33:45. At this time, however, Rachel was already pregnant with Benjamin, see *Targum J.* on Genesis 32:25. *Pirkey Rabbi Eliezer* 37 (87a). See *Esther Rabbah* 7:8.

48. See Genesis 32:25, Alshich *ad loc.* See my pamphlet, "The Jew," Collegiate Hashkafa Series, Young Israel, New York, 1973, pp. 5,6.

49. Genesis 35:1,7,15, *Midrash Lekach Tov ad loc., Bereshit Rabbah* 78:16, Radal, Maharzav *ad loc.*

50. *Sifri* on Deuteronomy 33:12. Benjamin was born in the year 2208, while Reuben was born in 2193, Judah in 2195, and Joseph in 2199. See *Seder HaDorot.*

51. *Sotah* 37a, *Tosefta, Berakhot* 4:16, *Mekhilta* on Exodus 14:23, *Zohar* 2:158b. Also see *Zohar* 1:89a, that Judah was given dominion because his name is identical to the Tetragrammaton, except for the *Dalet,* which stands for David. Regarding Simon and Levi, see *Targum J.,* Rashi, *Midrash HaGadol, Midrash Lekach Tov,* on Genesis 49:6.

52. *Bereshit Rabbah* 99:1. It was not in Joseph's portion, since the other brothers were punished because of him, Radal *ad loc.* 99:3. Joseph was sold at the age of 17 in the year 2216, and Benjamin was eight years old at the time.

53. Genesis 38:29, 46:12, Ruth 4:18-22. This took place in the year 2228. Judah's rule was enhanced at this time, see *Sotah* 37a, *Tosefta, Berakhot* 4: 16.

54. *Sanhedrin* 56b, *Tosefta, Avodah Zarah* 9:4, *Yad, Melakhim* 9: 1.

55. *Bereshit Rabbah* 67:8.

56. *Yerushalmi, Sanhedrin* 4:7 (22b), *Karban HaEdah ad loc.* (4:8), *Tanchuma B, VaYeshev* 17, *Esther Rabbah* 4:6, *Yafeh Nof ad loc.* It was also in this court that a decree was issued against premarital intercourse, see *Avodah Zarah* 36b.

57. Genesis 43:8, 44:14, 44:18, *Bereshit Rabbah* 84:17. Judah was sent by Jacob to establish an academy in Egypt, see *Targum J.,* Rashi, on Genesis 46:28, *Bereshit Rabbah* 95:3, *Tanchuma, VaYigash* 11.

58. *Targum J.,* Rashi, *ad loc., Megillah* 16b. See Psalm 78:67, and also see note 52.

59. Rashi *ad loc., Bereshit Rabbah* 98:8, *Sifri* on Deuteronomy 33:12, *Rashi, Zevachim* 54b, s.v. *"Velka."*

60. *Targum,* Rashi, *Midrash Agadah, ad loc.,* Rashi on Deuteronomy 12:14, Rashi, *Zevachim* 53b *"Toref,"* Bertenoro, *Middot* 3:1 (end), *Zevachim* 5:4.

61. *Zevachim* 53b

62. *Zevachim* 55b, *Tosafot Yeshenim, Yoma* 12a.

63. *Seder Olam Rabbah* 3, *Seder HaDorot* 2331, *Midrash Pinchas ben Yair*

(Midrash Tadsheh) 8, Bachya on Exodus 1:6. See BaMidbar Rabbah 13:8, Targum J. on Exodus 6:16, Shir HaShirim Rabbah 4:7. Levi had already been chosen by Jacob as the "tithe" of his twelve children, see Pirkey Rabbi Eliezer 37 (87a).

64. Sotah 12a, Maharitz Chajot ad loc, Shemot Rabbah 1:13,19, Shir HaShirim Rabbah 2:8, Kohelet Rabbah 9:17, Yad, Melakhim 9:1, Tshuvot Makom Shmuel 23.
65. Tanchuma B, VaArah 4, BaHaAlotecha 13; Yad, Avodat Kokhavim 1:3, Issuery Biah 13:2.
66. Mekhilta on Exodus 14:22.
67. Sifri on Numbers 9:5, Sifri, Targum J., Rashi, on Deuteronomy 33:8-10, Midrash Tehillim 1:14.
68. Rashi on Deuteronomy 33:12.
69. Yoma 12a, Megillah 26a, Zevachim 53b, 118b.
70. Mountains refer to Jerusalem, see note 73.
71. Pirkey Rabbi Eliezer 36 (84b), Rashi, Radak, on Joshua 15:63.
72. Mekhilta on Exodus 13:11. See VaYikra Rabbah 17:6, Devarim Rabbah 5:14, Yerushalmi, Shevi'it 6:1 (16a). See Sanhedrin 91a, with regard to their complaint to Alexander the Great, that there were African tribes who were descendants of the Canaanites. The Hittites, Jebusites and Amorites were all descendants of Zidon, Genesis 10:16. The Jebusite was one of the tribes promised to Abraham, Genesis 15:21. Also see Ezra 9:1.
73. Sifri, Rashi, Hirsch, ad loc.
74. See chapter 7, note 20.

7. DEDICATION

1. Sifri on Numbers 10:32, Deuteronomy 12:5, 33:12, Rashi on Numbers 10:32, Tosafot, Bava Kama 82b, s.v. "VeAin."
2. Siyach Yitzchak on Yoma 12a, Petach Eynayim (Chidah) on Zevachim 54b. See Megillah 26a, Yad, Tumat Tzaraat 14:11, Bet HaBechirah 7:14, Ralbag on Joshua 12:5. Cf. 1 Kings 11:32, Tosafot Yom Tov on Negaim 12:4, Zevachim 5:4. All tribes are partners in Jerusalem, Avot Rav Natan 35:3, Rashi on Deuteronomy 12:14. From Rambam on Negaim 12:4 (end), however, there seems to be an indication that Jerusalem may actually be an international city, since he derives it from Isaiah 56:7, "My house is a house of prayer for all peoples." See Minchat Chinuch 177:4, that the ground was divided but not the air space, cf. Zevachim 54a.
3. Joshua 10:3,5, 12:10.
4. Joshua 10:12-14.
5. Joshua 10:5. See Chapter 6, note 18.
6. Shalshelet HaKabalah (Jerusalem 5722) p. 225, Seder HaDorot 2478.
7. Pa'at HaShulchan 3:14, Bet Yisrael ad loc. 3:33. See Arkhin 9:6 (32a).
8. Ralbag on Judges 19:10, Abarbanel on Judges 1:8, Radal on Pirkey Rabbi Eliezer 36:78; Midrash Pinchas ben Yair, quoted above in Chapter 6, note 18. Others, however, maintain that Joshua himself conquered Jerusalem.
9. See Bava Batra 118a,b, Rashi on Numbers 26:54, HaGra on Joshua 17:14.

10. See Malbim, HaGra, on Joshua 15:8, Radak on Joshua 18:28.
11. *Yoma* 12a, *Megillah* 26a.
12. *Rashi ad loc.* See Chapter 6, note 24.
13. See Chapter 6, note 18.
14. Regarding the question when the episode of the concubine in Givah occurred, see *Seder HaDorot* 2516, 2764, 2811.
15. See Rashi *ad loc.*, Rashi, *Sanhedrin* 44b, s.v. *"Avikha Emori."*
16. *Sotah* 10a, *Tosafot Shantz ad loc.* David did not yet know that Jerusalem was the chosen city, see Ibn Ezra on Psalm 51:20, Rashi, *Makkot* lla, s.v. *"Nasa."* Until Psalm 51, there is no mention of Jerusalem at all. In Judges 17:57, we find that David also brought Goliath's head to Saul, while in Josephus, *Antiquities* 6:9:5, we find that he brought it to his own house. See Malbim on Judges 17:57. This may be a hint to the tradition that the Philistines had lived in Jerusalem and were protected by a covenant.
17. Sifri, Ramban, on Deuteronomy 12:5. It may be that the city must be ascertained logically, while the place of the Altar is to be revealed by a prophet.
18. *Ibid.,* Abarbanel on 2 Samuel 24:24. See Rashi, *Makkot* 11a, s.v. *"Nasa."*
19. Radak on Psalm 132:2.
20. *Zevachim* 55b, *Sifri* on Deuteronomy 33:12, Rashi, *Makkot loc. cit.* See 1 Kings 8:16.
21. *Ibid.* Another sign was the fact that Jerusalem was the only city divided between two tribes, see *Tosafot Yeshenim, Yoma* 12a, s.v. *"Ma Haya,"* *Sanhedrin* 111a.
22. *Sanhedrin* 20a, Rashi, *Tosafot, ad loc. s.v. "Shtey," Tzemach David* 2892, *Seder HaDorot* 2889; Radak on 2 Samuel 5:3, 1 Chronicles 11:4.
23. See Chapter 6, note 18. Cf. Rashi, Radak, Abarbanel, on 2 Samuel 5:6, *Pirkey Rabbi Eliezer* 36. See *Midrash Tehillim* 18:24.
24. *Midrash Pinchas ben Yair,* quoted in Chapter 6, note 18.
25. There is considerable evidence that the Jews lived in peace with the Hittites, see Radak on 2 Samuel 11:3, *Kiddushin* 76b. Also see Judges 1:26, 1 Samuel 26:6, 1 Kings 10:29,11:1, 2 Kings 7:6,1 Chronicles 11:41.
26. 2 Samuel 5:17, 1 Chronicles 11:3, Rashi on 1 Chronicles 14:8. This valley was to the south of Jerusalem, see Joshua 15:8. The *Metzudah is* identified with *Metzudot Tzion,* and it was on the eastern side of the mountain. Psalm 2 was said at this time, see Radak on Psalm 2:1, 2 Samuel 5: 17.
27. See Radak *ad loc.,* 1 Chronicles 16:1. Psalm 105 was said at this time, see Ibn Ezra, Radak, on Psalm 105:1, and also see I Chronicles 16:8. See *Bet Yosef* on *Tur, Orach Chaim* 50, s.v. *"BiZman."*
28. 1 Chronicles 16:39, 22:29, I Kings 3:4. See Chapter 2, note 6.
29. 2 Samuel 8:7, Rashi, Radak, *ad loc.*
30. Rashi on Deuteronomy 12:10.
31. Also 1 Chronicles 17:1.
32. Radak *ad loc.* See 1 Kings 5:17, 1 Chronicles 28:3, Abarbanel on 2 Samuel 7:13.
33. 2 Samuel 24, 1 Chronicles 21. See *Zohar* 2:125b, Ramban, *Or HaChaim, Paneach Raza,* on Exodus 30:12, Radak on 1 Samuel 15:4, 2 Samuel 24:1, *Midrash Tehillim* 17:4. See note 31.

34. *Yad, Bet HaBechirah* 2:1, *Targum* on 1 Chronicles 21:15, 2 Chronicles 3:1. See *Zevachim* 62a.

35. *Midrash Shmuel* 30, *Pesikta* 11 (43a), Radak on Psalm 51:16. There are only two places where David says, "I have sinned before God," one being here, 2 Samuel 24:10, and the other being with regard to Bathsheba and Uriah, 2 Samuel 12:13. In *Berakhot* 62b, we find that David was tempted to count Israel because he called God a Tempter (1 Samuel 26:9, see Radak *ad loc.*) with regard to Saul. Thus, there are two places where the scripture says of David, "His heart smote him," here (2 Samuel 24:10) and with regard to Saul (1 Samuel 24:16). It might be that because he called God a Tempter that he was tempted with Bathsheba, and this entire episode then was decreed to happen.

36. 1 Samuel 11,12.

37. *Avodah Zarah* 4b. See *Shabbat* 55b that whoever says that David sinned is mistaken.

38. *Yerushalmi, Peah* 1:1 (5a), *Sanhedrin* 10:1 (49a), *Zohar* 2:106a, *Emunot VeDeyot* 5:6, *Yad, Tshuvah* 3:14.

39. It is significant to note that Psalm 51 was said with regard to Bathsheba; Psalm 51:20 is the first mention of Jerusalem as a place of sacrifice, and indeed, the very first mention of Jerusalem in the Book of Psalms. It is thus evident that the episode involving Bathsheba is closely related to the revelation of the chosen place to David.

40. Rashi, Bachya, *Chizkuni, ad loc.*, *Berakhot* 62b, *Tanchuma, Ki Tisa* 9, *Pesikta* 2 (18b), *Zohar* 2:125b. It is important to note that the half shekel was intended as an atonement for the Golden Calf. It is taught in *Avodah Zarah* 4b that the main purpose of the episode involving the Golden Calf was also to teach the power of repentance. Regarding the relationship of the half shekel and the Golden Calf, see *Yerushalmi, Shekalim* 2:3, *Midrash HaGadol* on Exodus 30:11.

41. Exodus 38:26,27; Rashi on Exodus 30:15.

42. *Sifri* on Deuteronomy 12:5.

43. 2 Samuel 24:25, 1 Chronicles 21:25; Abarbanel on 2 Samuel 24:25, *Zevachim* 116b, *Pirkey Rabbi Eliezer* 36 (85b), *Sifri* on Numbers 6:26, Deuteronomy 12:6, Rashi, *Yoma* 12a "*Eleh,*" Rashi on Deuteronomy 12:14, Tosafot, *Ketubot* 99a, s.v. "*Natan,*" *Bekhorot* 50a, s.v. "*DeMizdavana.*"

44. I Chronicles 22:2 f., 29:2 f.

45. *Succah* 53a, Rashi, *Makkot* 11a, s.v. "*SheKara,*" Maharsha, *Succah* 49a, 53a. Rashi writes that David dug these foundations even before he bought the place from Arnon.

46. *Yerushalmi, Sanhedrin* 10:2 (52b), *Megillah* 1:1 (1b). See I Chronicles 27:33, Rashi, Radak, on 1 Chronicles 28:19. This was based on a scroll handed down from the time of Moses, see *Midrash Shmuel* 15 (end), *Agadat Bereshit* 37. Others, however, state that it was revealed to the prophets Nathan and Gad, see Rashi, *Succah* 51b, s.v. "*HaKall.*" See Rashi, *Eruvin* 104a, s.v. "*Ka Mosif.*" Also see *Iggeret Moshe, Orach Chaim* 39.

47. *Eruvin* 104a, *Pesachim* 86a, *Succah* 51b, *Zevachim* 33a, 62a, *Chulin* 83b, *Bekhorot* 17b.

48. 1 Kings 1:38,39
49. 1 Kings 3:1, Abarbanel *ad loc.* There were three walls around Jerusalem, see 1 Kings 9:15,19, Josephus, *Antiquities* 8:2:1, 8:6:1. There is also a mention of building the walls of Jerusalem in Psalm 51:20.
50. See *Pesachim* 54a, *Bereshit Rabbah* 1:4.
51. See *Targum*, Ralbag *ad loc.*, *Kuzari* 2:14 (17a). Also see *Josephus, Antiquities* 7:13:4, 7:3, 8:2.
52. *Zevachim* 62a. As before, the place of the Altar had to be revealed through a prophet, see note 17.
53. According to traditional Jewish chronology, the second Temple stood for 420 years, see *Seder Olam Rabbah* 28, *Yoma* 9a, *Yerushalmi, Yoma* 1:1, *Tosefta, Zevachim* 13:3, Rashi, *Avodah Zarah* 9a, s.v. "*Ki Mayanta.*" According to this tradition, the second Temple was built in 350 B.C.E., while according to secular historians it was built in 516 B.C.E., or 166 years earlier. Josephus also has a different chronology, see *Antiquities* 20:10, Wars 6:10. For a discussion of this, see *Tzemach David* 2:3842, *Seder HaDorot* 3828. The 420 years include 34 of Persian rule, 180 of Greece, 103 of the Hasmonians, and 103 of Herod. See commentaries on Daniel 9:25, *Seder HaKabalah* (Abraham ben Daud) p. 6.
54. *Taanit* 4:6 (26a).
55. See Chapter 5, note 19.
56. *Bava Batra* 60b, *Tosefta, Sotah* 15:12-14, *Orach Chaim* 560: 1.
57. *Moed Katan* 26a, *Tosefta, Nedarim* 1:4, *Orach Chaim* 561.
58. *Yalkut* 2:1009.
59. *Taanit* 30b.

8. REBIRTH

1. *Sanhedrin* 98a, *Or HaChaim* on Numbers 24:17; *Emunot VeDeyot* 8:5,6. See *The Real Messiah* (NCSY, New York, 1973) p. 65 [vol. I p. 253 of this work].
2. *Sanhedrin* 98a, Maharsha *ad loc.* "*Ad SheTikhla.*"
3. Ramban on Song of Songs 8:12, Radak on Psalm 146:3, *Derishat Tzion* 1:2 (p. 90).
4. *Sanhedrin* 98a.
5. *Tshuvot Chatam Sofer, Yoreh Deah* 234, *Petach HaDevir* 3:319d, *Din Emet* (Responsa at end of volume) 2, *Mateh Aaron* 2:274c, *Pitchey Tshuvah, Yoreh Deah* 251:4. Also see *Tshuvot Chatam Sofer, Orach Chaim* 203.
6. *Berakhot* 49a, *Tanchuma, Noah* 11. Also see *Midrash* quoted in *Sheveiley Emunah* 10:1 (93d), *Megillah* 17b, Maharsha *ad loc.*
7. *Iggeret Teimon* p. 30. See Joel 3:1,5.
8. Radak *ad loc.*, *Eruvin* 43b, *Eduyot* 8:7, *Targum J.* on Deuteronomy 39:4, *Pirkey Rabbi Eliezer* 43. Also see *Yad, Melakhim* 10:2, *Kereiti U'Peleiti*, end of *Bet HaSafek*.
9. *Yad, Melakhim* 1:3. See Chapter 4, note 1.
10. *Yad, Tshuvah* 9:2. See *Targum*, Abarbanel on Isaiah 11:2, Mahari Kara, *Kli Paz*, on Isaiah 52:13; *Tanchuma, Toledot* 14, *Agadat Bereshit* 45. "Coming of the Messiah" is the time when the Messiah attains this spirit of prophecy and realizes his mission, see *Arba Meot Shekel Kesef* (Cracow, 5646) p. 68c.

11. *Mekhilta* on Exodus 12:1, *Tanchuma, Bo 5;* Rashi, Radak, on Jonah 1:3, *Zohar* l:85a, 1:12la, 2:170b, *Emunot VeDeyot* 3:5, *Kuzari* 2:14, Ibn Ezra on Joel 3:1, *Tshuvot Radbaz* 2:842. The only one who apparently disputes this is Abraham Abulafia, see *Sefer HaCheshek (Ms.* JTS 1801) p. 32a ff.

12. *Yoma* 9b, *Kuzari* 2:24 (40a).

13. *Sifri,* Ramban, on Deuteronomy 18:15.

14. Thus, if the generation is not worthy of prophecy, it cannot exist, even though there might be worthy individuals. See *Sanhedrin* 11a, *Berakhot* 57a, *Succah* 28a, *Bava Batra* 134a; *Tosefta, Sotah* 13:4. *Pirkey Rabbi Eliezer* 8 (20b), *Avot Rabbi Natan* 14:1. Also see *Taanit* 30b, *Bava Batra* 121a (end), *Tosafot ad loc. s.v. " Yom,"* *Mekhilta* to Exodus 12:1, *Sifra* on Leviticus 1:1; *Yerushalmi, Taanit* 3:4 (15a), *Shir HaShirim Rabbah* 2:27, Rashi on Deuteronomy 2:16.

15. *Yad, Melakhim* 11:4. See *Yerushalmi, Maaser Sheni* 5:2 *(29b),Tosafot Yom Tov,* Rashash, *Malechet Shlomo ad loc., Shnei Luchot HaBrit, Bet David* 1:37b, *Petil Tekhelet* (in *Shloshet Sifrey Tekhelet,* Jerusalem, 5723) 8:2 (p. 160). Cf. *Megillah* 17b (end). We find that the Messiah will reveal himself on the Temple roof, *Yalkut* 2:499.

16. Rambam, Bertenoro, *Tosafot Yom Tov,* on *Sanhedrin* 1:3, Rambam on *Bekhorot* 4:3, *Yad, Sanhedrin* 4:11. For discussion, see Radbaz on *Yad, Sanhedrin* 4:11, *Tshuvot Ralbach, Kuntres HaSemichah, Tshuvot Yaakov BeRab p. 199, Bet Yosef, Choshen Mishpat* 295, *Birkey Yosef, Chosen Mishpat* 64, *Shach, Yoreh Deah* 242:22, *Sema, Choshen Mishpat 1:9, Minchat Chinukh* 491, Yaakov Emden (Maharibatz), *Sanhedrin* 14a. In the year 5298 (1538 C.E.), Rabbi Yaakov Berab restored this ordination, granting it to four scholars, Rabbis Joseph Caro, Moshe di Trani, Joseph Sagis, and Moshe Cordevero, but it was later discontinued.

17. *Eruvin* 43b, Maharitz Chajot *ad loc, Kereiti U'Peleiti, Bet HaSafek,* end; Rashash, *Sanhedrin* 13b.

18. See commentaries ad loc., *Yalkut* 2:620, *Kuzari* 3:73 (77a).

19. Ezekiel 38, 39.

20. Zechariah 12:2, 14:2, Radak *ad loc., Yalkut* 2:578.

21. See *Succah* 52b, *BaMidbar Rabbah* 14:2, Radak on Zechariah 2:3; *Bereshit Rabbah* 99:2, 73:5, 75:6; *Bava Batra* 123b, from Obadiah 1:18; *Or HaChaim* on Numbers 24:17. Also see Isaiah 11:13, Ramban on Exodus 17:9 (end), Ezekiel 37:16, Rashi, Radak, Ibn Ezra, on Zechariah 12:10. See Chapter 7, note 32.

22. *Pirkey Rabbi Eliezer* 31 (72a).

23. Jeremiah 3:17, *Shemot Rabbah* 23:11, *Avot D'Rabbi Natan* 35:9.

9. EYE OF THE UNIVERSE

1. *Tanchuma, Kedoshim* 10, *Pesikta Rabatai* 10:2, *Zohar* 2:157a, 2:222b, Ramban on Genesis 14:18, *Shalshelet HaKaballah p.* 31, *Likutey Torah* (R. Shneur Zalman of Liadi) *Masai* 91b.

2. *Yoma* 5:2 (53b), *Va Yikra Rabbah* 20:4, *Pesikta* 26 (171a), *Zohar* 1:71b (end), 1:231a, *Zohar Chadash* 28a; *Yad, Bet HaBechirah* 4:1, Rashi on Job 39:28. See *Likutey Moharan* 61:6, from Job 31:35.

3. *Tosefta, Yoma* 2:12; *Yoma* 54b, *Pirkey Rabbi Eliezer* 35 (82b), *Midrash*

Tehillim 91, *Zohar* 1:131a, 1:86b,87a, Ramban, Bachya, on Genesis 28:19. Also see *Zohar* 1:231a, 222a, *Tikuney Zohar* 67 (98a). God's Name is inscribed on this stone, see *Targum* J. on Exodus 28:39, Ecclesiastes 3:11.

4. *Bereshit Rabbah* 5:8. Creation began at a single point, *Bereshit Rabbah* 4:2.

5. *Moreh Nebukhim*, introduction to part 2, #16; *Or HaShem* 1:1:16, *Shefa Tal* 1:3 (Hanau 5372) p. 13c in note, *Pardes Rimonim* 2:7, *Amud HaAvodah, Vikuach Shoel U'Meshiv* 99. See note 7. Also see my book, "Tefillin" (NCSY, New York, 1973) p. 42 [pp. 261-262 in this volume]. Cf. *Toledot Yaakov Yosef* 197c, *Tzafnat Paneach* 26d, 68d, *Sefer Baal Shem Tov, Ekev* 72, *Bereshit* 41.

6. *Bereshit Rabbah* 50:2, *Targum*, Rashi, on Genesis 18:2, *Zohar* 1:127a.

7. For a similar argument, see *Yad, Yesodey HaTorah* 1:7, 2:5, see Commentary *ad loc.*

8. *Shabbat* 89a, *Bereshit Rabbah* 48:11.

9. *Pitchey Chakhmah VaDaat* 4, *Shefa Tal* 3:1.

10. *Zohar* 3:90b.

11. It is thus written, "He makes peace in His high places" (Job 25:2), see Rashi *ad loc.*, *Bereshit Rabbah* 12:8, *BaMidbar Rabbah* 12:8, *Bahir 11, 59,* 153. Also see *Chagigah* 12a, *Bereshit Rabbah* 4:7, Rashi on Genesis 1:8.

12. The word *Bereshyt* can thus be read as *Bara Shyt* — "He created the *Shyt*" — the *Shyt* being the foundation and drainage pit of the Altar, see *Succah* 49a. Note that *Shyt* is masculine, while *Shetiyah is* feminine, both words sharing the same root. The *Shetiyah* was the foundation of both the physical and spiritual worlds, see *Yoma* 54b. It was a place of constriction *(tzimtzum)* of spiritual forces, cf. *Likutey Moharan* 61:6.

13. *Bereshit Rabbah* 8:3. Note that the Jew was also created on the spot, since key events in the lives of the Patriarchs occurred here, see Chapter 6, notes 28, 45, 49.

14. *Avot Rabbi Natan* 31:3, Saadya Gaon on *Sefer Yetzirah* 4: 1, *Tikkuney Zohar* 17a.

15. Cf. *Metzudot David* (Radbaz) 266.

16. See Chapter 6, note 4.

17. Isaiah 59:2, Rambam, *Shemoneh Perakim* #8, *Reshit Chakhmah* 1:7 (22d), *Nefesh HaChaim* 1:18.

18. See Chapter 5, note 15.

19. See *Shabbat* 33a, 137b, *Pesachim* 68b, *Taanit* 27b, *Megillah* 31b, *Nedarim* 31b, *Avodah Zarah* 3a, *Tosefta, Berakhot* 6:18, *Yebamot* 2:6, Commentaries on *Avot* 1:2.

20. *Shabbat* 88a, Rashi on Genesis 1:31.

21. *Kohelet Rabbah* 2:7, *Tanchuma, Kedoshim* 10, Rashi on Ecclesiastes 2:5, *Sichot HaRan* 60.

22. *Tzioni ad loc., Sodey Razia* (Bilgorai 5696) p. 35a, *Megalah Amukot* 121,128,131, 134, 178.

23. *Taanit* 5a, Rashba (in *Eyin Yaakov)* ad loc., *Chagigah* 12b, *Tanchuma, Pekudey 1, Zohar* 1:80, 1:183a, 2:59a, Ramban on Genesis 14:18; *Yerushalmi, Berakhot* 4:5 (35b), Ibn Ezra on Psalm 76:3, Rashi on Genesis 28:17, *Targum*, Rashi, on Psalm 122:3.

24. Zohar 1:87a, 3:90b.

25. *Derekh HaShem* 2:5:4, 3:2:5

26. *Yad, Yesodey HaTorah* 2:9, *Moreh Nebukhim* 1:69, *Likutey Amarim* (Tanya), *Shaar Ha Yichud VeHaEmunah*

27. Deuteronomy 12:11, 14:23, 16:2, 16:6, 16:11, 26:2. See I Kings 8:29. Also see Chapter 6, note 1.

28. See *Sichot HaRan* 40.

29. Jerusalem is thus identified with *Yesod*-Foundation, the Attribute that unites Male and Female, see *Etz Chaim, Shaar HaArat HaMochin* 5 (p. 126), *Shaar Kitzur ABYA* 1 (p. 393). Cf. *Zohar* 2:184b, *Mavo Shaarim* 4:2:7 (p 165), *Shaarey Gan Eden* 89a, *Siddur Rabbi Shneur Zalman of Liadi* p. 53d, 59b, 62c, *Torah Or* 37d, *Likutey Torah, Ekev* (16c,d).

30. *Taanit* 5a. See *Pardes Rimonim* 8:26, *Shnei Luchot HaBrit, Torah SheBeKtav,* beginning of *VaYechi* (3:66b), *Likutey Torah* (R. Shneur Zalman), *Pekudey* (4a).

31. *Succah* 55b. Regarding these seventy directing angels, see *Targum J.* on Deuteronomy 32:8, Genesis 11:7,8, *Pirkey Rabbi Eliezer* 24, Ibn Ezra on Zechariah 1:8, *Derekh HaShem* 2:4:8.

32. See Bachya on Deuteronomy 4:7, *Tshuvot Rivash* 157, *Elemah Rabatai, Eyin Kall* 1:2, *Pardes Rimonim* 32:2, *Metzudot David* (Radbaz) 2, *Shomer Emunim* (HaKadmon) 2:64,65, *Kisey Melekh* (on *Tikuney Zohar* 22) 94b #50.

33. *Berakhot* 7a, *Otzar HaKavod ad loc., Siddur Rabbi Shneur Zalman of Liadi* p. 136c.

34. *Likutey Moharan* 26.

35. For details, see "The Jew," Collegiate Hashkafa Series, Young Israel, New York, 1973.

36. See note 31.

37. This was thus the place of the creation of Adam, the father of the entire human race.

SABBATH Day of Eternity

Aryeh Kaplan

Why the Sabbath?

There is a miracle in Shabbos.

Even if you have never felt it yourself, it is there. It is one of the most important ingredients of Jewish survival.

It is no exaggeration to say that the Jew has survived two thousand years of persecution and humiliation largely because he had the Sabbath. It was one factor that not only made him survive, but kept him alive, both spiritually and morally.[1]

Without the Sabbath, the Jew would have vanished. It has been said that as much as the Jew has kept Shabbos, so has Shabbos kept the Jew.

As long as Judaism exists as a vibrant, vital force, the Sabbath is its most outstanding ritual practice.

In order to understand this, you would have to experience a true traditional Shabbos. You would see a change take place, almost like magic. Take the poorest Jew, the most wretched person, and the Sabbath transforms him, as if by a miracle into a man of dignity and pride. He might be a beggar all week long, but on this one day, he is a true king.

There are hundreds of thousands of Jews who keep the Sabbath, with the number growing every year. To understand what Shabbos means, you must live it with them.

I remember once spending Shabbos with a poor working man in Williamsburg. He was a simple but pious man who did not have very much in the way of worldly goods. Seeing his cramped, dreary apartment, you might have pitied him, but at his Shabbos table, he sat like a king.

He made a remark that has remained with me all these years. "I pity people who don't keep Shabbos. I really pity them. They don't know what they are missing. They have no idea at all."

There is a Sabbath prayer that reads: "Rejoice in your kingdom, you who keep the Sabbath." The miracle of Shabbos is the kingdom of every Jew.

There is a miracle in the Sabbath.

Let us look into it more deeply.

◆§ The Primary Ritual

Two of the major parts of Judaism are the ethical and the ritual.

We can all understand the importance of the ethical laws of Judaism. None of us have any difficulty comprehending why the Torah tells us not to kill and steal, or why we must not shame or hurt another person.

On the other hand, Judaism contains many ritual laws, rules that strengthen man's relationship with G-d. These include the holidays, the Kashrus laws, and such things as Tallis, Tefillin and the Mezuzah. It is, in large part, these rituals that separate Judaism from all other ethical systems.

Among the many rituals of Judaism, we find one prime ritual that stands above the rest.

That is Shabbos — the *Jewish* Sabbath.

More than Rosh Hashanah, more than Yom Kippur, more than keeping Kosher or attending services, the Sabbath is the one ritual that marks the Jew.

It is the only ritual mentioned in the Ten Commandments.

Think about if for a moment. Of all the many rituals of Judaism, only one is mentioned in the Ten Commandments.

Many people claim that, to be a "good Jew," one need only observe the Ten Commandments. But if you do not keep the Sabbath, then you are only keeping nine of them.

At this point, the question must be forming in your mind, "But why? What is so special about the Sabbath? Why does it merit a place in the Ten Commandments? Why is it so important?"

The question becomes even stronger when we realize that, in ancient times, when Jews administered their own system of Justice, when capital punishment was administered, violating the Sabbath was a major crime, punishable, in extreme circumstances, by death.

The Torah openly states (*Ex.* 31:14), "You shall keep the Sabbath, for it is holy to you; any one who profanes it shall be put to death. For whoever does any work on that day shall be cut off from his people."

Put to death. . .Cut off from his people. . .Very strong terms indeed. But why?

In Torah law, we find that the penalty for violating the Sabbath was to be stoned to death, the worst possible form of execution. The Sabbath violator was put in the same category as the person who betrays his faith and his people.[2]

Jewish law treats one who does not keep the Sabbath as one who abandons Judaism for another religion.

The Talmud flatly states, "Breaking the Sabbath is like worshiping idols."[3]

In many respects, one who willingly and flagrantly does not keep the Sabbath is no longer considered part of the Jewish community.[4], [5]

But why should this be so?

One way of understanding it can be grasped by studying those authorities who take a more lenient view. They write that in modern times, one may extend to a Sabbath violator the privileges of being a Jew, for a very interesting reason. They state that no one would violate the Sabbath if he truly understood its meaning. Therefore, unless we have contrary evidence, we assume that a person violating the Sabbath is doing so out of ignorance, and therefore we treat him with sympathy and understanding rather than harshness.

All this highlights one point: *The Sabbath is the most important institution of Judaism.* It is the primary ritual, the very touchstone of our faith.

Not only is the Sabbath the only ritual appearing in the Ten Commandments, but it is also repeated more often in the Torah than any other commandment.

Our great prophets hardly ever mentioned any ritual. Their task was to admonish Israel with regard to faith and morality. But still, they placed a great emphasis on the Sabbath.[6]

Throughout the Talmud, the Midrash, and the other great classical Jewish writings, we find that the Sabbath has a most central place in Jewish thought.

Classical Judaism does not recognize such divisions as Orthodox, Conservative and Reform. There were basically only two kinds of Jews, The Sabbath Observer (*Shomer Shabbos*), and the Sabbath Violator (*MeChallel Shabbos*).

There is absolutely no question that the Sabbath plays a most central role in Judaism. But we are still left with our original questions.

How does the Shabbos create such an atmosphere?

Why is it so important?

What makes it so central to Judaism?

Why is a person who violates the Sabbath counted as an apostate?

What is the real meaning of the Shabbos?

✥ A Day of Rest?

Most of us think that we understand the Sabbath. It seems very simple. It is nice to have a day of rest, especially if one works hard all week. Everyone needs a day of rest, both for physical renewal and for spiritual relaxation.

Many of us hold on to this simple notion. We feel that the Sabbath was given as a day of rest for the weary worker. But this notion would imply that if we do not feel particularly tired, there is no need to keep the Sabbath at all, in fact, all too many of us use this as an excuse not to keep Shabbos.

But this simple "Day of Rest" explanation of Shabbos is really very weak — and the more we examine it, the weaker it becomes. In fact, it fails to explain any of the questions we have just raised.

It may be nice to have a day of rest, but why should it have such an important place in Judaism?

Why is it so central to our tradition?

The Ten Commandments are fundamental to Judaism. They contain some of its most important religious principles and ethical concepts. How did a mere "day of rest" sneak in?

If you are not tired on Shabbos, why is it so important to rest? Why not just take a day off whenever you do get tired instead?

If we look into the Ten Commandments themselves, it

becomes even more puzzling. The first Commandment tells us to believe in G-d. The second confirms G-d's unity and warns against idol worship. The third cautions us to respect G-d, and not use His name lightly. If one truly believes in G-d, then He is to be respected.

The very next commandment tells us to keep the Sabbath. Somehow, it seems to be out of place.

The first three commandments deal with our most basic concepts of G-d. Why does the Sabbath immediately follow? What does a mere "day of rest" have to do with our most basic beliefs?

The mystery deepens when we look at the text of the Commandment of Sabbath. As it appears in the Book of *Exodus* (20:8-11), it reads:

> *Remember the Sabbath day*
> *to keep it holy.*
> *Six days shall you work*
> *and do all your tasks.*
> *But the seventh day is a Sabbath*
> *unto the L-rd your G-d.*
> *You shall do no manner of work. . .*
> *For in six days,*
> *G-d made heaven, earth and sea*
> *and all that is in them,*
> *and He rested on the seventh day.*
> *Therefore, G-d blessed the Sabbath day*
> *and made it holy.*

The Commandment calls Shabbos, "a Sabbath unto the L-rd." Exactly what does this mean?

The Commandment also tells us that our Sabbath is supposed to symbolize G-d's rest on the seventh day of creation. Why is this important enough to be mentioned in the Commandment?

The Ten Commandments appear twice in the Torah, once in the Book of *Exodus*, and once in *Deuteronomy*.

It we look at the version in *Deuteronomy*, the question becomes still more difficult. Here the Commandment reads (*Deut.* 5:12-15):

Observe the Sabbath day
and keep it holy
as G-d commanded you. . .
And you shall remember
that you were a slave in Egypt
and G-d took you out
with a mighty hand and an outstretched arm.
Therefore, G-d commanded you
to keep the Sabbath day.

In this version of the Commandment, an entirely different reason is given for the Sabbath.

Here we find that the Sabbath is meant to recall the Exodus rather than Creation.

What is the connection between the two?

What does the Sabbath have to do with the Exodus?

If we say that the Sabbath is merely a "day of rest" and a time to relax after a week's work, how can we even begin to understand these things?

The truth is that we can't, and if we really want to gain a real understanding of the Shabbos, we must re-examine the most basic ideas of Judaism.

◄§ A Question of Belief

Judaism begins and ends with G-d.

It is essentially a way of life that brings man to G-d.

One who denies G-d, rejects the very basis of Judaism, and is totally cut off from it.

All this may seem very fundamental and obvious, but it is one thing to say that you believe, and it is another to understand exactly what you believe.

Suppose a person were to say, "I believe in G-d." Suppose that in the very next breath, he were to point to a statue and say, "This is the G-d I believe in!"

Such a person would be an idolater. He certainly does not believe in G-d, much less so in a Jewish sense. What he believes in is idolatry, not G-d.

We know that G-d is not a statue. But what is He?

This is a very difficult and complex question to discuss, but we do have certain concepts about G-d which form a fundamental part of all of Jewish tradition and teaching.

G-d is as real as anything else in the world.

He is One and unique.

He is absolutely incorporeal, having neither body, shape nor form.

Anyone who says that he believes in G-d but denies these truths, is fooling himself. He may say that he believes in G-d, but what he really has done is set up an idol and called it G-d.[7]

Let us clarify this point with an example.

You are standing in a room with Mr. Jones. You make a statement: "Mr. Smith is indeed absent." You point to Mr. Jones and say, "This is Mr. Smith."

Saying that Mr. Jones is Mr. Smith does not make it so; neither does saying that Mr. Jones is G-d make it so.

If you say that you believe in G-d, but do not believe that He is as real as you or I, or that He is One, then you really do not believe in G-d, at least, not the Jewish concept of G-d. You are really speaking of something else.

But how do we, as Jews, define G-d?

We find the answer in the very first verse of the Torah. It says:

"In the beginning, G-d created the Heaven and the Earth."

Here we have a definition of G-d.[8]

G-d is the Creator of all things.

He is the One who brought all things into existence.

This has some very important implications.

As Creator of all things, G-d must be both greater than all creation and distinct from it. Therefore, we, as Jews, reject the philosophy of pantheism.

As Creator, G-d's existence cannot depend on any of his creatures. Our definition therefore rejects any concept of G-d as an abstract ethical force or social convention.[9]

If a person says that he believes in G-d, but does not believe that He is Creator, then he does not really believe in the Jewish concept of G-d.

But there is another point in our belief in G-d.

Some people think that G-d created the world and then

forgot about it. They may claim to believe in G-d, and even admit to some abstract Creator, but they insist, at the same time, that His existence has no bearing on their lives. To them, G-d is a remote philosophical abstraction.

We see G-d as much more than this.

When G-d introduced Himself in the Ten Commandments, He said (*Ex.* 20:2), "I am the L-rd your G-d, Who took you out of the land of Egypt, from the house of bondage."

G-d was telling us that He is involved in the affairs of man and has a profound interest in what we do.[10]

G-d Himself gave the Exodus as an example. It was here that the entire Jewish people experienced G-d. To them, G-d was no mere abstraction. They saw His deeds to such an extent that they were actually able to point and say, "This is my G-d."[11]

Here again, one who does not accept G-d's involvement and interest in the affairs of men cannot be said to believe in the Jewish concept of G-d. He is violating the first of the Ten Commandments.

In the light of these concepts, we can now understand the significance of the Sabbath.[12]

Faith requires more than mere lip service. It must also involve action in the form of our steadfast adherence to G-d's will. The Hebrew word for faith is *Emunah*. It comes from the same root as *Uman* — a craftsman. Faith cannot be separated from Action. But, by what act in particular do we demonstrate our belief in G-d as Creator? The answer now becomes obvious.

The one ritual that does this is the observance of the Sabbath. It is the confirmation of our belief in G-d as the Creator of all things.

We now understand what the Talmud means when it says that one who does not keep the Sabbath is like an idol worshiper. Violation of the Sabbath is an implicit denial of faith in G-d, the Creator.

We can also understand why the Sabbath violator is considered outside the Jewish community. Judaism exists as a community striving toward G-d. One who denies G-d, as we know Him, cuts himself off from his community.

For the Jew, belief in G-d is more than a mere creed or catechism. It is the basis of all meaning in life, for if the world does not have a Creator, then what possible meaning can there be in existence! Man becomes nothing more than a complex physiochemical process, no more important than an ant or a grain of sand. Morality becomes a matter of convenience, or "might makes right." It is the belief in G-d that gives life purpose and meaning. It is also what gives us a standard of right and wrong. If we know that G-d created the world, and did so for a purpose, then we also realize that everything that furthers this purpose is "good," and everything that runs counter to this purpose is "evil."

The essence of Judaism is purpose and morality. One who does not actively believe in G-d as creator of the universe divorces himself from these two most basic values. He, therefore, casts himself outside of Judaism.

This also explains the reason Sabbath violation incurs the death penalty. For life itself involves purpose. A purposeless life is, in reality, no life at all. In a sense, therefore, one who does not keep the Sabbath is not really considered alive in the first place. The existence of the death penalty in such a case is not a mere vindication, but the confirmation of an already existent situation.

In a positive sense, the Sabbath is the focus of Jewish belief.

Once each week, the Jew spends a day reinforcing his belief in G-d. As long as Jews keep the Sabbath, G-d remains an integral force in their lives. Their faith is like a rock, and nothing can shake it. All the waves of persecution and prejudice break before this rock of faith. With this belief, they not only survive, they flourish.

For one day each week, the Jew can see himself in G-d's eye, and before G-d, every man is a king.

This is as true today as always. Many of our leaders bewail the decline of Judaism. But this decline is only to be found where the Sabbath is neglected. Among the community of Sabbath observers, Judaism is the same living and vital force that it always was.

৶§ Sabbath of the Exodus

Once we see G-d as Creator, it is obvious that His creation has purpose.

It should also be obvious that eventually He would reveal this purpose to man.

This immediately brings us to the Exodus.

It is the Exodus that makes Judaism unique. G-d revealed Himself to an entire people, and literally changed the course of nature for a forty-year period. This was an event unique in the history of mankind.[13]

The Torah itself speaks of this when it says (*Deut.* 4:34), "Did G-d ever venture to take a nation to Himself from another nation, with a challenge, with signs and wonders, as the L-rd your G-d did in Egypt before your very eyes? You have had sure proof that the L-rd is G-d, there is no other."

There are other religions in the world, but none of them can match the powerful beginnings of Judaism. The others all began with a single individual, who claimed to have spoken to G-d or arrived at Truth. This individual gradually spread his teachings, forming the basis of a new religion. Virtually every great world religion follows this pattern.

Judaism is unique in that G-d spoke to an entire people, three million people at the same time, who saw with their own eyes and heard with their own ears. That one historic, traumatic experience is the solid bedrock of Jewish faith.

The Exodus not only made us uniquely aware of G-d, but it also showed Him profoundly involved in the affairs of man.

The impact of the Exodus remained imprinted on the Jewish mind throughout our history. We saw every persecutor as Pharaoh, with G-d standing on the sidelines ready to repeat the miracle of the Exodus. We were thus able to withstand a long, gloomy exile.

We usually associate the Exodus with Passover. But it is just as intimately connected with the Sabbath.

One of the important miracles of the Exodus was that of the Manna.

For forty years, some three million people were literally fed by a miracle. This miracle, a lesson for the ages, dramatically demonstrates G-d's involvement in the day-to-day life of each one of us.

In order that the Jews not forget that it was a miracle, the Manna was presented in a most unique way. It only appeared six days a week, but was absent on the Sabbath. The miracle of the Manna paralleled the miracle of Creation.

When Moses told the Jews about the forthcoming Manna, he said (*Ex.* 16:26), "You shall gather it for six days, but on the seventh day, the Sabbath, there shall be none."

This also answers another important question. How do we know which day was the Sabbath? Who counted it from the time of Creation?

The answer is that G-d Himself revealed the exact day of the Sabbath in giving the Manna.[14]

Thus, the Torah says (*Ex.* 16:29), "See, G-d has given you the Sabbath. Therefore, He gives you two days' food every sixth day. . .let no man go out on the seventh day."

From then on, for over three thousand years from the Exodus until our own day, the Sabbath has been faithfully kept.

We recall the Exodus and the miracle of the Manna every time we celebrate the Shabbos.

The two Challahs on the Shabbos table represent the double portion of Manna that fell each Friday.[15]

The Sabbath tablecloth represents the dew that covered the ground before the Manna fell. The Challah cover is the dew covering the Manna to protect it.[16]

During the entire period of the Exodus, we lived with a unique intimacy with G-d.

The Torah says (*Deut.* 8:3), "G-d fed you with Manna that neither you nor your fathers had known — to teach you that man does not survive by bread alone, but lives by every word that comes from the mouth of G-d."

On the Sabbath, we seek to revive and deeply feel this close relationship with G-d, and live by the Word.

Sabbath Rest

Many of us realize the importance of the Sabbath, but have confused ideas about how to keep it.

After all, rest has many connotations. For some, it may mean a relaxing game of golf. For others, it may be an afternoon watching television. Others may think of rest as reading a good book, painting a picture, or writing a poem.

Somehow, these ideas do not seem to fit the Jewish idea of Shabbos.

The Sabbath is supposed to remind us of the drama of creation. But exactly how does this work? How does the Sabbath bring us to recall this?

There is another thing about the Sabbath that many of us seem to find difficult to understand. There is a whole body of ritual law — *Halachah* — surrounding the Sabbath. This consists of a set of very stringent rules. They comprise two major tractates of the Talmud, *Shabbos* and *Eruvin,* and include almost 200 chapters in the *Shulchan Aruch,* the unabridged code of Jewish Law.

Most of us are hardly aware that this body of law exists.

If we are aware of some rules, we do not understand them at all. Because of this lack of understanding, we often fail to observe these rules completely.

If we think of the Sabbath as a "day of rest" from a hard week's work, then these rules do not make any sense at all.

These rules involve ritual laws. Many things are forbidden even where no physical effort is involved. It is not only forbidden to make a bonfire, it is even forbidden to throw the smallest stick into a flame. One may not pluck a single blade of grass, write down a telephone number, or put a pot on the stove to boil, even though none of these things involve much physical effort. We are told that riding a car is "work," even though walking certainly involves more effort.

In the Torah, we find an account of a man found gathering some sticks on the Sabbath.[1] He was not working very hard, but was found guilty of breaking the Sabbath and therefore punished by death.

What does all this mean?

Why are we forbidden to do so many things even when little or no physical work is involved?

It is obvious that the restrictions of Shabbos are not directed at physical work, but rather some form of ritual work.

Clearly, we must delve further into the Sabbath and fathom its meaning.

The Torah calls the Sabbath an everlasting sign between G-d and Israel.[2]

The Sabbath involves both G-d and the Jewish people. In order to understand its rules, we must look more deeply into both of these ideas.

ᴥᵃ§ G-d's Rest

As we discussed earlier, the concept of the Sabbath is intimately bound to the concept of G-d's rest after the act of creation.

Before we can hope to understand the Sabbath, we must first understand the meaning and significance of G-d's rest. But this itself presents some difficulties.

What does the Torah mean when it says that G-d rested?

Was He tired? Had He worked too hard? Was Creation an exhausting task?

Is the Torah so naive that it looks at G-d in such anthropomorphic and human terms? Does it really assume that G-d needed a rest after six days of hard work, just like any other laborer?

Of course not. The Bible itself says (*Isa.* 40:28), "Do you not know? Have you not heard? The L-rd, the everlasting G-d, Creator of the wide world, grows neither weary nor faint."

G-d did not rest because He was tired or overworked. Even creating a universe is not hard work for G-d. Our Sages teach us that it involved less effort than to pronounce a single letter.[3]

G-d rested in another sense. He rested when He stopped creating — when He no longer interfered with His world. This gives us an insight into the Torah's definition of Sabbath rest.

We rest in a Sabbath sense when we no longer interfere with the world. In this way, we emulate G-d's rest on the Sabbath, when He stopped interfering with His world.

During the six days of Creation, G-d asserted His mastery over the universe by actively changing it. On the Sabbath, He "rested" by no longer asserting this mastery.

We emulate G-d by relinquishing our mastery over the world on the Sabbath.

We now have a new understanding of work that makes the entire concept of the Sabbath make sense.

This is our definition:

Work, in the Sabbath sense, is an act that shows man's mastery over the world by means of his intelligence and skill. [4]

We now also have a definition of rest:

Rest, in the Sabbath sense, is not interfering with nature nor exhibiting mastery over it. It is a state of peace between man and nature.

We can now understand the Sabbath ritual. We must leave nature untouched. We must not demonstrate our mastery over nature, nor change it in any way.

We must not intervene in the natural process. Any change or interference, no matter how trivial or small, is a violation of this rest.

Heavy work, and physical labor, such as plowing and building, are still work in this sense. But it also includes many things that require no effort at all — things like lighting a match, plucking a rose, or frying an egg.

These may not require much effort, but they are symbols of man's dominance over nature.

The Sabbath is much more than a mere "day of rest" from a hard week's work. It is a symbol of our belief in G-d's creation. On Sabbath, the process of creation stopped completely.

We emulate G-d's rest with our Sabbath. Therefore, even the most trivial act of interference with creation can be considered work and a violation of the Sabbath.

◂§ The Day of Eternity

The Sabbath is called both holy and blessed. This is intimately tied to the Sabbath of creation and to the concept of rest. The Fourth Commandment thus reads (*Ex.* 20:11): "For in six days, G-d made heaven, earth and sea, and all that is in them, and He rested on the seventh day. Therefore, G-d blessed the Sabbath day and made it holy."

To understand the deeper significance of the Sabbath, we must first understand the Sabbath of creation. Why did G-d rest after six days? Why did G-d set aside a day when He specifically stopped working?

This becomes even more puzzling when we look at the account of creation. As we go through the six days, we find that each one brings a higher level of creation. First there is inert matter, then plants, then animals, and finally man. We would expect the seventh day to continue this sequence and produce something even higher. Instead, we find nothing. . .

We can understand this in terms of a Midrash.[5] In the account of creation, the Torah says (*Gen.* 2:2), "G-d finished on the seventh day."

The Midrash asks an obvious question. If G-d rested on the seventh day, how could He have finished on the very same day? If He did nothing on the Sabbath, then obviously, He finished on the sixth day.

The Midrash gives us a most profound answer. It says that *on the Sabbath, G-d created Rest.*

In order to understand this, we must introduce a still more fundamental concept:

The more something resembles G-d, the closer it is and the more it partakes of Him. Indeed, the ultimate purpose of Judaism is such an emulation of G-d.[6]

G-d dwells in Eternity, in a realm beyond change and time. He Himself told His prophet (*Malachi* 3:6), "I am G-d, I do not change."[7] Serenity and tranquility are therefore an imitation of G-d's attributes.

On the Seventh Day, G-d added this dimension of tranquility and harmony to the world. It was no longer in a process of change, and therefore was able to partake of G-d's serenity. As such, it became holy and blessed.[8]

The Sabbath thus became the day of eternity. In this way, the world was then able to partake of G-d's timelessness.

In a sense, G-d descended to the world on the Sabbath of creation. It is interesting to note that the word *Shabbos* is related to the word *Sheves*, to dwell. On the Sabbath, G-d made the world His dwelling place.

The Sabbath thus brought about an integral harmony between G-d and His world. Rather than continuing to change the universe, G-d brought it into harmony with Himself.

The *Zohar* tells us that the mystery of the Sabbath is Unity.[9] On the Sabbath, G-d created Harmony between Himself and the universe.

When man observes the Sabbath, he too partakes of G-d's eternity. He enters into a state of harmony with both G-d and the world. Man is then in a state of peace with all creation.

This immediately explains why the concept of peace is so important on the Sabbath. One of the most common Sabbath greetings is *Shabbat Shalom*/Sabbath peace, for the main idea of the Sabbath is peace; not just peace between man and his fellow, but peace between man and all creation.

⋽ To Be a Man

This also gives us a deeper insight into how the Sabbath recalls the Exodus. Both symbolize freedom.

All week long, man lacks a certain freedom. He is bound to the material world and is a slave to its pressures. He may show his dominance over nature by taking bread from the ground, but this is also part of the curse (*Gen.* 3:19), "By the sweat of your brow shall you eat bread." Man's act of asserting his dominance over nature makes him a slave to it.

On the Sabbath, man is freed from this slavery. He can exist in harmony with his world and need no longer battle it.

All week long, man is ruled by his need to dominate the world. People are usually defined by their occupations. One is a plumber, another a nurse, or a brickmason, or a writer, or a housewife. A man's occupation is, in fact, the way in which he exercises his dominance over nature. But somehow, his most basic humanity is submerged by his occupation.

On the Sabbath, all this is changed. Every man is a king, ruling his own destiny. He is no longer defined by his occupation. He is a man— in the fullest sense of the word.

On the Sabbath you can be a man..

You can also be a Jew. . .

More than at any other time, the Jew can live as a Jew on the Sabbath. He divorces himself from everything else in the world and turns to G-d. He looks into the window of Eternity and feels the closeness of G-d.

The main Sabbath ritual is negative action. One observes the Sabbath by *not* doing. As long as one does not do any of the forbidden categories of work, he is actually fulfilling the Mitzvah of keeping the Sabbath.[10]

One can therefore observe the Mitzvah of keeping the Sabbath literally every second of the day, even while sleeping. All that is required is that one *not* do any work. The Sabbath is unique in this respect, giving a person the opportunity to be totally immersed in a Mitzvah for an entire day, without any positive effort on his part.

It is told that the Hasidic leader, the Lentcher Rebbe, once said, "The Succah is one Mitzvah into which you can enter, even with your boots." When Rabbi Yaakov Yitzchak of Pshiska, known as the "Holy Yid," heard this, he remarked, 'You can walk out of the Succah — but you spend every instant immersed in the Sabbath."

The unique aspect of the Sabbath is in fact that through it we can partake of G-d without any positive effort. All we must do is refrain from work, and G-d does the rest.[11]

In a sense, this is what the Torah means when it says (*Ex.* 31:13), "You shall keep My Sabbaths. . .that you may know that I am G-d, *Who makes you holy."* At all other times, one must strive to make *himself* holy, by doing the various Mitzvos. But on the Sabbath, one need only refrain from doing — and G-d does the rest. It is then *He* Who is the One making the person holy.[12]

The Midrash tells us that all the days were paired off except the Sabbath. Sunday was paired with Monday, Tuesday with Wednesday, and Thursday with Friday. Only the Sabbath was left without a mate. When the Sabbath complained, G-d proclaimed that the Jewish people would be his mate.[13]

On the Sabbath, you can be a Jew in the fullest sense of the word. Every second of the day can infuse you with the unique closeness to G-d that is the essence of Judaism.

◄§ When All Will Be Sabbath

The great hope of the Jewish people is the Messianic Age which will be followed by a time of universal harmony. It will be a time when man will learn to live at peace, both with his fellows and with nature. It will mark the end of all war, injustice and exploitation.

In the Talmud[14] the Messianic Age is called *Yom SheKulo Shabbos* — the day when all will be Sabbath.

As the Bible describes it (*Micah* 4:4), "Every man will sit under his vine and beneath his fig tree, and none will make them afraid."

The coming of the Messiah will herald the greatest revolution in the history of mankind. It will mark the ultimate triumph of man over evil.

One of the great problems with revolutions is that they usually fail. The new regime is usually as corrupt as the old one. The revolutions know what they wish to destroy, but they most often have no idea with what they wish to replace it. They never have a chance to really get the feel of the new order. Then, when they finally seize power, they are too busy with the details of administration.

The Sabbath is a rehearsal for revolution.

On every Sabbath, we partake of the Future World — of the peace and harmony of the Messianic Age. The Jew who keeps Shabbos knows the meaning of true harmony and tranquility. He knows how to use it and how to elevate himself with it.

When the Messianic revolution comes, he will not be unprepared. By observing the Sabbath, he will be ready for the Day When All is Sabbath.

The Sabbath keeps us aware of our final goal in life. It is very easy to become engulfed by the worldly. The Sabbath constantly reminds us of a higher reality.[15]

The Shabbos teaches us to plan ahead. Everything we eat on the Sabbath must be prepared beforehand. The same is true of Eternity. When speaking of the Future Reward the Talmud says, "He who prepares on Friday, will eat on the Sabbath."[16]

Every time we prepare for the Sabbath, we are also reminding ourselves to prepare for the World When All is Sabbath. We remind ourselves that our stay in this world is but a preparation for something much more lofty.

The Torah calls Shabbos (*Ex.* 31:17), "an eternal sign." The author of *Reshis Chochmah* writes that this means that it is a "sign of Eternity." On Shabbos, the door opens a crack, and we see a spark of the Eternal. We feel a breeze blowing from the Future World When All is Sabbath. The Shabbos feeling is a sign of the Future, when man and G-d will be in total harmony.[17]

The Fourth Commandment tells us to "Remember the Sabbath."

Remember. . .

Sabbath Work

One of the most confusing things about the Sabbath for most people is the concept of Sabbath work. Many of us think of work as heavy physical labor, or else, as going about our usual occupations. As we have seen earlier, this is not true in the case of the Sabbath. Here, the prohibition is not against actual labor as much as against ritual work. We have also seen that in order to understand the Sabbath, we must define ritual work as any act in which man interferes with nature and shows his mastery over it.

Still, this does not provide us with any details. It does not tell us, in particular, what things are forbidden and which ones are permitted. At best, it provides us with an overall philosophy of ritual work. For the particulars, we must search further.

~§ The Unwritten Torah

With the exception of a few cases which we will discuss later, the Torah does not specify exactly what types of work are forbidden. There are some hints and allusions, but no clear picture is provided.

However, it is important to realize that the Torah really consists of two parts.

First of all, there is the Written Torah (*Torah SheBeKesav*), with which we are all familiar. This is the Torah that we keep in the ark, consisting of the Five Books of Moses, the first five books of the Bible.

However, there is also the Unwritten or Oral Torah (*Torah SheBaal Peh*), consisting of the oral tradition given to Moses at Sinai.

The Torah was not meant to be a mere book, lying on a

shelf. It was meant to be part of the everyday life of an entire people. As such, it could only be transmitted by word of mouth. The Oral Torah was handed down from teacher to disciple for almost 1,500 years. During the time of the Roman persecutions, it became very difficult to maintain the academies where the Oral Torah was taught, and it was feared that it would be forgotten and lost. Because of this, it was finally put into writing some 1,700 years ago to form what we call the Talmud.

The Talmud itself says that the laws of the Sabbath are only alluded to by a hairbreadth in the Written Torah, but rise like mountains in the Oral Law.[1]

One reason for this was because the Sabbath was a weekly affair. Every Jew knew quite well what was permitted and what was forbidden on the Sabbath. Every family was an academy where the Sabbath laws were taught. It was only when new or different questions arose that the Sages had to be consulted.

In a sense, this is still true today. It is very difficult to write about the rules of the Sabbath, even though we shall attempt to do so in the next section. However, in written form, they seem very difficult and complex. This is really a misleading impression. The best way, by far, to learn the rules of Sabbath is to spend a few weekends with someone who observes it, for the Sabbath is much more than a mere set of rules. It is really a totally different way of life. The only way one can really learn a way of life is by living it. Put it in writing, and it seems difficult and formidable.

It is for this very reason that the detailed laws of Shabbos were not included in the Written Torah. They could only be learned as a way of life, and this essentially *was* the Oral Tradition.

However, there are several important allusions to the rules of Shabbos in the written Torah. These teach us a number of important lessons and bear close examination.

◄§ The Tabernacle

One of the first things that the Jews did in the wilderness after receiving the Torah was to build a tabernacle to G-d. This was to be a permanent sign of G-d's presence among them, as

G-d Himself told Moses (*Ex.* 25:8), "They shall make Me a sanctuary, and I shall dwell among them." The Tabernacle was a sign of Israel's dedication to G-d.

Just before G-d told Moses to start building the Tabernacle, He repeated the commandment of the Sabbath.[2] The Torah also tells us that before building the Tabernacle, Moses gathered the entire Jewish nation and repeated this command-ment.[3]

The Oral Torah uses this allusion to provide us with a most important lesson regarding the Sabbath. All work on the Tabernacle had to cease on the Sabbath. Even the slightest effort toward completing the Tabernacle had to be aban-doned.[4]

We, therefore, see that every type of work that could possibly have been needed to complete the Tabernacle was forbidden on the Sabbath, for if any of these types of work were permitted, it could be used as a step in completing the Tabernacle. The fact that absolutely no progress was permit-ted indicates that every step was forbidden.

If we then want to know what types of work are forbidden on the Sabbath, we need only analyze the building of the Tabernacle and find every possible type of work that went into it. The Oral Torah does this and teaches us that there are thirty-nine categories of Sabbath work. We will discuss them all in the following section.

Thus, for example, the Tabernacle required all sorts of woodwork and metalwork. Every category of textile-making was required for its hangings. Leather was used for its roof, and this needed all leather-making operations. Many plant prod-ucts were used for such things as dyes, and these required all sorts of agricultural and cooking activities. Material had to be carried from the outside camp, and written records had to be kept.[5]

All of these things constitute ritual work.

The building of the Tabernacle represented a total commit-ment of the Jewish people to G-d. As such, its building included every possible skill they could muster. Thus, the Torah clearly states that its building included "all manner of skilled work."[6]

Every one of man's skills went into building the Tabernacle. It is precisely these skills that may not be used on the Sabbath.[7]

If we understand the significance of the Tabernacle in a deeper sense, we can understand why it was chosen as a vehicle to indicate the precise nature of Sabbath work.

Our Sages teach us that the Tabernacle was intended to be a microcosm of all creation.[8] It was built to indicate that it is man's responsibility to elevate and sanctify all creation.[9] The Tabernacle represented man's partnership with G-d in bringing the world toward its final goal. Thus, in a sense, its building paralleled G-d's act of creation.[10]

Each of the thirty-nine categories of work that went into the Tabernacle is the counterpart of some aspect of G-d's creation. The cessation of these was therefore an exact counterpart of G-d's rest.[11]

In refraining from these thirty-nine categories of work, we are also paralleling G-d's rest on the Sabbath of creation.

ᴥᔆ The Sanhedrin

The Torah was meant to be a dynamic force guiding an entire people for all times, and therefore, it needed a body entrusted with its interpretation.

This body was the Sanhedrin, which for over 1,600 years served as both supreme court and legislative body of the Jews. Until it was abolished by Roman repression some 1,600 years ago, it was the final interpreter and legislating body of Jewish law. To some extent, it was the abolishment of the Sanhedrin that eventually led to the necessity of putting the Talmud down in writing.

The authority of the Sanhedrin is derived from the Torah itself, as we find (*Deut.* 17:9-10), "You shall go. . .to the judges then in office, seek their guidance, and they will render judgment. You must abide by their decision rendered from the place chosen by G-d. You must also carry out all their instructions."

The Torah is speaking of the Sanhedrin.

This body had a twofold authority. First of all, it was the keeper of the Oral Torah, and was charged with its interpretation. As such, it functioned as the supreme court of Jewish law.

Secondly, it had the authority to legislate religious law. Since this authority was derived from the Torah itself, it was as binding as Biblical law. Once legislation was passed, it could only be repealed by the Sanhedrin itself.[12]

Such legislation was most often aimed at maintaining the spirit, as well as the letter, of the law.[1][3] A prime rule given to the Sanhedrin was to "make a fence around the Torah."[14]

Taking the Sabbath as an example, one could refrain from the forbidden categories of work in the literal sense, but still violate the Sabbath in spirit. The Torah therefore states (Ex. 23:12), "Six days shall you do all your tasks, and on the seventh day you shall rest." The Torah is telling us that we must rest according to the spirit of the law as well as according to its letter. Besides abstaining from actual work, one must preserve the general aura of the Sabbath.[15]

The Thirty-Nine Categories of Sabbath Work

1. Carrying
2. Burning
3. Extinguishing
4. Finishing
5. Writing
6. Erasing
7. Cooking
8. Washing
9. Sewing
10. Tearing
11. Knotting
12. Untying
13. Shaping
14. Plowing
15. Planting
16. Reaping
17. Harvesting
18. Threshing
19. Winnowing
20. Selecting
21. Sifting
22. Grinding
23. Kneading
24. Combing
25. Spinning
26. Dying
27. Chainstitching
28. Warping
29. Weaving
30. Unraveling
31. Building
32. Demolishing
33. Trapping
34. Shearing
35. Slaughtering
36. Skinning
37. Tanning
38. Smoothing
39. Marking

✒ The Categories

In order to present some idea of Sabbath rest, we will here outline the thirty-nine categories of ritual work. This is only the barest of outlines, and is meant to present the spirit, rather than the details of the law. For the latter, the appropriate codes should be consulted.

These are the thirty-nine categories:

1. Carrying

This category involves carrying in a public place.

This is one of the few categories of work that is actually mentioned in the Torah. It is also the very first type of work that was prohibited.

As we discussed earlier, the initial commandment of the Sabbath was given in connection with the Manna. But what possible type of work was involved in gathering a portion of Manna for one's family? Obviously, this is carrying. Thus, when Moses told the people (*Ex.* 16:29), "Let no man leave his place on the seventh day," he was telling him that they could not carry the Manna.[1]

The Torah also gives an account of a man who was put to death for gathering wood on the Sabbath. Here again, according to some commentators his violation of the Sabbath involved carrying.[2]

In a third place, the Prophet Jeremiah specifically warns his people not to carry on the Sabbath. He says (*Jer.* 17:21-22), "Take heed and carry no burdens on the Sabbath. . .Also do not carry any burden out of your houses on the Sabbath."[3]

Carrying is really the prototype of all other types of Sabbath work.[4] As mentioned earlier, the definition of such work is any act where man demonstrates his mastery over nature. But the first act by which man demonstrates such mastery is by taking things from nature and carrying them where he needs them. This was the deed of the man gathering wood. Therefore, if we are to relinquish our mastery over nature, the first requirement is that we not carry anything away.

In a sense, by not carrying, we also relinquish our ownership of everything in the world. A main sign of ownership is that one may take something wherever he pleases. On the Sabbath, we give up something of this ownership. Nothing may be removed from the house. When a man leaves his house, he may carry nothing but the clothing on his back. It is G-d, not man, who owns all things.

This category absolutely forbids all carrying in the street.

Even such trivial things as a key or a handkerchief must be left at home. Certainly pocketbooks, purses, wallets and keychains may not be carried. The only thing one may carry outdoors are things that are actually worn.

We can get some idea how serious carrying on the Sabbath is from the following law. When Rosh Hashanah falls on the Sabbath, the Shofar is not sounded. This was legislated by the Sanhedrin for a most interesting reason. Suppose that a synagogue has only one Shofar, and it became lost or damaged. Imagine the embarrassment and breach of ceremony involved in not being able to sound the Shofar on this most solemn day of Rosh Hashanah. How great the temptation to carry a replacement Shofar from another synagogue or from someone's house! But this would involve a gross violation of the Sabbath. To avoid this problem the Sanhedrin decreed that the Shofar never be sounded on the Sabbath at all.[5]

Carrying in a private home is permitted on the Sabbath. It is only in a public domain that it is forbidden. When a semi-public domain is involved, the Rabbis prohibited carrying to it from a public domain and vice-versa without an Eruv.

The spirit of the law, however, forbids the carrying or handling of unnecessary objects, even indoors. The Sanhedrin therefore legislated the categories of *muktzeh,* things which may not be handled on the Sabbath. These include such useless things as pebbles and stones. They also include things which may not be used on the Sabbath, such as pencils, candles and money.[6]

The spirit of the law also forbids the transfer of ownership, even inside a building. The Sanhedrin legislated a prohibition against all forms of buying, selling, trading and other commerce for a variety of reasons. The Sabbath must be a day when all business stops.[7]

It is interesting to note that the prohibition against commerce is one of the few types of legislation actually recorded in the Bible. Thus, we find (*Nehemiah* 10:32), "If the (non-Jewish) natives of the land bring any goods or food to sell on the Sabbath day, we will buy nothing from them on the Sabbath or on any holy day."[8]

The Thirty-Nine Categories of Sabbath Work □ 135

2. Burning

This involves making a fire or causing anything to burn.

Even throwing a toothpick into a fire is considered a violation of the Sabbath under this category.

This is another category of work mentioned specifically in the Torah, as we find (*Ex.* 35:3), "You shall not light a fire at home on the Sabbath day."[9]

The use of fire is one of the prime ways in which man demonstrates his mastery over nature. Indeed, the use of fire is one of the cornerstones of human civilization. It is fire that allows man to extract energy, his most basic requirement, from nature. Thus, in a sense, it is also a prototype of Sabbath work.[10]

Obviously, this category forbids such acts as striking a match or turning on a stove.

It also prohibits smoking on the Sabbath.

An automobile engine works by burning gasoline. Turning on the ignition and stepping on the accelerator causes it to burn. It is therefore forbidden to drive a car on the Sabbath.

Heating a piece of metal so that it glows is also in the category of burning.[11][11] When an electric light is turned on, its filament is heated white hot, producing light. This is therefore forbidden on the Sabbath.

In general, any use of electricity violates the spirit of the Sabbath, since it involves extracting energy from nature. According to many authorities, electricity has the same status as fire with regard to the Sabbath. In any case, the practice of all observant Jews is to avoid turning any electrical appliance on or off. Since a telephone also works by electricity, it also should not be used.[12]

3. Extinguishing

This includes extinguishing or lowering a flame in any way. As such, it is the opposite of burning.

Thus, for example, one may not turn down the gas on Shabbos. Similarly, it is forbidden to turn off the lights or any other electrical appliance.

The Sabbath, however, may be violated wherever there is any possible danger to human life. Therefore, in case of fire, anything necessary must be done where life may be endangered.[13]

4. Finishing[14]

This includes completing any useful article, even where no other category of work is involved.

It includes all forms of repairs and adjustments.

For example, putting together a machine is in this category, even when no other type of work is done.

It is similarly forbidden to put together any other article, unless it is made to come apart.

Smoothing a stone and planting wood is also in this category. It therefore precludes all forms of sculpture and shopwork. Sharpening a knife is also in this category.

This heading also forbids us to cut or tear paper in any way. To take a very mundane example, one may not tear toilet paper on the Sabbath. Religious Jews therefore only use pre-cut paper.[15]

Putting the finishing touch on any article is also in this category. Thus, for example, one may not put new laces into shoes.

Any form of adjustment comes under this heading. Thus, one may not wind a clock or set a watch.[16]

It is similarly forbidden to tune any kind of musical instrument. The Rabbis forbade the use of all musical instruments on the Sabbath.[17]

Blowing up a balloon or water wings also comes under this category.

The same is true of setting the sails on a boat. For this reason, the Sanhedrin forbade the riding of small boats on the Sabbath. (One may, however, ride a large ship piloted by non-Jews, as long as he does not embark or disembark on the Sabbath.) There is a special rabbinic enactment that swimming is not permitted on the Sabbath.[18]

5. Writing[19]

This includes all forms of writing and drawing.

Typing, printing, and using a rubber stamp all come under this heading.

The main objective of writing is the keeping of records, and therefore, the spirit of the law forbids any activity normally requiring a written record. Thus, the Sanhedrin forbade all sorts of business activity, as well as marriage and divorce on the Sabbath.[20]

Calculations and measurements are also included, since they also normally involve writing.

Gambling and playing games of chance also are included in this category.

6. Erasing[21]

This includes erasing or destroying any form of writing.

Breaking apart or tearing through words or letters also is included in the spirit of this category.

Although it is permitted to tear a package to get the food inside, this should be avoided when it involves tearing through the writing on the package.

Likewise, when words are stamped on the edge of a book (as in the case with most library books), these letters are separated when the book is opened, and this should not be done unless the book is urgently needed.[22]

7. Cooking[23]

This includes all forms of cooking and baking.

Even boiling water falls under this category.

It also includes any form of heat treatment of non-foods.

Thus, melting metal or wax and firing ceramics are all included.

The prohibition against cooking does not prevent us from eating hot food on the Sabbath. Indeed, part of our Sabbath joy (Oneg Shabbos) consists of eating hot food. However, this must be prepared in such a manner that no act of cooking actually takes place on the Sabbath.

In order to prevent one from forgetting and adjusting the flame, the stove must be covered with a tin or blech. This must also cover the controls, making it impossible to adjust the flame. Hot cooked food may then be kept on this tin.

Under some conditions, it is also permitted to reward food that is already cooked.[24] These laws appear very complex when put in writing, while being very simple in actual practice. The best thing is to see how a true Sabbath observer prepares hot food for Shabbos.

8. Washing[25]

This includes washing or bleaching a garment in any manner.

It also includes removing any spot or stain from clothing. Wringing out a wet garment also falls under this heading.

9. Sewing[26]

This includes all forms of sewing and needlework.

Pasting, taping and stapling paper are also included. Thus, one may not seal an envelope nor attach a postage stamp on the Sabbath.

Fastening something with a safety pin, however, is permitted, since this is only a temporary fastening.

10. Tearing[27]

This includes undoing any form of sewing.

It also includes tearing a garment.

Separating glued papers falls under this heading.

11. Knotting[28]

This includes tying any permanent knot.

Tying a bow, however, is permitted. Therefore, for example, one may tie shoes on the Sabbath.

12. Untying[29]

This includes untying any permanent knot.

If a knot is not made to be permanent, however, it may be untied. This is true even if it is a permanent-type knot. Thus, for example, if one's shoes accidentally become knotted they may be untied.

13. Shaping[30]

This includes cutting any object to a desired shape.

Cutting material for a dress would fall under this category. So would cutting out pictures or newspaper articles.

Working wood or metal on a lathe or mill also falls under this heading.

Foods are not included in this category, and may be cut to be served.

14. Plowing[31]

This includes any work that improves the ground.

Digging up a garden and fertilizing it fall under this heading. Also included is raking a lawn.

15. Planting[32]

This includes all forms of planting and gardening.

Also included is anything that encourages plants to grow. Thus, one may not water plants on the Sabbath.

It is likewise forbidden to place cut flowers in water, or even to change their water.

16. Reaping[33]

This includes cutting or plucking any growing thing.

Agriculture is again one of the main ways in which man shows his dominance over nature. This category is therefore also one of those mentioned in the Torah, as we find (*Ex.* 34:21), "Six days shall you work, but you shall rest on the seventh; in plowing and in harvesting, you shall rest."

Such activities as plucking a flower and plucking a fruit from a tree come under this heading. The same is true of mowing a lawn.

It was also legislated that we do not handle any growing flowers or plants. It is also forbidden to climb a tree or smell a growing flower.

Fruit which falls from a tree on the Sabbath may not be used on the same day.

The use of animals as well as plants is forbidden since there is the concern that one might forget and inadvertently pluck a branch for use as a switch.

17. Harvesting[34]

This includes all harvesting operations such as binding grain into sheaves or bales.

Gathering fallen fruit into piles or placing them into baskets also falls under this heading. This is even true in a private enclosed yard where carrying is permitted.

18. Threshing[35]

This includes all operations where food is separated from its natural container.

Both solid and liquid foods are included.

The prime example is threshing grain to remove it from its husk.

Squeezing a fruit for its juice is also included. The same is true of milking a cow.

19. Winnowing[36]

This includes all activities where food is separated from its inedible portions by means of the wind.

The prime example is winnowing grain, where it is thrown up in the air, allowing the chaff to blow away.

20. Selecting[37]

This includes separating unwanted portions of food by hand.

Thus, for example, if one is eating berries, he may not pick out the bad ones before eating the good ones.

One may, however, eat the good ones and leave the bad. It is likewise permitted to peel fruits and vegetables for immediate consumption.

This category also forbids one to pick the bones out of fish. This is one reason for the custom of eating Gefilte Fish on Shabbos, since its bones are already removed.

If one must remove something inedible, a small amount of food should be removed along with it.

The spirit of this category also forbids all sorts of sorting and filing activities.

21. Sifting[38]

This includes separating the unwanted portions from food by means of a sieve.

It includes the sifting of flour and the straining of liquids.

22. Grinding[39]

This includes all grinding and milling operations. The prime example is milling grain.

Grinding coffee or pepper, filing metals, and crushing

substances in a mortar, all fall under this heading.

Its spirit also forbids the grating of cheeses and vegetables and the grinding of fish and meat, as well as herbs used for medicine.

The Sanhedrin therefore legislated to forbid the use of all non-vital medicines and treatments except for a sick person.

An initial exception, however, was made in cases of acute pain and actual illness, where necessary medical treatments may be used.

Where life is actually in danger, the Sabbath may be violated in any necessary manner. Our Sages teach us that it is better to violate one Sabbath in order that another may live to keep many.

23. Kneading[40]

This includes combining a powder with a liquid to form a dough or paste.

The primary example is making a dough or batter for bread or cake.

Also included would be making instant puddings, even where no cooking is required.

24. Combing[41]

This includes combing wool or cotton in preparation for making it into thread.

25. Spinning[42]

This includes all thread-making and rope-making activities. Making felt is also included.

26. Dyeing[43]

This includes changing the color of any object or substance.

Dyeing clothing, painting, and mixing paints and dyes all come under the heading.

The spirit of this law also prohibits the use of lipstick and eyeshadow. However, there are permanent cosmetics that can be put on before the Sabbath and last the entire day.

27. Chainstitching[44]

This includes all crocheting, knitting, and braiding activities.

Also included are basketweaving and net making.

The prime example involved setting up a loom for weaving. A chain of threads was looped across the loom, to hold the warp.[45]

28. Warping[46]

This includes setting up the warp on a loom, even when no actual weaving is done.

29. Weaving[47]

This includes all weaving operations.

Also included are all sorts of needlework, such as embroidery, needlepoint, and rug hooking.

30. Unraveling[48]

This includes unraveling any woven or knitted material.

31. Building[49]

This includes all building and assembling activities.

All building repairs come under this heading, even driving a nail into a wall.

Also included is pitching any kind of tent.

The spirit of the law even forbids the opening of an umbrella (even when it will not be carried outside), since it affords the same protection from the elements as a tent.

32. Demolishing[50]

This includes undoing any building operation.

Thus, for example, even a temporary tent may not be taken down on the Sabbath.

Taking apart any kind of machinery is also included.

33. Trapping[51]

This includes capturing or restricting the freedom of any living creature.

The prime example is trapping an animal. However, even catching an insect in one's hand comes under this heading.

34. Shearing[52]

This includes removing hair, wool or feathers from any living creature.

Also included are such things as haircutting, shaving and cutting one's fingernails. Eyebrow plucking is also forbidden.

The spirit of the law also forbids the combing of hair on the Sabbath, since this normally also pulls out hairs. Using a soft brush, however, is permitted.

35. Slaughtering[53]

This includes the killing of any living creature.

Swatting a fly or mosquito is also included, as is wounding or bruising an animal or human being.

Deadly snakes and wasps, which pose a danger to human life, may be killed on the Sabbath. This is another case where human life overrides all other considerations.

36. Skinning[54]

This includes skinning any animal to obtain its hide.

37. Tanning[55]

This includes all tanning and softening processes used to make hides into leather.

Also included is any process that softens or improves leather. Rubbing oil or saddle soap into leather thus comes under this heading.

38. Smoothing[56]

This includes all smoothing and polishing operations.

The prime example is the preparation of leather, where the hair is removed and the surface rubbed smooth.

Shining shoes is also included under this heading.[5][7]

The same is true of polishing silver or any other metal.

39. Marking[58]

This includes marking or scoring lines on a surface in preparation for cutting or writing.

It applies even when such marking does not come under the category of writing.

⋅≈ A Concluding Word

After reading through the thirty-nine categories of work, you might have come to feel that keeping the Sabbath is an impossibly complex task.

We warned you of this earlier. The Sabbath is more than a mere set of rules. It is another way of life completely, totally divorced from weekday life. When put in handbook form, a different life style may seem very difficult and complex. When lived, however, it is really very easy.

A good example is going off to college. Every university prints a catalog, telling of all its rules and regulations and including a list of courses. If your sole impression of campus life were to be based on this catalog, it would seem impossibly complicated. After all, it takes a 200-page book just to describe it! But once you get there, you learn to live it.

The same is true of Shabbos. You learn to keep the Sabbath by reading books, but that makes it seem impossibly difficult. It is almost like learning about love from a marriage manual. You have to live to see its true dimensions of beauty.

A Taste of Light

Imagine that you are about to take a trip to another world.

You are preparing for a most exciting experience. It will be a totally different place, and you are looking forward to things you have never seen or experienced before.

But it *is* different, and you will have to adjust to it. Your experiences here will be of little use to you once you get there.

You are given an instruction manual, telling you how to live on this new world. It is a thick book, filled with detailed charts and lists. You read it through and are left very confused and distressed. How can one understand this new world? How will one possibly adjust to all these complex conditions and rules? Before you have started, you are almost ready to abandon the trip completely.

But you make up your mind and decide to go through with the trip. You get there, and as you expected, find it very difficult to adjust, but then the days pass, and you become used to your new world. After a while, all your questions and apprehensions have vanished.

A while later, you look at your instruction manual again. This time, you read it in a new light. Most of it now seems very obvious. Things look very different now that you have experienced them.

For many of us, the Sabbath is a new world.

We have difficulty understanding and really feeling its significance. Reading a book like this only seems to complicate the matter. It is talking of a world that seems very alien. We read, but somehow do not understand.

When put in writing, keeping the Sabbath seems like an impossibly difficult task. How can one remember all the rules and regulations, much less observe them? How can one possibly keep the Sabbath in this modern day and age?

It is not as difficult as it sounds. Hundreds of thousands of Jews all over the world keep the Sabbath, and the number is increasing every year. And, for most of them, observing it is one of the easiest and most enjoyable things possible.

But there is really only one way to learn about the Sabbath. That is by trying it.

You may struggle through it on your own for a few weeks. A much easier way is to spend a few Sabbaths with an observant family and learn how to feel the mood, or you might spend a weekend or two at a Shabbaton. But gradually, you will learn the feeling of Shabbos, and once you really feel it, you will never forget it.

Many things in this book may now seem strange. But once you have the feel of the Shabbos, they will be very obvious. It will be like reading a guidebook of your own hometown. Once you live there, it no longer appears strange.

But Shabbos must also be a do-it-yourself project. In order to really feel the Shabbos, you cannot wait for it to come to you. You must get into it. The Torah tells us (*Ex.* 31:16) "to make the Sabbath." Every person must make his own Shabbos. You must prepare yourself and get into the mood. Only then will you be able to feel its true significance, for Shabbos is not an intellectual exercise. If it were, meditating about it would be enough. We might provide explanations, but true understanding only comes from doing and feeling.

In a way, Shabbos is like love. You can talk about love for the rest of your life, but if you have never experienced it, you will never understand it. Once you have been in love though, no further discussion is necessary.

Shabbos is a bond of love between ourselves and G-d.

To understand it, you must experience it.

◄§ Do It Yourself

The Shabbos mood begins with its preparation. The Commandment says, "Remember the Sabbath day to keep it holy." Our Sages teach us that in order to truly keep it holy, we must remember it all week long and prepare for it. If you see something you will enjoy on Shabbos, by all means set it aside for use on the Sabbath.[1]

The preparations for Shabbos reach their peak on Friday afternoon. You then direct most of your activities toward Shabbos. Recall the lesson of our Sages, "He who prepares on Friday, will eat on Shabbos."[2] Anticipate it as you would an important visitor. After all, Shabbos is the Queen of all creation.[3]

Eat lightly on Friday afternoon. Work up an appetite for the Shabbos meal.

Make sure that you will have the tastiest possible food for Shabbos. If possible, do something to help prepare the meal. Make sure that everything will be just right for the Shabbos Queen.

Clean up your room and tidy your belongings. Put away all weekday things. Prepare your surroundings to reflect the Shabbos mood.

Take a relaxing bath or shower. Cleanse your mind and soul along with your body.

Put on your best clothes. Dress as if for an important occasion. If possible, have special Shabbos clothing set aside.

Many of our *Tzadikim* (pious people) have the custom of reading the *Shir HaShirim* (Song of Songs) just before Shabbos. It is the most beautiful love poem ever written, telling of the love between G-d and His people. Read it if you have time, and try to feel this love.

Prepare the table for the Shabbos meal. Cover it with a fine white tablecloth. Set it with your best china and silver in honor of the Queen.

Set aside two Challahs, *Lechem Mishneh* of Shabbos, and cover them with a clean napkin or special cover. Prepare the wine for Kiddush along with a special goblet set aside as a Kiddush cup. If possible, try to have a silver one.

Make sure that candles will be lit in the room where you will eat. If there is no one else to light them, do it yourself. Light them 18-20 minutes before sunset and gaze at their light for a few moments. Feel them radiate the light of Shabbos.

As the Shabbos arrives, treat it as an honored guest. Wrap

yourself in a hush of serenity. Try to raise the plane of your life. Direct your conversation, and even your thoughts, toward a higher level.

Now is the time to gather and pray. If you have a synagogue within walking distance, join with their Sabbath service. By no means destroy the Shabbos spirit by riding in a car. It violates both the law and mood of Shabbos. If there is no convenient synagogue, find a quiet corner and pray by yourself.

If you can read Hebrew, go through the service in our ancient, sacred language. Even when you do not understand the words, listen to their sound and feel them on your tongue. Imagine these same sounds spoken by Abraham, Moses, Isaiah and David. Let your mind relax and allow the words to become part of you. Let the Holy Language and the Holy Day bind themselves together and surround you with light on all sides. A siddur with an accurate and modern translation will help make the words even more meaningful.

If you cannot read Hebrew, say the prayers in English. Ponder their meaning and let them penetrate your being. When you say "Blessed are You," you are not just saying words. Think for a moment about this "You." Don't just say the prayers — address them to G-d.

Walk quietly home from synagogue. You might gaze at the stars and recall the Psalmist's words (*Ps.* 8:4), "When I see Your heavens, the work of Your fingers, the moon and stars which You have established. . .What is man, that You think of him, or the son of man, that You remember him?" Do not forget the answer. . .G-d does indeed remember.

Enter the house with a Shabbos greeting — "Shabbat Shalom," or "Good Shabbos."

Sing *Shalom Aleichem* and the Kiddush. As you say the words, let the Shabbos enter into you. Drink the Kiddush wine and let it lull you into a state of Shabbos serenity.

Wash your hands with a blessing, and remain silent until the blessing over the Challahs is said. Dip it in salt, and chew the portion slowly, relishing every morsel. Keep in mind that you are eating it as an offering to G-d.

Take a moment and enjoy the Shabbos meal. Perhaps you

too will taste the "special seasoning" that Shabbos adds to the food.[4]

Let your mood be both happy and reflectful. Hum a tune. If you can, sing the *Zemiros* (Table Hymns) from a prayer book, or any Jewish song.

Close the meal with the *Birkas HaMazon* (Grace After Meals). Thank G-d for giving you food and for the special blessing that comes with this day.

After the meal, it is a time to relax. Use this time to learn about G-d and His teachings. Read the portion that will be read from the Torah that particular week. Take a quiet stroll.

Now is a time to be alone with G-d for a while. Take a calm walk alone, or sit in your room. Ask G-d to help you feel the holiness of Shabbos.

Reflect a moment on your life. Ask yourself: What am I doing and where am I going? What does life mean to me? What am I doing wrong, and how can I improve myself? Ask G-d to help you find answers.

Be happy that you're alive.

Shabbos is a time to get together. If you know others who keep Shabbos, gather together with them. Use the long winter Friday nights and summer Saturday afternoons as a time of companionship. Sing songs and tell stories. Use it as a time to learn together. Strengthen your bond of friendship.

As the evening draws to a close, let the serenity of Shabbos overwhelm you. "Sabbath sleep is a delight."[5] As you prepare yourself for the night, say the *Shema* and place yourself in G-d's hands. Fall asleep in Shabbos rest.

Begin the Sabbath day in the same mood. Spring out of bed, and make prayer your first order of the day. Let the morning service awaken you, both physically and spiritually. Make the second Sabbath meal at noon as much of a banquet as the first the night before. Spend the day in deep awareness of Shabbos. Let study and friendship help you keep the mood.

As the sun begins to set, you should feel a change. The Queen is preparing to leave. The third Sabbath meal is a time of sweet longing for a day that is about to close.

When the skies are dark and the stars appear, Shabbos is over. It is time for *havdalah,* the prayer that ushers in a new week. Inhale the spices and enjoy a last taste of Paradise. Gaze at the twisted candle, and meditate about how this day will brighten the coming week.

Do all this, and you will begin to feel the spirit of Shabbos. You might not feel it all the first time, but do not be discouraged. If you truly seek, it will eventually be yours. The task is not difficult, but you must persevere. You are on the quest of Eternity. Eventually you will find it.

We have a promise.

G-d Himself told His prophet. (*Isa.* 58:13 f.):

> *If you trample not the Sabbath,*
> *do no business on My holy day;*
> *Call the Sabbath a delight,*
> *and honor G-d's holy day;*
> *Keep yourselves from daily tasks,*
> *from weekday interests,*
> *speaking mere words.*
> *Then will you find joy in G-d,*
> *soar the earth's heights,*
> *take in Jacob's heritage —*
> *G-d Himself has said it.*

NOTES

WHY THE SABBATH?

1. *Kuzari* 2:34, 3:10. Cf. *Abarbanel* on *Moreh Nevuchim* 2:31.
2. *Sanhedrin* 7:4 (55a).
3. *Eruvin* 69b, *Chullin* 5a; *Yad Shabbos* 30:15.
4. See *Yoreh Deah* 2:5, 119:7.
5. *Pri Megadim, Eshel Avraham* 55:4, *Mishneh Berurah* 55:46.
6. *Isa.* 56:1, 58:13; *Jer.* 17:21; *Ezek.* 20:23; *Neh.* 13:15.
7. See *Kesef Mishnah, Lechem Mishneh,* on *Yad, Tshuvah* 3:7.
8. *Emunos VeDeyos* 1:1, *Yad, Yesodey HaTorah* 1:1,5.
9. *Yad,* loc. cit. 1:4, *Nimukey Mahari* and loc. Cf. *Radak* on *Jer.* 10:10, *Yerushalmi, Berachos* 1:5 (9b), *VaYikra Rabbah* 26:1.
10. *Ramban* ad loc.; *Sefer HaChinuch* 25. Cf. *Kuzari* 1:1,2.
11. *Ex.* 15:2.
12. See *Moreh Nevuchim* 2:31, 3:32, 3:41; *Sefer HaChinuch* 32, *Ibn Ezra, Bachya,* on *Ex.* 20:8, *Ramban* on *Deut* 5:15, *Menoras HaMaor* 159, *Akedas Yitzchok* 4:55; *Sh'nei Luchos HaBris,* loc. cit. 2:10b. Cf. *Mechilta* on *Ex.* 31:14.
13. *Moreh Nevuchim* 2:35.
14. *Kuzari* 1:85, Cf. *Mechilta* on *Ex.* 20:11, *Bereishis Rabbah* 11:2, *Rashi* on *Gen.* 2:3, *Tiferes Yisroel* (*Manaral*) 40.
15. *Ex.* 16:22; *Berachos* 39b, *Shabbos* 117b.
16. *Ex.* 16:13, *Um.* 11:9; *Tosefos, Pesachim* 100b "*SheAin,*" *Turey Zahav* (*Taz*); *Orech Chaim* 271:12.

SABBATH REST

1. *Numbers* 15:32 ff.
2. *Ex.* 31:17, cf. *Eruvin* 96a.
3. That is, the physical world was created with the letter *Hei,* the easiest letter to pronounce. *Bereishis Rabbah* 12:2, *Etz Yosef* ad loc. See also *Menachos* 29b, *Rashi* on *Gen.* 2:4; *Mechilta* on *Ex.* 20:11.
4. Dayan I. Grunfeld, *The Sabbath* (Feldheim, N.Y. 5720), p. 19. Cf. *Shabbos* 12:1 (102b) according to *Maggid Mishneh* on *Yad, Shabbos* 9:13. Also see *Alshich* on *Jer.* 17:21, *Maleches Shlemah* on *Shabbos* 1:1.
5. *Bereishis Rabbah* 10:10, *Rashi* on *Gen.* 2:2.
6. *Derech HaShem* 1:2,2, cf. *Sotah* 14a, *Maharsha* ad loc.
7. *Yad, Yesodey HaTorah* 1:12, *Moreh Nevuchim* 1:11.
8. *Sefer Baal Shem Tov, Bereishis* 82; *Maggid Devarav LeYaakov* 135; *Maor VaShemesh* on *Ex.* 31:16. Cf. *Sefer HaChinuch* 32.
9. *Zohar* 2:135b.
10. Cf. *Makkos* 3:15 (23b).
11. *Ohr HaChaim* on *Ex.* 31:16.
12. *B'nai Yesasechar* 4:1.
13. *Maor VaShemesh* loc. cit.
14. *Talmid* 7:4.

15. *Sefer HaChinuch* 32; *Ephodi* on *Moreh Nevuchim* 2:31,
    Derech HaShem 4:7:2.
16. *Avodah Zarah* 3a, see *Akedas Yitzchok* 55 (201b).
17. *Reshis Chochmah, Shaar HaKedushah* 3 (New York, 5728) p. 131a.

SABBATH WORK

1. *Chagigah* 1:8 (10a), *Tosefos Yom Tov* ad loc.
2. *Ex.* 31:12, *Rashi* and ad loc.
3. Ibid, 35:1.
4. *Mechilta, Rashi,* ad loc.; *Shabbos* 70a, 97b; *Yerushalmi,* 7:2. Also see
   Rashi, Beitzah 13b, *Chagigah* 10b "*Mach'sheves.*"
5. *Chayay Adam* 9:1. See *Shabbos* 49b, *Tosafos* ad loc.
   "*KeNeged,*" ibid.
6. *Ex.* 35:33. See *Targum* ad loc., *Rashi* on *II Char.* 26:15, *Ibn Ezra* on *Ex.*
   26:1.
7. We are thus proscribed from doing *Maleches Mach'sheves,* literally,
   "skilled work." See *Beitzah* 13b, *Chagigah* 10b, *Rashi* ad loc.,
   "*Mach'sheves,*" *Tosafos* ibid.
8. *Tanchuma, Pekudey* 2; *Zohar* 2:162b.
9. Cf. *Mesilas Yesharim* 1.
10. *Berachos* 55a; *Zohar* 2:152a, 2:324b, *Rambam* on *Ex.* 31:2.
11. *Tanchuma* loc. cit.
12. See *Yad,* Introduction; *Mamrim,* chapters 1 and 2.
13. *Shnei Luchos HaBris, Torah SheBaal Peh* "*Amnam,*"
    2:240b; *Maharal Beer HaGolah* 1. Cf. *Chullin* 106a, *Tanna DeBei Eliahu* 15.
14. *Avos* 1:1.
15. *Yad, Shabbos* 21:1; *Rashi, Shabbos* 14b "*Talmud Lomar,*" *Yoma* 74a
    "*Shabaton,*" *Rambam* on *Lev.* 23:24.

THE THIRTY-NINE CATEGORIES

1. Cf. *Rashi, Ibn Ezra,* ad loc., *Eruvin* 17b, *Tosefos, Shabbos* 2a "*Yetzias.*"
2. *Num.* 15:32, *Shabbos* 96b.
3. See *Beitza* 12a, *Yerushalmi, Shabbos* 1:1 (1b).
4. Cf. *Tikuney Zohar* 24 (69b), 30 (73a); *Etz Chaim, Shaar
   HaMelachim* 7; *Maleches Shlemah* on *Shabbos* 1:1; *Alshich* on *Gen.* 2:1,
   commenting on *Bereshis Rabbah* 11:6.
5. *Rosh Hashanah* 4:1 (29b), *Yad, Shofar* 2:6.
6. *Raavad,* on *Yad, Shabbos* 25:12. Cf. *Shabbos* 124b.
7. See *Rashi, Beitza* 37a "*MiShum,*" *Tosefos, Shabbos* 113b "*Shelo.*" Others,
   however, hold that it is forbidden because one might keep a written
   record, cf. *Yad, Shabbos* 23:12, 13, *Rambam* on *Beitza* 5:2, *Ralbag* on
   Neh. 10:31. Also see *Pri Megadim, Eshel Avraham* 307:14.
8. Cf. *Neh.* 13:15-18. See *Rashi, Beitza* 27b "*Ain*"; *Tiferes Yisroel, Beitza*
   3:27, 5:21.

9. See *Yebamos* 6b, *Sanhedrin* 35b.
10. See *Derech Mitzvosecha (Chabad)* 89a.
11. *Yad, Shabbos* 12:1.
12. *Shaalos U'Tshuvos Maharsham* 2:247; *Levushey Mordechai, Orach Chaim* 47; *Pri Sadeh* 1:81.
13. See *Orach Chaim* 334.
14. *Yad, Shabbos* 10:16-18, 23:4-9; *Chayay Adam* 44.
15. *Ch. A.* 29:5.
16. *Mishneh Berurah* 338:15.
17. *Orach Chaim* 338.
18. Ibid. 339:2.
19. *Yad,* 11:9-17, 23:12-19; *Ch. A.* 36.
20. *Shabbos* 148a. See note 7.
21. *Yad,* 11:17; *Ch. A.* 38.
22. *Magen Avraham* 340:6, *Mishnah Berurah* 340:17.
23. *Yad,* 10:1-6, 22:1-10, *Ch. A.* 22.
24. *Orach Chaim* 253, 254.
25. *Yad,* 0:10-11, 22:15-20, *Ch. A.* 22.
26. *Yad,* 10:9, 11, *Ch. A.* 28.
27. *Yad,* 10:10, *Ch. A.* 29.
28. *Yad,* 10:1-6, *Ch. A.* 26.
29. *Yad,* 10:7-8, *Ch. A.* 27.
30. *Yad,* 11:7, *Ch. A.* 36.
31. *Yad,* 7:3, 8:1, 21:2-4, *Ch. A.* 10.
32. *Yad,* 8:2, 21:5, *Ch. A.* 11.
33. *Yad,* 8:3-5, 21:6-10, *Ch. A.* 12.
34. *Yad,* 8:6, 21:11, *Ch. A.* 13.
35. *Yad,* 8:7-10, 21:12-16, *Ch. A.* 14.
36. *Orach Chaim* 319:7, *Ch. A.* 15.
37. *Yad,* 8:11-13, 21:17, *Ch. A.* 16.
38. *Yad,* 8:14, 21:32, *Ch. A.* 18.
39. *Yad,* 8:15, 21:18-31, *Ch. A.* 17.
40. *Yad,* 8:16, 21:33-36, *Ch. A.* 4b119.
41. *Yad,* 9:12, *Ch. A.* 23.
42. *Yad,* 9:15, *Ch. A.* 25:1-2.
43. *Yad,* 9:13-14, 22:23, *Ch. A.* 24.
44. *Shabbos* 13:1 (105a), *Tosafos Yom Tov* ad loc.; *Yad,* 9:16, *Chayay Adam* 25:3.
45. This category specifies making *two* loops (*nirin*). This is because a single loop or slip knot is permitted on the Sabbath. It is only when these are made into a chain of loops, such as in a chainstitch, that this constitutes a violation. See *Minchas Chinuch* 32:17. Also see *Tiferes Yisrael, Shabbos* 18.
46. *Yad,* 9:17-18, *Ch. A.* 25:4-5.
47. *Yad,* 9:18-19, *Ch. A.* 25:6.
48. *Yad,* 9:20, *Ch. A.* 25:7.
49. *Yad,* 10:12-14, 22:25-33, *Ch. A.* 39.
50. *Yad,* 10:15, *Ch. A.* Ibid.
51. *Yad,* 10:19-25, *Ch. A.* 30.

52. *Yad,* 9:7-9, 22:13-14, *Ch. A.* 21.
53. *Yad,* 11:1-4, *Ch. A.* 31.
54. *Yad,* 11:5-6, *Ch. A.* 32.
55. Ibid.
56. Ibid., *Chayey Adam* 35.
57. *Tiferes Yisrael* loc. cit. 30, *Mishnah Berurah* 327:15.
58. *Yad,* 11:17, *Chayey Adam* 34:1, *Minchas Chinuch* 32:36.

A TASTE OF LIGHT

1. *Beitza* 15b; *Mechilta, Ramban* on *Ex.* 20:8; *Chayay Adam* B 1:1.
2. *Avodah Zarah* 3a.
3. *Shabbos* 119a, *Babba Kamma* 32b; *Pesikta Zutrasa,*
   BaShalach 16:5, *Sefer Chasidim* 149, *Tiferes Yisroel*
   (Maharal) 40.
4. Ibid.
5. *Yalkut Reuveni, VeEsChanan; Shnei Luchos HaBris, Mesechta Shabbos*
   (Jerusalem 5720): 7b.

TZITZITH
A THREAD OF LIGHT

ARYEH KAPLAN

Introduction

by Rabbi Pinchas Stolper

How can we learn to control our passions so that we will rule over them, and not allow them to rule over us? How are we to avoid the self-deception which so often tells us that truth and beauty are synonymous, and that human fulfillment and physical pleasures are one and the same thing?

The Torah wants us to arrive at the conclusion that discipline and self-control are the key to human happiness. It gives us the tools with which to prevent our eyes and our hearts from enticing us into thinking that life is the pursuit of pleasure — the pursuit of beauty, and physical things. The Torah wants to keep us from traveling the wrong road on which we will find suffering, frustration, evil and the suppression of our highest and most noble aspirations.

Our Sages teach us that, "He who carefully observes the commandment of Tzitzith will be able to behold the 'Face' of the All-Present God" (Menachoth 436), because God does not want us to "explore after our heart and after our eyes, after which we go astray". As Rashi says, "The eye sees, then the heart desires, and then the body sins." But God does not want us to be misled by our eyes and our hearts — therefore, he has given us a visible reminder of Himself and His Laws. Tzitzith, which means to *appear in visible form* (Hirsch), remind us that the animal in us seeks gratification only from physical things which can be seen and felt, while our truest, greatest and most meaningful attainments and relationships are with or from God who is unseen and invisible.

The Tzitzith and the Tallith are reminders of the fact that clothes are the first visible characteristic which distinguish man from the animal — clothes remind us of the need to conceal the animal in ourselves and be constantly aware of the invisible God and His commands.

In this deep and moving book Rabbi Aryeh Kaplan has again taken us beyond simple and superficial meanings. Here, he delves deeply into the mystery of the commandment of Tzitzith to reveal the link between Tzitzith, the sin of the first man, and the ability of mankind to overcome sin and reach toward God. Here we are introduced to an understanding of the connection between clothes, the sexual urge, self control and the story of the serpent. Here we begin to realize that God has instilled within us the ability to choose freely so that we will not function as mindless robots. Instead, we have within us the ability to overcome evil and gain mastery over ourselves in order to create a new world in which mankind will rule his instincts, overcome the beast in himself, and create a society of the spirit in which good and truth will prevail and in which war, hatred and evil will be banished forever.

Why Tzitzith

Have you ever thought about the really important questions in life? Have you ever asked yourself why you were born? What is the purpose of life? What are your responsibilities? Have you ever tried to develop a philosophy of life and then live by it? One of the world's greatest philosophers came to the conclusion that "the unexamined life is not worth living."[4] Have you ever examined *your* life?

Of course, we all know the main problems is not so much developing a philosophy of life, but living up to it. If we think, we know what is right and what is wrong. But when it comes down to the crunch, we tend to forget.

Deep down, every Jew realizes that Judaism offers a philosophy of life that is without equal. One does not have to be overly sophisticated to realize that a philosophy of life that has survived for over three thousand years, and has dealt with every possible human problem in every possible society, must have an overriding validity. Looking at it that way, the fact that it originated with God seems almost perfectly obvious.

Yet, in the heat of everyday life, there are many things that draw us away from God and Judaism. There are friends who pull us to conform, good times that beckon, and a desirable world of pleasures that tempts us away, even from the truths that we recognize. Above all, there is the strong itch of desire that sweeps us along, often against our very will.

We may know what is right, but there are so many things that make us forget. It is so very hard to remember.

God realized this, so He gave us a commandment to serve as a constant reminder. The Torah clearly spells this out when it says, "They shall be your Tzitzith, and you shall see them and remember all of God's commandments and obey them, and not stray after your heart and eyes, which lead you to immorality."

In the simplest sense, then, the Tzitzith serve as a reminder. We bind them to our garments just as one might tie a string around his finger [5] or belt[6] in order to remember something. Some say that the Tzitzith is reminiscent of a lash,[7] serving to remind us that we are ultimately accountable for all our deeds and misdeeds.[8] We wear them as a constant reminder that we must obey God's commandments, and not be led astray by our desires.

This is also apparent from the context in which the commandment was given. Immediately before God gave the commandment of Tzitzith, the Torah tells of a man who committed a most serious sin. The Midrash explains that God then taught Moses that this man had sinned "because he did not have anything to remind him constantly of his responsibility." In response to this, He gave the commandment of Tzitzith.[9]

Along with this immediate benefit, the Torah also tells us of a long-term effect.[10] Here God speaks to us directly, "In order that you remember and keep all My commandments, and be holy to your God." That is, if we allow the Tzitzith to be a constant reminder, keeping us from being misled by worldly temptations, we will form the habit of remembering God's commandments. This in turn will ultimately lead us to become holy; that is, immersed in the Godly, rather than in our worldly desires.[11]

The commandment ends with a mention of the Exodus from Egypt: "I am God you Lord who brought you out of the land of Egypt, to be your God - I am God you Lord."

One thing the Torah is telling us here is why the commandment of Tzitzith, as well as other commandments, were given to the Jews in particular, and not to all people. There is a special bond between God and the Jew which was forged at the Exodus. God here says, "I. . .brought you out of Egypt to be your God." The unique miracles of the Exodus had this specific purpose — to forge this bond between God and Israel. God therefore repeats, "I am God your Lord" - now and forever.[12]

The Exodus was a unique event in the annals of history. It was the only time that God ever revealed Himself to an entire people, literally changing the course of both nature and history. The Torah therefore asks us, "Did God ever venture to take a nation for Himself; from the midst of another nation, with a challenge, with signs and wonders, as God your Lord did in Egypt before your very eyes? You have had sure proof that God is the Lord; there is no other" (*Deuteronomy* 4:34). The Exodus made every Jew uniquely aware of God and showed Him to be profoundly involved in the affairs of man.[13]

The Exodus and events surrounding it made Judaism unique among religions. Other faiths began with a single individual who claimed to have a special message. He gradually gathered a following and his disciples converted others, creating a new religion. That is the pattern followed by almost every great world religion.

The only exception to this is Judaism. God brought the entire Jewish people out of Egypt, and ultimately brought them to the foot of Mount Sinai where they all heard His message. It is most interesting to note that the very first words of the Ten Commandments are, "I am God your Lord who brought you out of the land of Egypt, from the house of slavery" (*Exodus* 20:2, *Deuteronomy* 5:6). This was both the culmination and the realization of the drama of the Exodus.

It is because of the unique bond forged at the Exodus that the Jew in particular must keep the commandments of the Torah. Through the commandments, this bond is strengthened and renewed, preserving the Jew and maintaining him on a high spiritual level. God therefore tells us, "I am God your Lord, who brought you out of the land of Egypt, and you shall observe all of My rules and laws and keep them - I am God" (*Leviticus* 19:36,37).

The Exodus thus places a very special responsibility on the Jew. God rescued us from slavery, and in a very special sense, became our Master. In the Torah He says, "The Children of Israel are My servants, whom I brought forth out of the land of Egypt - I am God your Lord" (*Leviticus* 25:25).

Therefore, in a sense, the Tzitzith are an insignia that we wear, proclaiming that we are God's subjects.[14] It is because of the Exodus that we are God's subjects in this very special way.

The Torah alludes to this in telling us to wear Tzitzith to be "holy to your God." The word "holy" means two things: First that we are close to God; and second, that we are separated from things that are ungodly.[15] We wear Tzitzith as a sign of our special relationship with God, as the ones who accepted His Torah. God reiterates the concept of this relationship when He says, "You shall be holy to Me, for I, God, am Holy, and I have set you apart from all other peoples, that you should be Mine" (*Leviticus* 20:26).

But we must understand the reason for all this. Why are the Jews so unique? Why did God have to choose a particular group of people as His own special servants Why, in short, are the Jews the "chosen people"?

God needed a special group of people who would undertake to lead the rest of humanity and show them the way. Looking at the generations before Abraham, God saw that humanity as a whole could not maintain a high moral and spiritual level. He therefore chose Abraham and his children, the Jews, as His special representatives, to proclaim His teachings to all the world. This is what God told us through His prophet, "I, God, have called you in righteousness. . .and have set you as a covenant of the people, as a light for the nations" (*Isaiah* 42:6). Israel's special mission is to bear witness to God, as we again find, "You are My witnesses," says God," and My servants, who I have chosen" (*Isaiah* 43:10).[16]

Although the Jew constantly fulfills this mission, the main time of its fruition will be in the Messianic Age. When all Jews are brought back to God by the Messiah (*Mashiach*), they in turn will influence all mankind in this direction. This is one of the main prophecies of the Messianic Age (*Isaiah* 2:2-4):

> It shall come to pass in the end of days
> that the mountains of God's house
> shall be set over all other nations
> and lifted high above the hills
> and all nations shall come streaming to it.
> Many people shall come and say:
> Come, let us go up to God's mountain

to the house of Israel's God
and He will teach us His ways
and we will walk in His paths.
For out of Zion shall go forth the Torah
and God's words from Jerusalem.
And He will judge between nations
and decide between peoples.
And they will beat their swords in plowshares
and their spears into pruning hooks.
Nation shall not lift up sword against nation
neither will they practice war anymore.

From this we learn that the Jews will be in a unique position of moral leadership in the Messianic Age. But who among the Jews will be in a position to exert such leadership? Who will be the ones deemed capable of spreading God's word to the rest of the world?

Our sages teach us that it will be those individuals who are careful to observe the commandment of Tzitzith. Regarding this, the prophet foretold, "In those days, ten men of each language will grasp the corner of [a garment containing Tzitzith, worn by] a Jewish man, and they will say, 'Let us go with you for we have heard that God is with you' " (*Zechariah* 8:23).[17]

What Are Tzitzith?

[This chapter is somewhat technical, and may be skipped on the first reading.]

If you have ever worn a Tallith or *Tallith Katan*, you are probably aware of the Tzitzith or tassels hanging on each of the four corners. If you look more carefully you will see that they are made of eight strings, or more accurately, four strings doubled over to make eight. You will also notice that they are attached through a small hole near the corner and that they contain five knots and four groups of windings between the knots.

If you take the trouble to count the windings, you will see that the group nearest the corner has seven windings, the next, eight, the next eleven, and the last one, thirteen. (See figure 1)

Look closely at the individual strings, and you will notice that they are each made of two threads, tightly twisted together.

All this shows that Tzitzith are more than simple strings. There are set rules as to how they must be made, and each of these rules has a reason. We must first explore how these rules are derived from the Torah, and then delve more deeply into their significance. We will discover that they are not mere strings, the Tzitzith touch upon some of the deepest philosophical concepts of Judaism.

Before going into the rules of Tzitzith, it would be useful to review the two places where they are mentioned in the Torah. The first, which we have already quoted is (*Numbers* 15:38):

> Speak to the sons of Israel and say to them that they make Tzitzith on the corners of their garments for [all] generations; and they shall place on the corner Tzitzith a twist (*Pethil*) of blue [wool].

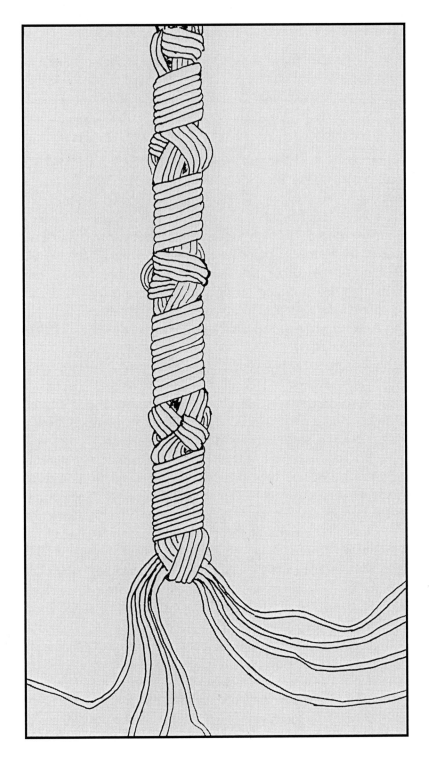

The second reference is (*Deuteronomy* 22:11,12):

> You shall not wear *Shaatnez* (a mixture of) linen and wool together.
>
> [But] you shall make tassels (*Gedilim*) on the four corners of your garments, with which you cover yourself.

First we must define the terms used by the Torah. There are three basic words that need definition: Tzitzith, *Pethil*, and *Gedilim*.

The word Tzitzith only occurs in one other place in the Bible, where we find, "The form of a hand came forth, and I was grasped by a lock of hair (Tzitzith) on my head" (*Ezekiel* 8:3). Referring to this verse, the Talmud tells us that Tzitzith are a group of freely hanging strings, resembling a lock of hair.[18] We thus have the first requirement of Tzitzith: They must contain a number of loose strings. This part of the Tzitzith is called the *Anaf*.

The Torah then tells us, "You shall place on the corner Tzitzith a twist (*Pethil*) of blue [wool]." We will discuss the question of the blue in a separate section, but the word *Pethil* or "twist" has a very special significance. It means a "twisted string," but it also has three other connotations:

The first connotation of the word *Pethil* is that of a winding; from this we derive the fact that one of the strings must be wound around the rest.[19] The Torah therefore states that it should be placed "*on* the corner Tzitzith." The Tzitzith refer to the loose threads and the *Pesil* or winding is placed over and around them. The threads are first hung to form loose strings or Tzitzith. Then we take another string and wind it "on" them. In ancient times, when the blue thread was still used, it was the string used to make most of the winding.

The second connotation is that of two threads twisted together.[20] This is one reason why each of the Tzitzith strings is made out of two threads twisted together like a rope. Most authorities also agree that whenever a string is mentioned in Jewish law, it is always defined as one twisted out of two or more threads. Tzitzith follow this rule.[21]

The third connotation of the word *Pethil* is almost a combination of the first two. The word means both "joined" and "bent," and therefore, it also denotes a double string. From this we learn that the strings are doubled. This is the reason we make the Tzitzith out of four strings, and then double them over to make eight.[22] We find a number of other places where a blue thread was used, such as in priestly garments; there, too it was placed through a hole and doubled over.[23]

Finally, the Torah says, "You shall make *Gedilim* (tassels) on the four corners of your garment." This immediately tells us that Tzitzith are only worn on a four-cornered or rectangular garment. This is why both the Tallith and *Tallith Katan* are rectangular in shape.[24]

The word *Gedilim* itself teaches us another important fact about the Tzitzith. Whereas the word Tzitzith refers to loose hairs or strings, the word *Gedil* means hair or strings bound together to form a tassel, braid or rope.[25] Obviously, a single string, even if doubled and twisted, would not be called a *Gedil* or tassel. (As we have already seen, the word *Pesil* already has this connotation.) It must therefore refer to a minimum of two doubled strings. The word used in the Torah - *Gedilim* - is plural therefore, there must be a "'doubled tassel" in each corner. This is an allusion to the fact that the Tzitzith must contain four doubled strings. *Gedil* in singular is two, and *Gedilim* in plural is four.[26] Of course, aside form this allusion, this is also known from tradition.[27]

Recapitulating, we now see that the Tzitzith have two basic parts. The first part consists of loose strings, alluded to in the word Tzitzith. This is called the *Anaf*.

The second part consists of the upper section, where the strings are tied together with the winding. This is called the *Gedil*. For aesthetic reasons our sages decreed that the *Gedil* consist of one third of the length of the entire Tzitzith, and the *Anaf* the other two-thirds.[28]

◄§ The Knots

The derivation of the knots in the Tzitzith involves a number of interesting concepts. Basically, the fact that the Tzitzith must be knotted to the garment is knows from oral tradition, as handed down from the time of Moses.[29]

There is, however, an important allusion to be found in the Torah. In the Biblical quotation which refers to *Gedilim*, you will notice that the commandment for Tzitzith comes right after the prohibition against *Shaatnez*. The laws of *Shaatnez* are fairly well known. Most of us are aware that the Torah forbids us to wear any garment containing both wool and linen. Even today, we must be careful of this, since many woolen garments, especially men's suits, contain linen as a stiffener in the lining or collar. Linen thread is also used occasionally to sew on buttons, and this must be replaced before a woolen suit can be worn. A network of "Shaatnez Laboratories" exists, whose sole purpose is to examine garments and ascertain that they do not contain *Shaatnez*. Many major clothing chains will send garments to these laboratories for free testing and rectification where necessary.

Everything in the Torah has a reason, even its order, so the fact that the commandment of *Shaatnez* is right next to that of Tzitzith comes to teach us something. According to Talmudic tradition, the laws of *Shaatnez* are set aside when one must place the blue woolen Tzitzith thread in a linen Tallith. The juxtaposition of the two commandments comes specifically to teach us this exception.[30] This was, however, only true when the blue thread was still in use.[31]

We must now take into account still another rule, that the prohibition of *Shaatnez* only applies when the linen and wool are permanently attached together. Thus, the very tradition that the commandment of Tzitzith can override that of *Shaatnez*, teaches us that the Tzitzith must be permanently attached to the garment. The simplest way of attaching the strings in a permanent way is by tying them on with a double knot.

Since this is a fairly complex argument, it is useful to see how it is presented in the Talmud:[32]

> Rabba said: We thus learn that the upper knot is Biblical in origin (*DeOraitha*).
> For if we were to say that it is only of Rabbinical

origin (*DeRabanan*), why must the Torah permit the use of [woolen] Tzitzith on a linen garment?

It would obviously be [permitted, since the two are not permanently attached], and a single knot is considered a [permanent] attachment.

We therefore see that it is Biblical in origin.

According to most commentaries, this "upper knot" refers to the double knot at the end of the windings.[33] According to this interpretation, this knot is also necessary to hold the windings in place. Unless knotted at the end, the windings would not be a permanent, integral part of the Tzitzith.[34]

Therefore, according to the primary law, the Tzitzith only require one double knot at the end of the windings. Some authorities also require a knot near the corner, before the windings. According to this opinion, the Tzitzith must have at least two knots, one before, and one after the windings.[35]

It is a most ancient custom to include five knots in Tzitzith.[36]

There are many reasons given for this custom. Some say that they are meant to represent the five books of the Torah: Genesis (*Bereishith*), Exodus (*Shemos*), Leviticus (*VaYikra*), Numbers (*BeMidbar*), and Deuteronomy (*Devarim*). In this manner, the Tzitzith recall "all of God's commandments."[37]

Others say that the five knots are reminiscent of the five senses, indicating that they all must be dedicated to God.[38]

Still another source indicated that they represent the first five words of the *Sh'ma: Sh'ma Yisrael Adonoy Elohenu Adonoy* - "Hear O Israel, God is our Lord, God is. . ." The final word, *Echad* - One - is then indicated by the windings, which bind all the threads together into *one* unit.[39] A number of other reasons are also given; they will be discussed later.[40]

The Torah does not specify the number of windings required in the Tzitzith. All that is required is a single triplet (*Chulya*), consisting of three windings.[41] Indeed, in a dire emergency, one may make such minimal Tzitzith, tying a double knot, making the three windings, and then tying another double knot.[42]

Rabbinical law, however, requires that one-third of the

Tzitzith consist of windings, and the other two-thirds of the loose strings, as discussed earlier. Since it is the custom to have five double knots in the Tzitzith, there are four groups of windings separating the knots. The accepted practice is for the first group to be made with seven windings, the second with eight, the third with eleven, and the fourth with thirteen. We will discuss the reason for this custom in a later section.[43]

There are a number of other laws regarding Tzitzith that bear mentioning. First of all, one cannot make Tzitzith out of just any strings. They must be made either of wool or of exactly the same material as the Tallith. They must also be spun especially to be used in Tzitzith. This is true even of the two strings that are twisted together to make each cord. In this respect, Tzitzith are no different from any other ritual object that must be made specifically for its intended ritual purpose.[44]

◅§ Measurements

There is another group of rules involving the dimensions of the Tzitzith and the measurements associated with them. Before beginning to explain them, however, there are several general concepts that must be understood.

In many places where the Torah requires something to be used for a ritual purpose, a certain measure or *Shiur* is required. These measures are known from the Oral Torah, which was transmitted from master to disciple from the time of Moses, and finally set in writing in the Talmud. Thus, when the Torah requires us to eat something (such as Matzah on Passover) we must eat a piece at least as large as an olive. This is the measure or *Shiur* for something to have the status of food. In the case of a beverage, the measure is a *Revi'ith*, approximately three fluid ounces. With regard to Tzitzith, we will discuss the measures involved in such things as cloth and thread.

All Talmudic measurement of length are presented in terms of a "finger" or *Agudel*, the width of an average thumb. There is some question as to the precise length of a "finger," but the majority of authorities agree that it lies somewhere between 3/4 inch and one inch.[45]

Other measurements are then defined in terms of this "finger." Those most often used are:

Agudel	"finger"		3/4 inch- 1 inch
Tefach	handbreadth	4 "fingers"	3-4 inches
Ama	cubit	6 handbreadths	18-24 inches

Making use of these measurements, we can discuss the measure used in cloth and thread.

A piece of woven material does not have the status of cloth unless it measures at least three "fingers" square, that is, three "fingers" by three "fingers."[46] Anything less than this is considered a useless scrap, and has no status in Jewish law.

In the case of thread or string, the measure is a "double span" or *Sit Kaful*, double the distance between the forefinger and middle finger when the hand is spread out. This is approximately equal to four "fingers" in length.[47] Anything less than this is also considered a useless scrap, and has no status in Jewish law. Therefore, in order for a piece of string or thread to have any ritual status, it must be at least four "fingers" long.

There is, however, one exception to this rule. The measure of a piece of string that is part of a garment is a "single span" or *Sit*. This equals two "fingers." When a piece of thread is part of a garment, it must be taken into account even if it is only two "fingers" long.[48]

Keeping all this in mind, we can now understand some of the measurements involving Tzitzith.

First of all, each part of the Tzitzith must contain a significant length of string. The shortest such section is the *Gedil* or wound section, which must therefore be at least four fingers long.

As discussed earlier, the wound portion or *Gedil* must comprise one-third of the length of the entire Tzitzith. Therefore, their entire length must be at least 12 fingers.

From this, we see that the length of the Tzitzith must be between 9 and 12 inches. We usually take the stricter view and require them to be a foot long.

The question still remains as to where on the garment the Tzitzith must be hung. The Torah simply tells us to place them "on the corner," but no exact distance is given. This distance is derived from the general laws regarding cloth and thread.

The Torah tells us to place the Tzitzith "*on* the corners of your garments." The Talmud interprets the word "on" to mean that a significant portion of the Tzitzith must actually be "*on* the corner," that is, in contact with it.[50] The Talmud states that this portion must be the length of a "thumb joint" or *Kesher Agudel*, a measure which is approximately two fingers.[51] The hole through which the Tzitzith string is attached must therefore be at least two fingers from the edge of the garment.

The reason for this is obvious. As mentioned earlier, when a string or thread is part of a garment, a significant length is two fingers. This is the amount of Tzitzith string that must be "on the corner." If the hole is placed any closer than this, the significant amount will not be "on the corner" but "beneath the corner."[52]

We also have a rule that a piece of cloth that is more than three fingers square must be taken into account. If the hole through which the Tzitzith are attached was more than three fingers from the edge, it would be separated from it by a significant piece of the garment. It would then no longer be "on the corner," but inside the main body of the garment. For this reason the hole of the Tzitzith must be no more than three fingers from the edge of the garment.[53]

We therefore see that the hole through which the Tzitzith are attached must lie between two and three fingers from the edge of the Tallith. If we wish to take into account all opinions regarding the length of a "finger," we would have to place it between 2 and 2 1/4 inches from the edge.[54] If it is at least 1 1/2 inches from the edge, however, the Tallith may be worn. (See figure 2)

◄§ Conclusion

From all this, we clearly see that the Tzitzith are much more than mere "strings." There is a richness of law and lore surrounding them that bespeaks a most profound depth. Furthermore, their structure in *Halakhah* (Jewish Religious

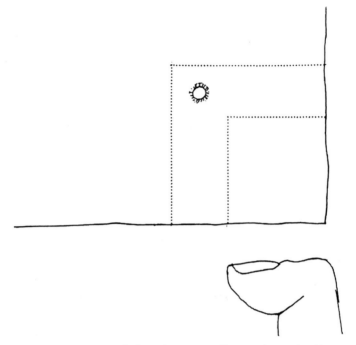

Law) involves some of the deepest discussions in the entire Talmud.

One point bears repeating. The strings used for Tzitzith must be spun especially for this purpose. Therefore, when one buys a Tallith, *Tallith Katan*, or Tzitzith to be put into a Tallith, it is most important that one make certain that the Tzitzith were made in the proper manner. This is especially true in the case of silk, rayon and nylon Tzitzith, where extreme caution must be exercised.

There are two ways in which we observe the commandment of Tzitzith. One is through the *Tallith Kattan* - the "small Tallith" - which we wear as part of our clothing. The second is the *Tallith Gadol* - the "great Tallith" - worn in the synagogue.

Of the two, the tallith worn in the synagogue is by far the most familiar. In many ways, however, the *Tallith Katan*, which is worn all day, is more important. We will therefore begin our discussion with the *Tallith Katan*.

The Tallith Katan

In proclaiming the commandment of Tzitzith, the Torah says, "You shall make tassels (*Gedilim*) on the *four corners* of your garments. . ." From this we learn that Tzitzith are only required on a four-cornered garment.[55]

In ancient times, many garments were four-cornered.[56] Clothing was not tailored as it is today, but most often consisted of a simple rectangle of cloth, direct from the loom, which was worn as a shawl, cape, tunic or toga. As late as the classical Greek period, the standard garments consisted of the *chiton* and *himation*, which were essentially rectangles of cloth, draped and fastened around the body. Similar garments were worn in Talmudic times. Since everyone wore four-cornered clothing, they fulfilled the commandment of Tzitzith merely by placing them on their regular garb.

Because we no longer regularly wear four-cornered clothing, we wear a special garment in order to fulfill this most important commandment.[57] One of the most important Jewish commentators, Rabbi Yitzchak Abarbanel, stated that this is the reason why the Torah states that we must "make Tzitzith. . .for all generations." Even though a time would come when four-cornered garments would not normally be worn, we must continue to wear a special garment in order to fulfill the commandment of Tzitzith.[58]

This special garment is the *Tallith Katan* - the "small Tallith." It is also sometimes called an *Arba Kanfoth* - literally "four corners" - or simply "Tzitzith." In Yiddish it was often referred to as a *Lahbsideckel*, or "body cover."

The *Tallith Katan* consists of a simple rectangle of cloth, with a hole for the neck. Two styles are shown in figure 3.

The *Tallith Katan* should be at least a cubit (or *Amah*) square on each side. According to our discussion on measurements, this would be between 18 and 24 inches. If possible, it is best to wear the larger size, and thus be covered according to even the stricter opinion.

You should wear the *Tallith Katan* all day long. It is worn under your shirt, preferable over an undershirt, and is put on the first thing in the morning.

If you do not wear a Tallith in synagogue, you should say the following blessing before putting on the *Tallith Katan*:[59]

בָּרוּךְ אַתָּה ה׳ אֱלֹקֵינוּ מֶלֶךְ הָעוֹלָם,
אֲשֶׁר קִדְּשָׁנוּ בְּמִצְוֹתָיו וְצִוָּנוּ עַל מִצְוַת צִיצִית

Barukh Atah Adonoy Elohenu Malekh haolam
asher kid'sha-nu be'mitzvo-thav vetziva-nu al Mitzvath Tzitzith.

Blessed are You, God, our Lord, King of the world,
who has made us holy with His commandments
and gave us the Mitzvah of Tzitzith.

If you put on the *Tallith Katan* before washing your hands, you can defer the blessing until later, taking hold of the Tzitzith when you recite it.[60]

If you normally wear a Tallith, according to most authorities, it is best not to say the blessing over the *Tallith Katan* at all. Instead, you should have in mind to include it when you say the blessing over the Tallith.[61] The *Tallith Katan* should be worn all day long. Some people also wear it to sleep.[62]

It is also a custom for some people to keep their Tzitzith exposed, in order that they constantly fulfill the injunction, "and you shall see them."[63] This, however, is not a strict requirement, and the Tzitzith may be worn completely under one's clothing.[64]

Since the *Tallith Katan* is always worn, the Mitzvah of Tzitzith is one Mitzvah that is observed most constantly. It is the first commandment that we observe in the morning,[65] and continues throughout the day. As such, it is a constant reminder of our obligation as Jews, and of our allegiance to God.

Through the *Tallith Katan*, the Mitzvah of Tzitzith is one of the very first observances that we teach a child. In many communities, it is a custom to present a child with his first *Tallith Katan* on his third birthday; from then on, it is constantly worn.[66]

The *Tallith Katan* is also one of the least expensive ritual objects that you can purchase. Its cost is negligible, and yet, its spiritual benefits can be priceless.

The Tallith

The second, and more familiar manner in which we fulfill the commandment of Tzitzith is through the Tallith, which is worn primarily during the morning prayer services.[67]

The fact that we pray in a Tallith is alluded to in the verse, "The prayer of a poor man, when he enwraps himself [in a Tallith] and pours out his words before God" (*Psalms* 102:1). When we stand before God like beggars, in prayer and supplication, we are to wrap ourselves in a Tallith.[68]

There are a number of diverse customs regarding the Tallith. In some communities, young men do not begin wearing a Tallith until they are married.[69] In others, the Tallith is worn immediately after Bar Mitzvah. In all such cases, one follows the custom of his congregation.

An important point must, however, be made. In congregations where many teenagers do not wear the *Tallith Kattan*, they *must* wear a Tallith for the morning service. It is most important that Tzitzith be worn during this service.

A Tallith should be large enough so that one can drape it over his shoulders, with two corners in front and the other two in back.[70] A good Tallith should therefore measure at least four feet by six feet and be large enough to cover the individual down to his waist. As an absolute minimum, it must measure one cubit or *Amah* (24 inches) in width.

Although a Tallith can be made of any type of cloth, it is preferable to make it of pure white wool.[71] Whenever the Torah speaks of a garment, the reference is usually to either a woolen or linen garment.[72] (Now that we do not have the blue wool to place in the Tzitzith, a linen Tallith is not used.[73]) Therefore, when one wears a woolen Tallith, he is performing the Mitzvah exactly as it was done in Biblical times, and such a Tallith is considered a "garment" in the fullest sense of Torah usage. Besides, wearing a woolen Tallith has become the hallmark of the individual who is sophisticated and observant in the best possible Jewish sense.

On weekdays, when Tefillin are worn, the Tallith is put on first.[74] There is a general rule that the Mitzvah performed most often takes precedence. Judaism is more a religion of steadfastness than one of dramatic highlights. Therefore, since the Tallith is also worn on the Sabbath and holidays, while the Tefillin are not, the Tallith takes precedence.[75]

Before putting on the Tallith, you should check the Tzitzith and make sure that they have not become torn. If they are tangled, you should separate them, so that they hang down like "loose hairs."[76] In many places, it is a custom to place the folded Tallith on one's shoulder while doing this.

Just before you put on the Tallith, you should say, "I am now about to fulfill God's commandment to wear Tzitzith on my garment, in order that I remember and observe all His commandments." There is also a longer declaration found in most prayer books.

The Tallith is put on while standing. You should hold the Tallith over your head and say the blessing:

בָּרוּךְ אַתָּה ה' אֱלֹקֵינוּ מֶלֶךְ הָעוֹלָם,
אֲשֶׁר קִדְּשָׁנוּ בְּמִצְוֹתָיו וְצִוָּנוּ לְהִתְעַטֵּף בַּצִּיצִית.

*Baruch Atah Adonoy Elohenu Melekh haolam asher
kid'sha-nu be-mitzvo-thav vetziva-nu le-hithatef ba-Tzitzith.*

Blessed are You God, our Lord, King of the world,
who made us holy with His commandments
and bid us to enwrap ourselves in Tzitzith.

You should then drape the Tallith over your head, and cast the corners over you left shoulder. This is what the Talmud means when it states that one should enwrap himself with a Tallith, "as the Arabs (Ishmaelites) enwrap themselves."[77] There are a number of customs regarding this.

You should stand wrapped in this Tallith in this manner long enough to walk four cubits, or approximately four seconds.

While enwrapped in the Tallith, it is customary to say (*Psalm 36:8,11*):[78]

מַה יָּקָר חַסְדְּךָ אֱלֹקִים, וּבְנֵי אָדָם בְּצֵל כְּנָפֶיךָ יֶחֱסָיוּן: יִרְוְיֻן מִדֶּשֶׁן
וְנַחַל עֲדָנֶיךָ תַשְׁקֵם: כִּי עִמְּךָ מְקוֹר חַיִּים, בְּאוֹרְךָ נִרְאֶה אוֹר:
מְשֹׁךְ חַסְדְּךָ לְיֹדְעֶיךָ וְצִדְקָתְךָ לְיִשְׁרֵי לֵב:

How precious is Your love, O God,
    man finds shelter
    in the shadow cast
    by the corners of Your [Tallith].
They feast on the riches of Your house,
    You let them drink Your rivers of delight.
For the source of life is with You,
    by Your light, we see light.
Bring Your love to those who know You,
    by Your light, we see light.
Bring Your love to those who know You,
    Your charity to upright hearts.

Since this is said while your head is covered with the Tallith, you will have to learn it by heart.

You should then rearrange the Tallith so that two Tzitzith are in front, and two in back. You are thus surrounded by Tzitzith.

In many communities, it is customary for married men to cover their heads with the Tallith. Unmarried boys, however, even when they do wear a Tallith, never cover their heads with it.[80]

It is also a very ancient practice for the one leading the service (the *Shliach Tzibur* or *Chazzan*) to wear a Tallith. As we shall see, there is a most profound significance underlying this custom.

In order to beautify the Mitzvah, many observant Jews place a border or *Atarah* of pure silver on the Tallith. This is done to make the observance as beautiful and meaningful as possible.

Now that you know something of the Halakhic structure of Tzitzith and how to put them on, you might like to make a pair yourself.

Make Your Own

There is nothing very mysterious about making a Tallith, or *Tallith Katan*. Each one is simply a rectangle of cloth. Tzitzith are a bit more involved, but are so easy to put in that even a young child can do it.

To make a Tallith, all you need is a good piece of pure white woolen cloth. It should be 4 feet by 6 feet in size.

For a *Tallith Katan*, you can use any sort of cloth, although wool is still best. It should measure at least 18 by 36 inches, and preferably 24 by 48. Cut a T-shaped hole for the neck.

For both a Tallith and *Tallith Katan*, you then make a hole approximately two inches from each edge (measured perpendicularly, not diagonally). Through this hole the Tzitzith are placed.

It is a good idea to hem both the Tallith and the hole, so that they will not tear. When doing so, you must use a thread made of a different material than the Tallith.[81] For example, if you are making a Tallith out of wool, you should sew the hem with cotton or silk. If you are making a cotton *Tallith Katan*, sew the hem with silk or rayon thread (but not wool). In no case, however, should you use linen thread, since together with the woolen Tzitzith, this would constitute *Shaatnez*.

You are now ready to place the Tzitzith in the Tallith or *Tallith Katan*.

◂§ Making Tzitzith

Whether or not you make your own, there are occasions when you may want to put Tzitzith on a Tallith or *Tallith Katan*. You might buy a Tallith and desire to put in your own Tzitzith or replace the ones already in. The Tzitzith may have become worn or torn and might need replacement. In any case, it is useful to know how to make them.

You can buy Tzitzith from any good Jewish book store, or your rabbi or adviser can order you a set. Look for rabbinical certification stating that they are made of thread spun especially for Tzitzith. Your rabbi can serve as your guide in this area.

The package of Tzitzith will contain 16 strings, four for each corner. Four of these strings will be longer than the rest, and they are usually wound around the others. One of these longer strings is used in each corner as the *Shamash* or "servant" string; this is the one you will use to make the windings.

Separate the strings and you are ready to begin:

1. Take all four strings and place them through the hole. Adjust them so that they are all even (except for the *Shamash*, which remains longer on one side). The four strings are now doubled into eight.
2. Make a double knot, with four strings on each side. (It does not matter whether you make a square knot or a granny knot.) Before making the first knot, you should say, "I am doing this to fulfill the commandment of Tzitzith," or *LeShem Mitzvath Tzitzith* in Hebrew.
3. Take the *Shamash* and wind it around the other seven strings. Make seven windings.
4. Make another double knot.
5. Eight windings.
6. A double knot.
7. Eleven windings.
8. A double knot.
9. Thirteen windings.
10. A final double knot.

Your Tzitzith are now complete. It's as easy as that! Your Tzitzith should contain five knots and four groups of windings. The total number of windings should be 39.

Now that we have explored some of the basics of Tzitzith, we can look into their deeper significance.

A DEEPER LOOK

*"Open my eyes, that I may behold
the wonders of Your Torah."*

(Psalms 119:18)

Clothing

One of the most obvious points about Tzitzith is the fact that they involve a commandment directly related to clothing. They are not a Mitzvah in their own right as are Tefillin, but one that pertains to the garments we wear. If we are to understand fully the meaning of Tzitzith, we must first explore the significance that clothing plays in human society.

Of all living creatures, man is unique in the fact that he covers his body with clothing. *Homo Sapiens* is the only species that wear clothing. The reason for this has been the subject of study for philosophers, sociologists, anthropologists, psychologists and ethnologists for many years, and they have come up with some interesting theories. Even more fascinating is the fact that their conclusions often agree with those taught by our great religious sages.

The most obvious reason for wearing clothing might appear to be to provide protection from the elements. However, when anthropologists studied primitive tribes in even the warmest climates, they found that people still wore clothing as a matter of course. The human practice of wearing clothing seems to be universal, even where there is no need for protection from the elements.[1]

What was discovered was that people covered their sexual organs in virtually every human society. Let us now see how this agrees with the Torah view.

One of the most intriguing stories in the Torah is that of Adam's sin. We all know the story: How the serpent tempted Eve to eat of the Tree of Knowledge (*Etz HaDaath*), and, as a result, both Adam and Eve were cursed and driven out of the Garden of Eden. Taken superficially, this is an intriguing story;

but on a deeper level, it provides us with a profound insight into human psychology.

The existence of a walking, talking serpent might seem difficult to understand, but our sages teach us that it was the very incarnation of evil. In order for man to have free will, at least the possibility of evil had to exist.[2] Before Adam sinned, evil was not part of man, but something external. It was therefore represented by the serpent, an entity external to man. It was only after man sinned that evil became an integral part of this being.[3] From then on, man's battle with evil became as much a battle with himself as one against an external force.

Before Adam sinned, the Torah says of him, "And they were both naked, the man and his wife, and they were not ashamed" (*Genesis* 2:25). Our sages comment that they were not ashamed because they had no sexual desire.[4] Sex was as natural a body function as eating and drinking. It was something completely under man's control. Sexual pleasure may have been something that they could enjoy, but it was not the overwhelming passion that it is today, where it drives people to foolish and even destructive acts. Sex, like the serpent, was something external to man. Man could enjoy it when he wanted to, but he was not driven by it.

Since sexual desire was not an integral part of man's nature, there was no shame in exposing the sexual organs. They were no different that his eyes, ear, hands or feet. They were not something that could arouse another individual, or in any way make one feel like a sex object.[5] Indeed, so innocent and natural was the sexual act, that Adam and Eve did not even feel compelled to perform it in private.[6]

The external incarnation that led them to sin was represented by the serpent. It is a well known fact that in almost every culture the serpent represents some sort of phallic symbol. To a large degree then, the serpent represents sexual temptation. Our sages teach us that the main temptation the serpent used to lure Eve was that of sex.[7]

As soon as man sinned, he began to have an Evil Urge or *Yetzer HaRa*. Evil was no longer something outside of himself, but an integral part of his being. It was now a force that man could overcome only with the greatest difficulty.

Our sages teach us that, "The Evil Urge exists mainly in the area of sex."[8] Very often, it is sexual temptation that leads a person away from religion and godliness in other areas. It is often the strongest barrier standing in the way of an individual's spiritual perfection.

On the other hand, the individual who can completely control his sexual desires is counted as one who can control all his emotions. Here again, our sages teach us that a person is only called a Tzadik or saint when he can control his sexual passions.[9] The main path to holiness is through self-mastery, and the most difficult area for such mastery is sex. To achieve such self-mastery takes great internal strength, to which our sages allude when they say, "Who is strong? He who overcomes his passions."[10]

As soon as man sinned, his sexuality was aroused. Immediately after Adam and Eve ate from the Fruit of Knowledge, the Torah tells us, "The eyes of both of them were opened, and they knew that they were naked. They sewed fig leaves and made themselves loincloths" (*Genesis* 3:7). The major commentators explain that now that their sexual desires were aroused, they were ashamed to stand naked. They had begun to view others as sex objects, and were themselves ashamed to be seen in that light.[11]

It is interesting to note how closely the opinions of social scientists parallel the Torah. Where science seeks with an unprejudiced eye, it is merely another way of approaching truth. In this particular area, honest investigation had discovered a truth revealed in the Torah thousands of years ago.

Even more interesting is the fact that some of these concepts are indicated by the very etymology of the Hebrew language. Hebrew is called the "Holy Tongue" (*Lashon HaKodesh*), and as such, even its grammatical and etymological rules teach us important lessons. In the area under discussion, we see an important case in point.

First of all, the Hebrew word for "garment" is *LeBHUSH* (לְבוּשׁ) (The capitalized letters indicate those actually used in the Hebrew spelling.) This comes from the word *BUSH* (בּוּשׁ), which means "to be ashamed."[12] The very structure of the

Hebrew language indicates that clothing is worn because of shame.

Another Hebrew word for garment is *BeGeD* (בֶּגֶד). This has the same root as the word *BaGaD* (בָּגַד), meaning "to rebel."[13] This indicates that man wears clothing because he originally rebelled against God. Before man sinned and rebelled, he was perfectly content and unashamed of being nude.

God also understood that in his fallen state man had a need for clothing. The Torah states that before ejecting man from the Garden of Eden, "God made garments of skins for Adam and his wife, and He clothed them" (*Genesis* 3:21).

From all this, we see that the main function of human clothing is to act as barrier against sexual desires. As such, it is particularly related to the sense of sight. The purpose of clothing is to cover the body in order that it not be visible as a source of sexual arousal.

We can now understand the purpose of Tzitzith.

Here again, we can actually see this in the etymological structure of the word. The word *TziTzith* (צִיצִית) has the same root as the word *TzuTz*, (צוּץ), meaning "to look."[14] Tzitzith are therefore something that relate specifically to the sense of sight, something to look at.

The Torah says of the Tzitzith, "You shall *see* them, and not stray after your heart and after *your eyes*, which had led you to immorality." The Talmud explains that the injunction not to stray "after your eyes" refers to visual sexual stimulation.[15] Clothing in general acts as a natural barrier to such arousal, and the Tzitzith serve to reinforce this barrier.

None of this, however, is meant to imply that sex is something dirty or evil. To the contrary, Judaism looks upon sex as something beautiful and pleasurable. The Torah views sexual relations between husband and wife as something normal, desirable, and the one act that does the most to strengthen the bond of love between them.[16] But at the same time, the Torah realizes that when misused, sex can be a most destructive and debilitating force. Historians tell us of entire civilizations that have fallen as a result of sexual corruption, and here again, this view is reflected in our Torah's teachings.[17]

The type of sex that the Torah proscribes is that which is irresponsible, exploitative and destructive. The commandment of Tzitzith was given as a safeguard against such activity.

In the Talmud, we find a most interesting story that illustrates this:[18]

There was a man who was most careful to observe the Mitzvah of Tzitzith. Once he heard that there was a harlot in a port city who charged 400 gold pieces for her services. He sent her the 400 gold pieces and arranged a rendezvous.

When the appointed time came, he traveled to her city, and waited outside her door. Her attendant informed her that the man who had sent 400 gold pieces had arrived and was waiting outside. The harlot replied, "Let him enter."

She arranged seven beds, six of silver, and the seventh of gold. Next to the beds, she placed seven ladders, six of silver, and the uppermost of gold. Finally, she disrobed and sat herself on the highest bed.

The man was beginning to undress when suddenly his four Tzitzith began to slap him in his face. He slipped down and sat on the ground.

The woman joined him and also sat on the ground. She exclaimed, "By Jupiter! I will not let you leave me until you tell me what you find wrong with me."

The man replied: "I [swear] by the Divine Service that I have never seen a woman as beautiful as you! But our God has given us a commandment known as Tzitzith. [In the section dealing with the commandment,] it is written, 'I am Hashem your God,' two times. 'I am' the One who will eventually reward - and 'I am' the One who will eventually punish. [The Tzitzith] appeared to me like four witnesses [who would testify against me for my sin]."

The woman said, "I [swear] by the Divine Service that I will not let you leave me until you tell me your name, your city, your rabbi, and the school where you studied Torah."

He wrote the information on a paper and left. The woman then sold all her possessions, giving a third of the proceeds to the government (to allow her to leave), a third to the poor, and keeping a third for herself. The only other thing she kept were her beds.

She then went to Rabbi Chiya's academy and said, "Rabbi, teach me and allow me to convert to Judaism."

The Rabbi demurred, saying, "My daughter, is it because you have set your eyes on one of my students?"

She then showed him the note [and related the entire story.] The Rabbi finally [agreed to convert her and] said, "Go, my daughter, and take what is yours. The same beds that you used for sin, you may now enjoy in a permissible manner."

The great commentator, Rabbi Moshe Alshech (1521-1593) explains that the Tzitzith did not actually slap him in the face physically.[19] Rather, they struck at him psychologically, as he later recounted, so that they suddenly seemed like four witnesses, ready to testify against him.

This account, however, shows dramatically how Tzitzith can help one master his sexual compulsions.

The passage of Tzitzith tells us to "look at them and remember all of God's commandments, and not stray after your heart and eyes." Sexual desire is the one thing that is most often responsible for leading a person away from religious observance. Sex is most readily available among those who are indifferent or antagonistic toward religion. In seeking to court the favor of those who will provide him with sexual outlets, one may be sorely tempted to give up such things as the Sabbath, Kashruth, and other important elements of Judaism. One who is drawn into a society of sexual promiscuity finds himself in an environment hostile to true Jewish values. This is not mere theory. There are countless cases of religious individuals who have left the ranks of religious observance in order to pursue their sexual infatuations.

The Talmud tells us that when the Torah says, "You shall not stray after your heart," the reference is to atheism.[20] This is also borne out by experience. There is nothing that will draw a person away from God more than sexual promiscuity. Many indeed are the Jewish youth who have given up God completely in order to gain some fleeting sexual pleasure. All too many are those who have sacrificed all the depth and meaning that they have gained from Judaism, for the dubious promise of sexual "freedom." And looming above this is the danger of intermarriage, which leads a tragic number of our youth away from Judaism completely.

If we look in the Torah, we find an important example of this. Soon after the Jews came near the borders of ancient Moab, the Torah relates, "Israel remained in Shittim, and the people began to behave promiscuously with the daughters of Moab. They invited the people to sacrifice to their gods, and the people came and ate and bowed down to their gods" (Numbers 20:1,2). This is one of the first recorded cases where sexual infatuation led many Jews to abandon the teachings of the Torah. Things have not changed very much since then.

The verse dealing with Tzitzith then says, "In order that you remember and keep all My commandments, and be holy to your God." Here again, the Torah is telling us that the main path to holiness is mastery of one's sexuality.[2][1] In protecting the individual from promiscuity, Tzitzith can lead him to holiness.

The verse ends with a reference to the Exodus. The Exodus represents both a physical and spiritual liberation, but in an important sense, it also involves the liberation from domination by one's sexual appetites. When the Torah speaks of forbidden sexual activity, it introduces the section with the statement, "You shall no longer do what was done in the land of Egypt where you dwelt" (Leviticus 18:3). Egypt was known as a place of extreme sexual immorality. When the Jews left Egypt, this was one of the things that they were to leave behind.[22] In serving to check our passions, the Tzitzith tend to reinforce this aspect of the Exodus.

The Tzitzith may seem like simple strings, but they can affect an individual's entire lifestyle. It is now useful to look even more deeply into their true significance.

God's Tallith

Rabbi Yochanan said: If it were not written [in the Bible] it would be impossible to say. But we are taught that God wrapped Himself [in a Tallith] like a prayer leader and showed Moses the order of prayer. He said, "Whenever Israel sins, let then proceed in this manner, and I will forgive them."

Talmud Rosh HaShanah 17b

In this short lesson, Rabbi Yochanan is presenting us with a most remarkable teaching. According to most commentators, the Biblical verse to which he is referring is, 'The Ancient of Days (*Atik Yomin*) sat there, His garment was white as snow, and the hair of His head was like pure wool" (*Daniel* 7:9).[23] It is also closely related to the verse, "He covers Himself with light as a garment" (*Psalms* 104:2).[24]

This is a very difficult lesson to understand. How can we say that God performs a physical act like putting on a Tallith? We know that it is a fundamental principle of Judaism to realize that God has no body, shape or form.[25] God is in no way physical, and nothing physical can apply to Him at all. To suggest anything physical such as a body or Tallith with relation to God would go against the very foundations of our belief.

Still, in the Torah and in many other places, we see that God is spoken of as if He had a human body. In countless verses, we find expression such as "the hand of God" or "the eyes of God." Numerous other parts of the body are also mentioned with relation to God. All such references are called *anthropomorphisms* - expressions where we borrow terms from human experience when speaking of God.

Obviously, all such expressions must be understood allegorically rather than literally. Our sages teach us that God borrows terms from His creatures to express His relationship to the world.[26] A physical allegory may be used to express a very profound philosophical relationship between God and His creation. Thus, for example, when the Torah speaks of "God's hand," it is speaking of His expression of power and of His providence in guiding the world's destiny. Similarly, when it speaks of "God's eyes," it is alluding to the fact that He is aware of everything that happens in the world. The same is true of all other such anthropomorphisms.

Anthropomorphisms such as "hand" and "eye" are fairly simple to understand. But when we try to understand the full richness of such allegories in our sacred literature, we find ourselves in a much more difficult situation. One of the greatest Jewish thinkers, the Rambam (Maimonides), states that a full interpretation of these would involve some of the deepest mysteries of Judaism.[27] This is an area where many of our greatest sages over the centuries have delved, explaining and expounding these deep concepts.

It is obvious that when our sages teach us that God wears a Tallith, they are providing us with a profound lesson concerning God's relationship to us. In speaking of Tzitzith, the Torah says that the reason for this commandment is so that "you should remember all of God's commandments." Obviously, then, this lesson also has something to do with the significance of the commandments. Let us try to understand it more completely.

◆§ The Problem of Evil

One of the questions that philosophers and thinkers have puzzled over for centuries is the problem of evil. If God is all good, why does He allow evil to exist? Why is it possible for people to harm each other? Why are such things as wars and concentration camps possible in a world created and ruled by God?

This is a question that is adequately treated by our great sages and teachers. But before we can begin to delve into their explanations, we must first try to answer an even more basic question:

194 □ Tzitzith

Why did God create the world?

Obviously, it would be utterly naive to believe that we could ever fully answer this quesiton. God is so high above us that we can no more understand His motives than a fly can understand the work of a great mathematician around whom it buzzes. God is so high that we cannot even begin to comprehend His purpose.

Yet, we can understand God's reasons to the extent that they have been revealed by Him in the Torah. The account of creation ends with the words, "God saw everything that He had made, and it was very good" (Genesis 1:31). This and similar passages teach us that God's purpose in creation was to do good. In order to express His love and goodness, God had to create a world. This essentially is what the Psalmist means when he sings, "God is good to all, His love rests over all His works" (Psalms 145:9).

But since God is infinitely and ultimately good, it would stand to reason that if He wanted to give good to His creation, it would have to be the highest possible good. What is that? What is the highest ultimate good?

The answer should be perfectly obvious. This ultimate good is God Himself. God thus created a world to which He could give of Himself.

But how is this possible? In what way can God give of Himself? How can a mere man partake of God?

The answer is not difficult if you really think about it. We can partake of God by resembling Him to the greatest possible degree. The more we resemble Him, the more we partake of the ultimate good that is God.

It is for this reason that God gave man free will. If man did not have free will, he would be poles apart from God. He would be little more than a robot or puppet. God, on the other hand, is absolutely free to do as He wills, since there is nothing that can hold Him back. In giving man free will, God gave him the ability to imitate God and thus ultimately partake of Him.

Therefore, just as God chose good as a matter of free will, so can man. But in order for this choice to be real, God had to create the opposite of good. He therefore created the possibility of evil, so that man would be free to choose between good and its opposite. God Himself speaks of this when He tells His prophet, "I form light and create darkness, I make peace and create evil - I am God; I do all these things" (*Isaiah* 45:7).[28]

Although evil does not fulfill God's primary purpose in creation, it does fulfill His purpose in a secondary way. In a sense, it is like the peel of a fruit or the shell of a nut. They are in themselves useless, but they serve the secondary purpose of preserving the fruit until it is used. The same is true of evil. It does not serve God's primary purpose of bestowing good, but it does not fulfill the secondary purpose of making it possible. Because of this analogy, the forces of evil are often referred to as the "husk" or *Klipah* in relation to God's purpose.[29]

God's ultimate purpose, however, is to do good, and to bring about a world "where all is good."[30] The destiny of evil is to be transformed ultimately into good.[31] Slowly but surely, the world must reach the level of perfection planned by God.

◆§ Providence

The major task of perfecting the world belongs to man. The Psalmist said, "The heavens belong to God, but the earth He gave to the sons of man" (*Psalms* 115:16). It is man's responsibility to use his God-given free will for good and thus bring about a world conforming to God's plan. In so doing, he becomes a partner with God, and is thus able to partake of Him in yet another sense.

But God does not leave things to chance. There is also an element of Divine Providence. Although God gave individuals free will, He still influences the large scale course of history. Even though He does not determine the conduct of individuals, the collective wills of nations and societies are largely determined by God. This is what scripture means when it say, "The king's heart is in God's hand. . .He turns it however He wills" (*Proverbs* 21:1).[32]

God also guides the destiny of each individual to fulfill His purpose. Man might have free will, but God interacts with him to bring about His goal. He thus might place an individual in a certain predicament, cause him to meet a propitious friend, or otherwise give him opportunities to act in a way that helps lead the world toward God's ultimate goal.[33]

In a way, the situation is very much analogous to the game of a master chess player. Although his opponent has complete free will, the master knows how to counter each move, and thus bring the game to any conclusion he desires. Using this analogy, we can say that God is the ultimate Master, and His game involves all mankind. The stakes are the ultimate triumph of good.

All this comes under the general heading of what we call Divine Providence or *Hashgacha*. It is what we mean when we say that God is "King of the universe." His providence is constantly at work, guiding the world toward His goal.

Besides this primary providence, however, there must also be secondary elements of providence that God uses specifically to deal with evil. If you think about it, it is obvious that there are two such secondary elements.

First, there is an element of providence that allows evil to exist. Since God's purpose requires the existence of evil, He must, in a sense, hold Himself back from utterly destroying it. Therefore, although God is constantly guiding the world toward good, He still allows evil to exist as long as it serves His purpose. It is of this element of providence that our sages speak when they teach us, "When one comes to defile himself, [God] opens the way for him."[34]

The second element of providence is that which protects from evil. Wherever man comes in contact with evil, God must at least give him the power to be able to overcome it. Furthermore, the power that God gives to evil must not be allowed to become part of His providence and thus make it malignant. It is of this second element of God's providence that our sages speak when they say, "Man's [evil] urge becomes stronger each day, and if God did not help him, he would not be able [to overcome it]."[35]

We therefore see that in order for evil to exist, God must interact with it in two basic ways: First, He must allow it to continue to exist; and second, He must not allow it to overcome the good.

Both of these concepts are alluded to in the beginning of the prophet Ezekiel's vision. He writes, "I looked, and behold, a stormy wind came out of the north, and a great cloud, and flashing fire. It was surrounded by a glowing light (Nogah). From its midst was the likes of the Chashmal, from the midst of the fire. And in its midst was the form of four Chayoth... (Ezekiel 1:4).

These verses are among the most mysterious in the Bible, as in this entire vision of Ezekiel. It involves such deep concepts that our sages proscribed its exposition.[36] We must therefore confine our remarks to the explanations offered by our great commentators and sages. This passage does, however, involve some of our topics under discussion, and we will treat it in that context.

Ezekiel begins this account by saying, "The Heavens were opened, and I saw a vision of God" (Ezekiel 1:2). He was looking at an allegory of the very topics that we are discussing. In a sense, he was seeing beyond the mere appearances of this world, and achieving an understanding of God's purpose and providence that underlies it.

The first things that the prophet saw were "a stormy wind...a great cloud and a flashing fire." Our sages teach us that these allude to the forces of evil that God allows to exist.[31][7] These are the forces that separate man from God, and the prophet had to break through them before he could actually see a "vision of God."

The next thing that the prophet saw was a "glowing light," Nogah in Hebrew. This alludes to the element of God's providence that sustains evil. It is merely a glimmer of God's light, like the after glow that remains in the sky after the sun has set. While pertaining to night and darkness, it still retains a glimmer of daylight. This is often referred to as the "glowing husk," or Klipath Nogah.[38]

Then the prophet describes seeing "the likes of the Chashmal." The word Chashmal is virtually untranslatable, even though most English translations render it as "electrum" (meaning amber), and in modern Hebrew it is used as the word for electricity. The Chashmal actually represents a spiritual force, which is involved in the element of providence that protect from evil. The Chashmal thus stands as a barrier between good and evil.[39]

The final thing that the prophet saw were "four Chayoth."

The word *Chayoth* literally means "living creatures," and the reference is to a certain type of angel particularly associated with God's providence. It is well to keep the *Chayoth* in mind, since we will return to them in our discussion of Tzitzith.

৵ God's "Garment"

When the Torah uses an anthropomorphism, speaking of God as if He were a man, it is usually making use of a human attribute in its most abstract sense. If we understand what function a certain thing has with relation to man, then, in its most abstract sense, this same function usually applies toGod's relationship to the world. Thus, a man works with his hands. Therefore, when we speak of "God's hands," we are referring to His activity. Similarly, man hears with his ears, so when we speak of "God's ears," we are referring to the fact that He hearkens to our prayers. The same is true of all other anthropomorphisms.

If we wish to understand what is meant by God's garment we must go back to our discussion of the function of clothing with respect to man. We can then take this function in its most abstract sense.

As we noted earlier, the main function of human clothing is to serve as a barrier against passion. Much evil would result if man's sexual passions were left unchecked, and in this respect, man's clothing provides protection from this evil.

Taking this in its most abstract sense, we can then say that God's "garment" is also the force that protects from evil.

We can also see this from clothing's secondary function. Man's apparel also serves to protect him from the elements. We can thus say that clothing serves as protection from a hostile environment. The environment hostile to Godliness is, again, evil. In this sense also, we can abstract it to say that God's "garment" is the element of His providence that protects against evil.

This would mean, however, that God's "garment" is identical to the *Chashmal* that we discussed earlier. Both are the elements of His providence that protects from evil. It is therefore not at all suprising that our sages do indeed identify the *Chashmal* with God's "garment," also pointing out that the numerical value or *Gematria* of the word *Chashmal* (חַשְׁמַל) is the same as that of *Malbush* (מַלְבּוּשׁ), the Hebrew word for "garment."[40] (A general discussion of *Gematria* appears in a later section, where this particular one is worked out.)

From this discussion, we can also understand the account of Adam's sin on a somewhat deeper level.

When the serpent was tempting Eve, he said, "On the day that you eat of it. . .you shall be like God, knowing good and evil" (*Genesis* 3:5). On its surface, this is a very enigmatic statement. Equally puzzling is the question of how Adam and Eve, who possessed extraordinary intelligence, could have succumbed to the serpent's argument in the first place.

But as we discussed earlier, the goal of man's creation was that he should strive to imitate God. The serpent therefore argued that God Himself was the Creator of evil, and therefore He "knew good and evil." If Eve were to eat of the Tree of Knowledge, she, too, would "know good and evil," and in this way would resemble God. The serpent contended that in doing this, Eve would fulfill God's purpose in creation, since she would be imitating Him.

The fallacy in this argument, of course, was that God had specifically commanded man not to partake of the tree. One does not fulfill God's purpose by going against His expressed word.

This also explains another enigmatic passage in the same account.

After Adam had sinned and was punished, the Torah says, "God made leather garments for Adam and his wife, and He clothed them. And God said, 'Behold, man has become like one of us. . .'' (*Genesis* 3:21,22).

This last expression is most difficult to understand. What does God means when He says, "Man has become like one of us"? This is especially difficult in light of the fact that man had just sinned and been punished. Even more enigmatic is the question of what this has to do with the fact that Adam and Eve had just been given clothing.

But God was saying that, now that man had sinned and was subject to evil thoughts, he needed a protection against evil. In this respect, he had become like God, who also wears a "garment" serving a similar purpose. Here again, however, this resemblance was not a positive one. What God actually wanted was that man resemble God in overcoming evil, and not that he should succumb to it and need to be protected against it.

⋖§ The Tallith

We can now look into another question that people often ask. We know that the Torah contains 613 commandments, 248 do's and 365 don'ts. But why? Why is it necessary to have so many laws? Isn't it enough for people to have a general idea of what is right and then adhere to it?

There are many people today who argue that we should do away with laws completely. They say that all that is necessary is that people be good and love one another. They point out that at times laws can be harsh. Why then, did God give so many laws in the Torah?

The answer, of course, is because there is evil in the world. If men were perfect, then we would need few, if any, laws. People would live in total peace with one another, without any rules or regulations. This is indeed true of animals, who live in total harmony with other members of their species, without anything remotely resembling formal law. It is all part of their intrinsic nature.

The same was true of Adam before he sinned. He was innocent of any evil, and therefore did not need a multitude of rules and laws. All that was required was that he obey his one commandment not to eat of the Tree of Knowledge. That one commandment was enough to give him free will and thus enable him to achieve perfection and a closeness to God.[41] It was only after man sinned that he needed an entire complex of law.

The commandments therefore serve as a safeguard against the forces of evil. They restrict man's relationship with his neighbor so that one individual does not harm another. They constantly remind us of our obligation to God, so that we do not become swallowed up in evil.

We therefore see that to a large degree, the commandments of the Torah serve to protect us from evil. They are, in this respect, the element of God's plan that serves as a barrier against the forces of evil. This is what God meant when He said, "I have created the Evil Urge (*Yetzer HaRa*), but I have created the Torah as a remedy for it."[42]

The Torah's commandments are the element in God's scheme that serve as a barrier against evil. But, as we have discussed earlier, this is also the concept of God's "garment."

God's Tallith is therefore the sum total of all the commandments in the Torah. This is what our sages mean when they say, "He who keeps the commandments grabs the Divine Presence. This is the meaning of Tzitzith. . ."[43]

As we shall see in the section on *Gematria*, the commandment of Tzitzith alludes to all 613 commandments. Our sages similarly teach us that, "The commandment of Tzitzith is equal to all the commandments"[44]

This is also what the Torah means when it speaks of the Tzitzith and says, "You shall see them and not stray after your heart and after your eyes." The commandment of Tzitzith alludes to God's Tallith, which in turn, represents the entire structure of the commandments, standing as a barrier against evil.

After Adam sinned, the Torah says that, "They knew that they were naked, and they sewed together fig leaves and made themselves loincloths." There is a tradition that what they actually made were Tzitzith.[45] Rashi further more explains that when the Torah says, "They knew that they were naked," it means that they knew that they were naked" of the one commandment that God had given them."

As soon as man sinned, he realized that he would need the entire structure of commandments, alluded to in the Mitzvah of Tzitzith. As soon as he realized that he was naked of his original commandment, he made himself Tzitzith, the one commandment that includes all the others.

The Midrash tells us that the first time that God is said to have appeared wearing a Tallith was when He gave Moses the first commandment, the one involving the Jewish calendar.[46] God was beginning to teach Moses the way of the commandments, and when He started, he showed Moses the Tallith that alludes to them all.

As mentioned earlier, one place in the Bible where God's

Tallith is alluded to is in the verse, "He covers Himself with light as a garment" (*Psalms* 104:2). Here again, the allusion is to the light of the Torah and its commandments, as we find elsewhere, "A commandment is a lamp, and the Torah is light" (*Proverbs* 6:23).

◆§ *Four Corners*

The main element of God's plan that serves as a barrier against evil is the array of commandments in the Torah. But even though the commandments are Divine in origin, they do not serve their purpose unless they are fulfilled by man. In this sense, God's Tallith is not whole unless it is completed by man.

Man's role in completing God's garment of commandments is represented by the Tzitzith on the four corners of His Tallith.

In general, we know that the Tallith is only worn because of the Tzitzith that it contains. Without the Tzitzith, the Tallith is nothing more than a square piece of cloth. The same is true of God's Tallith. Unless fulfilled by man, the commandments do not serve their purpose.

In this sense, the Tzitzith, being loose threads, are like the unwoven portion of the tallith. As such, they represent the incompleteness in God's garment. This unwoven part is left for man to complete.[47]

The tallith is therefore made in the form of a rectangle or square. Our sages teach us that a four-sided figure is the archetype of something that is manmade.[48] The square shape of the Tallith alludes to the fact that the main responsibility to complete God's Tallith lies in the hands of man.

The bond between God and man involves all levels of creation. Man is the goal of God's creation, and all the spiritual worlds exist only for his sake. There are essentially four levels in the spiritual plane, alluded to by the four letters in God's ineffable Name (יְ־הֹ־וָ־ה, Y-H-V-H). The four corners of the Tallith allude to these levels, and thus, to the spiritual link between God and man.

In Ezekiel's vision, after he saw the *Chashmal*, which was God's "garment," he saw the four angels called *Chayoth*. These four angels are the four Tzitzith on the corners of God's Tallith.[49] This is why the prophet saw them attached to the

Chashmal, which represents God's Tallith. Our sages further more teach us that the *Chashmal* exists primarily for these angels,[50] just as the Tallith is worn primarlity for the Tzitzith that it contains. As we know, God's providence is directed primarily through these angels; therefore, they also represent the link between God and man.

Since the Tzitzith represent the bond between God and man, they hang down below the Tallith. God's Tallith is high above our reach, but His Tzitzith hang down like a lifeline that we can grasp hold of.[51] They reach down to us so that we may complete God's Tallith, while at the same time perfecting ourselves.

The Tzitzith therefore have five knots, representing the five books of the Torah. The Tzitzith begin with the knots, since the first step in bringing the commandments within man's reach is the Torah. These knots bind the Tzitzith to the Tallith, just as the Torah and its commandments bind man to God.[52]

◄§ *The Eight Strings*

There is a song that we sing on Passover night that teaches us many important lessons about numbers. You may have sung "Who Knows One?" (*Echad Mi Yodea*) many times, but have you ever thought of the significance behind the words? This song, in short, tells of the particular significance that each number has to the Jewish people.

When we ask "Who knows eight?" the song replies, "Eight days for circumcision." The particular significance of the number eight is the fact that the ritual of circumcision is always performed on the eighth day.

Circumcision - the *Brith* or Covenant - is the most ancient ritual of Judaism. It was the covenant that God made with Abraham as soon as he was chosen to be the father of the Jewish people. But what is its significance?

A major clue comes from the fact that circumcision is always performed on the eighth day. Let us stop for a moment and consider the significance of the number eight.

We all know that we live in a three-dimensional world. Our universe contains three dimensions, length, breadth and height. Take this a step further, and you see that each dimension has two directions. Therefore, there are a total of six primary directions in our physical world: up and down, right and left, forward and backward.

Rabbi Yehudah Low (1525-1609), the famed Maharal of Prague, points out that this is one of the main reasons why the world was created in six days.[53] To complete a three-dimensional world, God spent six days, one for each primary direction.

The Maharal goes on to explain that this is also the reason for the Sabbath. We can think of the six primary directions as six lines, all emanating from a single central point. The Sabbath then represents this center point. As such, it is what connects the six directions, and thus unifies our three-dimensional world.

We can then see that the number seven represents the perfection of the physical world. In resting on the seventh day, God completed and perfected His creation, binding it all together with a central purpose. This is one reason why the number seven appears in so many places in Jewish lore.

But beyond the physical, there is the transcendental. What number pertains to this? What number do we use when we wish to transcend the physical completely? It should be obvious that this is the number eight.

A good example of this is the miracle of Chanukah. The fact that one night's supply of oil continued to burn was a miracle that transcended the mere laws of nature. We are dealing with a miracle that goes beyond the physical. For this reason Chanukah is an eight-day festival.

The same is true of the splitting of the Red Sea, the greatest miracle ever. This also took place on the eighth day of the drama that was the Exodus. As we know, one reason we celebrate the seventh day of Passover is that the Red Sea was split on that day. Since the Exodus actually began on the day before Passover, the splitting of the Red Sea was on the eighth day of this drama. Here again, this was because it was a miracle that transcended the mere physical.[54]

Circumcision is also performed on the eighth day, essentially for the same reason. Circumcision represents God's covenant with Abraham. Through this, God was establishing the fact that Abraham and his children would be living on a plane that would transcend the mere physical. From that time forward, the Jew would have a direct link to the spiritual realm.[55]

The fact that circumcision was to be performed on the sexual organ is also of particular significance. In the act of reproduction, man comes in contact with the transcendental in a most unique way. Through the sexual act, one can begin the process of birth, thus drawing down a soul from the highest spiritual realm. The fact that the circumcision of the sexual organ is associated with the number eight is indicative of its link to the transcendental.

On a more mundane level, circumcision also serves as an indelible bodily sign, and a constant reminder that one must remain master of his sexual passion.[56] But, as we have seen, this is closely related to the former reason.

This is the significance of the eight strings of the Tzitzith.[57] They indicate that the Jew has a link with the transcendental. Through the commandments, man can achieve a unique relationship with God. The eight strings bind us to God's "garment," and they indicate that we are bound to something that goes far beyond the realms of the physical world.[58]

The eight strings are bound by the five knots, representing the five books of the Torah. The only link that the strings have with the Tallith is through the knots. This indicates that there is only one way to achieve the transcendental; that is through the five books of the Torah.

There are a number of other important parallels between circumcision and Tzitzith.[59]

Most obvious is the fact that they both serve as a reminder that we must master our sexual infatuations.

Less well known is the fact that they both ultimately originated with Abraham.[60] Regarding circumcision, God told Abraham, "This is My covenant. . .every male among you shall become circumcised. . .he that is eight days old shall be circumcised" (Genesis 17:10,12). The origin of Tzitzith with Abraham, however, is not as well known.

One of the important events in Abraham's career was his battle with the four kings, as described in the 14th chapter of

Genesis. Although this was an actual battle, it also symbolized Abraham's fight against all the forces of evil in the world. After the battle, Abraham was blessed by Shem, son of Noah (Melchizedek), who declared, "Blessed be Abram of God Most High, Maker of heaven and earth" (*Genesis* 14:19). In conferring this blessing, Shem was also ordaining Abraham as the bearer of all the traditions that had been handed down from the times of Adam and Noah.[61]

Immediately after this, Abraham was invited to take his share of the spoil from the battle. His immediate reply was, "I have lifted my hands to the Lord, God Most High . . . that I will not take a thread or a shoelace . . ." (*Genesis* 14:22,23). Our sages teach us that because Abraham said, "I will not take a thread," his children were later given the thread of Tzitzith.[62]

The reason for this is the same as before. The eight threads of Tzitzith represent man's link with the transcendental. By disdaining all worldly gain — even as little as a thread — Abraham was demonstrating that his main interest was in the Godly and spiritual. His children were therefore worthy of Tzitzith, which are indicative of this link with the extra-mundane.

◄§ God's Attributes

If we go back to our song, "Who Knows One?" in the last stanza we find another number that is important to our discussion. That is the number 13. The song asks, "Who knows thirteen?" and replies, "Thirteen are the Attributes."

There are two definitions of these thirteen Attributes.

One reference is to the thirteen attributes or rules that our sages used to explain the Torah. You might recall seeing Rabbi Yishmael's enumeration of these thirteen rules in the prayer book, as part of the daily morning service.[63] The main purpose of these thirteen rules is to bring the general laws elucidated in the Torah down to the level of practical application.

The second reference here is to the Thirteen Attributes of God's mercy. These are the Attributes proclaimed by God when He forgave the Jews for the sin of the Golden Calf.

They are cited in the Torah, "God (1), merciful (2) and gracious (3), slow (4) to anger (5), and abundant in love (6) and truth (7). Keeping mercy (8) to the thousandth generation (9), forgiving sin (10), rebellion (11), and error (12), and cleansing (13)" *(Exodus 3:46).* [64]

Another place where these Thirteen Attributes appear is in the words of the Prophet, "Who is a God like you (1), who pardons sin (2) and overlooks rebellion (3) to the remnant of His heritage (4). He retains not His anger forever (5), for He desires mercy (6). He will again have mercy on us (7). He will subdue our sins (8), and cast all our errors in the depths of the sea (9). You will show truth to Jacob (10), love to Abraham (11), as sworn to our fathers (12) from days of old (13)" *(Micah 7:18-20).* [65]

The number thirteen, however, is also very important with respect to Tzitzith. Tzitzith contain five knots and eight strings, which together yield a total of thirteen. We will come across this again in our discussion of Gematria.[66]

This is related to both definitions of the thirteen Attributes given above. The Tzitzith represent God's link with man, and man's responsibility to complete God's Tallith. God's Tallith furthermore represents the sum total of the commandments. God's Tallith, however, only represents the commandments in their most abstract form. Before they can be fulfilled by man, they must be applied to actual situations. The rule used to apply the commandments to practical situations are precisely the thirteen principles through which the Torah is expounded. These are therefore represented by the Tzitzith, which link the abstract Tallith of God to the concrete problems of man. In this manner the thirteen knots and strings in the Tzitzith allude to the thirteen principles used in explaining the command- ments.[67]

On a more abstract level, God's Tallith also represents His providence in protecting against evil. This element of provi- dence, however, does more than just battle evil and protect us from it. Since it serves as the link between good and evil, it is the element that allows us to elevate evil and transform it into good. This is the concept of repentance. Despite the sin and evil a person may have done, a lifeline remains whereby he can repent and return to God. The vehicle of such forgiveness of sin is God's Thirteen Attributes of Mercy.

The five knots and eight strings of the Tzitzith also represent these Thirteen Attributes of Mercy.[68] Both represent the thread that links man to God's protection against evil. Through the Tzitzith of God's Tallith, an individual can pull himself out of the mire of sin and return to God.[69]

This brings us back to Rabbi Yochanan's statement, quoted at the beginning of this section. As you recall, Rabbi Yochanan said that, "God wrapped Himself [with a Tallith] like a prayer leader."

If we look at the context of this statement, we see that Rabbi Yochanan is speaking of the time when God forgave Israel for the sin of the Golden Calf. God "wrapped Himself with a Tallith" precisely when he proclaimed the Thirteen Attributes of Mercy.

Rabbi Yochanan is teaching us that God wrapped Himself with a "Tallith;" the five knots and eight strings of His Tzitzith represented the Thirteen Attributes of Mercy that God was then proclaiming.[70]

There is a third way in which the number thirteen represents the bond between God and man. These are the thirteen special commandments that serve especially to bind us to God. They are:[71]

1. Belief in God.
2. Fear of God.
3. Love of God.
4. Belief in God's unity.
5. Study of Torah.
6. Wearing Tefillin.
7. Wearing Tzitzith.
8. Affixing the Mezuzah.
9. Circumcision.
10. Sabbath observance.
11. Prayer.
12. Festival observance.
13. The Sh'ma.

These are the thirteen commandments that serve as a

particular bond between man and God. Of course, all the other commandments also bind man to God, but they do so in a more general manner. These thirteen commandments, however, are the ones that particularly serve this primary purpose; they, too, are represented by the five knots and eight strings of the Tzitzith.

From this, we can also begin to understand the reason there are 613 commandments. One major purpose of the commandments is to elevate all worldly things to the Godly.[72] This pertains particularly to the mundane things in the world, representing the six days of creation. We, therefore, have 600 commandments, one hundred for each day of creation.

In addition, we have the thirteen special commandments whose primary purpose is to link man to God. The total then is 613 commandments.[73]

Numbers

Do you know how to write Hebrew numbers? If you do, you probably know that classical Hebrew did not have separate number symbols, but represented them with a letter of the alphabet. It was a system something like the Roman numerals, but much simpler. The numerical value of letters of the Hebrew alphabet are given in the table following.

The fact that Hebrew uses letters instead of numerals opens a very interesting possibility. If each letter in a word represents a number, then the word as a whole must also have a numerical value. We refer to this when we speak of the numerical value, or *Gematria,* of a word.

Looking into it more deeply, we realize that there is an important reason for this relationship. As mentioned earlier, Hebrew is the Holy Tongue *(Lashon HaKodesh),* and even its linguistic structure can teach us important lessons.

In this case, the lesson is fairly clear. Both words and numbers convey information. In the case of words, this is obvious. A statement such as, "David eats bread," tells us something, and thus conveys information. We communicate with words, and through them, we convey information to one another.

Numbers also convey information. When I say 3 + 5 = 8, I am making a statement of fact, very much like the statement, "Roses are red." I am telling you something, and thus communicating information. As you might know, we communicate with computers entirely by means of numbers and symbols. There is also an entire language of higher mathematics.

Although numbers communicate information, they do so in a much more abstract manner than words do. When I speak of the number three, it can equally well refer to three apples, three people, three nations, or three abstract concepts.

NUMERICAL VALUES OF LETTERS

Aleph	א	1	Lamed	ל	30
Beth	ב	2	Mem	מ	40
Gimel	ג	3	Nun	נ	50
Dalet	ד	4	Samech	ס	60
Heh	ה	5	Eyin	ע	70
Vav	ו	6	Peh	פ	80
Zayin	ז	7	Tzadi	צ	90
Cheth	ח	8	Kof	ק	100
Teth	ט	9	Resh	ר	200
Yod	י	10	Shin	ש	300
Kaf	כ	20	Tav	ת	400

We can therefore say that the numerical value or *Gematria* of a word conveys its more abstract connotations.[74] When two otherwise unrelated words have the same numerical value, we can expect them to be connected in an abstract sense, or on a higher spiritual level.

The link between numbers and words is a link between the abstract and the concrete. As we have seen, this is also the significance of Tzitzith. We might therefore expect numbers to play an important role in Tzitzith, and this is indeed the case. In our discussions, we have already spoken of four corners, five knots, eight strings, 39 windings, and 613 commandments. We have also noted that detailed measurements are important to Tzitzith, and there also, numbers are involved. As we shall now see, the numerical value of words also plays an important role in Tzitzith.

Our sages teach us that the numerical value of the word Tzitzith is 600. Taken together with the five knots and eight strings, this gives us 613, the total number of commandments. The Tzitzith thus remind us of "all of God's commandments."[75]

To get a feel for it, let us actually go through this *Gematria*. Taking the word Tzitzith (צִיצִית) we have:

צ	Tzadi	=	90
י	Yod	=	10
צ	Tzadi	=	90
י	Yod	=	10
ת	Tav	=	400
			600

We see that in the abstract, the word Tzitzith alludes to the general commandments. These are the ones that serve as a link to God in an overall manner. The five knots and eight strings allude to the thirteen commandments that particularly serve to bind us to God. This gives us the total of 613.

To take another example, in our discussion of the mysterious word *Chashmal* (חַשְׁמַל), we pointed out that it represented the elements of God's providence that protected against evil. We also mentioned that it was identical to God's "garment," because both *Chashmal* and *Malbush* (מַלְבּוּשׁ), the Hebrew word for garment, have the same numerical value.[76]

Let us now work this out. Taking both *Gematrios* simultaneously, we have:

Chashmal חַשְׁמַל					*Malbush* מַלְבּוּשׁ			
ח	Cheth	=	8		מ	Mem	=	40
ש	Shin	=	300		ל	Lamed	=	30
מ	Mem	=	40		ב	Beth	=	2
ל	Lamed	=	30		ו	Vav	=	6
			378		ש	Shin	=	300
								378

Another very important place where *Gematria* comes into play is in the case of the Tzitzith windings. As discussed earlier, the windings allude to God's unity, which binds everything together. It is therefore customary to make 39 windings, the numerical value of *Hashem Echad* — "God is One." Let us look at the *Gematria* in detail.[77]

Hashem יהוה

י	Yud	=	10		
ה	Heh	=	5		
			15	15	
ו	Vav	=	6		
ה	Heh	=	5		
			11	11	
				26	26

Echad אחד

א	Aleph	=	1		
ח	Cheth	=	8		
ד	Dalet	=	4		
			13		13
					39

This *Gematria* immediately gives us the reason for the 39 windings. But if you look carefully at the subtotals, you will also see the reason for the number of windings in each group. Just as a reminder, the groups have 7, 8, 11 and 13 windings respectively.

The first group contains seven windings in accordance with the Talmudic injunction that no group contain less than this number.[78] As we discussed earlier, this represents the perfection of the physical world, which was created in seven days

The second group has eight windings, alluding to the transcendental.[79] Together, the first two groups have a total of 15 windings, the numerical value of the first two letters of God's Name.

The third group has eleven windings. This is the numerical value of the last two letters of God's Name. The first three groups thus have 26 windings, the total numerical value of God's Name.

Finally, the last group has thirteen windings. This is the maximum allowed in any group, and is also the numerical value of *Echad,* the Hebrew word for "one." This also alludes to the Thirteen Attributes, and the fact that this is the numerical value of *Echad* — one — indicates that these Attributes are all manifestations of God's ultimate unity.

The word *Echad* also alludes to the Tallith in another manner. *Echad* (אֶחָד) is spelled *Aleph, Cheth, Dalet.* Aleph (א) has the numerical value of one, alluding to the one Tallith containing the Tzitzith. Cheth (ח) is eight, representing the eight strings. Finally, *Dalet* (ד) is four, alluding to the four corners of the Tallith.

The final thing that we will examine in this section is sort of a reverse *Gematria.* As you now well know, each of the four Tzitzith has eight strings. This gives us a total of 32 strings on the four corners. The number 32, however, written in Hebrew is *Lamed Beth* — the letters that spell out *Lev* (לֵב), the Hebrew word for heart. Thus, the Tzitzith represent the heartstrings, constantly beating, yearning, and drawing one toward God.

A THREAD OF BLUE

*You shall place on the Tzitzith
of [each] corner a thread of blue. . .*

A Thread of Blue

Very often, people ask, "Where is the blue thread in the Tzitzith?"

We read the section dealing with Tzitzith twice daily in our prayers and each time, we read the words, "You shall place on the Tzitzith of [each] corner, a thread of blue." But when you look at the Tzitzith that people wear, you never seem to find this blue thread. Of course, the stripes that are often put on the Tallith are supposed to allude to the blue thread,[1] but still, the thread itself is missing. If the Torah tells us to put a blue thread in the Tzitzith, why don't we do so?

Our sages teach us that adding the blue thread is preferable, but its absence does not invalidate the Tzitzith. Tzitzith made only with white threads are perfectly valid.[2]

The great commentator, Rabbi Moshe Alshech, explains that this is why the Torah says, "They should make Tzitzith on the corners of their garments *for all generations.*" The commandment of Tzitzith applies to all generations, even when there is no blue. Regarding the commandment of the blue thread, however, the Torah does not say "for generations." When the blue is available, it should be used; but if it is not available, this does not prevent us from fulfilling the commandment of Tzitzith.

We do not add the blue thread today because the art of dyeing it has been lost. This particular blue is known in the Torah as *Techeleth,* and according to tradition, can only be obtained from an animal known as the *Chilazon.* [3] Since we no longer know the precise identity of this animal, we cannot dye the blue thread properly.

Even in ancient times, not everybody wore the blue thread in his Tzitzith. The *Chilazon* was a very rare animal, and even a single thread of this blue wool was very expensive.[4] For this reason, there was a time when almost no one at all wore it in Jerusalem.[5]

With the destruction of the second Temple, *(Beth HaMikdash*, the supply of this particular blue dye virtually disappeared.[6] Still, a small supply was maintained by a handful of individuals who knew where to find the *Chilazon.* [7] It appears that the blue *Techeleth* dye was used to some extent until the eighth century C.E.[8] The city of Tyre was the center of the ancient dyeing industry, and it is probable that whatever blue dye was available during this period came from there. It is quite possible that the conquest of Tyre by the Moslems around this time dried up the supply of *Techeleth* completely.[9]

The blue thread used in the Tzitzith was a special color known as *Techeleth.* There appear to be, however, several opinions as to the precise shade of blue that was used. According to the Rambam (Maimonides), it was the color of a clear noon sky,[10] similar to a pale indigo.[11] Rashi, on the other hand, writes that it was the color of the evening sky,[12] closer to a greenish blue or aquamarine.[13] Later authorities asserted that it was a dark grey-blue.[14]

Just any blue dye could not be used for the blue thread of Tzitzith. It had to be a special dye that came from an animal known as the *Chilazon.* There is no continuous tradition regarding the identity of the *Chilazon,* but according to most sources, it was a snail[15] that lived in the Mediterranean between Tyre and Haifa.[16] Our sages state that it is a boneless invertebrate,[17] and that, "When the *Chilazon* grows, its shell grows with it."[18] There are also illusions to the fact that it has two feelers[19] and a snakelike body.[20] We also know that the animal itself was blue in color.[21]

The fact that the *Chilazon* can be identified with a species of snail is not at all surprising. It is well known that a number of snails played an important role in yielding the beautiful blue and purple dyes that made Tyre famous in ancient times. Of particular importance were the conchlike snails of the Murex and the Purpura families. Even today, fine dyes can be obtained from such species as the Purple Shell *(Murex trunculus, Murex brandaris, Purpurea patula)*, the Purple Whelk *(Purpurea lapillus)*, and the Purple Fish *(Murex purpurea)*. All of these produce a purple or blue dye by means of special glands at the roof of their gill cavity.[22]

It is interesting to note that a number of our great sages have identified the *Chilazon* as the Purple Shell or Purpura.[23] This is a fairly large carnivorous Mediterranean snail, distinguished by a blue or purple shell containing rather large spines. It yields a creamy white fluid that turns purple when exposed to light. When mixed with soda, sea water and other chemicals, various shades of blue can be obtained from it. There is, however, another important opinion regarding the identity of the *Chilazon,* and this involves a fascinating modern story.

One of the greatest European rabbis of the last century was Rabbi Gershon Henoch Leiner (1839-1890), of Radzin, Poland. By the age of thirteen, he was already a Talmudic scholar of repute, and for his Bar Mitzvah, he delivered a discourse that dazzled the leading rabbis of Europe. He was accepted as rabbi of Radzin at a young age, and before he was thirty, he had already published his *Sidrey Taharoth* (Order of Purity), one of the greatest works ever written on the complex laws of ritual purity.

In 1887, Rabbi Gershon Henoch set out on a new quest — to rediscover the identity of the *Chilazon,* the animal used to dye the blue in the Tzitzith. Utilizing his encyclopedic knowledge of all Judaic literature, he wrote a small pamphlet, *Shefuney Temuney Chol* (Hidden Treasures of the Sand), exploring all the Talmudic and Midrashic traditions regarding the *Chilazon.* On the basis of this research, he felt certain that he would recognize the animal if he saw it.

The Rabbi was not content merely to search in books, and he began a year-long pilgrimage to various ports to try to find the *Chilazon* in the flesh. His search finally led him to the world famous aquarium in Naples, Italy. Like a fascinated child, he gazed at the many tanks, looking for a creature that would satisfy all the necessary criteria. Finally, he found an animal that he believed to be the *Chilazon.* [24]

The creature that he discovered was the common cuttlefish *(Sepia officinalis),* a member of the octopus family. His identification was so precise that he even provides us with the animal's Latin name. It is well known that the cuttlefish exudes a blue-black ink when frightened or attacked, and this has long been used to make a brown dye known as sepia. Rabbi Gershon Henoch experimented with the raw blue-black dye, and found that it would impart a dark blue color to wool. This, along with a number of other criteria, convinced him that the cuttlefish was the lost *Chilazon.*

From his own words, it is clear how excited the rabbi was with his discovery. He could reinstate a Mitzvah that had not been practiced for over a thousand years. He then wrote another book, *Pethil Techeleth* (A Thread of Blue), telling of his discovery. Since the usual codes of Jewish Law omit the details of how the fish is to be used, he included in his book a complete codification of these rules. He was now ready to introduce his discovery to the community at large.

By late 1889, the Rabbi had set up facilities for a rather large scale production of his blue wool, and within the course of a year, close to fifteen thousand people were wearing it in their Tzitzith. Since Rabbi Gershon Henoch was close to the Polish followers of Rabbi Nachman of Breslov, many of them also began to wear his blue.

All this did not go unnoticed by the other European rabbis, and many of them actively opposed this innovation. Correspondence ranged far and wide, disputing Rabbi Gershon Henoch's evidence. In response to this criticism, he wrote a third book on the subject, *Eyn HaTecheleth* (The Color of Blue), attempting to answer all those objections. Meanwhile, more and more people were wearing the blue, and it seemed as if it would finally take hold.

The movement came to an untimely halt, however, for on December 17, 1890 (4 Teveth, 5651), Rabbi Gershon Henoch passed away. Without his energetic leadership, the *Techeleth* movement died with him. Only his own followers and a small group of Breslover Chasidim continued to wear the blue thread. Less than a decade after his death, the author of the *Aruch HaShulchan* was able to write that an attempt to reintroduce the blue had been made, but it had not been accepted by the community at large.[25]

Although we do not wear the blue, it is interesting to note how it was worn during the brief period when it enjoyed a renaissance. Most of the people who wore *Techeleth* followed the opinion codified by Rabbi Gershon Henoch.

There are three major opinions regarding the number of blue threads that were worn in Tzitzith.

The Rambam (Maimonides, 1135-1204) maintained that only half a string was dyed, so that just one of the eight strings was blue. This opinion was also accepted by the Kabbalists.[26]

The Raavad (Rabbi Avraham ben David of Posquieres, 1123-1198) held that an entire string was dyed, so that when doubled, two of the eight strings were blue.[27]

Finally, Rashi maintains that the blue and white were equal, two threads of each, so when doubled, four threads were blue, and four white.[28]

Rabbi Gershon Henoch felt inadequate to decide among these giants but since the Kabbalists agreed with the Rambam, he personally accepted this view.[29] He also wrote that the windings should be made exactly as we make them with all white threads, with one exception. Since he was now using the blue, the rule that the windings had to be subdivided into triplets *(Chulyoth)* had to be observed.[30] The first and last windings were made with a white thread, while all the others were blue.[31]

We do not follow Rabbi Gershon Henoch's opinion, but the story teaches us a very important lesson. The blue is not required for the Tzitzith, and they are perfectly valid without it. The most that the rabbi could accomplish was to provide a more perfect manner of observing this commandment. Even so, the rabbi and thousands of his followers spared neither expense nor effort in obtaining this blue dye.

We thus see how priceless this observance was to our ancestors. A mere thread — but of infinite value.

NOTES

WHY TZITZITH?

4. Socrates, in Plato's *Phaedo*.
5. Alshech on Numbers 15:39.
6. *Tur Orach Chaim* 24.
7. *Zohar* 1:175a; Bach, *Orach Chaim* 24, s.v. *Tzitzith*.
8. *Menachoth* 44a; Rashi on Numbers 15:40; *Reshith Chochmah, Shaar HaKedushah* 6 (141c); *Pri Etz Chaim, Shaar Tzitzith*, note #1 (Ashlag, 5526) p. 81; *Likutey Moharan* 7:4. Cf. *Tikuney Zohar* 18 (37a).
9. *Tanna DeBei Eliahu Rabbah* 26 (104a); Ramban, *Baale Tosafoth*, on *Numbers* 15:32. The Abarbanel, however, writes that this was one of the first commandments given to the Jews.
10. Abarbanel on *Numbers* 15:40 (36b); Alshech *ibid.*
11. *Sifri* (115), Malbim, Or *HaChaim*, on *Numbers* 15:40; *Reshith Chochmah, Shaar HaKedushah* 6 (141a).
12. Cf. *Sifri* (115), Rashi, Malbim, on *Numbers* 15:41; *Zohar* 3:176a.
13. Kuzari 1:89; *Yad, Yesodey HaTorah* 8:1; *Moreh Nevukhim* 2:35.
14. *Menachoth* 43b, Rashi, *Tosafoth ad loc. s.v. Choshen, Pesikta Zutratha.* Sforno, Abarbanel, Or *HaChaim* on Numbers 15:39. Bachya *ibid.* quoting *Bahir* 93; *Sefer Ha-Chinukh* 386; *Zohar* 3:174b *Etz Chaim, Shaar HaShemoth* 7 *(p.* 343); *Derekh Hashem* 4:6:6.
15. See *Tosafoth, Kiddushin* 2b s.v. *DeAsar.*
16. These passages refer either to Israel or to the Messiah. In either case, the enlightenment of all peoples will be through Israel.
17. *Shabbath* 32b; Sifri, Bachya (83b); *Etz Chaim, loc. cit; Likutey Ha1achoth, Tzitzith* 3:9 (38a).

WHAT ARE TZITZITH?

18. *Menachoth* 42a; *Sifri,* Rashi, *loc. cit.; Tosafoth, Menachoth* 39b s.v. *O'Gedil, Yad, Tzitzith* 1:1. According to the second explanation in Rashi, *Menachoth* 39b s.v. *U'Poslehah,* however, we derive this *from the word Pesil.* Also see *Tosafoth ibid. U'Poslehah, Shita Mekubetzeth #l; Nimukey Yosef (Rif, Hilchoth Tzitzith 12b) s.v. Anaf.* Also *see* Rashi on *Numbers* 15:38; *Sifethey Chachamim ad loc. #5;* Rashbam, *ibid. For a deeper reason for* this, see *Zohar 3:174b; Etz Chaim, Shaar HaChashmal* 3; *Shaar HaKavanoth, Tzitzith* 2 (p. 27); *Pri Etz Chaim, Tzitzith;* 3 (p. 67); *Likutey Moharan* 8:8.
19. Rashi, *Menachoth* 39b s.v. *U'Poslehah, in first* explanation; *Tosafoth Ibid.* "*U'Poslehah"; Rashi on Deuteronomy 32:5; Yad, Tzitzith* 1:2,3, *P'er HaDor (Tshuvoth Rambam)* 21, 47, quoted in *Kesef Mishneh Tzitzith* 1:7; *Zohar* 3:175a; *Pesil Techeleth* 7 (p. 147). See note 25.
20. Sifri, Targum Yonathan, Malbim *ad loc.; Tosafoth, Yebamoth* 4b s.v. *VeAmar.* Also see *Orach Chaim* 11:2; *Turey Zahav ad loc.* ll:Z; *Eruvin* 96b, *Rokeach* 361 (p. 246). *The* word *Pesil* has the connotation of two things bound together, as we find in Rashi on Numbers 19:15; Genesis 39:8. The Rambam, however, does not require this, *cf. Yad, Tzitzith* 1:10, *Kesef Mishneh ad loc.; P'er HaDor* 22; *Chatham Sofer* on *Orach Chaim* 11:2.
21. This is true of the threads used to weave the priestly garments, and

Raavad, *Tzitzith* 1:10 derives this requirement in the case of *Tzitzith* from this fact. *Cf. Yoma 7lb. It is* also true with regard to the Biblical prohibition of *Shaatnez,* and this also relates to *Tzitzith,* see *Tosafoth, Menachoth* 39b s.v. *Kaher, Nidah* 6lb s.v. *Shua; Ran, Betza* (Rif 7b) s.v. *MiDeOraitha.*

22. *Tosafoth, Menachoth* 38a s.v. *HaTecheleth,* end; *Ibid.* 39b s.v. *U'Poskhah, Yebamoth* 5b s.v. *U'Poslehah.* See *Shabbath* 2:3 (28b), Rashi *ad loc. s.v. SheKifluha; Betza* 32b. *Cf. Menachoth* 42a, *Yad, Tzitzith 1:6; Orach Chaim* 11:12. The *Levush (HaTecheleth* 11:4), however, writes that this is the most logical way to attach the Tzitzith, and that the derivation from the word *Pesil* is merely an allusion.

23. See Rashi on Exodus 28:37, *39:31; Yad, Kley HaMikdash* 9:2. *Cf. Yoma* 72a, according to *Tosafoth, Menachoth* 38a s.v. *HaTecheleth.*

24. *Menachoth* 43a; *Zevachim* 18b; Sifri (234) on Deuteronomy 22:12; *Yad, Tzitzith* 3:1; *Orach Chaim* 10:1.

25. Sifri (115) on Numbers 15:38, (234) on Deuteronomy 22:12; *Tosafoth, Menachoth* 41a s.v. *Beth Shamai; Nimukey Yosef, Hilchoth* Tzitzith (Rif *12b) s.v. Tanya;* Rosh, *Hilkhoth Tzitzith* 12; *Baal HaTurim* on Deuteronomy 22:12. See 1 Kings 7:17; *Targum* on Exodus 28:14, 22, 24, 39:15, Judges 15:13, Isaiah 5:18; Gittin 69a; *Betza* 32b; Bertenoro on *Shabbath* 10:6. There is, however, another opinion that maintains that the word *Gedil* refers to the windings, see Rashi, *Menachoth* 39b s.v. *U'Poslehah,* second explanation, 39a s.v. *Chut, Yebamoth* 5b *s.v.U'Poslehah.* For the difficulties with this explanation, see *Tosafoth, Menachoth* 3b O *Gedil, s.v. U'Poslehah.*

26. *Menachoth* 39b; *Yebamoth* 5b; Rashi, *Menachoth 42a s.v. KeDidan, Sanhedrin* 89b s.v. *U'Perusho, Yoma* 72a s.v. *Kelil* According to this opinion, the reference is to the four strings before they are doubled. Another opinion, however, holds that it refers to the strings after they are doubled, and only to the white strings. Since there are an equal number of blue strings according to this view, the total number is eight. See *Tosafoth, Bechoroth* 39b s.v. *Kama, Menachoth* 38a, s.v. *HaTecheleth 41b s.v. Bais Shamai.*

27. Sanhedrin 89a; *Kesef Mishneh, Tzitzith* 1:1, *Sefer HaKobets, ibid.; Beth Yosef, Orach Chaim* 11 (l6b) s.v. *U'R. Y. Cf. Sefer HaMitvoth, Shoresh 2; Magid Mishneh, Kesef Mishneh, Ishuth 1:2.*

28. *Menachoth* 39a; *Yad, Tzitzith* 1:8; *Orach Chaim* 11:14 in *Hagah.* If this requirement is not met, the Tzitzith are still valid, Maharshal on *Sefer Mitzvoth Gadol* (Smag), *positive* commandment *26; Turey Zahav* 11:15. In *Chayay Adam* 11:19, however, we find an opinion that this is actually a Rabbinical law.

29. Rashi, *Menachoth* 39a s.v. *Kesher, Tosafoth Yeshenim, Yebamoth* 4b s.v. A. *Avel.*

30. *Yebamoth* 4a,b; *Sifri* (233) on Deuteronomy 22:11.

31. *Tur Orach Chaim* 11 (17a); *Orach Chaim* 9:1.

32. *Menachoth* 39a. *Cf. Sanhedrin* 89a.

33. Rashi, *Menachoth* 39a s.v. *Kesher, Tosafoth ibid.; Smag,* positive 26; *Magen Avraham* 11:19; *Turey Zahav* 11:14; *Mishneh Berurah* 11:64; HaGra on *Orach Chaim* 11:13. *Others,* however, *interpret* this to *refer to*

the knot nearest *the* Tallith, *see* Rashi, *Sanhedrin 88a s.v. Kesher, Shitah Mekubetzeth, Menachoth 39a #6; Tosafoth ibid. s.v. Kesher, Levush (HaTechekth)* 11:14. Rashi states that there is a dispute as to whether or not this knot is actually required by the Torah *(DeOraitha) see Tosafoth, Sanhedrin 39a s.v. Kesher, Chidushey HaRan ibid.* According to the Rambam, *Yad Tzitzith* 1:2, it would appear that this knot is not required, but see *Beth Yosef, Orach Chaim* 11 (17a) s.v. *VaYikach.*

34. *Tosafoth, Menachoth* 39a s.v. *Kesher.* The majority opinion is that the knot is tied with *four* strings on either side as we do it. Rabenu Tam, however, would tie the knots with the string used in the windings opposite the seven others. See *Shitah Mekubetzeth, Menachoth* 39a #13 end; *Rosh, Hilkhoth Tzitzith 15, Maadney Yom Tov ad loc. #20; Diverey Chamudos ibid.* 20; *Mordecai, Hilkhoth Tzitzith 940 (1d); Beth Yosef, Orach Chaim* 11 (17a) s.v. *U'Kathuv, Perisha ibid.* 11:17.

35. *Shitah Mekubetzeth, Menachoth* 38a #6, *Nimukey Yosef, Hilkhoth Tzitzith* (Rif 12b) s.v. *Keshara DeYaved; Kesef Mishneh, Tzitzith 1:9* end; *HaGra, Orach Chaim* 11:13 s.v. *Shelm, Mishneh Berurah* 11:64.

36. See *Targum Yonathan* on *Numbers* 15:38.

37. *Zohar* 3:228a; *Baal HaTurim* on *Numbers* 15:38; *Tur Orach Chaim* 24; *Orach Chaim* 24:1.

38. *Bachya* on *Numbers* 15:38 (83a).

39. *Tikuney Zohar* 10 (25b) Cf. *Menachoth* 43b, that the commandment of Tzitzith is supposed to remind us of the Sh'ma.

40. According to Rashi, the reason for the custom of five knots was so that together with the eight strings and the numerical value of Tzitzith, it should add up to 613. See below, part 2, note *75; Rashi, Menachoth* 39a s.v. *Min, Shitah Mekubetzeth #10; Tosafoth bid. s.v. Lo. Tosafoth* also *presents* an opinion that the five knots were actually required because of the blue. Three of the four groups of windings consisted of a triplet of white combined with one of blue, while the fourth one was a triplet of white alone. The four groups were thus composed of the seven triplets required by Talmudic law. Since each group was fastened on both sides by a knot, the Tzitzith automatically contained five knots.

41. *Menachoth* 39a, *Yad, Tzitzith* 1:9.

42. *Magen Avraham* 11:19; *Mishneh Berurah* 11:66. The additional windings, however, must be completed as soon as possible, in order to fulfill the requirement that they comprise one third of the Tzitzith.

43. *Orach Chaim* 11:14; *Magen Avraham* 11:22. See below, part 2, note 77.

44. *Menachoth* 42a; *Orach Chaim* 1:11.

45. This is the equivalent to the length of six barleycorns laid side by side, or two, end to end. *Yad*, Sefer Torah 9:9. Various opinions of the length of a "finger" are: .787 in. or 2 cm. (Misgereth HaShulhan HaSefardi, Chabad); .866 in. or 2.2 cm. (Chalath Aaron, end); .935 in. or 2.375 cm. (T'shuvoth Meshiv Davar 24); .952 in. or 2.417 cm. (Kitzur Shulhan Aruch); .959-984 in. or 2.437-25 cm. (T'shuvoth Imrey Yosher 88) 1.033 in. or 2.625 cm. (Darkey T'shuvah); 1.036 in. or 2.632 cm. (Toldoth Sh'muel); 1.082 in. or 2.78 cm. (Levush Malchuth, according to Chatham Sofer). See Shulchan Melachim, p. 7a.

46. *Kelim 27:2; Shabbath 26b, 79a; Yad, Kelim 22:1, Shabbath 18:13.*

47. This is a "double span," or *Sit Kaful; Shabbath* 13:4 (105b) *Tosefta 10:2.* According to *Rashi (Ibid. 106a),* this is *the distance* between the thumb *and* forefinger when extended. Many *authorities maintain* that the single span" or *Sit* is two fingers. See *Rambam* on *Orlah 3:2, Shabbath 13:4, Kelim 13:4, Shiltey Giborim, Shabbath (Rif 38a) #2; Rav Hai Gaon, Kelim 13:4; Aruch Sit.* This would make the "double span" equal to four fingers, or a single handbreadth. Another opinion, however, states that a span or *Sit* is two handbreadths, and a double span, four. See *Yad, Shabbath 9:7,10,13,* 15, 18:13; HaGra on *Orlah 3:2.*
48. *Orlah 3:2,3.*
49. *Tosafoth, Menachoth* 4lb s.v. *Bais Shamai, Bechoroth* 39b s.v. *Kama,* Rashi ibid. s.v. *Achath, Orach Chaim* 11:4. Others, however, hold that the entire Tzitzith need be only four fingers long, Rashi, *Menachoth 41b s.v. Meshulasheth; Yad, Tzitzith 1:6. The Levush (HaTechekth)* 12, 1, 3, maintains that the entire requirement of any length is only based on Rabbinical law. Also *see Chayay Adam* 11:16.
50. *Menachoth* 42a; Rashi *ad loc. s.v. SheTehey, Shitah Mekubetzeth ibid. #5;* Radal *ad loc.; Hagahoth Maimoni, Tzitzith 1:6 #2,* HaGra on *Orach Chaim* 11:9 *MiShum.* There are, however, a number of other interpretations to this statement.
51. *Menachoth* 42a, *Yad, Tzitzith 1:6, Orach Chaim* 11:9. This is approximately two fingers, cf. *Beth Yosef, Orach Chaim* 11 (16a) s.v. *VaYaaseh,* quoting Mahari Ibn Chabib; *Rav Shulchan Arukh* 11:16.
52. *Sefer Mitzvoth Gadol (Smag),* positive commandment 26; *Beth Yosef, loc. cit.; Orach Chaim* 11:9.
53. *Menachoth* 42a; *Beth Yosef loc. c;t.*
54. According to *the* opinion *that* a finger is one inch, it must be at least two inches from the edge. But according to those who maintain that a finger is 3/4 inch, since it can be no more than 3 fingers, the maximum distance it may be from the edge is 1/4 inches.

THE TALLITH KATAN

55. See note 24.
56. *Tosafoth, Arkhin* 2b, s.v. *HaKol, Tosafoth Yeshenim, Shabbath* 32b s.v. *BeAvon,* Abarbanel on Numbers 15:38.
57. *Menachoth* 41a, *Tosafoth Pesachim 113b s.v. VeAin, Tosafoth Yeshenim loc. cit.; Rokeach 361 (p.* 247); *Orach Chaim* 24:1.
58. *Abarbanel, loc. cit.*
59. *Nimukey Yosef, Hilkhoth Tzitzith (Rif 12a) s.v. Amar, Kol Bo* 22; *Orach Chaim 3:6 in Hagah.*
60. *Tosafoth, Menachoth* 36a s.v. *U'KeSheHigia, Berachoth 14b s.v. U'Manach, Orach Chaim* 8:10.
61. *Darkey Moshe, Orach Chaim* 8:3, *Aruch HaShulchan* 8:16, *Mishneh Berurah* 8:24; *Darkey Chaim VeShalom* 32.
62. *Darkey Chaim VeShalom* 38.
63. *Orach Chaim* 8:11; *Magen Avraham* 8:13; *Mishneh Berurah* 8:26.
64. *T'shuvoth Mahari Bruno* 96.
65. *Likutey Halachoth, Tzitzith 3:1 (35b), Netilath Yadayim* 4:8.

66. *Sukkah* 42a; *Arakhin* 2b; *Tosefta Chagiga* 1:3, *Orach Chaim* 17:3; *Shaarey T'shuvah* 17:2; *Likutey Halachoth* loc. cit.

67. *Tosafoth, Berachoth* 14b s.v. *U'Meniach; Yad, Tzitzith* 3:11; *Orach Chaim* 24:1. Cf. *Midrash Tehillim* 35:2; Ibn Ezra on Number 15:39; Bachya *ibid.;* Smag, positive 26; *Zohar* 3:226b; *Shaar HaKavanoth, Tzitzith 1* (p. 24).

68. *Zohar* 3:273a; *Tikuney Zohar* 11 (26b), 21 (55b). Cf. *Metzudoth* Tzion ad loc.

69. *Tashbatz* 462; Maharil, *Hilchoth Nisuin* (Jerusalem, 5729) p. 65a; quoted in *Be'er Hetiv, Orach Chaim* 17:4; *Darkey Chaim VeShalom* 37. See note

70. *Orach Chaim* 8:4,10:12; *Turey Zahav* 10:9; *Mishneh Berurah* 10:37. Cf. *Midrash Abkir* on Exodus 14:29; *Midrash Tehillim* 6:1; *Yalkut* 2:723; *Tosafoth, Arakhin* 2b s.v. *HaYodea, Hagahoth Maimonioth Tzitzith* 3:9 #20.

71. *Turey Zahav* 9:8; *Mishneh Berurah* 9:16. Cf. *Shabbath* 153a; *Bach, Orach Chaim* 24 s.v. *BeKol;* Rashi, *Menachoth* 38b s.v. *Midey.*

72. *Shabbath* 26b; *Yebamoth* 4b; *Menachoth* 39b.

73. *Tur Orach Chaim* 9 (12a); *Orach Chaim* 9:6. Cf. *Tosafoth, Menachoth* 40a s.v. *Sadin.*

74. *Orach Chaim* 25:1.

75. *Berachoth* 51b; *Pesachim* 114a; *Sukkah* 54b, *Megillah* 29b; *Beth Yosef, Orach Chaim* 25 s.v. *VeAchar; Turey Zahav* 25:1.

76. *Menachoth* 42a, *Orach Chaim* 8:7.

77. *Magen Avraham* 9:2; *Rav Shulchan Arukh* 8:5; *Ba'er Hetiv* 8:3; *Mishneh Berurah* 8:4. Cf. *Tosafoth, Arakhin* 2b *HaYodea,* from *Moed Katan* 24a; *Rokeach* 361 (p. 248); *Shaar HaKavanoth, Tzitzith* 2 (p. 32), *Pri Etz Chaim, Tzitzith 1 (p.* 65). See also *Ben Ish Chay (Halachoth) Bereshith* 5, *T'shuvoth Lechem Shlomo* 13, *Darkey Chaim VeShalom* 34

78. *Pri Etz Chaim, Tzitzith* 6, note 1 (p. 81).

79. See note 70.

80. *Magen Avraham* 8:3. Cf. Rashi, *Kiddushin* 29b s.v. *DeLo; Beth Yosef, Orach Chaim* 8 (9a) *U'Mechase.*

MAKE YOUR OWN

81. *Orach Chaim* 15:6.

CLOTHING

1. Cf. Abarbanel on Genesis 3:8.

2. See below, note 23.

3. *Nefesh HaChaim* 1:6, note s.v. *VeHaInyan* (6a).

4. Cf. Rashi, Sforno, Abarbanel ad loc.; Ramban on Genesis 2:9. See notes 6 and 11.

5. Cf. Alshech on Genesis 2:25.

6. *Ibid.* Cf. *Bereshith Rabbah* 18:6; *Maharazav* ad loc.; *Idem.* 85:2.

7. *Shabbath* 146a, Rashi ad loc. s.v. *KeSheBa, Yebamos* 103b; *Avodah Zarah* 22b; *Bechoroth* 8a; *Tosefta Sotah* 4:5; *Akedath Yitzchak* 9 (73b).

8. *Zohar* 3:15b. Cf. Rashi, *Megillah* 31a s.v. *Korin; Turey Zahav, Orach Chaim* 622:4.

9. *Zohar 159, Nitzutzey Or ad loc.* 5 and 6.
10. Avoth 5:1.
11. Sforno, Or *HaChaim, Abarbanel, Alshech ad loc.; Moreh Nebukhim* 1:2; Rashi *on Genesis* 3:11; Tikuney *Zohar 58; Reshith Chochmah, Shaar HaKedushah* 16 (196b); *Likutey Halachoth, Netilath Yadayim* 4:12; *Ben Ish Chay, introduction to Bereshith.*
12. Abarbanel on Genesis 2:25. *Cf. Shabbath* 77b.
13. *Zohar* 3:175a, 3:276a. *Cf.* Sahnedrin 37a, *Yerushalmi Peah* 1:1 (5a); *BeMidbar Rabbah* 10:1; *Agudath Bereshith* 42; *Reshith Chochmah, Shaar HaKedusha* 6 (142c); *Degel Machaneh Ephraim, Sh'lach* (58b); *Likutey Halachoth, Tzitzith* 5 :10 (45b).
14. *Sifri* (115), Rashi, Rashbam, *on* Numbers 15:38, *Zohar 3:174b, Akedath Yitzchak* 77 (4:43b). See *Bahir* 92, that the 32 *strings* of *the Tzitzith* are called watchers. *Cf. Maaloth HaSulam* on *Zohar* 3:301a.
15. *Berachoth* 13a.
16. *Cf.* Exodus 21:10, Rashi *ad loc.; Niddah* 3lb
17. *Cf. Yerushalmi Sotah* 1:5 (6a); *Bereshith Rabbah* 26:10; *VaYikra Rabbah* 23:9; *Tanchuma Bereshith* 12; Rashi on *Genesis* 6:13.
18. *Menachoth* 44a, *Sifri* (115) on Numbers 15:41.
19. *Alshech* on Numbers 15:41 (31d). *Cf. Iyun Yaakov* (in *Eyn Yaakov) ad loc.*
20. *Berachoth* 13a.
21. Rashi on Leviticus 19:2; *VaYikra Rabbah* 24:6.
22. *Sifri,* Rashi *ad loc.*

GOD'S TALLITH

23. *Mesorath HaShas ad loc. Cf. Zohar 3:140b, Derekh Mitzvothekha (Chabad) Tzitzith* (15b); *Likutey Halachoth, Tzitzith* 2:2; *Bach, Orach Chaim* 24 *s.v. BeKol.*
24. Maharsha *ad loc. Cf. Zohar* 1 :13b; *Tikuney Zohar* 21 (55b) Also see *Bereshith Rabbah* 1:6, 3:4; *Sh'moth Rabbah* 50:1; *Deuarim Rabbah* 2:37; *Tanchuma VaYak'hel 6.*
25. Thirteen Principles #3.
26. *Mechilta* (65a); Rashi, *on* Exodus 19:18; *Tanchuma Yithro* 13; *Bereshith Rabbah* 27:1; *Koheleth Rabbah* 2:24; *Yad, Yesodey HaTorah* 1:9.
27. Rambam on *Sanhedrin* 10:1, Seventh Principle.
28. In this entire discussion, we follow the outline of *Derech HaShem* 2. For further details, see *God, Man and Tefillin* (NCSY, New York, 1973) p. 35ff.; *The Handbook of Jewish Thought,* Chapter 3.
29. *Sefer HaYashar 1.*
30. Kiddushin 39b; *Yad, T'shuvah* 9:1.
31. *KaLaCh Pith'chey Chochmah* #2.
32. Ralbag, *Metzudoth David, ad loc.; Yad, Teshuvah* 6:5; *Moreh Nebukhim* 2:48; *Berachoth* 55a, Rashi *ad loc. s.v. Tzerichim; Emunoth VeDeyoth* end of 4:7 (68a); Radak *on* Jeremiah 10:23; Maharatz Chayoth *on Megillah* 11a.
33. *Makkoth* 10a; *Shabbath* 104a.
34. *Yoma* 38b.
35. *Kiddushin* 30b.

36. *Chagigah* 2:1 (11b). *See Moreh Nebukhim,* Introduction to part 3.

37. *Zohar* 3:227a; *Etz Chaim, Shaar Klipath Nogah* 2 (p. 381). Cf. Rashi, Malbim, *ad loc.*

38. *Etz Chaim, Shaar HaChashmal 2 (p. 293), Shaar Klipath Nogah 3 (p. 352), Shaar Kitzur ABYA 2 (p. 395). Cf. Zohar 3:227a; Likutey Amarim (Tanya)* 1:1 *(6a).*

39. *Etz Chaim, Shaar HaTzelem 3 (p. 51), Shaar HaChashmal 1 (p. 291);Shaar Kitzur ABYA 6 (p.* 401); *Mavo Shaarim 6:2:3;Shaar HaKavanoth,Inyan Levishath Begadim (pp. 12,13); Pri Etz Chaim, Shaar HaTefillah 3 (p.* 19).

40. See notes 39 and 76.

41. *Derekh HaShem 1:3:6; Adir BeMarom* (B'nai Brak, 5728) p. 11.

42. *Kiddushin 30b; Bava Metzia* 16a.

43. *Zohar* 1:23b. For *the* meaning of God's Tallith, see *Shaar HaKavanoth, Tzitzith* 2 (p. 28); Pri *Etz Chaim, Tzitzith* 3 (p. 68a). Also see *Tana DeBey Eliahu Zuta* 23 (51b); *Tikuney Zohar* 21 (55b); Bachya on Numbers 15:38; *Likutey Moharan* 8:8. For other explanations, see Rashba, *Berachoth* 6a; *Beer HaGolah* (Maharal) 4 (3sb).

44. See note 2, part 1.

45. *Zohar 1:28b* Cf. *Kli Yakar* on Numbers 15:38.

46. *Pesikta* 5 (55a); *Pesikta Rabathai* 15 (78a); *Yalkut* 1:191; *Rokeach 242 (p. 139).*

47. *Meshech Chochmah* on Numbers 15:38.

48. *Yerushalmi Nedarim* 3:2 (9a); *Bahir* 114, *Elemah Ralbothai* (RaMaK) 1:4:14 (29b); *Avodath Yisroel* on *Numbers* 15:38.

49. *Baal HaTurim,* Abarbanel, Bachya, on *Numbers* 15:38; *Targum Yonathan* on Numbers 15:40; *Zohar* 3:226b, 227a; *Tikuney Zohar* (10:25b).

50. According to the Talmud *(Chagigah* 13b top) the etymology of the word *Chashmal is Chayoth Esh Memalleloth,* or "*Chayoth* of Fire, speaking." *Cf. Zohar* 2:81b 3:228a; *Tikuney Zohar* 19 (28b); *Shaar HaHakdamoth, Orchey HaKinuyim, Kaf (p.* 220).

51. Bachya on *Numbers 15:38 (83c); Noam Elimelech ibid.* Cf. *Zohar 3:175b; BeMidbar Rabbah* 17:9.

52. *Likutey Halachoth, Netilath Yadayim* 4:11. Cf. *Zohar 3:228b.*

53. *Tifereth Yisrael* 40. Cf. *Sefer Yetzirah 4:3.*

54. For the relationship of this to Tzitzith, see Rashi on Numbers 15:41; *Sifsey Chachamim, Gur Aryeh,* Bachya *ad loc.* Also see Rashi, *Menachoth* 43b s.v. *Domeh LeYam; Smag,* positive 26 (p. 109a).

55. *Tifereth Yisrael* (Maharal) 1, 2. *Cf. VaYikra Rabbah* 27:10; *Derekh Mitzvothecha* (Chabad) 9b.

56. *Cf. Moreh Nebukhim* 3:49.

57. The eight strings allude to the eight days of circumcision, cf. Bachya on Numbers 15:38 (83a); *Menorath HaMaor* 3:3:4:3 (125).

58. This is also the reason why the total number of strings on all four corners is 32, alluding to the 32 *Nesivoth Chochmah* (Paths of Wisdom). Cf. *Bahir* 92, *Zohar* 3:175a, 3:227a, 3:301a; Bachya on Numbers 15:38, Rekanti, *Shlach* 38c, *Tzitzith* 10a; *Reshith Chochmah, Shaar HaKedushah* 7 (l4ld); *Pardes Rimonim* 23:9; Pri *Etz Chaim, Tzitzith* 6 (p. 81); *Nahar Shalem p.* 71. For a general discussion of the 32 *Nisivoth,* see *Sefer Yetzira* 1:1 ff Also see note 80.

59. Tzitzith thus allude to *Yesod* (Foundation) the Sefirah associated with the reproductive organ, cf. *Tikuney Zohar* 21 (55b); *Pri Etz Chaim, Tzitzith* 2 (p. 66).

60. *Menorath HaMaor* 3 :3 :4:3 (125).

61. *Nedarim* 32b, Ran *ad loc. s.v. u'Malki Tzedek; Pirkey Rabbi Eliezer* 8 (18b); Radal *ad loc.* 8:17.

62. *Sotah* 17a; *Chulin* 89a; *Bereshith Rabbah* 43:9; *Tanchuma, Lech Lecha* 13; *Zohar* 3:175b.

63. Taken *from* the introduction to *Sifra (Torath Kohanim),* cf. *Tur Orach Chaim* 50. For the relationship between these and the Thirteen Attributes of Mercy, *see Zohar* 3:228a; *B'nai Yesas'char, Rosh Chodesh* 4:3, *Tamuz* 3:7.

64. *Etz Chaim, Shaar Arich Anpin* 9; *Zohar* 2:4b, 3:131b Also see Rashi, Ibn Ezra, Ramban, *Baaley Tosafoth, Sforno ad loc.; Tosafoth Rosh HaShanah* 17b *s.v. Shalosh; Sefer Chasidim* 250; *Makor Chesed ad loc.* 250:3.

65. *Zohar 3:131b Etz Chaim ibid.; Tomer Devorah* 1.

66. See note 75. The *Zohar,* however, speaks of thirteen *Chulyoth* or triplets that make up the 39 windings. See *Zohar* 3:227a; *Tikuney Zohar* 10 (25b).

67. *Zohar 3:228a*

68. *Ibid.*

69. *Likutey Halachoth, Tzitzith* 5:8.

70. Ibid.

71. *Zohar 3:257a.*

72. *BeMidbar Rabbah* 17:8. Note that this exposition is given with regard to

Tzitzith in particular.

73. *Zohar* 3:227a. The hundred commandments for each day are very much like the hundred blessings mentioned on *Menachoth* 43b. For another derivation of the number 613, see Rabbi Azriel on *Shir HaShirim,* quoted in Bachya on Numbers 15:38 (83b); *Reshith Chochmah, Shaar HaKedushah* 6 (142d).

NUMBERS

74. Cf. *Likutey* Amarim (Tanya) 2:1 (77a).

75. *BeMidbar Rabbah* 13:21; *Tanchuma, Korach* 12; *Zohar* 3:227a; *Rashi on Numbers* 15:39; Abarbanel *ibid.;* Rashi *Shevuoth* 29a, *Menachoth* 43b *s.v. Shekula;* Rabenu Gershom, *Menachoth* 41a, end; Tosafoth *Ibid.,* 39a *s.v.* VeLo. Cf. Ramban on Numbers 15:39, and on Sefer *HaMitzvoth, Shoresh* 1.

76. See above, note 39.

77. *Perishah, Orach Chaim* 11:22; *Machtzith HaShekel* 11:22; *Ba'er Heteiv* 11:24; *Mishnah Berurah* 11:70. Also see *Shaar HaKavanoth, Tzitzith* 6 (47a); *Yam Shel Sh'lomo, Yebamoth* 1:3; *Magen Avraham* 11:22.

78. *Menachoth* 39a; *Tosafoth ad loc. s.v. Lo;* Raavad, *Tzitzith* 1:7; HaGra on *Orach Chaim* 11:14 s.v. VeNohagin.

79. Cf. *Pri Megadim, Eshel Avraham* 11:22.

80. *Zohar 3:175b; Likutey Halachoth, Tzitzith* 1 (32b), 5:23. See *Baaley Tosafoth* on *Numbers* 15:38. Also *see note* 58.

1. *Pri Megadim, Mishbetzoth Zahav 9:6; Taamey HaMinhagim 15.*
2. *Menachoth* 4:1 (38a); *Yad,* Tzitzith 1:4. However, *see HaMaor HaKatan, Shabbath* (Rif 11b), who holds that Tzitzith are not valid without the blue thread. See Pri *Megadim,* Introduction, s.v. Tzitzith; *Pethil Techeleth* 5 (p, 110).
3. *Tosefta, Menachoth 9:6; Shefuney Temuney Chol 2 (p.* 12). This requirement is questioned, however, in *Tifereth Yisrael.* Introduction to *Seder Moed, K'lelay Bigdey Kehunah (p. 14b)*
4. *Menachoth* 44a.
5. *Ibid.* 40a.
6. *Cf. Shaar HaKavanoth, Tzitzith* 4 (p. 37), *Pri Etz Chaim, Tzitzith 5 (p.* 77).
7. *Sifri* (354) on Deuteronomy 33:19.
8. From Raavad, *Tzitzith* 1:7, it would appear that Rav Natrunai Gaon, who died in 761 C.E., still had *Techeleth (Seder HaDoroth p.* 69a, *Shalsheleth HaKabalah* 36b). *Cf. Shefuney Temuney Chol p.* 9. It also appears that Rabbi Shimon Kiira, author of *Halachoth Gedoloth* also had *Techeleth cf. HaMaor HaKatan loc.* cit., and he, too, lived between 678 and 703 C.E. See *Pethil Techeleth, p.* 44. The earliest statement regarding the absence of *Techeleth* appears in *BeMidbar Rabbah,* 17:8; *Tanchuma Shlach* 15; but see *Shefuney Temuney Chol p. 9;* Also see Rambam on *Menachoth* 4:1; *Sefer HaChinukh* 386; *Rokeach* #361 (p. 247); HaGra on *Orach Chaim 9:1.*
9. *Pethil Techeleth p.* 44. *Cf.* Shabbath 26a, that this dye came from Tyre.
10. *Yad,* Tzitzith 2:1, *Kley HaMikdash* 8:13. In his commentary on *Berakhoth* 2:1, *Kelayim 9:1,* the Rambam writes that it is like the color of *Tarshish,* the precious stone mentioned in Exodus 28:29. See *Chulin* 91b, Rashi *ad loc. s.v. VeGeviasi;* Rabenu Gershom ibid., that this is a Mediterranean blue. See *BeMidbar Rabbah* 2:7.
11. The Rambam indicates that this is similar in color to Isatis; Yad, Tzitzith 2:1, Rambam on Shevi'ith 7:1, *Megillah* 4:7. This is most probably *Isatis Tinctoria* or Woad, a well known plant that produces a blue dye. In his commentary on Kelayim 2:5, however, the Rambam identifies this with the color *of Techeleth,* and states that it is Indi[go]. On Shabbath 9:5, he furthermore states that *Isatis is* skyblue. We also find in the Talmud that *Techeleth* resembled a dye known as *Kla Ilan, cf. Menachoth 4lb Baba Metzia 41b.* According to the *Arukh s.v. Kla* and the *Nimukey Yosef* (on *Baba Metzia,* Rif 34a s.v. *Ilan)* this *Kla Ilan is* indigo. (See Michael Sachs, *Beitrage zur Shprach und Alterthumsforshang,* Berlin 1852, 1:132, who identifies this with the Greek *Callainum.)* Also see *Tosafoth Chulin* 47b s.v. *Eleh;* Rabenu Yonah, *Berakhoth* (Rif 4b) s.v. *Rabbi Eliezer.*
12. Rashi on Numbers 14:41.
13. Rashi, Sota 17a s.v. *SheHa Techeleth* writes that it is not exactly the color of the sky, but more the color of the sea. In a number of other places, Rashi writes that *Techeleth is Yarok* or green; *cf.* Rashi on Exodus 25:4, Numbers 15:33, Berachoth 9b s.v. Techeleth, Gittin 3lb s.v. Sarbala. From *Yerushalmi, Berakhoth* 1:2 (7b), it also appears that it has a greenish color, *cf. Marah HaPanim ad loc. s.v. Magid, Tosafoth, Sukkah 31b s.v.*

HaYarok, Chulin 37b s.v. Eleh. See BeMidbar Rabbah 14:3; Midrash Tehillim 24:12.

14. Rabbi Gershon Henoch of Radzin, Shefuney Temuney Chol 3 (p. 36); Pethil Techeleth 2 (p. 65); Eyn Techeleth 26 (p. 126), all in Shlosha Sifrey Techeleth, Jerusalem 5723.

15. Aruch s.v. Chilazoni Tifereth Yisrael, Introduction to Seder Moed, K'laley Bigdey Kehunah p. 14b. Chidushey HaRan, Shabbath 107a (14:1), speaks of "our Chilazons who inhabit garbage heaps," most probably referring to the common European land snails. Also see Eyn Techeleth 20 (p. 115).

16. Shabbath 26a, Sifri loc. cit. The Rambam in Yad, Tzitzith 2:2, writes that it is found in the "Salt Sea," but the reference is not to the Dead Sea, but to salt water in general, cf. Rambam on Kelim 15:1, Tshuvoth Rambam 154. Also see Maadney Yom Tov, Rosh, Kelai Begadim (after Niddah) 7:10; Radal on Pirkey Rabbi Eliezer 18:45, notes 6 and 7; Torah Temimah on Numbers 15:38 #118; Shefuney Temuney Chol p. 28; Pethil Techeleth. It occasionally emerges on mountains near the sea, cf. Sanhedrin 91a; Rashi, Megillah 6a s.v. Al Yedey; Chulin 89a; T'shuvoth Radbaz 685. It was also found in Italy, cf. Targum on Ezekiel 27:7.

17. Yerushalmi Shabbath 1:3 (8a), Korban HaEdah, P'nai Mosheh, ad loc. s.v. VeHalo Chilazon. Also see Tosafoth Shabbath 73b s.v. MeFarek; Ritva, Shabbath 107a (14:1).

18. Devarim Rabbah 7:11; Shir HaShirim Rabbah 7:11; Pesikta 10 (92a); Midrash Tehillim 23:4; Yalkut 1:850, 2:691.

19. Kelim 12:1; Rosh ad loc. s.v. Chilazon, Shefuney Temuney Chol 2:5.

20. Bekhoroth 6:2 (38a), Targum Yonathan; Rashi, on Leviticus 21:20. Cf. Shefuney Temuney Chol 2:6.

21. Menachoth 44a; Shefuney Temuney Chol 2:1.

22. And therefore, it is not actually blood, cf. Tosafoth, Shabbath 75a s.v. Ki; Shefuney Temuney Chol 2:9.

23. Ravya on Berakhoth 3b, quoted in Torathan Shel Rishonim, Yerushalmi Berakhoth 1:2, who states that Techeleth is Pirpiron or Purpura. The Tifereth Yisrael loc. cit. also identifies it as the "Purple Snail," quoting Wilhelm Gesenius, Habraishes und chaldaishes Hanawortbuch Über dos Alte Testament (1812).

24. The story of the search and discovery are to be found in the introductions to Pethil Techeleth and Eyn Techeleth (p 29).

25. Aruch HaShulchan 9:12. For a discussion of some of the arguments raised against Rabbi Gershon Henoch's thesis, see Shulchan Melachim (Shaarey Shalom), Pethicha LeHilkhoth Tzitzith 5 (pp. 210a ff.)

26. Yad, Tzitizth 1:6, Kesef Mishneh ad loc.; P'er HaDor (Tshuvoth HaRambam) 21. Also see Shaar HaKavanoth, Tzitzith 4 (p. 39); Pri Etz Chaim, Tzitzith 4 (p. 7s).

27. Raavad, Tzitzith 1:6. Cf. Arukh s.v. Techeleth; Smag, positive 26.

28. Rashi, Menachoth 38a s.v. HaTecheleth, Shabbath 27b s.v. Salka Daata Amina KeDeRaba; Tosafoth, Menachoth 38a s.v. HaTecheleth.

29. Pethil Techeleth p. 144.

30. Menachoth 39a; Yad, Tzitzith 1:7; Pethil Techeleth p. 204.

31. Ibid.; Menachoth 38b.

TEFILLIN

ARYEH KAPLAN

Introduction

Hear O Israel, the L-rd is our G-d,
the L-rd is One.
And you shall love the L-rd your G-d
with all your heart,
with all your soul,
and with all your might.
And these words that I give you today
shall be on your heart.
You shall teach them to your children
and speak of them
when you are on the way
and when you are at home,
when you lie down,
and when you wake up.
And you shall bind them for a sign
upon your hand
and for Tefillin
between your eyes.
And you shall write them on the Mezuzah
of your doors and your gates.

(Deuteronomy 6:4-9)

This is the *Shema.*

It is the most important part of our prayer service.

It is recited by every believing Jew twice each day, in the morning and at night.

It is the first thing a Jew learns as a child, and his last words before he dies.

With the possible exception of the Ten Commandments, we

can say that it is the single most important passage in the entire Torah.

The *Sh'ma* contains five essential points:

1. Belief in G-d and His unity.
2. The love of G-d.
3. The obligation to repeat this lesson.
4. The commandment of Tefillin.
5. The commandment of the *Mezuzah*.

The commandment of Tefillin is repeated three other times in the Torah:

"And it shall be a sign on your hand, and a reminder between your eyes, so that G-d's Torah be on your lips; for with a strong hand G-d brought you out of Egypt." (Exodus 13:9)

"And it shall be a sign on your hand, and Tefillin between your eyes, because with a mighty hand G-d brought you out of Egypt." *(Ibid. 19:16)*.

"Therefore, take these words of Mine upon your heart and upon your soul, and bind them for a sign on your hand, and for Tefillin between your eyes. (Deuteronomy 11:18)

Obviously, a commandment repeated four times in the Torah is of more than ordinary importance.

The fact that it is included in the *Sh'ma* would indicate that the commandment of Tefillin must be significant indeed.

It would pay to explore it a little further.

Why Tefillin?

Have you ever truly loved?

Have you ever felt so close to another human being that every moment together was precious? Where every moment apart was one of longing? Where every letter and memento from this person was something to be treasured?

What if this person gave you a ring or a pin and asked you to wear it? Every time you looked at it or felt it on your finger, would it not remind you of this great love?

The greatest possible love is the love between G-d and man.

G-d told us through His prophet (Jer. 31:3), "I have loved you with an infinite world of love." To truly believe in G-d is to share this love.

To the best of our understanding, G-d's very act of creation was an act of love. It was a love so immense that the human mind cannot begin to fathom it. The Bible alludes to it, saying (Psalms 136:7), "To Him Who made the great stars, for His love is infinite."

This bond of love exists always, even when we do not deserve it. G-d is a Father Who loves His children even when they go astray. It is our duty, however, to strengthen this bond.

Tefillin are a sign of this bond of love.

Faith and love are very tenuous things. We can speak of them and think about them. But unless we do something about them, we tend to forget.

Tefillin serve to help us remember "and a reminder between your eyes."

If you would open a pair of Tefillin, you would find that they contain four parchments. One of these parchments consists of the *Sh'ma.* It contains the commandment to love G-d: "And you shall love the L-rd your G-d, with all your heart, with all your soul, and with all your might."

This commandment speaks of three types of love. You must love G-d with your heart, your soul, and your might.

The Tefillin mirror these three aspects of love.

"With all your heart." The hand Tefillin are worn on the left hand opposite the heart. We thus dedicate our heart, the seat of life, to the love of G-d.

"With all your soul." The head Tefillin are worn next to the brain, the seat of man's soul and intellect. We thus dedicate our mind to the love of G-d.

"With all your might." The hand Tefillin are bound to the arm, the symbol of man's strength. We thus dedicate all our powers to the love of G-d.[1]

Love is the basis of the entire Torah.

The Bible therefore tells us, "they shall be for a sign . . . that G-d's Torah be on your lips."

The essence of the Torah is its commandments, *Mitzvos* in Hebrew. The word *Mitzvah* comes from a root meaning "to bind." Every commandment or *Mitzvah* serves to draw us close to G-d and strengthen this bond of love.[2]

With every *Mitzvah* we forge a spiritual bond with G-d. In the case of Tefillin, this bond is physical as well as spiritual. We literally bind G-d's love symbol to our bodies. Thus, our sages teach us that the commandment of Tefillin encompasses all others.[3] Here, we can actually see and feel the bond.

Another important theme of the Tefillin is the Exodus from Egypt — "And it shall be a sign . . . because with a strong hand G-d brought you out of Egypt." The Exodus took place over 3000 years ago. But it still plays a most important role in Judaism.

To understand the reason for this, we must realize how Judaism differs from all other religions.

Other religions begin with a single individual. He claims to have a special message and gradually gathers a following. His followers spread the word and gather converts, and a new religion is born. Virtually every world religion follows this pattern.

The only exception is Judaism.

G-d gathered an entire people, three million strong, to the foot of Mount Sinai, and proclaimed His message. Every man, woman, and child heard G-d's voice decreeing the Ten Commandments. Thus was the bond forged between G-d and Israel.

This took place just seven weeks after the Jews left Egypt. It was the climax of the drama of the Exodus.

This was an event unique in the history of mankind.

It is most important not to forget. . ..

The Torah tells us (Deut. 4:9, 10), "Be very careful and watch yourself, that you not forget the things you saw with your own eyes. Do not let them pass from your minds as long as you live. Teach them to your children, and to your children's children. The day when you stood before G-d.. .."

The parchments in the Tefillin speak of the Exodus.

The Tefillin thus serve to bind us to our past, especially to this unique event in our history.

We can understand this on a deeper level. But first we must understand the true significance of the Exodus and Sinai. We must know what it means to say that an entire people heard G-d's voice.

To hear G-d's voice is no simple matter. Only prophets hear G-d's voice. What happened at Sinai was that an entire people, men, women and children, achieved the level of prophecy.

There are many ways to approach G-d.

You can approach Him on an intellectual level. You can ask questions and seek answers until you achieve some understanding of the Infinite. This is the realm of the philosopher.

You can seek G-d on a more intimate level, in prayer and in meditation. There may then come a time when your self ceases to exist and all your senses are numbed. Suddenly, a door seems to open, if only by the slightest crack. You catch a glimpse of the Divine, and discover something more wonderful than anything on earth. Somehow you feel a unique closeness to G-d. To describe it would be as impossible as to describe the beauty of a sunset to a blind man. But you know it is there. The door has been opened to you, and you have peered through the crack.

This is the level of the mystic.

But sometimes the door is opened all the way. A man experiences more than merely a glimpse. He hears a clear voice and receives a lucid message. This is the highest possible human bond with G-d. It is the level of the prophet.

At Sinai, every Jew attained this level.

Tefillin bring us back to this unique moment.

Not many of us can be philosophers. Very few of us can attain the level of the mystic. Prophets no longer walk the earth.

But we can remember. . ..

When we bind the Tefillin to our bodies, we relive the infinite bond of love that was forged at Sinai.

There were *Tzadikim* — saints — who achieved a mystical experience every time they put on Tefillin. They could feel the words of the parchments literally burning into their heart and soul.

We may never achieve this level.

But we can begin. . ...

G-d has given us the commandment of Tefillin and clearly spelled out how to do it.

Tefillin may seem like simple boxes and straps. But they are much, much more. . ..

What Are Tefillin?

As we mentioned earlier, the commandment of Tefillin appears four times in the Torah.

In each case, the Torah is telling us that certain words and concepts must be bound to our arm and to our head. We understand this to mean that the entire paragraph or *Parsha* containing this commandment must be included in the Tefillin. The Tefillin therefore contain four parchments, each one containing a paragraph with the commandment of Tefillin.

From the Torah itself, we therefore understand that the Tefillin must contain the following four *Parshos* or paragraphs. We usually refer to them by their initial Hebrew word:

1. *Kadesh* (Exodus 13:1-10), containing our obligation to remember the Exodus.
2. *VeHayah Ki YeViaCha (Ibid* 13:11-16), speaking of our obligation to transmit this tradition to our children.
3. The *Sh'ma* (Deut. 6:4-9), speaking of G-d's unity and our mutual bond of love.
4. *VeHaya Im Sh'moa (Ibid.* 11:13-21), declaring man's responsibility toward G-d.

There is one other thing that we can deduce from the Torah itself. When speaking of the hand Tefillin, the Torah calls it an *Os* — a sign — in the singular. When speaking of the head Tefillin, however, the Torah calls them *totefos* — usually translated simply as Tefillin — which is a plural word. Since the hand Tefillin is singular, all four paragraphs are written on a single parchment and put in one box. The head Tefillin, on the other hand, contains the four paragraphs written on four separate parchments and placed in four distinct boxes.

If you look carefully at a pair of Tefillin, you will notice that the one for the hand consists of a single box. The one for the head, however, is made up of four boxes pressed tightly together.

Beyond this, the Torah tells us nothing at all about the Tefillin. There is no description of them nor any hint as to how they must be made. The Torah merely outlines their contents and tells us nothing more.

It is most important to realize that G-d gave us the Torah in two parts.

There is the Written Torah *(Torah SheBeKesav),* which we keep in the ark. However, there is also the Unwritten or Oral Torah *(Torah SheBaal Peh),* consisting of the oral tradition handed down from Sinai.

The Torah was not meant to be a mere book, lying on the shelf. It was meant to be part of the everyday life of an entire people. As such, it could only be transmitted by word of mouth. The Oral Torah was handed down from teacher to disciple for almost 1500 years, until the harsh Roman persecutions finally threatened to extinguish it completely. Finally, some 1700 years ago, it was written down to form the Talmud.

The Talmud itself cites Tefillin as a prime example of a case where the full description of a commandment is found only in the Oral Torah.[4]

If you think about it, you will realize that it was not necessary to write a description of Tefillin in the Torah. One need simply look at an older pair. Tefillin were worn by virtually every adult male throughout Jewish history, and they themselves provided as permanent a record as any book.

There are ten basic laws regarding Tefillin contained in the Oral Torah, given to Moses at Sinai:[5]

1. The parchments must be made of the outermost hide *(Klaf)* of a kosher animal.[6]
2. They must be written with a permanent black ink.[7]
3. The parchments must be tied shut with the hair of a kosher animal.[8]
4. They must be placed in a perfectly square leather box.[9]
5. The box of the head Tefillin must be inscribed with the Hebrew letter *Shin.* On the right side of the box, this is the usual three-headed *Shin,* while on the left side, it must have four heads.[10]

6. The boxes must have a somewhat wider base. This is called the *Titura*. [11]

7. This base must contain an opening through which the straps are passed. This is called the *Ma'abarta*. [12]

8. The boxes must be sewn closed with thread made from the veins or sinews of a kosher animal.[13]

9. The Tefillin must be bound with leather straps, dyed black on the outside.[14]

10. The strap of the head Tefillin must be tied with a knot in the shape of the Hebrew letter *Dalet*. The hand Tefillin must be tied with a knot shaped like a *Yud*. [15]

These ten laws provide us with the basic form of Tefillin as we know them. We will discuss some of the reasons for them in the final section.

It is also interesting to note that Tefillin must be made entirely of animal products. These must all come from kosher animals. There is a profound reason for this which we will also discuss later.

The Tefillin contain the three Hebrew letters, *Shin, Dalet* and *Yud,* as a part of their basic structure. These spell out G-d's name *Sh-dai,* usually translated as Almighty. This is the same Name that appears on the *Mezuzah.* The Talmud says that this Name, spelled out in the Tefillin, is alluded to in the verse (Deut. 28:10), "And the peoples of the earth shall see that G-d's Name is called upon you, and they shall be awed by you."[16]

Tefillin can be made only by a duly ordained scribe or *Sofer.* There are four callings in Judaism that require ordination: that of the Rabbi, that of the *Shochet* for slaughtering kosher meat, that of the *Mohel* for ritual circumcision, and that of the *Sofer* or scribe.

Tefillin not made by such a duly ordained scribe are *posul* and unfit for use. Since such unfit Tefillin occasionally find their way to the market, particularly in Jewish gift shops, caution must be exercised in buying Tefillin. It is best to purchase Tefillin from a reliable scribe. Tefillin coming from Israel should contain a seal of certification from the Chief Rabbinate. (The seal must be removed before the Tefillin are used.)

You may have an old pair of Tefillin from your father or grandfather. There is always the possibility that the parchments may have deteriorated, and if at all possible, they should be opened and examined by an ordained scribe. The fee for this is usually very nominal. As a precautionary measure, our tradition advises that Tefillin should be checked in this way at regular intervals (at least twice during seven years).

If you cannot get to a scribe, you may use the Tefillin as long as there is no outward sign of deterioration.[17]

If you have a pair of Tefillin, put them on today. If not, buy, borrow or beg a pair, and put them on as soon as possible.

Make it a daily habit.

There are very few things in life that are more important.

Using Tefillin

On the day a Jewish boy reaches his thirteenth Hebrew birthday, he becomes Bar Mitzvah. It is automatic, and there is no need, as far as Jewish law is concerned, for lavish parties or elaborate synagogue rituals. Bar Mitzvah literally means "son of a commandment." From the day of his Bar Mitzvah, a boy has the duty of keeping G-d's commandments. One of the most important of these commandments is wearing Tefillin.

The first new obligation of Bar Mitzvah is putting on Tefillin for the first time. This is even more important than being called to the Torah in the synagogue.

Wearing Tefillin every day then remains a lifelong duty.

Tefillin are usually put on just before the morning prayer. If you wear a *Tallis,* it is put on before the Tefillin.

The Tefillin are normally worn during the entire morning service.

If for any reason you cannot say the morning prayers, you should put on Tefillin anyway.

You can fulfill the commandment of Tefillin by just putting them on and immediately taking them off. It need not take more than a few minutes. If possible, you should also say the *Sh'ma* while wearing the Tefillin.

If you cannot put on Tefillin in the morning, you can do so any time of the day until dark. If you have not put them on in the morning, you may say the afternoon *Minchah* prayer wearing Tefillin.

Tefillin are never worn at night.

Tefillin are also not worn on the Sabbath nor on festivals mentioned in the Torah, such as Rosh HaShanah, Yom Kippur,

Succos, Pesach or Shavuos. As regards Chol Hamoed (inter-mediate festival days), consult your rabbi.

Girls do not wear Tefillin, since it is a commandment having a specified time. We will discuss this in the last section.

It is customary to stand while putting on Tefillin. (Sephardic and Oriental Jews, however, put on the hand Tefillin while sitting.)

The Tefillin are put on the arm first. This is the Tefillin *shel yad* or hand Tefillin.

They are worn on the left hand. A left handed person, however, wears them on the right. If one is at all ambidexterous, a rabbinical authority must be consulted.

The *Ma'abarta* is where the strap passes through the Tefillin. This is placed on the arm closest to where the arm joins the body. The hand Tefillin is thus worn so that it appears to hang down from the strap.

The Tefillin is placed in the exact center of the biceps muscle. When you place your arm next to your body, the side of the box should touch your chest.

Before tightening the strap, you should say, "I am now about to fulfill G-d's commandment to put on Tefillin." There is also a longer declaration included in most prayer books. You then say the blessing:

בָּרוּךְ אַתָּה ה' אֱלֹקֵינוּ מֶלֶךְ הָעוֹלָם
אֲשֶׁר קִדְּשָׁנוּ בְּמִצְוֹתָיו וְצִוָּנוּ לְהָנִיחַ תְּפִילִין

Baruch Atah Ad-noy, El-henu Melech ha-Olom,
Asher kidsha-nu beMitzvo-sav VeTziva-nu le-hani'ach Tefillin.

(Bless You L-rd, our G-d, King of the world,
Who has made us holy with His commandments
and bid us to put on Tefillin.)

The strap is then tightened by pulling it toward the right. It is customary to wind it toward the body. (Chassidic and Sep-hardic Jews, however, wind it away from the body.)

The strap is wound seven times around the forearm .

The black side of the straps must always be on the outside.

Now wind the strap once or twice around the palm of the hand so that it can be held.

You are now ready to put the Tefillin on your head. These

are the Tefillin *shel Rosh* or head Tefillin.

The head Tefillin should be centered in the middle of the head and worn just above the hairline.

It is most important that no part of the box protrude below the hairline. You may notice some older men wearing Tefillin on their foreheads, but they are wearing them incorrectly. Although the Torah states that the head Tefillin are to be worn "between the eyes," the Oral Torah explains that this means in the middle of the head, above the hairline. If the hairline has receded, then the Tefillin should be worn just above the point of the original hairline.

The knot of the head Tefillin must be centered at the base of the skull, just above the hairline in back of the head.

The straps are then allowed to hang in front.

Here again, it is most important that the straps be worn with the black side out. This is especially true on the head itself.

Very long hair may make it difficult to wear the head Tefillin correctly. For this reason, some religious Jews wear their hair short.

Before tightening the straps of the head Tefillin, say the following blessing:

בָּרוּךְ אַתָּה ה׳ אֱלֹקֵינוּ מֶלֶךְ הָעוֹלָם
אֲשֶׁר קִדְּשָׁנוּ בְּמִצְוֹתָיו וְצִוָּנוּ עַל מִצְוַת תְּפִלִּין:

Baruch Atah Ad-noy, El-henu Melech ha-Olom,
Asher kidsha-nu beMitzvo-sav VeTziva-nu al Mitzvas Tefillin.

(Bless You L-rd, our G-d, King of the world,
Who has made us holy with His commandments,
and given us the Mitzvah of Tefillin)

Then tighten the straps and say:

בָּרוּךְ שֵׁם כְּבוֹד מַלְכוּתוֹ לְעוֹלָם וָעֶד

Baruch Shem Kavod Malchu-so LeOlom VaEd.

(Blessed is the Name of His glorious Kingdom forever and ever.)

(Sefardim and some Chasidim omit this second blessing completely.)

You are now ready to complete the windings of the hand Tefillin. There are several customs regarding how to do this, given in figures 1-4. Most American congregations, however,

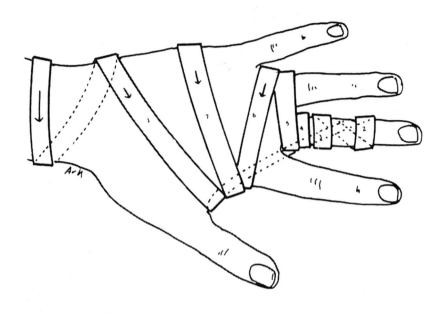

Figure 1. Windings on Hand, Ashkenazic Custom

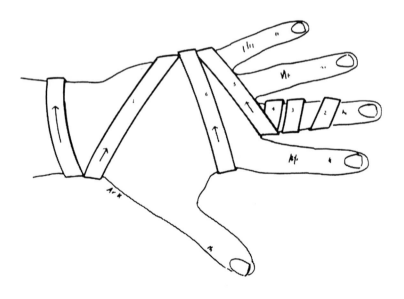

Figure 2. Chasidic Custom

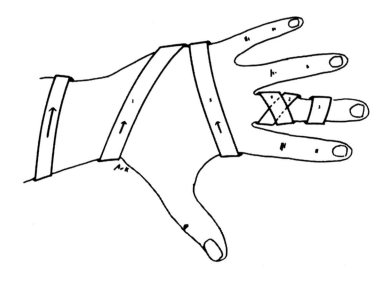

Figure 3. Chabad (Lubavitch) Custom

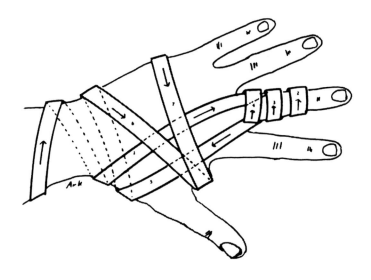

Figure 4. Sefardic Custom

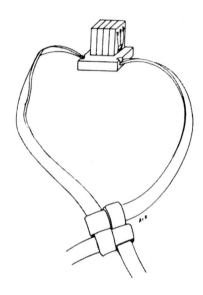

Figure 5. Head Tefillin, Ashkenazic Custom
Knot is in the shape of a double *Dalet*

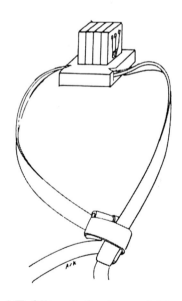

Figure 6. Head Tefillin, Sefardic and Chasidic Custom
Knot is in th ehape of a single *Dalet*

Figure 7. Hand Tefillin, Ashkenazic Custom
Yud shaped knot must touch *Bayit*

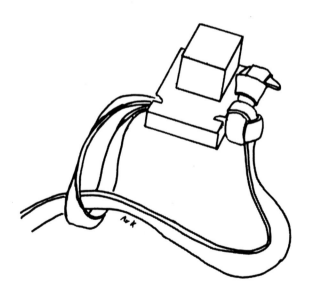

Figure 8. Hand Tefillin, Sefardic and Chasidic Custom

follow the Ashkenazic rite, shown in figure 1, and we will discuss this in detail.

Wind the strap around your hand, passing it between your thumb and forefinger. (Winding # 1)

Then wind it around the middle joint of the middle finger, and then twice around the lower joint.

The three windings around the middle finger are common to all rites, and symbolize the threefold bond of love between G-d and Israel. In a sense, they form a threefold wedding ring.

While making these windings, it is customary to repeat the following verses from the Book of Hosea (2:21-22). We are speaking to the Divine Presence of G-d:

וְאֵרַשְׂתִּיךְ לִי לְעוֹלָם. וְאֵרַשְׂתִּיךְ לִי בְּצֶדֶק וּבְמִשְׁפָּט
וּבְחֶסֶד וּבְרַחֲמִים. וְאֵרַשְׂתִּיךְ לִי בֶּאֱמוּנָה וְיָדַעַתְּ אֶת ה':

I will wed You to me forever.
I will wed You to me with right and justice,
   with love and mercy.
I will wed You to me with faith. . . and you shall know G-d.

The windings are then completed as in figure 1.

The rest of the strap is wound around the palm of the hand (winding #7) and loosely tied so that it can stay in place without being held.

Customs vary regarding the windings on the hand, and you should follow that of your synagogue. The only requirement is the three windings around the middle finger.[18]

When you remove the Tefillin, you reverse the process. First unwind the three coils from the finger, then remove the head Tefillin, and finally take off the hand Tefillin. If you wear a *tallis,* it is removed after the Tefillin.

You should always treat the Tefillin with the reverence due a sacred object, especially while wearing them. You should not engage in idle conversation while wearing Tefillin.

In general, it is very easy to observe the Mitzvah of Tefillin. It need not take more than a few minutes each day. But the true depth of this observance involves some of the most profound depths of Judaism.

We will now begin to explore these depths.

A Deeper Look

◈§ G-d's Tefillin

Rabbi Avin bar Rav Ada said in the name of Rabbi Yitzchok, "Where do we find that G-d wears Tefillin?"

It is written (Isa. 62:8), "G-d has sworn by His right hand, and by the arm of His strength."

"His right hand" is the Torah, as it is written (Deut. 33:2), 'from His right hand came a fiery law for them."

"The arm of His strength" is Tefillin, as it is written (Psalm 29:11), "G-d gives strength to His people."

But where do we find that the Tefillin are Israel's strength?

It is written (Deut. 28:10), "And the people of the earth shall see that G-d's Name is called upon you, and they shall (see your strength) and be awed by you."

We learned that the great Rabbi Eliezer said, "This is speaking of the Tefillin on the head."

Rabbi Nachman bar Yitzchok asked Rabbi Chiyah bar Avin, "And what is written in the Tefillin of the Master of the world?"

He replied that it contains the verse (I Chr. 17:21), "Who is like Your people Israel, a nation one on earth, whom G-d went to redeem for Himself for a people, to make Himself a name, by great and tremendous things."

(Talmud Berachos 6a)

It is written that G-d told Moses (Ex. 33:23), "I will take away My hand, and you will see My back, but My face shall not be seen."

Rabbi Chana bar Bizna said in the name of Rabbi Shimon Chasida, "We learn that G-d showed Moses the knot of His head Tefillin."

(Ibid. 7a)

We have here one of the most mysterious teachings in the entire Talmud. We are taught that G-d wears Tefillin containing the praise of the Jewish people. We are furthermore taught that when Moses asked G-d to show him the secret of Divine Providence, G-d showed him the knot of His Tefillin.

What does all this mean?

We know that G-d is not a material Being, and that he has neither body, shape nor form. We certainly cannot imagine Him wearing Tefillin in any physical sense.

But still, our sages were most certainly teaching us an important lesson when they say that G-d wears Tefillin. What message does this most remarkable lesson contain? As we mentioned earlier, the commandment of Tefillin encompasses all other Mitzvos.[1] As such, it forms the basis of our understanding of all other commandments.

Somehow, this lesson appears to teach us about the relationship between G-d and the Jewish people. Exploring this concept further will lead us to a deeper insight into this relationship.

⋅§ The Purpose of Creation

Why did G-d create the world?

There is a limit to how deeply we can probe, but our sages give us some insight into this question.

To the best of our understanding, G-d created the world as an act of love.[2]

It was an act of love so immense that the human mind cannot begin to fathom it. G-d created the entire world as a vehicle upon which He could bestow His good.[3]

But G-d's love is so great that any good that He bestows must be the greatest good possible. Anything less would simply not be enough.

But what is the greatest good? What is the ultimate good that G-d can bestow on His creation?

If you think about it for a moment, the answer should be obvious.

The ultimate good is G-d Himself. The greatest good that He can bestow is Himself. There is no greater good than achieving a degree of unity with the Creator Himself.

It is for this that G-d gave man the ability to resemble Himself.

The first ingredient of this was free will.

Just as G-d acts as a free Being, so does man. Just as He operates without prior restraint, so does man. Just as G-d can do good as a matter of His own choice, so can man. According to many commentators, this is the meaning of man being created in the "image" of G-d.[5]

But there is another necessary ingredient.

There must be a Way to reach G-d. Only G-d Himself could provide this way.

This way is the Torah.

Thus, our sages teach us that the Torah is the blueprint of all creation.[6]

The Torah provides the means through which man can partake of the G-dly, and therefore fulfills His purpose in creation. Thus, the Psalmist said (Ps. 16:11), "You have let me know the path of life, in Your presence is the fullness of joy, in Your right hand, bliss forever."

The Torah itself says (Deut. 6:24,25), "And G-d has commanded us to keep all these laws . . . for our good always. And it shall be righteousness for us if we keep all these Mitzvos before the L-rd our G-d, as He commanded us."

But there is still a third ingredient.

We need someone to follow this plan and receive G-d's Goodness.

This brings us to G-d's Tefillin.

◦§ The Tefillin

In many places the Torah speaks of G-d as if He had a body. We find such anthropomorphisms as "G-d's hand" and "G-d's eye."

What does this mean?

We know that God is absolutely incorporeal, and has neither body, shape nor form.

But our sages teach us that G-d borrows terms from His creatures to express His relationship with the world.[7]

But what do these terms represent?

We find a hint in Elijah's introduction in the *Tikuney Zohar,* [8] where he says:

> Love is the right hand,
> > Power is the left,
> Glory is the body,
> > Victory and Splendor are the two feet. . .
> Wisdom is the brain,
> > Understanding is the heart . . .
> And the Crown of all
> > is the Place where Tefillin rest . . .

G-d created the world with infinite wisdom. Thus, the Bible says (Ps. 104:24), "How great are Your works, O G-d, You made them all with wisdom."

But there is something that must come even before wisdom. There is something even higher.

What is the very first ingredient of creation? What comes even before wisdom?

The answer is purpose, and the will and desire to create.

Just as a Crown rests on top of the head, purpose and will stand above Wisdom.

The Crown of all creation is G-d's purpose. [9]

Elijah said, "The Crown of all is the place where *Tefillin rest.*"

This means that G-d's Tefillin are intimately bound to His purpose.

In the quotation at the beginning of this section, the Talmud asked what are in G-d's Tefillin. It answers that it contains the concept of Israel, the Jewish people.

G-d's Tefillin are His concept of Israel. [10]

When Elijah says, "the Crown of all is the place where Tefillin rest," he is saying that the concept of Israel is bound to G-d's purpose in creation.

We can readily understand this in terms of our earlier discussion. G-d's purpose in creation was to bestow good, and He created the Torah as the means through which man attains this good. Thus, the only ones who can reach the ultimate Good are those who accepted the Torah.

The ones who accepted the Torah are the Jewish people.

G-d's original purpose required someone to receive His

Good. In accepting the Torah, Israel became that someone. Thus, the concept of Israel was essentially the first ingredient of creation.

This is what our Sages mean when they say that the world was created for the sake of Israel.[11] It is also what is meant when they teach us, "the concept of Israel preceded all else."[12]

The Jewish people are G-d's Tefillin.

When we say that G-d wears Tefillin, we are saying that His ultimate purpose is bound up with the concept of Israel.

The straps emanate from the Tefillin and emanate to the right and to the left. This represents the two opposing forces of G-d's Providence, love and strength.[13] Good comes from G-d's love, while punishment comes from His strength. These two forces come together to form the structure of G-d's justice. This is the knot of His head Tefillin.

Moses asked G-d to reveal the ultimate depth of His purpose (Ex. 33:18), "Show me, I beg, Your glory." G-d replied that such perception is beyond the power of any man (Ibid. 33:20), "You cannot see My face, for man cannot see Me and live." However, G-d did agree to show Moses His back, that is, the purpose underlying His justice. He thus told Moses (Ibid. 33:23), "I will take away My hand, and you shall see My back, but My face shall not be seen."

Our sages teach us that Moses wanted to understand the true purpose underlying G-d's Justice. He asked G-d, "Why do the good suffer and the wicked prosper?"[14]

G-d then showed Moses the knot of His head Tefillin. This is where Love and Strength are bound together, forming the bond of G-d's Justice.

The straps of the head Tefillin then hang down the front of the body. This indicates G-d's purpose guiding the forces of history, down to even the lowest level. But here again, G-d's purpose requires that these forces of history be intimately linked with Israel's destiny. G-d thus guides man to bring about His ultimate purpose in creation.

Thus, the Torah says: (Deut. 28:10), "And the peoples of the earth shall see that G-d's Name is called upon you and shall be in awe of you." The Talmud, quoted at the beginning of this section, tells us that this refers to the Tefillin on the head. For the head Tefillin indicate that the Jewish people are the essential ingredient of all creation.

This purpose is not at all obvious. We must probe deeply before we can perceive it. This is one reason why the Tefillin are black, indicating that G-d's purpose is dark and hidden. The white parchments are only to be found when one penetrates this black barrier.

Summing up, the "place where Tefillin rest" indicates G-d's ultimate purpose.

His Tefillin are the Jewish people, uniquely bound to this purpose.

⊸§ The Hand Tefillin

When we speak of G-d's hand, we are speaking of His action in the world.

G-d's hand is at work, guiding the forces of history and the destiny of each individual. Although each individual has free will, G-d guides the general course of history toward His ends.[15] The collective wills of societies are determined by G-d and governments are steered by His hand. This is what the Bible means when it says (Prov. 21:1), "The king's heart is in G-d's hand . . . He turns it wherever He wills."[16]

The ultimate goal of the historic process is the perfection of society as a vehicle for G-d's goodness.

This goal is what we call the Messianic Age, and it is the focus of the entire historical process. It is one of the basic beliefs of Judaism and gives us complete optimism in the ultimate future of mankind.

The Jewish people have a twofold role in G-d's plan.

First of all, they are His prime instruments in bringing about the perfection of this world. Through their observance of the Torah, they are able to provide an example of G-d's teachings to all mankind. Thus, G-d told His prophet (Isa. 42:6), "I the L-rd have called you . . . for a light unto the nations."

Secondly, the Messianic Age will be a time when the Jewish people will be justified before all the world. For three thousand years we have remained devoted to G-d in the face of every possible persecution and suffering. In the Messianic Age, we will be recognized as the true suffering servants of G-d.

The prophet thus said: (Isa. 62:8), "G-d has sworn by His right hand, and by the arm of His strength, surely I will never again give your corn to be food for your enemies, and strangers will never again drink your wine for which you labored. But those who have garnered it shall eat it and praise G-d, and those who have gathered it shall drink it in the courts of My sanctuary."

This is a prophecy of the Messianic era.[17]

But if you look back at the Talmudic quotation at the beginning of this section, you will see that this is also the verse from which the Talmud derives the fact that G-d wears Tefillin.

The hand Tefillin indicate that Israel's destiny is uniquely bound to everything that G-d does in the world. G-d's hand is at work, guiding the world toward the realization of this destiny.

We see this in the very commandment of Tefillin. The Torah says: (Ex. 19:16), "It shall be for a sign on your hand, and for Tefillin between your eyes, for with a mighty hand, G-d brought us out of Egypt." We have here a direct link between the Tefillin and G-d's action.

In short, G-d's Tefillin represent the Jewish people. They are worn on His head and arm, representing Israel's unique relationship to His purpose and action.

Between G-d And Man

It is written (Genesis 1:27), "And G-d created man in His image, in the image of G-d, He created him."

Perceive this. When a man wears Tefillin, a voice proclaims to all the angels of the Chariot who watch over prayer, "Give honor to the image of the King, the man who is wearing Tefillin."

The Torah says of this man, "God created man in His image."

For this man is wearing the same Tefillin as the Master of the world.

(Tikuney Zohar 47, 83b)

☙ ☙ ☙

As we discussed earlier, Tefillin exemplify all the other commandments. If we can understand the meaning of Tefillin, we can perceive the deeper implication of all the other Mitzvos in the Torah. We know that the Tefillin are a symbol, reminding us of our faith in G-d and of the bond of love between us. We also know that they help us recall the Exodus.

There are some who think that Tefillin are nothing more than symbols. They think the same of the other Mitzvos.

However, mere symbolism is not enough to explain all the detailed laws regarding Tefillin. The *Shulchan Aruch,* the main code of Jewish law, contains twenty long chapters with all the intricate rules concerning the making and wearing of Tefillin. If even a single word is misspelled or a letter deformed, the Tefillin are *posul* and absolutely useless. And this is in the parchments, which are completely hidden in the Tefillin boxes.

If it is mere symbolism, then why all this attention to detail?[18]

Why not just hang a picture of Tefillin on the wall and merely look at it?

Why not simply meditate on Tefillin and their inner meaning?

Why do we have to actually wear such intricate ritual objects?

But, as we mentioned earlier, the greatest good that G-d can offer us is our ability to approach G-d and resemble Him. When we wear Tefillin, we are projecting ourselves in the image of G-d wearing Tefillin. This is more than mere symbolism. It is an imitation of the Divine.

This is the meaning of the quotation at the beginning of this section.

The author of the *Yesod VeShoresh HaAvodah*[19] comments that this is the reason for all the detailed laws of Tefillin. Every detail of the Tefillin we wear has a counterpart in the Tefillin on high.

There are some people who find it difficult to understand how a mere physical act, such as wearing Tefillin, can bring one close to G-d. They would say that the best way to accomplish this would be through meditation and contemplation, or through philosophical speculation.

These might be helpful, but they can never bring man to this goal. G-d told His prophet (Isa. 55:9), "As the heavens are higher than the earth, so are My ways higher than your ways, and My thoughts, than your thoughts."

But this does not really solve the problem.

If we cannot draw close to G-d through such spiritual exercises as meditation and contemplation, how can we do it through a mere physical act such as wearing Tefillin?

In order to understand this, we must ask another simple but profound question.

Why did G-d create the physical world?

This is really a difficult question. G-d Himself is certainly spiritual, and so is the Good that He has to give. The entire purpose of creation is essentially spiritual in scope.

Then what necessity was there in creating a physical world at all?

In order to answer this question, we must ask still another question.

What is the difference between the spiritual and the physical?

We speak of the two concepts, the spiritual and the physical, and realize that there is a difference between the two. But precisely what is it?

The answer is really quite simple. The main difference between the spiritual and the physical involves the concept of space. Physical space exists only in the physical world. In the spiritual domain, there is no concept of space as we know it.

But still we speak of things being close or far apart in the spiritual world. What does this mean?

We cannot be speaking of physical distance, for there is no physical space in the spiritual realm.

But in a spiritual sense, closeness involves resemblance.[20]

Two things that resemble each other are spiritually close. On the other hand, two things that differ are far apart in a spiritual sense.

This has very important implications. In the spiritual world, it is impossible to bring two opposites together. Because they are opposites, by definition they are poles apart.

But spiritual things can be bound to the material, just as the soul is bound to the body.

Two opposites can be brought together when they are both bound to the same material object. For in the physical world we can literally push two opposites together.

Thus, for example, man has both an urge for good and an urge for evil, the *Yetzer Tov* and the *Yetzer HaRa*. In a purely spiritual sense, these are poles apart. Without the material, they could never be brought together in a single spiritual entity. It is only in a physical body that they can be brought together. Although they are at opposite poles spiritually, they come together in the physical man.[21]

G-d and man are also worlds apart — "as the heavens are higher than the earth." On a purely spiritual plane, it would be totally impossible for the two ever to be brought together. All the meditating and philosophizing in the world cannot bridge this gap.

It is only here in the physical world that G-d and man can come together. In some ways, both can bind themselves to the same physical object or action. In this way, they are almost physically pushed together.

Here again, we can use Tefillin as an example.

The physical Tefillin we wear are a counterpart of the Tefillin on high. In each detail, they parallel God's spiritual Tefillin. And because they *resemble* these Tefillin, they are spiritually very close to them.

But as we discussed in the previous level, G-d's Tefillin are on the very Crown of creation. They exist at the very highest transcendental level.

When a man wears Tefillin, he therefore binds himself to the very highest spiritual level. He achieves a closeness to G-d that even the deepest meditation could not accomplish.

Of course, when a man wears Tefillin and also contemplates their significance, his very thoughts are elevated close to G-d. But even the physical act in itself can bring a man to the loftiest heights.

We can also understand this in a much simpler sense.

It is G-d's will that we wear Tefillin. Our physical Tefillin are therefore intimately bound to G-d's will.

But as we mentioned in the previous section, G-d's will is the Crown of existence, the very first stage in creation. Thus, our physical Tefillin are bound to the very highest transcendental level.

But when a man wears Tefillin, he is also bound to them.

Suddenly, this man has something in common with the Crown of existence. Both his body and G-d's will are intimately bound to the same physical object, in this case, Tefillin. Through the physical, he can literally push himself into contact with the G-dly.[22]

The same is true of all the other Mitzvos. As we mentioned in the first section, the word Mitzvah comes from a root meaning "to bind." Through the physical act of doing a Mitzvah, we literally bind ourselves to G-d.

We can now understand the reason for all the detailed laws

of Tefillin. In order to create this bond, our Tefillin must conform exactly to their counterpart on high. The slightest deviation breaks this link.

A good analogy is that of a radio. A radio is specifically designed to receive a particular type of signal. Every element in it is needed for this. Cut a single wire, remove a single capacitor, no matter how small, and you no longer receive the signal.

There are precise rules by which a radio must be built. These include all the laws of electromagnetism and circuits. If these are not exactly followed, the radio will not function.

Tefillin are our receiver for a spiritual signal. As such, they must be designed to receive this particular kind of signal. Violate a single rule, and they become like a radio with a transistor removed. The bond just no longer exists.

We can carry the analogy still further. You would have to have an extensive scientific education to even begin to understand how a radio works. You would have to know calculus and differential equations and all the complexities of electromagnetic theory. But still, even the youngest child can turn on a radio.

The same is true of the *Mitzvos.* A lifetime of study might lead you to begin to understand their significance. But anyone can put them on and receive the signal.

In the following sections, we will explore the meaning of a number of rules governing Tefillin. In doing so, we must bear in mind that this is not mere symbolism, but an analogue of the very forces underlying the purpose of creation.

We must also keep in mind that everything discussed here reflects only a very small fraction of their true significance.

Let us now examine one seemingly trivial example.

By A Hair

G-d Himself gave existence to the side of Evil and allows it to exist.

We must therefore not take it lightly, but safeguard ourselves so that it does not denounce us.

We give the side of Evil a small place in our most holy realm. For all its power ultimately comes from the Holy.

This is the mystery of the hair of the Calf inside the Tefillin.

This hair is allowed to show on the outside, but so short as not to cause defilement.

We must bring this hair into our highest sanctuary and give it a place, in order that it not denounce us.

(Zohar, Pekudey 237b)

❀ ❀ ❀

If you look carefully at the head Tefillin, you will see four very short hairs, coming out near the base, between the third and fourth sections.

In the section "What are Tefillin," we mentioned that one of the basic rules of Tefillin require that the parchments be tied with the hair of a kosher animal. The Tefillin may be perfect in every other respect, but if this hair is missing, they *are posul* and unfit for use.

It is customary to use the hair of a calf to bind the parchments. It is also necessary to pass these hairs through a small opening in the Tefillin so that they be visible on the outside. The length of hair showing on the outside is less than the length of a barleycorn.[23]

This is certainly one of the strangest rules involving Tefillin. Yet, the significance of this hair leads us to understand some of the most profound concepts of Judaism. It is intimately bound to the question of good and evil.

Again, let us begin our discussion with a question.

Why does G-d allow evil to exist? Why did He allow for the possibility of evil in the first place?

In order to understand this, we must go back to an earlier discussion. As we mentioned earlier, one of the most profound ways in which man resembles his Creator is in his possession of free will. This free will is one of the most basic ingredients of creation.

But just as man must have free will, he must also have freedom of choice. A man locked up in prison may have the same free will as anyone else, but there is little that he can do with it. For man to resemble his Creator to the greatest possible degree, he must exist in an arena where he has the maximum freedom of choice. The more man resembles G-d in His omnipotence, the closer he can resemble Him in his free choice of the good.

To make this freedom of choice real, G-d also had to create the possibility of evil.[24] If nothing but good were possible, it would produce no benefit. To use the Talmudic metaphor, it would be like carrying a lamp in broad daylight.[25]

The *Zohar* thus states, "The advantage of wisdom comes from folly, just as that of light comes from darkness. If there were no darkness, then light would not be discernible, and would produce no benefit. . . . Thus, it is written (Eccl. 7:14), 'G-d has made one thing opposite the other.'"[26]

G-d therefore told His prophet (Isa. 45:7), "I form light and create darkness, I make peace and create evil.'

Originally, G-d gave Evil just barely enough power to exist. Its existence literally hung by a hair. It was only man's evil deeds that strengthened it and allowed it to grow.

This is the hair in G-d's Tefillin.

It is the hair of a calf. The Golden Calf is one of archetypes of Evil.

Hair itself is something dead. You can cut your hair and

not feel a thing. Yet, it emanates from the living. Its root stems from life.

The same is true of evil. Although it in itself is dead, it ultimately stems from the Source of all life. Nothing can exist without G-d.

G-d's very purpose required the existence of evil. Thus, the hair is right inside His head Tefillin.

But it is only a hair. Evil is only given a hairsbreadth of G-d's life force.

This hair ultimately connects all evil to the Holy. Therefore, it is also the channel through which all evil can be brought back to the Holy and redeemed.

No matter how much evil a man does, G-d's hand is always open to receive him when he repents. When a man returns to G-d, all the evil he has done can be turned to good.[27]

Here again, the Tefillin play a profound role.

The main good that G-d offers us is in a transcendental realm beyond this life. It is where man experiences the closeness to G-d that was His ultimate purpose in creation. This is called *Gan Eden,* Paradise, and the World to Come.

However, for the man who has done evil and remained far from G-d, this is also a time when he must face his Maker. He must experience the burning shame of one who has rebelled against G-d. This burning shame is what we call the fires of *Gehenom.* [28]

The Talmud[29] teaches us that a man who is not utterly sinful experiences *Gehenom* for a mere moment and is then redeemed. This is alluded to in the passage (1 Sam. 2:6), "G-d kills and revives, He brings one down to *Sh-ol,* and brings him up again." It is also the meaning of the verse (Zech. 13:9), "I will bring . . . them through fire, and refine them like silver, and assay them like gold."

This is only true, however, when a person wears Tefillin. The hair of the Tefillin serves as a bond, linking even the evil man to the Holy, and through it he can be redeemed. A sinner who wears Tefillin may descend to *Gehenom,* but he is immediately purified and refined. All the evil he has done can be redeemed and returned to the Holy.

By A Hair □ 267

The man who never wears Tefillin does not have this means of redemption.

The Talmud calls him a sinner with his body — the hair binding the material to the spiritual has been broken.

We are taught that the man who does not wear Tefillin cannot escape *Gehenom* unharmed. The Talmud says that "his soul is burned and the ashes scattered under the feet of the righteous," as alluded to in the verse (Malachi 3:21), "And you shall tread upon the wicked, for they shall be ashes under the soles of your feet." They might leave *Gehenom,* but they remain so filled with unredeemed evil that they cannot fully return to the Holy.[30] They do not have this one hair of the Tefillin, and cannot redeem their evil.

This hair therefore remains a lifeline, keeping one in contact with the Holy at all times.

Even if a man sins, as long as he maintains the link of the Tefillin. he can still bring himself back to G-d.

As long as you maintain this hairsbreadth of Godliness, you can always return. . .

The Mystery of Tefillin

Now that we have explored some general aspects of Tefillin in depth, we can look at some of its details.[31] As we have already mentioned, every single detail is intimately linked with the very mystery of creation and existence.

In this section, we will present some very deep concepts. But it is important to remember that all this is less than a drop in the ocean of Truth.

The number four is very closely linked with Tefillin. There are four parchments inside four boxes. The shape of Tefillin is a four-sided square. The head Tefillin knot is in the shape of a Dalet, the fourth letter of the Hebrew alphabet. There is an unusual four-headed *Shin* on the head Tefillin.

The number four represents the four stages through which all creation is brought into existence. These are represented by the four letters of the Tetragrammaton, G-d's Name *Yud Kay Vav Kay.* They are: emanation, creation, formation, and completion, alluded to in the verse (Isa. 43:7), "All that is called by My Name, for My glory (1), I have created it (2), I have formed it (3), and I have completed it.(4) [32]

We will also come across the number seven, as in the seven windings around the arm. These represent the seven *Midos,* the emanations through which G-d guides the world. They are the seven steps linking G-d to His creation and represented in the seven days of creation. The seven emanations are also represented by the seven branches of the *Menorah.* They are alluded to in the passage (1 Chr. 29:11), "Yours, O G-d, are the greatness (1), the power (2), and the glory (3), the victory (4) and the splendor (5), for all that is in heaven and earth (6); Yours, O G-d, is the Kingdom (7)."[33]

Everything in the Tefillin is made from an animal product. Man is only perfected through his animal nature, that is, through his physical body. Man's main link with G-d is through the physical observance of His commandments.

Everything in Tefillin must be made only from kosher animal products. The physical can be raised to the Godly only when it is not intermingled with evil.

Tefillin begin with four parchments. These must be perfectly white. This alludes to the Infinite Light at the beginning of creation.

For any creation to exist, this Light had to be modulated and constricted. This is represented by the jet black letters written on the white parchment — "black fire on white fire."[34]

The fact that the letters are intelligent symbols teaches us that this modulation and constriction was through the supernal Intelligence.

The parchments are bound with the hair of a calf. This represents the power of evil, as discussed in the previous section. The very purpose of creation is bound by the necessity of evil in order to give man free will.

Ultimately, G-d's ways are hidden from man. We can sometimes see what G-d does, but only dimly perceive His purpose. The parchments are therefore hidden in a black box.

Scientists sometimes have to deal with a process that they cannot understand. They can, however, measure what goes into this process and what comes out. In such a case, they call this process a "black box." Tefillin are literally such a "black box."

The Tefillin must be square. Our sages teach us that the square is the archetype of that which is man made rather than natural.[35] The ultimate goal depends on man.[36]

The Tefillin boxes must be sewn with the veins of a kosher animal. Our sages teach us that there are 365 main veins in the body, corresponding to the 365 days of the year.[37] The boxes are sewn with twelve stitches, representing the twelve months of the year.[38] A most essential ingredient of creation is time, which makes our world an arena of activity. Only in such a world can G-d's purpose be fulfilled.

The head Tefillin are inscribed with the letter *Shin*. On

the right side, it is the usual three-headed *Shin,* while on the left, it contains four heads.

This *Shin* is the first letter of G-d's Name, *Sh-dai,* which is spelled out by the letters of the Tefillin. This Name is associated with channel of G-d's providence *(Yesod).* The *Shin* on the head Tefillin indicates that G-d's purpose governs all providence.

The two letters *Shin* on the head Tefillin have three and four heads respectively. This gives us a total of seven, representing the seven Midos, or emanations. They appear in letters, intelligent symbols, indicating that we are dealing with the intelligent reason and purpose behind all providence.

In the letter *Shin,* all the heads are connected to a single base. This shows that all forces are ultimately directed toward one goal.[39]

The two straps emanating from the head Tefillin to the right and left represent the two basic forces of creation, love and judgment. While sometimes G-d's love would dictate mercy, His judgment demands retribution. Ultimately, G-d's justice is a combination of the two. This is represented by the knot, binding the two sides together.

The straps are then allowed to dangle to the lower parts of the body. G-d's justice extends to even the lowest levels of creation.

The hand Tefillin are worn on the left arm. The right hand is love and the left is judgment. G-d's love is given freely, but His judgment is dictated by His purpose.

The head Tefillin have four compartments, while the hand Tefillin consist of just one. All four levels of existence are directed toward a single goal.

The hand Tefillin are bound with a knot in the shape of the letter Yud. This letter always symbolizes the ultimate good in the World to Come.[40] G-d's action is guided by His ultimate goal which is this Future World.

The Yud is also the final letter of the *Name Sh-dai,* the Name associated with G-d's providence. Together with the *Shin* of the head Tefillin, and the *Dalet* of its knot, the Tefillin spell out this Name.

The *Dalet* in the knot represents G-d's justice in all His actions.

The Yud represents the final stage, where this justice is expressed in deed.

The seven windings on the arm represent the seven emanations, paralleling the seven days of creation. It is through these seven stages that all things proceed from G-d.

The seven rings coiled in a descending spiral represent G-d's ways in guiding His world. They end in three rings around the middle finger, representing the threefold betrothal between G-d and Israel, as discussed in the first section. This betrothal is the goal of the entire process of history. The ultimate betrothal will take place in the Messianic Era and in the World to Come.

For Girls Only

I understand that there may be some girls reading this. They are most probably saying, "All this is very fine. Tefillin are a most wonderful way to bind yourself to G-d. But it is only for boys. Where do we come in?"

On a most simple level, the reason for the commandments is to establish a link with G-d. The most profound way to do this is to resemble Him.

There is one unique way that women resemble G-d in a way that no man could ever hope to. Only a woman can create within her body. Only a woman can bear a child. In this sense, a woman partakes of G-d's attributes more intimately than any man.

The Kabbalists teach us that the hand Tefillin represent the feminine element. The single hollow can be said to represent the womb, and the coils, the umbilical cord.

What man partakes of with an object, woman partakes of with her very body.

The box of Tefillin is called a *Bayis* — literally a house. The woman also has her *Bayis* — the home in which she raises a family. One could say that a woman's home is her Tefillin.

Women resemble G-d through their Tefillin, just as man does through his. The entire world is G-d's house, and the attribute that tends to it is called the *Shechinah* or Divine Presence. It is interesting to note that the word *Shechinah is* of the feminine gender. The Kabbalists call it the *Akeres HaBayis* — literally, the Mistress of the house.

There are two basic elements in Judaism, the home and the synagogue. Unlike other religions where the church is primary, Judaism treats the home and synagogue as being co-equal.

Some of our most important rituals belong exclusively to the home, such as the *Seder,* the *Succah,* the Sabbath table, and the Chanukah lamp. The continuity of Judaism rests on the home more than anything else. As our sages teach us, "If there are no lambs, there can be no rams."[41]

This *Bayis* — the home is a woman's Tefillin. It is her contribution to the overall picture of G-d's purpose.

It is interesting to note that G-d told Moses "This is what you must say to the family of Jacob and teach the sons of Israel." (Exodus 19:3)[42] If the Torah does not enter the Jewish home first, there can be no continuity of Judaism.

This spirit of Torah in the Jewish home *(Bayis) is* the same as the parchments of Torah in the Tefillin box *(Bayis).* But this is the domain of the woman.

Tefillin In The Classics

◄§ In The Talmud

Tefillin are Israel's strength. It is written (Deut. 28:10), "And the peoples of the earth shall see that G-d's Name is called upon you, and they shall be awed by you."

Berachos 6a

※ ※ ※

A man who washes his hands, puts on Tefillin, says the *Sh'ma* and prays is considered to have built an alter and offered sacrifice. He is also said to have truly accepted upon himself the yoke of heaven.

Ibid. 14b, 15a

※ ※ ※

Rabbi Jeremiah saw that Rabbi Zera was very jubilant. He asked, "Is it not written (Prov. 14:23), 'In seriousness there is profit?' " Rabbi Zera answered, "I rejoice for I have worn Tefillin today."

Ibid. 30b

※ ※ ※

Every single Jew is surrounded by seven *Mitzvos*. He has Tefillin on his arm and head, a *Mezuzah* on his door, and four *Tzitzis* on his garment. Thus, King David said (Psalm 119:164), "I will praise You each day with seven."

Tosefta, Berachos 6:31

A man must constantly touch his Tefillin and not take his mind from them.

Shabbos 12a

❀ ❀ ❀

One should be as dedicated in wearing Tefillin as Elisha, the Master of Wings. Once the government issued a decree that anyone wearing Tefillin should be put to death. Elisha defied the decree and publicly wore Tefillin. He was caught by one of the king's agents and captured. They asked him, "What is in your hand." Concealing his Tefillin, he replied, "A dove's wing." When they forced open his hand, they indeed found the wing of a dove in place of his Tefillin. From then on, he was called Elisha, the Master of Wings.

Ibid. 49a

❀ ❀ ❀

Many Jews risked their lives in order to wear Tefillin.

Ibid. 130a

❀ ❀ ❀

It is written (Eccl. 9:8), "Let your garments always be white, and let your head never lack oil." This speaks of the *Tzitzis* and Tefillin.

Ibid. 153a

❀ ❀ ❀

Man always needs a sign of his bond with G-d. The Sabbath itself is such a sign, but on weekdays, this sign is Tefillin.

Eruvin 96a

❀ ❀ ❀

One who does not wear Tefillin is counted among those banned by G-d.

Pesachim 113b

❀ ❀ ❀

Tefillin are called the glory of Israel.

Succah 25a

❁ ❁ ❁

It is said that Rabbi Yochanan ben Zackai never walked four steps without Tefillin.

Ibid. 42a

❁ ❁ ❁

Who is a sinner with his body? One who never wears Tefillin.

Rosh HaShanah 17a

❁ ❁ ❁

The students asked Rabbi Ada ben Ahavah, "Why were you worthy of such long life?" He replied, "One reason is because I always wore Tefillin."

Taanis 20b

❁ ❁ ❁

Abraham told the King of Sodom (Gen. 14:23), "I will not even take a thread or a shoe strap." Because of this, G-d gave Abraham's children the threads of *Tzitzis* and the straps of Tefillin.

Sotah 44b

❁ ❁ ❁

The *Mitzvah* of Tefillin encompasses all others.

Kidushin 35a

❁ ❁ ❁

G-d Himself showed Moses the knot of Tefillin.

Minachos 35b

❁ ❁ ❁

The knot of the Tefillin is worn at the top, signifying the elevation of Israel. It is toward the body, showing Israel's closeness to G-d.

Ibid.

❁ ❁ ❁

G-d so loved Israel that He surrounded them with *Mitzvos:* Tefillin on the arm and head, Tzitzis on their garment, and a *Mezuzah* on their door.

Ibid. 43b

❁ ❁ ❁

A man wearing Tefillin on his arm and head, *Tzitzis* on his garment, and a *Mezuzah* on his doorpost, is certain not to sin.

Ibid.

❁ ❁ ❁

One who does not wear Tefillin violates eight commandments.

Ibid 44a

❁ ❁ ❁

He who wears Tefillin is worthy of long life.

Ibid.

◆§ In The Midrash

It was a time of religious persecution and a man was being beaten to death. He said, "I defile their ban and risked my life to wear Tefillin. Let me now die doing the will of my heavenly Father."

VaYikra Rabbah 32:1

❁ ❁ ❁

It is written (Psalms 91:7), "A thousand shall fall at your side . . . it shall not come near you." Through the *Mitzvah* of Tefillin, one is guarded from evil by a thousand angels.

BaMidbar Rabbah 12:3

❁ ❁ ❁

It is written (Cant. 2:6), "Let His left hand be under my head, and His right hand embrace me." G-d thus embraces man who wears Tefillin.

Shir HaShirim Rabbah 2:17

🦋 🦋 🦋

It is written *(Ibid. 4:1),* "Behold you are beautiful My love." The beauty of Israel before G-d is Tefillin.

Ibid. 4:1

🦋 🦋 🦋

It is written *(Ibid. 8:6),* "Set Me for a seal on your heart, as a seal on your arm." The Tefillin are this seal of G-d.

Ibid. 8:4

🦋 🦋 🦋

It is written (Ex. 14:29), "And the waters were a wall to their right and to their left." The *Mezuzah* forms a wall to Israel's right, and the Tefillin to their left.

Mechilta ad loc.

🦋 🦋 🦋

Wearing Tefillin is like reading the Torah.

Pesikta Zutrasa, Sh'mos 13

🦋 🦋 🦋

The Jewish people said to G-d, "We would like to immerse ourselves in the Torah day and night, but do not have the time." G-d replied, "Keep the *Mitzvah* of Tefillin, and I will count it as if you spent all your time with My Torah."

Midrash Tehillim 1

🦋 🦋 🦋

The wicked say (Psalms 2:3), "Let us break their bands asunder and cast away their thongs." They "break their bands asunder" and abandon the Tefillin on their arms, and "cast away their thongs," the Tefillin on their heads.

Ibid. 2

❀ ❀ ❀

The Messiah will come to give the world *Mitzvos* such as Tefillin.

Ibid. 21

❧ In The Kaballah

Happy is the man who wears Tefillin and fathoms their mystery.

Zohar 1:129a

❀ ❀ ❀

When a man wears Tefillin and *Tzitzis,* he enters a realm where the Holy One Himself surrounds him with the mystery of the Highest Faith.

Ibid. 1:140b

❀ ❀ ❀

When a man places Tefillin on his arm, he should stretch out his hand as if to draw in the Community of Israel and embrace it with his right arm. Thus, it is written (Cant. 2:6), "Let His left hand be under my head, and His right arm embrace me."

Ibid. 3:55a

❀ ❀ ❀

The man who wears Tefillin is crowned as on high. He enters the perfection of Unity, and so resembles his Creator.

Ibid. 3:81a

❀ ❀ ❀

He who wears Tefillin is called a king on earth, even as G-d is called a King in heaven.

Ibid. 3:169b

❧ ❧ ❧

Man is bound to the Mother of Israel with two signs, the Tefillin and the Covenant of Abraham.

Tikuney Zohar 7a

❧ ❧ ❧

When a man wears Tefillin, a voice proclaims to all the angels of the Chariot who watch over prayer, "Give honor to the image of the King, the man who wears Tefillin."

Ibid. 55 (124a)

❧ ❧ ❧

A man wearing Tefillin is enveloped by the supernal Mind, and the Divine Presence does not depart from him.

Ibid. 69 (159a)

❧ ❧ ❧

When a man wakes up in the morning and binds himself with the holy mark of Tefillin, four angels greet him as he leaves his door.

Zohar Chadash, Teruman 41b

❧ ❧ ❧

The Tefillin straps are like chains binding the Evil One.

Tikuney Zohar Chadash 101b

❧ ❧ ❧

There was a pious man who was very careful about always wearing Tefillin. When he died, the angels on high eulogized him with the verse (Deut. 33:21), "He kept G-d's righteousness and His ordinance with Israel."

◄§ With The Chasidim

It is told that the saintly Rabbi Levi Yitzchok of Berdichov once saw a simple Jew drop his Tefillin. The man gently lifted them up and lovingly kissed them. The Rabbi then raised his hands and said, "Lord of the universe: The Jewish people are Your Tefillin. You have dropped them and let them lie on the ground for more than two thousand years, trampled by their enemies. Why do You not pick them up? Why do You not do as much as the most simple Jew? Why?"

☙ ☙ ☙

It is told in the name of the blessed Baal Shem Tov that the *Mitzvah* of Tefillin is so holy it can bring man to a yearning that will make him depart this world. He must therefore bind them with straps, holding body and soul together.

Sefer Baal Shem Tov, VeEsChanan 83

☙ ☙ ☙

Rabbi Nachman of Breslov once heard that the saintly Rabbi Levi Yitzchok of Berdichov was forced to wander about. He called his scribe and asked him to examine his Tefillin. He explained that a *Tzadik* like Rabbi Levi Yitzchok is the glory of his generation, and as such, is the Tefillin of the entire Jewish people. If a defect in our people's Tefillin forces him to so wander, all Tefillin must be examined for a blemish.

Yemey Moharnat 28b

☙ ☙ ☙

God desires that we wear Tefillin. Therefore, when we wear them, we are enveloped by His desire. This is true of all other *Mitzvos* as well.

Lekutey Moharan 34:4

☙ ☙ ☙

Tefillin can help a man master the perfection of speech.

Ibid. 38:1

❦ ❦ ❦

Tefillin can bring a person to Truth.

Ibid. 47

❦ ❦ ❦

The light of Tefillin illuminates the holiness of the Land of Israel.

Ibid.

❦ ❦ ❦

Every day, G-d grants us signs, showing us the way of truth. Through Tefillin you can attain the wisdom to recognize these signs.

Ibid. 54:3

❦ ❦ ❦

When you overcome evil desires, you break the seal of the Evil One. You are then worthy of the holy seal of Tefillin and the deep insight they provide.

Lekutey Moharan Tanina 5:7

❦ ❦ ❦

G-d's providence is revealed through Tefillin.

Ibid. 40

❦ ❦ ❦

The boxes of Tefillin represent wisdom, and the straps, the fear of G-d. You can only bind yourself to wisdom through the fear of G-d.

Ibid. 77

❦ ❦ ❦

The Tefillin straps encompass your faith, protecting it from the Outside Forces. When your mind and soul are thus safeguarded, you can attain a perception of the innermost Light.

Lekutey Eitzos, Tefillin 1

❁ ❁ ❁

Tefillin are the innermost Light and glory of Israel.

Ibid. 4

❁ ❁ ❁

Tefillin can bring your thoughts into the World to Come.

Ibid. 5

How Tefillin Are Made

1. The finest Tefillin are made from a single piece of leather. Here we see the first step in the process of making the hand Tefillin. A single piece of leather is pressed over a wooden form.

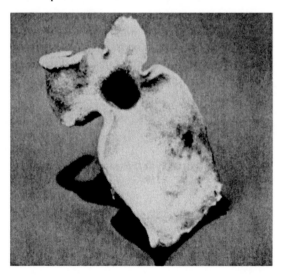

2. Another view of the Tefillin leather after initial forming.

3. The *Bayit* has now been formed and squared. It must be trimmed, smoothed, blackened and sown.

4. A completed *Bayit* of the hand Tefillin. Note the Yud shaped knot in the strap.

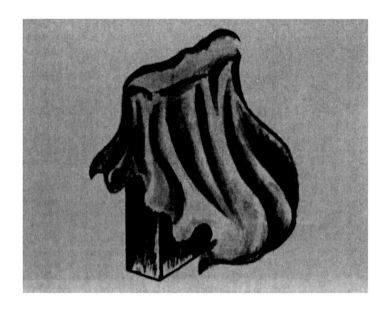

5. The head Tefillin require a much more complex process. Again, we begin by stretching the leather over a wooden form.

6. The four sections are then formed by stretching the leather over four separate wooden forms.

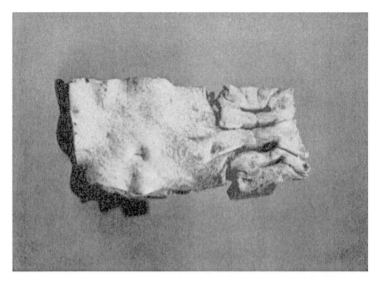

7. Bottom view of head Tefillin in initial stage. Note that even the four walls of the inner chambers are made of the same piece of leather.

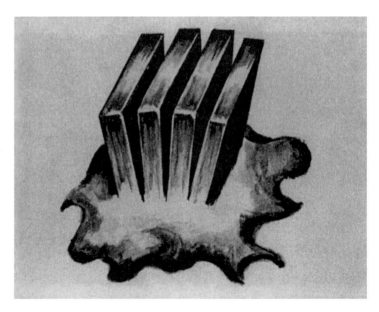

8. The separate sections are then pressed into a squared form.

288 □ *Tefillin*

9. The entire *Bayit* is then placed in a press to give it its final cubic form.

10. The *Bayit* pressed into its final form.

11. Another view of the *Bayit*. Note the four compartments for the four parchments. The *Bayit* must now be trimmed.

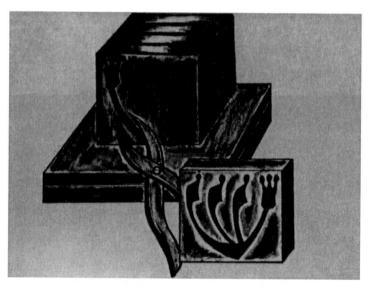

12. Pincers are used to draw out the *Shin* on the *Bayit*. The engraved mold illustrated on the lower right is then pressed onto the rough *Shin* to give it a perfect shape. On the right side. this is a usual three headed *Shin*, but on the left, it has four heads. This is the only place where a four-headed *Shin is* ever used.

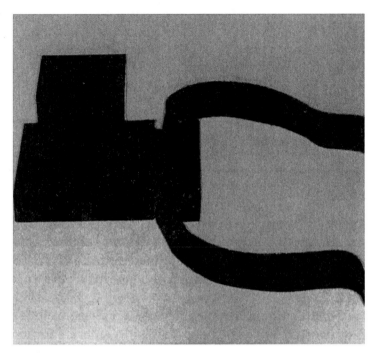

13. A completed *Bayit of* the head Tefillin.

The Knots of Tefillin

Occasions may arise when you may have to replace or adjust the straps (retzuos) of your Tefillin. This, of course, is best done by a duly ordained scribe (Sofer) or by your rabbi. In some cases, however, you may have to do it yourself.

The most common instance is when you have to loosen or tighten the straps of your head Tefillin to assure a perfect fit. This is shown on Plate 3. The procedure for permanently fixing the Yud shaped knot on the hand Tefillin is shown in Plate 5. Also included is the procedure for making the knots for right handed Tefillin, to be worn by left handed individuals (Plate 7).

If you are replacing the Tefillin straps, it is important to remember that these straps or retzuos must be made especially for Tefillin. They should therefore only be purchased from a most reliable source.

Before making any of the knots, you should say, "I am making this knot (kesher) especially for the Mitzvah of Tefillin."

In an emergency, you may take the straps from one pair of Tefillin and affix them on another. You can similarly transfer the straps from hand Tefillin to those of the head. To reverse this procedure and use the straps from the head Tefillin for that of the hand, however, is forbidden. The head Tefillin have a higher degree of holiness, and this may not be reduced. A number of pictures here are reproduced or copied from *The Tefillin Handbook,* by Rabbi Shmuel Rubeinstein (New York, 5730) with permission.

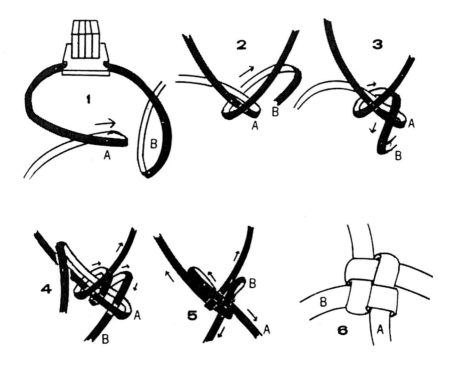

PLATE 1.
THE HEAD TEFILLIN KNOT: ASHKENAZIC CUSTOM

This plate indicates how to make the Ashkenazic or double *Dalet* type knot, shown in figure 5, page 27.

1. Place the strap through the Tefillin, and center it so that the left side of the strap extends some five inches further down than the right side. (Since the two straps are crossed in the knot, this will result in the right side being somewhat longer than the left.) Then form a loop on each side.
2. Slide the left loop (A) through the right (B).
3. Draw strap (B) through the loop in (A).
4. Loop (B) around, and draw it through the same loop (A) again.
5. Now slip strap (A) over strap (B) and through the loop it forms.
6. Pull both ends tight, and the knot or *Kesher* is complete.

The left hand strap should now reach to your belt, and the right strap a few inches lower. If the strap is too large or small for your head, adjust it according to the instructions on Plate 3.

The Knots of Tefillin □ 293

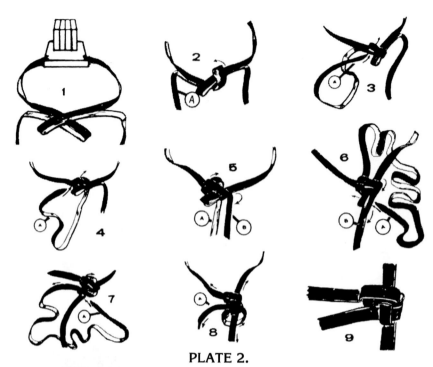

PLATE 2.
THE HEAD TEFILLIN KNOT: SEFARDIC CUSTOM

This plate indicates how to make the Sefardic or single *Dalet* knot, shown in figure 6, page 27.

1. Place the strap through the *Ma'abarta* of the Tefillin, and center it so that the right hand strap extends some fourteen inches further than the left. (The straps are not crossed in this type knot, and some eight to ten inches of the right hand side will be used up in making the knot.) Now loop both straps, placing the right loop over the left.
2. Fold the (lower) right loop over the left.
3. Slide the right strap (A) through the loop as shown.
4,5. Repeat this process, drawing strap (A) through the same loop again.
6. Slip strap (A) through lower loop as indicated. Then fold over strap (B) so that it is parallel to that loop.
7,8. Draw strap (A) through the same loop once again, tying down the folded over strap (B).
9. Pull both ends tight. When you put on the Tefillin, the left hand strap should reach your belt, and the right side, a few inches further. If the strap is too tight or loose on your head, adjust according to instructions on plate 3.

PLATE 3. ADJUSTING THE HEAD TEFILLIN KNOT

ASHKENAZIC CUSTOM

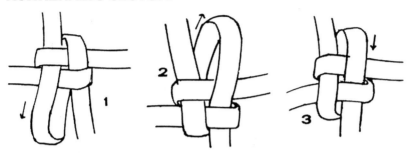

Tightening the head Tefillin.

Loosening the head Tefillin.

SEFARDIC CUSTOM

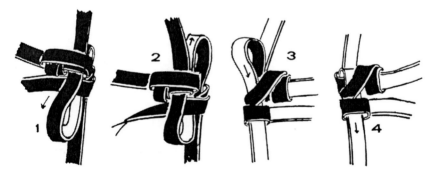

Steps for tightening the head Tefillin. Note that only the right hand strap is made to slide.

To loosen the strap, the exact opposite procedure is followed. The sequence is then 4,3,2,1.

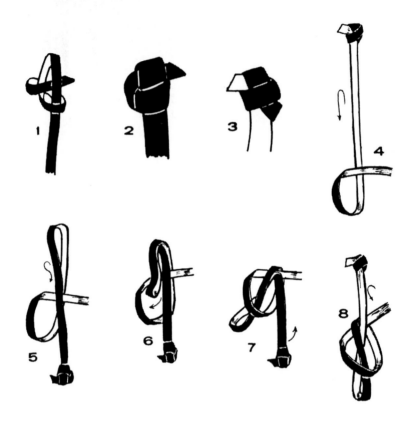

PLATE 4.
THE HAND TEFILLIN KNOT: ASHKENAZIC CUSTOM

1. The *Yud* shaped knot is made at the very end of the strap. It is actually a simple figure-of-eight knot.

2,3. Front and back views of the Yud shaped knot.

4. Make a loop approximately 12 inches from the Yud shaped knot.

5. Fold strap down, forming a second loop.

6,7. Fold over top of loop, bringing it through lower loop.

8. You now have a loose slip knot.

 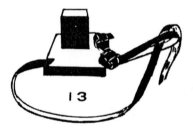

9, 10. Now bring the *Yud* shaped end through the right side of the loop. This stabilizes the knot so that it does not "slip."

11. Tighten the knot as indicated in diagram.

12. Then place the unknotted end of the strap through the *Ma'abarta,* from right to left.

13. Draw strap through *Ma'abarta* until Yud shaped knot is touching the Tefillin box or *Bayis.* Then draw loose end through loop. The Tefillin are now ready to wear. Tefillin made in this manner are meant to be wound *toward* the body.

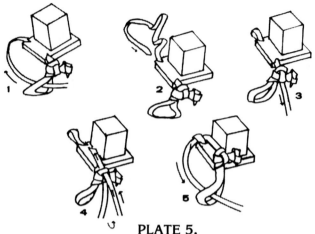

PLATE 5.
FIXING *YUD* TO *BAYIS*

The *Yud* shaped knot must always be in contact with the *Bayis* or Tefillin box. In Ashkenazic Tefillin, however, the strap has a tendency to slip, pulling the *Yud* away from the *Bayis*. Here is a procedure often used by *Sofrim* (scribes) to remedy this situation.

1. Remove strap *(retzua)* from loop.

2,3. Pass strap back through the *Ma'abarta* forming a new loop on the left hand side of the Tefillin.

4. Now bring the strap through the top of the Tefillin knot, as indicated.

5. Draw the strap through the new loop on the left hand side of the Tefillin, and pull it tight. This will permanently fix the *Yud* next to the *Bayis.* Then draw the loose end through the loop again.

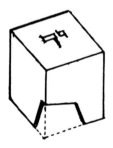

The Yud shaped knot should not be separated from the Tefillin even when they are put away. It is therefore customary to cut away the Tefillin cover so that it not separate the two. This is done in the manner shown in this illustration.

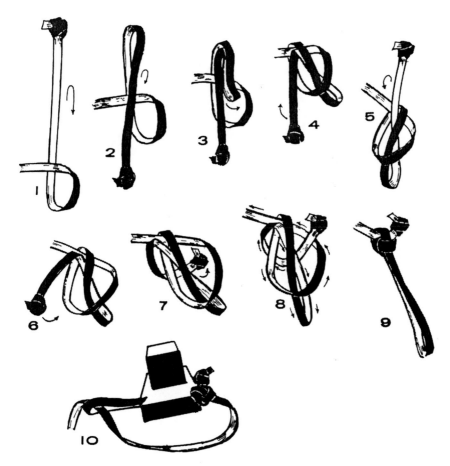

PLATE 6.
THE HAND TEFILLIN KNOT: SEFARDIC CUSTOM

1. Make *Yud* shaped knot as in figures 1-3, plate 4. Then make a loop approximately 12 inches from this knot.
2. Fold over strap, forming a second loop.
3,4. Fold over top of loop, and draw it through lower loop.
5. You now have a slip knot.
6,7. Now bring *Yud* shaped end through the left side of the loop. This stabilizes the knot so that it does not "slip."
8. Tighten the knot as indicated.
9. Draw the loop through the *Ma'abarta,* and then bring the loose end of the strap through this loop. The Tefillin are now ready to wear. Tefillin made in this manner are meant to be wound *away from* the body.

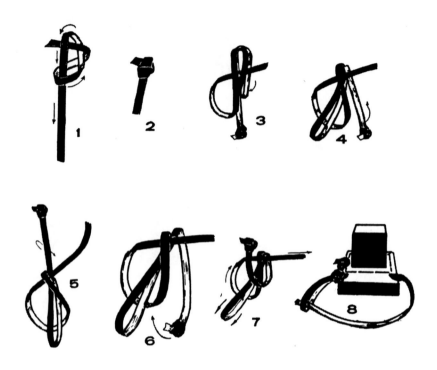

PLATE 7.
RIGHT HANDED TEFILLLIN,
FOR LEFT HANDED INDIVIDUAL

Tefillin are always worn on the "weaker" hand. A left handed individual must therefore wear Tefillin on his right hand. The knot for such Tefillin must be reversed accordingly.

ASHKENAZIC CUSTOM

1,2. The Yud shaped knot is a mirror image of that used in ordinary Tefillin. Instead of pointing to the right, the tip points to the left.

3-5. The slip knot is made as in figures 6-8, plate 4, except that it is a mirror image of that knot.

6,7. The strap is then drawn through the right side of the loop and tightened.

8. The loose side of the strap is then drawn through the Ma'abarta, and then through the loop. Note that the Ashkenazic knot for right handed' Tefillin is very much like the Sefardic knot for left handed Tefillin (Plate 6), except that the Yud shaped knot is reversed.

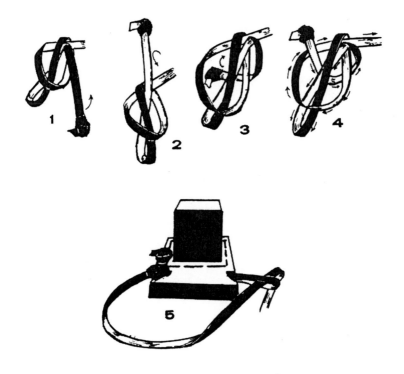

SEFARDIC CUSTOM

1-4. The Yud shaped knot is made as in figures 1,2, above. The knot is otherwise exactly the same as that for Ashkenazic left handed Tefillin, illustrated in plate 4.

5. The loop is then passed through the *Ma'abarta* as shown.

The Laws of Tefillin...
Some Final Questions

1. What is the earliest that Tefillin can be put on in the morning?

Tefillin can be put on as soon as it begins to get light in the morning. The sky should be light enough so that one can recognize a person's face from about four paces.[1]

2. What if I do not put on Tefillin in the morning? How late can I put them on?

You can put on Tefillin all day until sunset.[2] If you have not put on Tefillin until after sunset, you may do so until dark, but without saying the blessings.[3]

3. What if I do not have Tefillin in the morning?

You may pray without them, and put them on later when you obtain a pair.

When you put them on later in the day, you should say the Sh'ma or a Psalm.[4]

4. What if I take the head Tefillin out first?

You must still put on the hand Tefillin first.[5]

5. What if I accidently put on the head Tefillin first?

You need not take it off to put on the hand Tefillin.[6]

6. What if I accidently talk while putting on Tefillin?

If you talk between the time you say the blessing over the hand Tefillin and the time you have finished tightening the head Tefillin, you must repeat the entire process. You first loosen the hand Tefillin slightly, say the blessing over it, and then finish putting them on as usual.[7]

If you follow the Sefardic custom and do not usually say a blessing over the head Tefillin, you must do so in case of an interruption. Those who follow this custom, however, need not loosen the hand Tefillin again.[8]

If your talking involved your putting on of Tefillin, you need not repeat the blessing in any case.[9]

7. *What if I only have half a set?*

The hand and head Tefillin are each a separate *Mitzvah,* and therefore, each one may be put on alone.

If you put on the hand Tefillin alone, you say its usual blessing.

If you put on the head Tefillin alone, you must say both blessings.

If you follow the Sefardic custom, however, then you only say the blessing *Al Mitzvas Tefillin.*

The same is true if you have an injury and can only put on one of the pair.[10]

8. *What if I put on Tefillin more than once during the day?*

You must say a blessing each time you put them on.[11]

9. *What if I take my Tefillin off in the middle of the service?*

You need not repeat the blessing when you put them on for the remainder of the service.[12]

If you take them off to go to the bathroom, however, you must repeat the blessings, since it is forbidden to wear Tefillin in the bathroom.[13]

10. *What if I forget to say the blessing when I put on Tefillin?*

You may say them when you remember.[14] It is best, however, to move the Tefillin off to the side a bit before saying the blessing, and then to immediately replace them.[15]

11. *How long must I keep the Tefillin on?*

It is accepted practice to wear them during the entire morning service, until the very end.[16] It is particularly important that they be worn while you say the *Sh'ma* and *Shemonah Esreh.* [17]

12. *What if a strap tears?*

This is a somewhat complex question, and it is best that you consult your rabbi. The following, however, is a general guideline.

If the strap on the hand Tefillin tears, you may say a blessing over it if there is enough strap left to tie the Tefillin in place and wind it three times around the middle finger, even if there is not enough for the windings around the arm.[18] If it is shorter than this, you may put it on without a blessing, as long as there is enough strap left to bind the Tefillin on the arm.[19]

If the strap on the head Tefillin tears, you may put it on with a blessing as long as at least eight inches remains hanging down. If the amount hanging down on either side is shorter than this, you may still put it on, but without a blessing.[20]

In any case, whenever a strap tears, you must get it repaired as soon as possible.

13. What if the black rubs off or fades from my Tefillin?

If the black comes off the *Batim* (boxes) you may wear the Tefillin without a blessing.[21]

If the black fades or rubs off the straps, however, the Tefillin become unfit for use.[22] If some black color remains, however, you may wear them without a blessing.[23]

In any case, it is best to consult your rabbi. You should have the Tefillin reblackened as soon as possible, especially where the straps are involved.

14. What if my Tefllin become damaged?

Wherever any damage is evident, you must consult your rabbi or a competent scribe.

NOTES

WHY TEFILLIN

1. See *Sefer Mitzvos HaGadol (S'mag)*, positive commandments #3; *Orech Chaim* 25:5.
2. *Lekutey Moharan* 4:6. Cf. *Berachos* 6b, *Shabbos* 30b; *Rashi ad loc.* *"Mitzvos."*
3. *Kiddushin* 35a.
4. *Sanhedrin* 88b.
5. *Sefer HaChinuch* 421; *Yad, Tefillin* 1:3, 3:1.
6. *Orech Chaim* 32:7.
7. *Ibid.* 32:3. Cf. *Yerushalmi, Megillah* 1:9 (12a).
8. *Ibid.* 32:44. The *Yad* and *Sefer HaChinuch* list that the parchments must be wrapped in another blank parchment or cloth. We, however, follow the opinion of the *Rosh*, who states that this is not necessary. See *Magen Avraham* 32:60, *Biur Halachah Ibid.* *"VeKorachah."*
9. *Ibid.* 32:39. See *Minachos* 35a.
10. *Ibid.* 32:42.
11. *Ibid.* 32:44.
12. *Ibid.* Here we follow the opinion of the *Shulchan Aruch* which lists the *Titurah* and the *Ma'abarta* separately.
13. *Ibid.* 32:49.
14. *Ibid.* 33:3.
15. *Ibid.* 32:52. The *Rambam* holds that only the *Dalet* is required, but *Rashi* holds that the *Yud* is also obligatory. See *Biur HaGra ad loc.*, *Shabbos* 62a, *Rashi*, *Minachos* 35b *"Kesner,"* *Tosefos Ibid.* *"Elu,"* *Mordechai Halchos Tefillin.*
16. *Minachos* 35b.
17. *Orech Chaim* 39:10, *Mishnah Berurah* 39:28.

USING TEFILLIN

18. *Magen Avraham* 27:12. Cf. *Zohar* 3:228b, *Yad, Tefillin* 3:12.

A DEEPER LOOK

1. *Kiddushin* 35a.
2. *Cf. Maggid Devarav LeYaakov* # 102, *Likutey Monaran* #64.
3. *Emunos VeDeyos* 1:4 end, 3:0, *Sefer HaYashar* 1, *Pardes Rimonim* 2:6, *EtzChaim, Shaar HaKellalim* 1, *Reshis Chochmah, Shaar HaTshuvah* #1, *Sh'nei Luchos HaBris, Bais Yisroel* (Jerusalem, 5720) 1:21b, *Shomrei Emunim (HaKadmon)* 2:13, *Derech HaShem* 1:2:1.
4. *Derech HaShem, Ibid.*
5. Cf. *Mechilta on Ex.* 14:29, *Bereshis Rabbah* 21:5, *Shir HaShirim Rabbah* 1:46; *Yad, Tshuvah* 5:1.
6. *Bereishis Rabbah* 1:2; *Tanchumah, Bereishis* 1, *Pirkei DeRabbi Eliezer* 3, *Tana DeVey Eliahu Rabbah* 21, *Zohar* 1:5a, 1:24b, 1:47a, 1:134a, 1:205b, 2:161b, 2:200a, 3:35b, 3:69b, 3:178a; *Bahir* 5.

7. *Mechilta, Rashi* on *Ex.* 19:18, *Tanchuma, Yisro* 13; *Bereshis Rabbah* 27:1, *Koheles Rabbah* 2:24.
8. *Tikuney Zohar* 17a.
9. See *Shaarey Orah* # 10, *Pardes Rimonim* 23:20.
10. See *Maharsha ad loc., Beur HaGolah (Maharal)* #4, *Bechaya* on *Ex.* 13:16.
11. *Shemos Rabbah* 38:5, *Koheles Rabbah* 1:9, *Sifri, Ekev* 47, *Tana DeVey Eliahu Rabbah* 14, *Rashi* on *Gen.* 1:1. Cf. *Berachos* 32b, *Tannis* 3b.
12. *Bereishis Rabbah* 2:1.
13. *Derech Mitzvosecha (Chabad), Tefillin* #2; *Iyun Yaakov Minachos* 35b (in *Even Yaakov* #5). Cf. *Yerushalmi Sanhedrin* 1:1 (1b), *Tanchuma Bereishis* 5, *Rashi* on *Gen.* 1:26.
14. *Berachos* 7a.
15. *Yad, Tshuvah* 6:5, *Moreh Nevuchim* 2:48.
16. See *Ralbag, Metzudos David, Malbim ad loc., Yalkut* 2:959. Cf. *Berachos* 55a; *Rashi ad loc.* "*Terichim,*" *Yalkut* 1:860; *Emunos VeDeyos* 4:7 end; *Manaratz Chayos, Megillah* 11a; *Radak* on *Jer.* 10:23.
17. *Emunos VeDeyos* 8:8. Cf. *VaYikra Rabbah* 25:8.
18. See *Moreh Nevuchim* 3:26.
19. *Yesod VeShoresh HaAvodah* 2:8.
20. See *Amud HaAvodah, Hakdamah Gedolah* # 31; Rabbi Yitzchok Ashlag, *Hakdaman P'nimis,* part I, 1:4 (p. 15).
21. See Rabbi Moshe Chaim Luzatto, *Pischey Chochmah VoDaas* #3.
22. *Likutey Amarim (Tanya)* 1:4, *Likutey Moharan* 33:4, 34:4.
23. *Orach Chaim* 32:44.
24. Cf. *Midrash Tehillim* 36:4, *Zohar* 1:23a, 2:184a, *Akedes Yitzchak* 70 (3:145b), *Etz Chaim, Shaar HaMelachim* 5, *Sefer Baal Shem Tov, Shemos* #9.
25. *Chullin* 60b.
26. *Zohar* 3:47b.
27. *Yoma* 86b.
28. *Ikkarim* 4:33, *Nishmas Chaim* 1:13. See my article, "On Immorality and the Soul," in *Intercom* 13:2 (Sivan, 5732).
29. *Rosh HaShanah* 17a.
30. *Ramban, Toras HaAdam, Shaar HaGamul, "VeAchshav,"* (Jerusalem, 5715) p. 78a.
31. See *Shemoneh Shaarim, Shaar HaKavanos, Inyan Tefillin; Shaar Maamarey Rashbi* (Ashlag, Jerusalem, 5721) p. 273 ff.; *Pri Etz Chaim, Shaar HaTefillin; Shnei Luchos HaBris, Mesechta Chullin* 1:185b, *Derech Mitzvosechta (Chabad)* p. 16b ff., *Likutey Halachos (Breslov,)* *Hilchos Tefillin.*
32. In a Kabbalistic sense, these are the four worlds, *Atzilus, Beriah, Yetzirah* and *Asiyah,* being respectively the worlds of *Sefiros,* souls, angels and the physical.
33. These are the last seven of the Ten *Sefiros.* The first three denote mental activity, and the last seven, action.
34. *Yerushalmi, Shekalim* 6:1 (25b), *Shir HaShirim Rabbah* 5:9, *Zohar* 2:84a, 2:114a, 2:226b, 3:132a, 3:154b, *Tikuney Zohar* 56 (90b).
35. *Yerushalmi Nedarim* 3:2 (9a).
36. See *Bahir* 114, *Elema Rabosai (Ramak)* 1:4:14 (29b).

37. *Zohar* 1:170b, *Targum* J. on *Gen.* 1:27, *Makkos* 24a.
38. *Orach Chaim* 32:51.
39. *Bahir* 81.
40. *Minachos* 29b, *Rashi* on *Gen.* 2:4.
41. *Yerushalmi, Sanhedrin* 10:2, *Bereishis Rabbah* 24:3, *VaYikra Rabbah* 11:7, *Rashi* on *Isa.* 8:18.
42. *Rashi* says "the family of Jacob" refers to the Jewish women.

THE LAWS OF TEFILLIN

1. *Shulchan Aruch, Orech Chaim* 30:1.
2. *Orech Chaim* 30:2. See *Mishnah Berurah* 37:6.
3. *Pri Megadim, Eshel Avraham* 30:7, *Mishnah Berurah* 30:3.
4. *Mishnah Berurah* 58:5.
5. *Orech Chaim* 25:6.
6. *Shaarey Teshuvah* 25:10, *Mishnah Berurah* 25:22; *Teshuvos Yaabatz* 125, *Shiurey Brachah* 25.
7. *Orech Chaim* 25:9, *Magen Avraham,* 25:15, *Mishnah Berurah* 25:32.
8. *Ibid.*
9. *Orech Chaim,* 25:10.
10. *Orech Chaim,* 26:1,2.
11. *Orech Chaim,* 26:12.
12. *Ibid. in Hagah.*
13. *Magen Avraham,* 25:22.
14. *Pri Megadim, Eshel Avraham* 25:12, *Mishnah Berurah* 25:26.15.Cf. *Magen Avraham* 25:15.
16. *Orech Chaim,* 25:13.
17. *Orech Chaim,* 25:4.
18. *Orech Chaim,* 27:8, *Mishnah Berurah,* 27:44.
19. *Magen David* 33:6, *Chayay Adam* 14:8.
20. *Mishnah Berurah* 27:44.
21. *Mishanh Berurah* 32:184.
22. *Biur Halachah* 33:3 "*Retzuos.*"
23. *Ibid.* "*Retzuos*" #2.

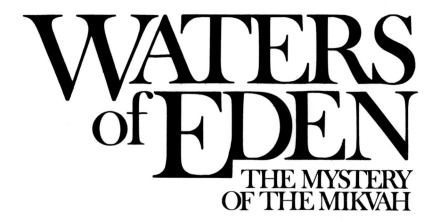

WATERS of EDEN

THE MYSTERY OF THE MIKVAH

ARYEH
KAPLAN

Introduction

*There are things that stand in heights of the universe,
yet people take them lightly.*

Talmud, Berachos 6b.

A friend of mine, who has visited Russia many times, tells of
a secret meeting he had with a young Jewish family in a
Russian city. After an involved discussion of the problems
facing the community, my friend gained the confidence of the
husband, a tall, sturdy man named Yaakov. As my friend was
preparing to leave, Yaakov said, "Wait, I have something that I
would like to show you." He took my friend to the clothing
closet. Before opening the door, almost instinctively, he
looked over his shoulder, as if to make sure that no
unwelcome eyes were watching. Satisfied that it was safe,
Yaakov opened the closet, moved aside a number of boxes,
and carefully lifted up a false floor. Under the floorboards there
was a staircase, leading to a small pool. "This is the city's
Mikvah," he proudly announced, "over forty families make use
of it."

Yaakov then told my friend of the dangers involved in
building that Mikvah. No religious facilities could be built
without express government permission. Otherwise it was
subject to the direst penalties. Besides, the house was
government property, and if caught, he would face a long
prison sentence for "defacing" it.

Gradually — almost cautiously — he began to tell how the
Mikvah was built. All the work had to be done in the utmost
secrecy. No one, even his closest friends and neighbors, could
know what he was doing. Only a small amount of digging
could be done under the house each day, so that the dirt could

be disposed of without arousing suspicion. Small quantities of cement — "for making minor repairs" — were purchased, until there was enough to line the Mikvah. A similar subterfuge had to be used to obtain pipes for the plumbing. In addition, the rigorous requirements of Jewish Law had to be satisfied. This is difficult enough under any circumstances, even if secrecy is not a paramount consideration.

Not until the Mikvah was completed did Yaakov dare tell anyone about it. At first, his closest friends shared the secret. Gradually, one by one, other families were invited to make use of the hidden Mikvah. Most of them did not believe it possible — but they came anyway. Before long, Yaakov's "top secret project" had become the community Mikvah.

A year after this meeting, Yaakov and his family were finally able to emigrate to Israel. All of his children had remained observant Jews, even though they were born and raised in Russia.

When asked why he had undertaken all the expense and danger to build a Mikvah, Yaakov explained, "Without it, I could not live as a Jew."

One of the most exciting, recent archaeological events in Israel was the excavation of the mountain fortress of Massadah. Here was the record of some of the last defenders of ancient Israel, who gave their lives eighteen hundred years ago for the holy soil.

Of all the fascinating discoveries on Massadah, one of the most important was the finding of not one, but two Mikvahs. Following the usual practice, one was most probably for men, while the other was for women.

Here were people fighting for their lives — pitted against the might of the entire Roman Empire. Yet, on the mountain top of Massadah, they found the time and resources to build two Mikvahs. As religious Jews, they knew that they could not exist without them.

While the Massadah excavations were in progress, two experts on Mikvah, Rabbi David Muntzberg and Rabbi Eliezer Alter, examined them. After meticulous study, these rabbis announced that the Mikvahs had been built according to the minutest requirements of Jewish Law — "among the finest of the finest, seven times seven." In the eighteen hundred years that have passed, neither the Mikvah nor its importance has changed.

In the past few years, the issue of conversion has received much publicity, especially in Israel. Even American news media have spoken of the term *Giur KeHalachah* — "conversion according to Jewish Law." Many people have begun to become aware of the fact that there are specific requirements involved in conversion to Judaism. One of these requirements is immersion in a Mikvah.

Conversion is a unique far-reaching experience. It involves a change of identity, and the assumption of a new status, namely that of a Jew. It follows, therefore, that the rituals involved in conversion include those things that are most basic to Judaism.

The fact that the Mikvah is a necessary element in conversion indicates that it is an important element of Judaism. Indeed, anyone versed in Jewish tradition knows this to be true. The use of Mikvah is one of the main factors that traditionally distinguishes the Jew from the non-Jew.[1]

Many people would be surprised to learn that the Mikvah is more important than the synagogue. This may not be obvious, since in many communities, synagogues have expensive, imposing buildings, while the Mikvah is small and poorly maintained. Yet, the Mikvah is more important. Jewish Law maintains that a congregation that does not have its own Mikvah does not even have the status of a community.[2]

This is not mere theory. In Israel, where religious authorities are particularly meticulous, the Mikvah is the first religious facility that is built in a new community. It is of primary importance. Synagogue services can be held in an apartment or store. The synagogue building is erected later, when the community is better organized and established.

Visiting A Mikvah

Many people have never seen a Mikvah, and even if you have seen a Mikvah, you might have missed many details. Therefore, at this point, it may be useful to paint an imaginary picture of a typical Mikvah.

At first glance, a Mikvah looks like little more than a small swimming pool. The water is usually about chest high, large enough for three or four people to stand in comfortably. For easy access, there are stairs leading into the water of the Mikvah.

If you look more closely, you will see a small hole, two or three inches in diameter, just below the water line of one wall of the pool. This hole may appear insignificant, but it is what actually gives this pool its status as a Mikvah.

Just opposite this small hole, you will notice a removable cover over a *Bor* or "pit," which is the essential part of the Mikvah. This *Bor* is a small pool by itself, and it is filled with natural rain water. The rain water must enter the *Bor* in essentially a natural manner, as will be discussed in a later section. Under certain conditions, spring water or melted snow or ice can also be used.

There are two other requirements for the *Bor* aside from containing natural rain water. First, it must contain at least forty *Sa'ah*. The *Sa'ah is* an ancient Biblical measurement, equivalent to approximately five gallons of water, so that the Mikvah contains approximately 200 gallons of rain water.

The second requirement is that the *Bor* must be a pit built directly into the ground. It cannot consist of any kind of vessel that can be disconnected and carried away, such as a barrel, vat or tub. Under some conditions, however, it can be built directly into the upper story of a building.

The *Bor* itself can be used for a Mikvah, but since it is very difficult to change its water, it is most often used as a source to give another pool connected to it the status of a Mikvah. This larger pool can be filled in any convenient manner from the ordinary city water supply, and its water can be changed as often as desirable. The only requirement is that it be connected to the water of the *Bor* by an opening at least two inches in diameter. By connecting the two pools and allowing their waters to mingle we give the water in the larger pool the status of the water in the smaller pool. The process of intermingling the waters of the two pools is known as *Hashakah;* this too will be discussed in more detail in a later section.

Now that we have some idea of what a Mikvah looks like, we can briefly mention its uses. There are three basic areas where immersion in the Mikvah is required by Jewish Law:

1. After a woman has her monthly period, she may not be intimate with her husband until she immerses in the Mikvah. This involves a Biblical law of the utmost severity.

2. Immersion in a Mikvah is an integral part of conversion to Judaism. Without immersion, conversion is not valid. This is required of men and women alike.

3. Pots, dishes and other eating utensils manufactured by a non-Jew must also be "converted" by immersion in a Mikvah before they can be used on a Jewish table. This is a special law in its own right, and does not necessarily have anything to do with Kashrus.

Besides these, there are other times when it is customary to use the Mikvah. For example, it is an established custom to immerse before Yom Kippur as a sign of purity and repentance. Many Chasidim immerse before the Sabbath in order to sensitize themselves to the holiness of the day. In this general context, immersion in a Mikvah is a process of spiritual purification and cleansing.

In ancient times, the Mikvah had another important function in relation to various types of *Tumah,* or ritual defilement.

Why Mikvah?

If we look at the commandments found in the Torah, we find that they fall into three major categories.

Firstly, there are what we would call moral and ethical laws, the need for which is fairly obvious. Thus, when the Torah tells us not to steal, kill, cheat or hurt another's feelings, we do not have to look far to understand the reasons for such rules. These are moral laws, and are necessary if men are to live together in harmony. These commandments are known as *Mishpatim* — translated literally, "judgments." Any person with good *judgment* should find this category of laws and commandments perfectly obvious.

Secondly, there are other commandments, which, while not morally necessary, fill an important need in strengthening Judaism. These are the rituals and festivals which reawaken us to important religious truths or commemorate key events in Jewish history. For example, few people would question the importance of observing Passover, which commemorates the Exodus from Egypt. Indeed, it is one of the best kept of Jewish holidays. The same is true of the Sabbath and other holidays. Similarly, commandments such as Tefillin and the Mezuzah serve constantly to remind us of God's presence. Commandments in this second category are known as *Edos* — literally, "witnesses." These are the practices that bear *witness* to the important concepts of Judaism.

The third category is the most difficult to understand. It consists of laws and commandments for which there is no apparent reason. The best-known example are the dietary laws, for which no explicit reason is given, either in the Torah or in Talmudic literature. These commandments serve to strengthen the bond between God and man, but the manner in which they do this is by no means obvious. Laws falling into this category of commandments are known as *Chukim,* translated literally as "decrees." These are commandments which we must obey as *decrees* of our God, whether or not we understand their reason.[3]

One of the most important commandments falling into this last category is that of Mikvah.[4]

It is obvious that this category of commandments is the most difficult to keep. The Talmud tells us that these are the laws that "the Evil Urge *(Yetzer HaRa)* and the nations of the world attempt to refute."[5] If we do not understand the reason for something, it is tempting to find excuses not to do it. When we try to explain our religion to non-Jews, the laws that do not have an obvious reason are the most difficult to justify. If a person is unsure of himself or is wavering in his Judaism, these laws will be the first to be abandoned. This may well explain why the use of the Mikvah has become one of the most neglected observances, and even — God forgive us — a joke in some circles.

The fact that a commandment does not have an obvious reason makes its observance all the more an act of faith. It indicates that we are ready and willing to obey God's commandments, even when we cannot justify them with logic. It shows that we are placing God above our own intellect.

In this spirit the Jewish people accepted the commandments. The Torah relates that when Israel accepted the Torah, their initial response was *(Exodus 24:7),* "All that God says, we will do and we will hear *(Na'aseh VeNishma)."* Our sages stress the fact that their first statement was "we will do," and only then did they say, "we will hear." This indicates that when the Torah was given, we were ready to keep the commandments and "do" them, before we "heard" any reason or logic for them.[6]

The Talmud illustrates this with an anecdote. A gentile saw the sage Rava engrossed in his studies. So involved was he that, although he had crushed his finger, causing it to bleed profusely, he was oblivious of the pain. The gentile remarked, "You are an impetuous people, allowing your mouth to precede your ears — and you are still not aware of what you are doing. At first you should have heard all the reasons, and then you could have decided whether or not to accept the Torah."

Rava replied, "We went into it with complete trust. Is it not written *(Proverbs 11:3),* "The integrity of the upright shall guide them?"[7]

When we keep commandments that have no apparent reason, we demonstrate our inner security as Jews. Even though we may not be able to justify these commandments to the world, we feel secure as Jews to continue observing them. We understand what the Torah means when it says, *(Deuteronomy 4:6),* "Observe and keep [the commandments], for this is your wisdom and understanding in the eyes of the nations." We do not observe the commandments because logic demands it, but simply because they were given by God. The required basis is the relationship between the commandments and their Giver. This is higher than any possible human wisdom.[8]

This may be one reason why a convert to Judaism must immerse in the Mikvah. The convert's first step into Judaism involves a ritual whose explanation is not apparent and obvious, and therefore, he must reaffirm the initial acceptance of the Torah, declaring, "I will do and I will hear." To abandon his gentile identity and to assume Jewish identity, he is required to participate in a ritual that is inexplicable to one who does not accept the basis of Judaism. By so doing, he demonstrates his status as one who keeps those commandments "that the Evil Urge and nations of the world try to refute."

The fact that we are required to observe certain commandments without awareness of their reason does not mean that there is no logic in their observance. The reasons involve deep concepts that are not immediately obvious. When we realize that there is a limit beyond which we cannot delve, we can begin to explain their significance.

In ancient times, one of the main uses of the Mikvah was for ritual purification. There were numerous things that would render a person *Tomeh* (ritually unclean). The main significance of such *Tumah* was that a person in that state was forbidden to enter the grounds of the Holy Temple in Jerusalem *(Bais HaMikdash)*. Violation was punishable by the severest penalties.[9] The Torah speaks of numerous things that make a person *Tomeh*, ritually unclean, and of a number of processes of purification. One act of purification that is required in all cases, is immersion in the Mikvah.[10]

The laws of ritual purity and impurity belong in the category of commandments known as *Chukim*, decrees for which no reasons are given. These laws were to be taken on faith, because they were given by God, as indicated by the teaching of our sages who said, "The dead body does not defile, and the water does not cleanse. Rather, God said, 'I have issued an order, and made a decree — and no man may violate My decree.'"[11]

From these words we see that the Mikvah involves some degree of spiritual purification. In a later section, we will define "pure" *(Tahor)* and "impure" *(Tomeh)* more carefully, and thus gain a greater insight into these concepts.

Up until this point, we have stressed the fact that there is no explicit reason given for the Mikvah and its associated laws. Nevertheless, we can strive to understand the significance of these laws.[12] However, we must realize that the reasons which will be discussed provide only an incomplete picture, and that the ultimate rationale of such commandments is beyond the grasp of human intellect. Therefore, no matter how deeply we probe, these reasons cannot serve to change or restrict these religious laws.[13] No matter how profound these reasons may be, we must realize that the Torah emanates from God, and that His commandments may involve many factors beyond the grasp of our mind and experience. With this in mind, we can begin to probe the reasoning underlying the Mikvah.

On the simplest level, we usually think of water as a cleansing agent. If one is bodily unclean, it is natural to wash with water. Therefore, when we think of purification and cleansing in the spiritual sense, we would also use water as the purifying agent. It is the special status of the Mikvah that allows us to cleanse ourselves spiritually, as well as bodily.[14]

If we look into the Torah more carefully, we find that the

Mikvah has a deeper significance than mere purification, particularly in two special areas.

The first involved the original consecration of Aaron and his sons as *Kohanim* or priests, which took place soon after the exodus from Egypt, and was administered by Moses. Aaron and his sons then served as priests in the *Mishkan* sanctuary built in the desert, and their descendants have retained this special status for all time. Even today, a *Kohen* is an individual whose lineage goes back directly to Aaron in an unbroken line.

The Torah tells us that the first step in the consecration of Aaron and his sons as *Kohanim* involved immersion in a Mikvah.[15]

Here, immersion did not involve "purification," but rather, a change in status — an elevation from one state to another. Aaron and his sons were originally no different than anyone else, but with this immersion they attained the new status of *Kohanim* or priests.

The second area where we see the special significance of Mikvah is in the Yom Kippur service in the Holy Temple *(Bais HaMikdash)*. This service is outlined in the sixteenth chapter of Leviticus. Although this special Temple ritual has not been performed for over 1900 years, its detailed retelling provides some of the most dramatic elements of our current Yom Kippur *Mussaf* service.

The most crucial part of this ancient Temple service was the entrance of the High Priest *(Kohen Gadol)* into the Holy of Holies — the special chamber in the Temple where the ark containing the original stone Tablets given to Moses was kept. This was the only time of the year when any human being was allowed to enter the Holy of Holies. The *Kohen Gadol* had to put on special white vestments before entering this most sacred room. After leaving the Holy of Holies, he would once again put on the "golden" vestments that he wore all year round.

On this most sacred of days, the *Kohen Gadol* would enter the Holy of Holies two times. This, in turn, would require that he change his vestments five times, since he would begin and end in his "golden" ones. Each time before he changed, he would have to immerse himself in a Mikvah.[16]

The *Kohen Gadol* was not impure or unclean in any way. He was rather undergoing a change in status, symbolized most dramatically by the changes of vestments. When he entered the Holy of Holies, he had a very different status than before — a unique status that would allow him to enter this room. This change in status was achieved through immersion in the Mikvah.

The immersion in ritual purification involves the very same concept. The water is not washing away any filth. Rather, the Mikvah is changing the individual's spiritual status from that of *Tomeh* (unclean) to that of *Tahor* (clean). Actually, this "purification" is a change of status rather than a "cleansing" process.

The most dramatic example of this change of status is in the case of conversion. Here again, there is no question of uncleanness or purification, but merely a change in status.[17] As in the examples mentioned earlier, this change in status comes about through immersion in the Mikvah. As the Talmud states, "as soon as [the convert] immerses and emerges, he is like a Jew in every way."[18]

How does immersion in a Mikvah change a person? This can best be understood on the basis of another Talmudic teaching, that "a convert who embraces Judaism is like a new born child."[19]

This has many important ramifications, especially with regard to the convert's (previous) non-Jewish family. In addition, it provides us with an important insight into the concept of Mikvah, that emerging from the Mikvah is very much like a process of rebirth.

Seen in this light, we see that the Mikvah represents the womb.[20] When an individual enters the Mikvah, he is reentering the womb, and when he emerges, he is as if born anew. Thus he attains a completely new status.

This is particularly true in the purification from ritual uncleanness. The womb is a place that is completely divorced from all concepts of *Tumah* and uncleanness. A baby enters the world in complete purity, and there is no way in which he can be defiled while in the womb.[21] Thus when an individual enters the Mikvah, he leaves all uncleanness and *Tumah* behind, and emerges as a new, purified person.

The identification of the Mikvah with the womb becomes somewhat clearer in view of the fact that the Torah describes the world's most primitive state as water. In the opening verses of the Torah, we find *(Genesis 1:2)*, "The earth was empty and desolate, with darkness on the face of the deep, and God's spirit fluttering *on the face of the water.*" On the second day of creation, the "upper waters" were divided from the "lower waters." Finally, on the third day, the waters were gathered into seas, so that dry land could appear.

In a sense, therefore, water represents the womb of creation. When a person immerses in the Mikvah, he is placing himself in the state of the world yet unborn, subjecting himself totally to God's creative power.[22]

We can see this from the etymology of the world *Mayim,* which is the Hebrew word for water. According to a number of authorities, it shares the same root as the word *Mah,* meaning "what."[23] When a person immerses in water, he is nullifying his ego and asking, "What am I?" Ego is the essence of permanence, while water is the essence of impermanence. When a person is ready to replace his ego with a question, then he is also ready to be reborn with its answer. Thus, when Moses and Aaron declared *(Exodus Z6:7)*, "We are *what,*" our sages comment that this was the greatest possible expression of self nullification and subjugation to God.[24] When a person enters the Mikvah, he subjugates his ego to God in a similar manner.[25]

We can also see this in a more prosaic manner. When a person immerses himself in water, he places himself in an environment where he cannot live. Were he to remain submerged for more than a few moments, he would die from lack of air. He is thus literally placing himself in a state of non-existence and non-life. Breath is the very essence of life, and, according to the Torah, a person who stops breathing is no longer considered among the living.[26] Thus, when a person submerges himself in a Mikvah, he momentarily enters the realm of the nonliving, so that when he emerges, he is like one reborn.[27]

To some degree, this explains why a Mikvah cannot be made

in a vessel or tub, but must be built directly in the ground, for in a sense, the Mikvah also represents the grave. When a person immerses, he is temporarily in a state of nonliving, and when he emerges, he is resurrected with a new status.[28]

The representation of the Mikvah as both womb and grave is not a contradiction. Both are places of non-breathing, and are end points of the cycle of life. Indeed, it is interesting to note that the Hebrew word *Kever*, which usually means a "grave," is also occasionally used for the womb.[29] Both are nodes in the cycle of birth and death, and when a person passes through one of these nodes, he attains a totally new status.

In one place, our sages liken a person who immerses in the Mikvah to seeds planted in the ground.[30] Even though such seeds may be *Tameh*, ritually unclean, the plants that grow from them have a new status, and are clean.[31] The seeds have been returned to their source, where they can once again begin the cycle of growth. When the new seedlings emerge from the ground, they retain no element of their previous ritually unclean state. The same is true of man. For him, the waters of the Mikvah are his womb and source, and when he emerges, he too is like a new individual.

We therefore see that immersion in the Mikvah represents renewal and rebirth. We will examine this concept in greater detail, but first, let us take a closer look at just what a Mikvah is.

WHEN THE MIKVAH IS USED

Niddah

The most general use of Mikvah is for the purification of a woman after her monthly period. Although this primarily involves married women, it has important ramifications for single girls as well.

According to the Torah's definition, a woman has the status of a "Niddah" from the time that she has her period until she immerses in a Mikvah. The Torah thus states *(Leviticus 15:19)*, "When a woman has a discharge of blood, where blood flows from her body, she shall be a Niddah for seven days." As we shall see, she retains this status until she immerses in the Mikvah.

The word Niddah comes from the word *Nadad*, meaning "removed" or "separated."[1] The very word therefore indicates that she must forgo all physical contact with her husband. The word Niddah does not refer to menstruation, but to this necessity for separation. Both the name and the status of a Niddah are retained by a woman until she changes this status by immersion in a Mikvah.

The Torah openly forbids any sexual contact between a man and any woman who has the status of a Niddah. We thus find the commandment *(Leviticus 18:19)*, "You shall not (even) come close to uncovering the nakedness of a woman who is 'unclean' as a Niddah."[2]

Sexual intercourse between a man and a woman with the status of Niddah is considered a most serious sin. The Torah tell us *(Leviticus 20:18)*, "If a man lies with a woman who is a Niddah, and uncovers her nakedness, . . . both of them shall be cut off from their people."

The expression, "they shall be cut off," refers to the penalty of *Korais*. This is the same penalty that we find for incest between brother and sister,[3] violating Yom Kippur, or eating bread on Passover.[4] The expression "cut off" does not refer to any type of mutilation or excommunication. Rather, this is a spiritual penalty, where a person is "cut off" from his spiritual source.[5] The individual loses the ability to feel and appreciate the spiritual and Godly, and thus becomes "cut off" from the most important elements of life as a Jew. The only way for a person to re-attach himself to his spiritual source is to sincerely repent before God with resolve never to repeat the act.[6]

The prohibition against sexual contact between a man and a woman who is a Niddah is a most serious one. This is perhaps best expressed in the words of the Prophet Ezekiel, who says *(Ezekiel 18:5, 6)*, "If a man is righteous, and would accomplish justice and charity. . .. He will not defile his neighbor's wife, nor will he approach a woman who is a Niddah." The prophet equates intercourse with such a woman to adultery with another man's wife.

The fact that a woman removes herself from the status of Niddah by immersion in a Mikvah is known primarily from the Oral Torah, which was transmitted by God to the Jewish people at Sinai, along with the written Torah.

Like many other things in the Oral Law, this too is alluded to in the written Torah. The Torah says regarding a Niddah *(Leviticus 15:28)*, "She shall count seven days, and then she shall be purified." After counting seven "clean days," a woman must undergo a normal process of ritual purification. As we have seen, the universal means of such purification is immersion in a Mikvah, and this is also required to remove the status of Niddah.[7] Even though the prohibition against sex for a Niddah is not directly related to ritual impurity *(Tumah)*, the means of changing this status is likened to a purification process.[8]

Another allusion to the fact that the status of Niddah is removed by water is found in the Torah's discussion of the immersion of vessels. The Torah states *(Numbers 31:23)*, "It shall be pure only if it is purged in water for a Niddah." According to the Talmud, this indicates that vessels must be immersed in a Mikvah, just like a Niddah.[9]

The fact that a Niddah had to immerse, was well established in the Oral Torah, even without these allusions. We see that the

Prophet takes it for granted when he says *(Zechariah 13:1)*, "On that day, a fountain shall be opened, for the house of David, and for the inhabitants of Jerusalem, for purging and for the Niddah."[10] From this, we clearly see that it was a well established fact that a Niddah required immersion for her purification.

Use of the Mikvah is one of the most important aspects of Jewish married life. In a sense, it is even more important for the marriage bond than the wedding ceremony and can be seen as a monthly renewal of the couple's marriage.

Like most of the laws involving Mikvah, those involving Mikvah are "decrees" or *Chukim,* for which the Torah gives no reason. Nevertheless, like all these laws, it has an innate underlying logic.

The Talmud, provides one "reason" that is related to our discussion. Since the rules of Niddah require a woman to be physically separated from her husband at least twelve days each month, the couple experiences a virtual honeymoon after the wife's immersion. Unlike many couples, whose sex life becomes almost dull and jaded after a number of years, a husband and wife keeping the rules of Niddah experience continual renewal.[11]

Many couples who begin to keep these strictures late in marriage report a new zest in their relationship. During pregnancy, when the Niddah cycle in interrupted, many couples eagerly anticipate a return to the separation periods and the monthly "honeymoon" that the Niddah laws provide.

The rules involving Niddah and Mikvah are fairly involved, and every engaged or married couple should attempt to familiarize themselves with them. Classes are held in many larger communities, and any competent rabbi would be happy to provide literature and other information for interested couples. In general, however, the main requirement is that a woman count seven "clean" days in the ritually prescribed manner after her period ends, and then remove her Niddah status through immersion in a Mikvah.

Although the laws of Niddah are usually discussed within the context of marriage, they are equally important to single girls. From the time a girl begins to menstruate, she assumes the status of Niddah, whether she is married or not.[12] From the time of her first period, until she immerses in the Mikvah with marriage, she retains this status.

This has many important ramifications. Judaism forbids premarital intercourse in the strictest terms. Even if a girl has not yet begun menstruating, or in the rare case where she has immersed since her last period, premarital intercourse is still forbidden. The Torah states *(Deuteronomy 23:18),* "There shall be no harlot among the daughters of Israel." According to the Torah's definition, harlotry includes all forms of premarital sex, and has nothing to do with payment for the act. Thus, any couple engaged in premarital intercourse is violating the commandment forbidding harlotry.

Conversion

Another important use of the Mikvah involves conversion. As we discussed earlier, immersion in the Mikvah is an integral part of the conversion process, without which a non-Jew cannot enter the ranks of Judaism. In the case of a male, immersion must be preceded by ritual circumcision, while for a woman, immersion itself represents the entire ritual of conversion.

When a convert embraces Judaism, he is actually repeating what the Jewish people did when they first came into existence.

The special relationship between God and Israel was established for all generations through an oath and a covenant. The Torah spells this out when it says, *(Deuteronomy 29:9-14):*

You are all standing before the Lord your God . . . to enter into the covenant of the Lord your God — and into His oath — which the Lord your God is making with you today — that He may establish you this day as His own people, and that He may be your God, as He promised you, and as He swore to your fathers, Abraham, Isaac and Jacob. It is not with you alone that I am making this covenant and oath . . . but also with those who are not here this day.

These verses mention two things with which the Torah was accepted, an oath and a covenant.

The oath was taken shortly after Israel crossed the Jordan and entered the Promised Land under Joshua. The entire nation of Israel stood between Mount Ebal and Mount Gerizim, and the oath was administered by the Levites. The oath, prescribed by the Torah, provides that the Levites should declare *(Deuteronomy 27:26),* "Cursed is he who does not uphold the words of this Torah and keep them and all the people shall say Amen."[15] With this, all generations of Jews became bound to keep the Torah as if each one had personally made an oath to abide by it.[16]

The covenant was made before the giving of the Ten Commandments at Sinai. It consisted basically of three things, circumcision, immersion in the Mikvah, and a sacrifice. [17]

The circumcision of all males took place before the first Passover, just prior to the Exodus from Egypt. The Torah states that the Passover could not be celebrated by one who was uncircumcised, and therefore all the males who celebrated the first Passover had to be circumcised. We thus find that *(Joshua* 5:5), "all the people who came out [of Egypt] were circumcised."[18]

The second part of the covenant was a sacrifice, that was brought on behalf of the entire Jewish nation just before the giving of the Torah. We thus find *(Exodus* 24:5-8), "And [Moses] sent young men of the children of Israel, who offered burnt offerings . . . to God. . . . And [the people] said, 'All that God has spoken, we will do and we will hear *(Na'aseh VeNishma).'* . . . And [Moses] said, 'This is the blood of the covenant that God has made with you.' "

The final part of the covenant consisted of all the people immersing in the Mikvah. Immediately before the Ten Commandments were given, we find that God told Moses *(Exodus 19:10),* "Go to the people, and sanctify them today and tomorrow, and let them *wash their garments.* And be ready for the third day, for on the third day, God will descend in the sight of all the people on Mount Sinai."

The command to "wash their garments" seems puzzling, until we look into the general laws regarding purification. There, we find that whenever a person is required to "wash his clothing," he is also required to immerse himself in the Mikvah. When the Torah states that an individual must wash his clothing, this means that he must purify his clothing *as well as* his body in the Mikvah. Thus, we know from tradition that an important part of the preparation for the receiving of the Ten Commandments consisted of immersion in the Mikvah.[19]

We find another allusion to this in a most beautiful parable given by the Prophet Ezekiel. He likens Israel to an abandoned child, who was cast aside by her parents at birth. God takes in this infant girl, caring for her and raising her to be a princess. God then says *(Ezekiel 16:8,9)*, "Your time was the time of love. I spread My garment over you, and covered your nakedness. I swore to you, and I entered into a covenant with you — says the Lord God and you became Mine. Then I washed you in the water. . . .." This washing refers to the immersion of the Jews before the giving of the Ten Commandments.[20]

When a person converts to Judaism, he must enter the covenant in the same manner as Israel did when they first accepted the Torah. The Torah thus says *(Numbers 15:15)*, "As you are, so shall the convert *(Ger)* be before God."[21] Every male who converts to Judaism must therefore undergo the special ceremony of ritual circumcision. If he is already circumcised, "blood of the covenant" *(Dam Bris)* must be drawn. Both men and women must then undergo immersion. When the Holy Temple *(Bais HaMikdash)* stood in Jerusalem, and the sacrificial system was in force, the third element of conversion involved bringing a sacrifice. This sacrifice, however, is not required now that the Temple is no longer standing and the sacrificial system no longer exists.

The ritual of immersion, as well as circumcision where required of a male, is not something a convert can do on his own. Since it involves a major change in a person's communal status it must be treated as a community function. Therefore, these rituals are administered by a three man rabbinical court. Unless done in the presence of such a court, conversion is not valid.[22]

Immersion in a Mikvah is not only the main ritual of conversion, but was also the means through which all Jews originally entered into the covenant with God. Mikvah has its roots at Sinai as one of the earliest Jewish rituals.

There is even evidence that the ritual of immersion goes back to the time of the Patriarchs. One of the main differences between Abraham and other religious people who lived before him is that Abraham was deeply concerned with others, and taught those around him concerning God. Not only did

Abraham spread God's teachings, he began the new faith that was to become Judaism. According to tradition, Abraham literally converted people to this new faith.[23] This tradition of converting others was followed by Isaac and Jacob.[24]

The question then arises, how did Abraham convert those who wished to enter his new faith? We find a hint in the story of the three angels who visited Abraham. Abraham's first remark to them was (Genesis 18:4), "Let now a little water be taken, and wash your feet." The Zohar explains that this alluded to the fact that Abraham had a Mikvah, and immersed the strangers in it.[25] The reason feet were specified for washing was because he suspected that they might be idolators, who "bow down to the dust of their feet."[26] According to this, the ritual of immersion in a Mikvah originated with Abraham.

Pots And Dishes

The last area where the use of a Mikvah is required by Jewish Law is for pots, dishes, and other eating utensils. Of all the uses of Mikvah, this is perhaps the least known, but is nevertheless of major importance.

Briefly, the law requires that any metal or glass eating utensil manufactured or owned by a non-Jew, be immersed in a Mikvah before it can be used for Jewish food.[27]

This rule has nothing to do with Kashruth. Rather, this immersion is a form of "conversion" for the utensils, very much like that required for a person who converts to Judaism.[28] Thus, it is even required for brand new utensils, that have never been used before. When a utensil has been used for non-Kosher food, it must be both "Kashered" (rendered Kosher), and immersed.[29] The rules for Kashering are too complex to be included here, and a competent rabbinical authority should be consulted where this is required.

Before the immersion of metal or glass utensils previously owned by a non-Jew, the following blessing is said:[30]

בָּרוּךְ אַתָּה ה׳ אֱלֹקֵינוּ מֶלֶךְ הָעוֹלָם
אֲשֶׁר קִדְּשָׁנוּ בְּמִצְוֹתָיו וְצִוָּנוּ עַל טְבִילַת כְּלִי (לרבים כֵּלִים):

Baruch Atah Ad-noy El-henu Melech HaOlam Asher Kid'shaNu BeMitzvoSav VeTzivaNu Al Tevilas Keli (Kelim).

Blessed are You O Lord, our God, King of the universe, Who made us holy with His commandments and commanded that we immerse a utensil (utensils).

This is similar to the blessing *Al HaTevilah* (upon immersion) said by both a Niddah and a convert when they immerse in the Mikvah.

The law requiring that utensils be immersed is derived primarily from the Oral Torah. [31] Nevertheless, it is alluded to in the written Torah in a most interesting context.

Toward the end of the Jews' forty years in the desert after leaving Egypt, shortly before they crossed into the Promised Land, they came near the land of Moab. The Torah tells us that *(Numbers 25:1,2),* "the people began to commit harlotry with the daughters of Moab. And [the Moabite girls] called the people to sacrifice to their gods, and the people ate and bowed down to their gods." As a result, war eventually broke out between the Israelites and the Moabites. The Israelites emerged victorious and brought back a considerable amount of spoil.

God then commanded them *(Numbers 31:22,23),* "The gold, the silver, the copper, the iron, the tin, and the lead — everything that comes through fire, you shall bring through fire — and it shall be pure only if it is purged in water for a Niddah. And everything that does not come through fire, you [need only] bring through water."

The Torah tells us that the metal utensils the Israelites brought back as spoil had to undergo a special purification before they could be used. If they were cooking utensils that were used over fire — which "comes through fire" — they would have to be Kashered (made Kosher) by heating in fire, as is indeed the law.[32] This, however, is not enough. Before these vessels could be used, they would also have to be "purged in water for a Niddah" — that is, immersed in the same kind of Mikvah required for a Niddah.[33] Utensils not used over fire need only be washed thoroughly and immersed.

From this we learn two things. First, we see that all metal utensils made by a non-Jew must be immersed before they can be used. Secondly, we learn that when vessels must be Kashered, this should be done before their immersion.

Our sages liken the table to an altar, and therefore, every utensil used on a Jewish table must be sanctified, just like vessels used on the altar of the Holy Temple *(Bais HaMikdash).* [34] This is part of a Jew's sanctifying every element of his life.

Like all the other laws involving Mikvah, this one is a *Chok* or "decree," for which no reason is given. Indeed, in introducing this rule, the Torah openly states *(Numbers 31:21),* "This is the decree *(Chukah)* of the Torah, which God commanded Moses." Nevertheless, this rule still has a degree of logic.

The use of metals represents one of man's major steps toward civilization. Rabbi Samson Raphael Hirsch explains that a metal utensil is therefore the most visible sign of man's intelligent mastery over the earth and its materials.[35] Not only the shape, but the use of the material itself proclaims this fact.

This explains why metal vessels have a special status. Since glass is processed and melted like metal, it also has this status.

Eating, on the other hand, is an activity that primarily belongs to the animal sphere of man's nature. When a metal utensil is used for eating, this therefore represents man's highest mental faculties being employed to serve his animal nature.

The Torah requires, however, that even the most physical of man's activities be elevated to the realm of the spiritual. Before using a metal utensil for eating, we must first sanctify and elevate it to a level of holiness by immersion in a Mikvah.

The vessel will, in turn, sanctify the food served in it. In this manner, a Jew's eating utensils become like the consecrated vessels of the Holy Temple, which sanctified anything that was placed in them.[36]

Customs

In the cases discussed earlier, Niddah, conversion and utensils, immersion in the Mikvah is required by Torah law. There are a number of other cases where immersion in a Mikvah is customary. In such cases, no blessing is said upon immersion.

It is customary for a repentant apostate to immerse in a Mikvah. A person who "converts" to another religion is still considered a Jew, and does not require any formal conversion when returning to Judaism. Nevertheless, it is customary for him to immerse, as a sign of repentance and spiritual rebirth.[37]

Immersion in the Mikvah is an act of self-renewal and rebirth, and therefore, it is customary to immerse as a sign of repentance. For this reason many religious Jews immerse before Yom Kippur, and indeed, this custom is brought in the codes.[38] Some also immerse before Rosh HaShanah.[39]

Since immersion in the Mikvah indicates a change in status, many people, particularly Chassidic Jews, follow the custom of immersing on Friday afternoon as part of their preparation for the Sabbath. The Sabbath is on a completely different spiritual level than the other days of the week, and immersion in the Mikvah indicates this change of status.[40]

It is customary to immerse three times when going to the Mikvah. One reason for this is because the word Mikvah occurs three times in the Torah.[41]

A DEEPER LOOK

The River From Eden

God planted a garden in Eden, to the east, and there He placed the man that He had formed. And God made the ground grow every tree that is pleasant to see and good to eat — and the Tree of Life in the middle of the garden, and the Tree of Knowledge of Good and Evil. And a river went out of Eden to water the garden, and from there it split, and became four headwaters. . .. And God took the man, and placed him in the Garden of Eden to work it and to watch it. And God commanded the man, saying, "From every tree of the Garden, you may eat. But from the Tree of Knowledge in the middle of the Garden, you may not eat — for on the day you eat from it, you will die.

Genesis 2:8-17

This account tells of how God created man, and then placed him in the Garden of Eden, which represents the perfected state of man. Man was given one commandment, to abstain from eating the fruit of the Tree of Knowledge. As the account ends, the serpent tempts Eve and both she and her husband eat the forbidden fruit. Man is then driven from the idyllic life of the Garden of Eden, and must live in the world outside. This represents the imperfect state of man today.

However, there is one puzzling element in this account. Right in the middle of the story, the Torah suddenly speaks of the river that came out of Eden, giving a detailed description of the river and its tributaries, interrupting the narrative for no apparent reason. This is all the more puzzling, since the river is never again mentioned in the entire account. Furthermore, the entire story of Eden teaches us a very important lesson about man and his condition, and in this context, the description of the river seems all the more out of place.

In order to explain the inclusion of the rivers, we first must grasp the concept of man's perfection, the concept of evil, and the idea of Adam's sin.

Every basic question that we can ask about Judaism begins with one fundamental question: Why did God create the world? Of course, to a large degree, this question is unanswerable. We cannot understand God, and we certainly cannot understand His reasons. Still, we can probe those reasons that God Himself revealed in His Torah and to His prophets.

What we learn from these sources is that God created the world as an act of pure altruism, in order to do good.[1] He created a world, and placed man upon it, in order that man be the recipient of this good.

What is this good that God desired to give man? Our sages teach us that God's intention would not be satisfied with giving anything less than the ultimate good.

But, what is the greatest possible good God can give to man? The answer is that the greatest possible good is God Himself. Therefore, the good that God destined for man was the ability to resemble Him and draw close to Him.[2]

In order for this to be possible, man had to be created with absolute free will. Otherwise, he would be little more than a puppet or a robot. With free will, on the other hand, man is created "in the image of God."[3] "Just as God acts as a free Being, so does man. Just as He acts without prior restraint, so does man.

Just as God can do good as a matter of His own free will, so can man. Just as man must have free will, so must he have freedom of choice. A man locked up in a prison has the same free will as anyone else, but still, there is little he can do with it. For man to resemble his Creator to the greatest degree possible, he must function in an arena where he has the maximum freedom of choice. The more man resembles God in His omnipotence, the closer he resembles Him in His free choice of good.

In order to make this freedom of choice real, God had to create the possibility of evil.[4] If nothing but good were possible, there would be no freedom of choice, and the good would produce no beneficial change. To use the Talmudic metaphor, it would be like carrying a lamp in broad daylight.[5]

Originally, however, this evil was not an integral part of man. Man was a perfectly integrated creature, who had no inner desire or compulsion to do evil. To the contrary, man's natural inclination was to live in perfect harmony, both with his environment and with his spiritual self. As such, man had no conflicts, frustrations, compulsions or lack of self control. He had the ability to build a perfect society, where each individual could grow, develop, and serve God to the best of his ability.

This was the state of man in the Garden of Eden. He lived an idyllic life, with no work or toil, with his mind free to contemplate wisdom, and his soul free to commune with God.[6] His food was right at hand, and he had need for neither clothing nor shelter.[7]

Evil was not part of man, but an outside force he could easily avoid. This was represented by the Serpent in the Garden, which was not part of man's makeup, but something outside of him. Man could debate with this evil or ignore it, like any other outside force. Evil urges and compulsions were not part of him, as they are now, so that now he cannot escape them, no matter where he goes.[8]

Man was given one commandment, not to eat of the Tree of Knowledge of Good and Evil. In this Tree, good and evil were intermingled, in such a manner that they could not be separated. Once man partook of this tree, the same became true of him.

At that moment, evil became an intrinsic part of his being. He now had a Yetzer HaRa, — an Evil Urge — that was part of his psyche, and no matter what he would do, he could not escape it.[9] Just like the Tree of Knowledge, man was now a mixture of good and evil, and he would have to spend all his days fighting this evil and attempting to overcome it.

Man's very essence now became filled with contradictions. His life became full of conflict and its resulting frustrations, making a perfect society all but impossible. Man's spiritual nature and animal nature became two opposites, in constant conflict, causing mental anguish and imperfection.

In man's perfected state, represented by the Garden of Eden, he would have been able to attain physical as well as spiritual perfection. Ultimately, he would have vanquished death and gained immortality. When man sinned and ate from the Tree, he lost this opportunity to gain immortality. God therefore said regarding the Tree of Knowledge *(Genesis* 2:17), "On the day that you eat of it, you will surely die."[10]

Since the entire world was created for the sake of man, when man fell, he brought the entire world down with him. Evil would no longer be concentrated in a single "serpent," but would now be diffused throughout all creation. Just like in the Tree of Knowledge, good and evil would be completely intermingled, and man would have to struggle to discern one from the other.

God eventually chose the Jewish people to recreate the state of Eden, and thus eventually elevate all mankind. To enable them to accomplish this, He gave Israel the Torah. For one thing, this gave man the ability to overcome the evil in himself,[11] it also gave him the ability to avoid evil, overcome it, and eventually elevate it to a state of good.[12]

This is a very important point. In his fallen state, man cannot attain good by himself, nor can he reach out to God on his own. The only way to attain good, approach God, or form a perfect society, is through the Torah. As a result of Adam's sin, evil has become such an integral part of man, reinforced by hundreds of generations of sin, that the only means for man to escape it and overcome it is through the specific remedy given by God, and that remedy is the Torah. Our sages therefore teach us that God said, "I have created the Evil Urge, but I have created the Torah as its remedy."[13]

One of the important commandments that God gave Israel was to build a Sanctuary *(Mikdash).* He thus told us *(Exodus* 25:8), "They shall make Me a sanctuary *(Mikdash)* that I may dwell among them." When Israel was in the desert, this Sanctuary took the form of the prefabricated Tabernacle *(Mishkan)* that was carried with them on their journeys. When they finally settled in the Promised Land, it was built as the Holy Temple *(Bais HaMikdash)* in Jerusalem.

But the question arises, why was it necessary to have a

special sanctuary? We know that, *(Isaiah 6:3),* "the whole earth is filled with His glory."

Our sages teach us that the reason for the Sanctuary was because the entire world had become intermingled with evil as a result of Adam's sin. When God chose Israel, He told them to build one Sanctuary where this evil would not enter. This Sanctuary was to be like a miniature Garden of Eden, devoted totally to the service of God, where everything pertaining to man's fallen state would be excluded.[14]

This explains the concept of *Tumah,* or ritual uncleanness. The main application of the rules regarding such ritual uncleanness was with regard to the Sanctuary or Holy Temple *(Bais HaMikdash).* [15] Normally, it made no difference whether a person was ritually clean or unclean. When he was in an unclean state, however, he was absolutely forbidden to enter the Holy Temple, under the severest of penalties. The Torah thus says *(Numbers 19:20),* "But the man who is unclean, and does not purify himself, that soul shall be cut off from the community if he defiles God's Sanctuary."[16]

But what is this concept of uncleanness? Obviously, such uncleanness is not physical. Rather it is a type of spiritual defilement that places a person in a state in which he is forbidden to enter the Holy Temple. We learn that it is spiritual when the Torah says *(Leviticus 11:44),* "*You* shall not make your souls unclean." Thus, ritual uncleanness is something that primarily involves the soul, rather than the body.[17]

Ritual uncleanness is often associated with sin. We find in God's words to His prophet *(Ezekiel 14:11),* "They shall no longer make themselves unclean through their sins." Uncleanness is ultimately related to evil and sin.[18]

Things that cause ritual defilement are primarily associated with death. Thus, many kinds of ritual defilement are caused by contact with dead bodies or dead animals.[19] Other causes of uncleanness are things that are associated with man's imperfection.

Ultimately, all uncleanness is a result of Adam's sin.[20] Death and all other human imperfection was a result of this sin. If man would have remained in his elevated state in the Garden of Eden, nothing would exist that could cause uncleanness .

This explains why a person who has been defiled by something unclean was not allowed to enter the grounds of the Holy Temple. The Temple represents a miniature Garden of Eden. When Adam sinned, he was driven from this Garden. Therefore, anything associated with this sin prevents him from entering the miniature Garden of Eden that is the Temple. When a man is in a state of *Tumah* or uncleanness, he may not enter the Temple grounds under the severest of penalties.[21]

But how does man purify himself and remove himself from this state of uncleanness? How does he disassociate himself from man's fallen state and reassociate himself with Eden?

This purification is primarily through water, through immersion in the Mikvah. Water is the primary connection that we have with the Garden of Eden.

The Talmud tells us that all the water in the world ultimately has its root in the river that emerged from Eden.[22] In a sense, this river is the spiritual source of all water. Even though a person cannot re-enter the Garden of Eden itself, whenever he associates himself with these rivers — or with any other water, — he is re-establishing his link with Eden.

We thus find a Midrash which tells us that after Adam was driven from Eden, he repented by sitting in this river.[23] Although he had been permanently barred from the Garden itself, he tried to maintain a link through this river.

Thus, when a person immerses in the waters of the Mikvah, he is also re-establishing a link with man's perfected state. He then loses the status of uncleanness *(Tumah)*, and is reborn into a state of purity, where he is permitted to enter the Holy Temple.[24]

This also explains why the Mikvah must be linked to natural water. Water must come to the Mikvah from its natural state, and must not come in contact with man in his state of spiritual exile. Similarly, it must not pass through anything that is capable of becoming defiled, since this would also break its direct link with the River from Eden.

Our sages thus teach us that the word MiKVaH (מִקְוָה) has the same letters as Ko(V)MaH (קוֹמָה), the Hebrew word for "rising" or "standing tall."[25] It is through the Mikvah that man can *rise* from things associated with his fallen state, and re-establish a link with the perfected state that is Eden.

We can now go back to our original question. The story of Eden is interrupted with a description of the "River that ran out of the Garden of Eden." In the beginning of this section, we questioned the significance of this river. By now the reason for the river is apparent. The Torah tells us that God planted a Garden, and in it, the Tree of Knowledge of Good and Evil. With it, the possibility was created that man would sin, and be evicted from Eden. Thus, even before God placed man in Eden, He established a link between the Garden and the world outside, namely the river which emerged from Eden.

The account of this river is therefore not an extraneous fact that merely interrupts the story. Rather, it is an important statement regarding man's condition in the world outside of Eden. Even though man has been expelled from Eden, a link remains. The concept of Mikvah is very closely associated with this link.

The Election of Israel

One of the most difficult questions regarding Judaism involves the concept of the "chosen people." If God created the world to bestow good on man, why did He not give all mankindaccess to this good? Why was the Torah, which is the main gateway to this good, only given to Israel? In short, why did there have to be a single "chosen people?"

The answer to these questions brings us back to Adam. When man was first created, all mankind was destined to be the "chosen people." If Adam had not sinned, then all of his children would have been worthy of partaking in the ultimate good that God destined for all mankind.[26]

When Adam sinned, however, the opportunity was lost for all his children to automatically be included in this concept. As a result of the evil that had become part of man's nature, the early generations forgot God almost completely. Only a few individuals kept alive the tradition of serving the one true God.

Our sages teach us that "there were ten generations from Adam to Noah. . ... All these generations continued to anger [God], until He finally brought the flood upon them."[27]

God gave mankind these ten generations to lift themselves back up to the state of Eden. If they would have done so, all mankind would again have had a chance to become the Chosen People. The Midrash thus teaches us that God intended to give the Torah to the generations of Noah.[28] That generation, however, was so evil, that it could not accept the Torah. Instead of having the waters re-establish their link with Eden, the generation of Noah was destroyed by them. If water could not rectify man by purifying him, it would do so by destroying all who were unworthy.

Soon after the flood, however, the world again reverted to paganism and corruption. With very few exceptions, man again forgot the rule of God. Again, there were ten generations, — this time from Noah to Abraham.

Although born into a pagan atmosphere, Abraham spent his life seeking and serving God. He realized that he could not live a truth while allowing others to be ignorant of it, he therefore became the first to publicly teach others about God and His law. Unlike other righteous men, Abraham was able to establish his faith among his descendants, until a self-sustaining group was formed. The Torah tells us that God said of Abraham *(Genesis 18:18, 19)*, "Abraham shall surely become a great and mighty nation, and all the nations of the earth shall be blessed by him. For I have known him, and I know that he will instruct his children and household after him, that they may keep God's way. They will observe righteousness and justice, in order that God may bring upon Abraham everything that He promised him."[29]

During Abraham's lifetime, the Tower of Babel was built and mankind was divided into many nations. This took place when Abraham was 48 years old.

In Abraham, God saw a force that could bring all mankind back to Him, and regain the status of the "chosen people." God therefore brought a spirit of unity into the world, influencing all mankind to act with one accord. Under the leadership of Abraham, they could all have been restored to the state of Eden. Instead, mankind united to build the Tower of Babel.[30]

Man then lost the opportunity for all humanity to become the "chosen people." Instead, mankind was divided into nations. The Torah thus says that *(Genesis 11:9)*, "[God] confounded the language of all the [people of the] earth, and ... scattered them abroad upon the face of the earth."

Each nation was then given its own language and mission. God decreed that the children of Abraham would also become a nation, with the special mission of serving God.[31] Regarding this, the Torah says *(Deuteronomy 32:8, 9)*,

*When the Most High gave the nations inheritance, when
  He separated the sons of man,
He set the borders of the peoples according to the number
  of Israel's children;
For God's portion is His people, Jacob, the lot of His
  inheritance.* [32]

The other nations, were given one last chance to gain the status of the "chosen people." The Midrash tells us that, before giving the Torah to Israel, God "offered" the Torah to all the other nations, who, in turn, "refused" to accept it.[33] God looked deeply into the essence of all these nations, and saw that none of them would be able to preserve the Torah for thousands of years and not abandon it. Thus, Israel alone was worthy to receive the Torah and become the chosen people.

The Torah is the means through which the Jew elevates himself back to the state of Eden. Therefore, the Jews had to immerse in a Mikvah before receiving the Torah.[34] Through the waters of the Mikvah, the link with Eden was re-established.

The same holds true for any person who converts to Judaism today. He must also re-establish this link with Eden, since this is a fundamental element of the concept of the chosen people. This is one reason why a convert to Judaism must immerse in the Mikvah.[35]

The final state, where all mankind will partake of God's good, is in the World to Come. At that time, all the world will once again be in the state of Eden. The prophet thus foretold *(Isaiah 51:3),* "[God] will make its desert like Eden, and its wastelands like the Garden of God." When this time arrives, the entire world will be clean, and uncleanness will cease to exist. God thus said *(Zechariah 13:2),* "*I* will cause . . . the spirit of uncleanness to be removed from the earth."

This will be a time when all mankind will attain the perfection that was originally destined for it. All the world will once again be in a state of harmony and perfection, and the strife and conflict that afflicts mankind will cease to exist. God thus told His prophet *(Isaiah 11:9),* "They shall not hurt nor destroy on all My holy mountain, for the earth shall be full of the knowledge of God, just like the waters cover the sea."[36]

Here again we find the concept of water. The knowledge of God is likened to "the waters that cover the sea." In the Future World, it will be as if the waters of Eden have covered all the world. Mikvah alludes to the "waters of knowledge," that will ultimately encompass all mankind.

The Holiness of Sex

Among the most difficult commandments to understand are those associated with Niddah and menstruation. The Torah tells us that from the time a woman has her period, until she immerses in the Mikvah, she has the status of a Niddah. During this period, all sexual activity and physical contact with the opposite sex is forbidden.

Like all other such laws, Niddah is a *Chukah* or "decree," for which no reason is given. Still, it does have a logical basis, which we will attempt to explore.

A common source of confusion is the fact that a taboo against a menstruating woman is found in many primitive societies. Many such societies place harsh restrictions on a woman during her monthly period. This has led some misguided writers to declare that the Torah laws regarding Niddah are merely an extension of these primitive beliefs and practices. In order to properly appreciate the significance of the Torah laws, we must contrast the reasons for them with the reasons for these primitive taboos.

First, however, we must understand the nature of menstruation. From the time a woman reaches puberty, she loses a relatively small quantity of blood at the end of her menstrual cycle each month. This blood loss, which is called the menstrual flow, is intimately related to the human reproductive process. Every month, a woman releases an ovum or egg, which, if fertilized, becomes an embryo which will grow into a new human being. The lining of the uterus (endometrium) thickens to accommodate the fertilized egg. It develops an increased blood supply with which to nourish the embryo if the egg is fertilized.

If the egg is not fertilized, after approximately two weeks, it is expelled. The uteral lining and its accumulated blood is also shed, and the expelled material is essentially what constitutes the menstrual flow. Thus, the menstrual cycle involves the construction and destruction of an enriched uteral lining.

This well-known fact is by no means that simple or logical. From a biological standpoint, it would be much more economical if the uteral lining would be reabsorbed instead of expelled. This would certainly be more esthetic and comfortable for the woman. She would then not have to lose a significant amount of her vital fluids each month.

Even more efficient, from a biological viewpoint, would be a situation that would allow the womb to remain in a constant state of readiness to nourish the fertilized ovum. Actually, there is no biological or medical reason why the uteral lining must be expelled and restored each month. There is no reason why the ovum has to "die" only to be replaced by another egg. Most biologists look upon this as an example of unexplained inefficiency in the human reproductive system.

To the primitive mind, which had no idea of the inner workings of the womb, the very idea that a woman should lose a portion of her vital fluids was both bizarre and frightening. They could not explain it logically, and therefore, they attributed it to some "evil force." According to most anthropologists, this is one of the main reasons so many taboos surround the menstruating woman in many primitive cultures.

We see, however, that all of our biological sophistication does not really help us understand this natural phenomenon. With all our scientific knowledge, it still remains an "unexplained inefficiency of the human reproductive system." In *The Second Sex,* Simone de Beauvoir writes of menstruation:[37]

> *This complex process, still mysterious in many of its details, involves the whole female organism, since there are hormonal reactions between the ovaries and other endocrine organs, such as the pituitary, the thyroid, and the adrenals, which affect the central nervous system, the sympathetic nervous system, and in consequence, all the viscera . . . The woman is more emotional, more nervous,*

more irritable than usual .. It is during her periods that she feels her body most bainfully as an obscure, alien thing; it is, indeed, the prey of stubborn and foreign life that each month constructs and then tears down a cradle within; each month all things are made ready for a child, and then aborted in the crimson flow.

When we look at menstruation in the light of human imperfection in general, it clearly fits the pattern. As a result of Adam's sin, man lost the ability to perfect himself, both spiritually and physically. As mentioned earlier, the clearest manifestation of this physical imperfection is man's mortality. Man wears out and dies. The human body does have the innate capability of constantly renewing itself; in theory at least, man has the potential of living forever. This, however, is something that he cannot attain as long as he is in his state of imperfection.

Another large area where human imperfection is evident is in the area of sex and reproduction. One manifestation of this is the menstrual cycle, which is inefficient, uncomfortable, and unesthetic.

Another manifestation of this imperfection is in childbirth itself. Rather than being the natural function that it should logically be, childbirth is often a most traumatic experience. The woman is hospitalized, as if she were experiencing a serious illness, rather than partaking in one of the most natural of bodily functions. The Torah openly states that this is a manifestation of man's imperfection, associated with the sin of Adam and Eve; as God told the first woman *(Genesis 3:16)*, "I will increase your anguish in pregnancy — with anguish you shall bear children. . . .." Far from being the natural biological function of continuing the species, pregnancy and childbirth have become painful and anguishing experiences .

A third aspect of the imperfection of man's reproductive process is evident in his general attitude toward sex. Rather than being a simple, natural biological function, sex is the source of man's greatest compulsions and frustrations. There have been many experiments, such as "free sex," which have attempted to "restore" sex to its status as a "natural" human function, but all of these have remained unsuccessful. Man's innate nature demands that he should have psychological conflicts with regard to sex.

One obvious area where man's lack of sexual integration is apparent, is with respect to his attitude toward his body. Of all creatures, man is the only one who experiences shame from his nakedness. This is one of the clearest indications of how Adam's sin affected his entire sexual makeup. Before the sin, the Torah says of man, *(Genesis 2:25),* "The two of them, the man and his wife, were naked, but they were not ashamed." After the sin, however, Adam was to declare *(Ibid. 3:10),* "I was afraid, because I was naked." This change dramatically indicates the fundamental change in man's attitude toward both sex and his body in his degraded state.[38]

Returning to our original discussion, it now becomes obvious why a woman is considered "unclean" when she has her period. This too, is associated with humanity's degraded state and expulsion from Eden. Indeed, our sages openly declare that menstruation is a result of humanity's sin.[39] Therefore, until the woman purifies herself from this ritual uncleanness, she is not allowed to enter the grounds of the Holy Temple, which is a miniature Eden. (This does not apply to going to the synagogue.)

This helps explain why a Niddah is forbidden to have any sexual contact with a man. According to Jewish teachings, sex is not something that is intrinsically shameful or "dirty." Quite to the contrary, it is one of the holiest of all human functions — provided that it is kept within the guidelines of Torah and not perverted. The Hebrew word for marriage is *Kiddushin,* which literally means "sanctification" or "holiness." When a man marries a woman, the words he declares to her are, "Behold you become holy to me with this ring. . .."[40] Interestingly, the opposite of marriage is prostitution and one of the words for a prostitute is *Kadeshah* — literally, a woman who has defiled her holiness, indicating the "other side" of this holiness, which is its perversion.[41]

One of the reasons sex is so holy is because it has the ability to accomplish something that is beyond the power of any other human function — namely, drawing a soul down to the world, and producing a living human being.

Incidentally, this explains why God's covenant with Abraham involved circumcision — an indelible mark on the organ of reproduction. As the father of the "chosen people," Abraham and his children would now be able to use this organ to bring the holiest souls into the world. Thus, it was only after Abraham circumcised himself that he was able to give birth to Isaac, and it is the sexual organ that bears the mark of God's covenant.[42]

The covenant of circumcision was one of the things that elevated Abraham and his children from the fallen state resulting from the expulsion from Eden. As a result of this covenant, the sexual act of the Jew enters the realm of the holy, and partakes of man's optimum state before his expulsion .

For precisely the same reason that a person who is ritually unclean cannot enter the Holy Temple, a Niddah cannot participate in sexual intercourse. Niddah represents the state of expulsion from Eden. As a result of the covenant of circumcision, however, the sexual act is one of holiness (Kedushah), and therefore, is associated with man's state before the expulsion. Therefore, as long as a woman is in a state of Niddah, she cannot participate in the holy act of sex.

On a simpler level, Niddah is a sign of the imperfection of the human reproductive process. As long as a woman is in a state of Niddah, she may not partake in this reproductive process.[43]

Intercourse between a man, and a woman who is in a state of Niddah is therefore very much like entering the Holy Temple while unclean. Both acts entail entering a representation of man's perfected state while associated with a representation of his fallen state. They both incur the same penalty, namely Korais, being "cut off," as does one who does not enter into the covenant of circumcision.[44]

The punishment of being "cut off" is particularly appropriate for sins such as these. Korais means that the individual is "cut off" from his spiritual source. This spiritual source is very intimately related to Eden. Two major areas where man gains access to his perfected spiritual state is through the Holy Temple and through the covenant of Abraham. Therefore, when a person perverts these vehicles, it is only fitting that he should be cut off completely from his spiritual source.

The punishment of being "cut off" is prescribed as a general punishment for sexual perversions, since all of these are perversions of the covenant of circumcision.[45] Likewise, this is the penalty for violating the Sabbath, Yom Kippur, and Passover, since all of these are times when man is elevated to a state of Eden.

This also explains the purification of a Niddah. Since Niddah is associated with the expulsion from Eden, its purification must involve something that re-establishes the connection with Eden, namely, the water of the Mikvah.

This has deeper significance on another level. Earlier, we spoke of how the Mikvah represents the womb, and how it is also connected to the River from Eden. Niddah, however, is a sign of the imperfection of the human reproductive process, especially the womb. Therefore, the purification and rectification of Niddah must be a return to the perfected "womb" that is the Mikvah.

The laws of Niddah, which force man and wife to separate for a period of almost two weeks each month, have the positive function of constantly renewing the sexual bond between them. This, also indicates the imperfection of human sexuality. In essence, this monthly separation is necessary to prevent the couple from becoming bored with sex. To an unmarried person, this may seem farfetched. Nevertheless, according to most marriage counselors, a significant reason for married couples drifting apart is because they simply become bored with each other, and bored with sex. A too common response is for one or both partners to seek sexual liaisons with individuals other than their spouse.

The husband-wife bond is essential for the rearing of human children. On the other hand, the very basic and essential relationship between husband and wife can fall apart through something as undramatic as simple boredom.

In this respect, the laws of Niddah also represent a solution to man's basic sexual imperfection. The monthly separation tends to renew the sexual relationship and thus stabilize the marriage bond. It is interesting to note that among families who observe the Niddah laws, infidelity is virtually unknown, and the divorce rate is significantly below the normal level. In a pragmatic sense, we can say that the structure of the Niddah laws is a system that actually works.

We therefore see that the laws of Niddah have two basic functions. First, the state of Niddah represents the imperfection of man's reproductive process, and therefore, precludes sexual contact until this status is removed through immersion in the Mikvah. On the other hand, it also represents one of the best cures known for this imperfection, which brings about the best possible sexual relationship, stabilizing the fundamental institution of marriage.

On another level, the fact that husband and wife cannot have any physical contact during the days of separation forces them to look upon each other as human beings, rather than as mere sex objects. During this period, they must communicate with each other on a spiritual level, rather than on a mere physical level. "The laws of Niddah insure that for a given period each month, respect, affection and all the other impulses and factors that bind two people, with the exception of the physical, be allowed to dominate the relationship of a married couple. While marriage demands sex, it is much more than sex. Only the Jew has succeeded in abiding by a formula that has made work in practice, the idea that sex is basic to marriage but must be restrained as well as preserved so that other factors could have their due and also that intimacy not become monotonous and unappealing."[46] In this context, the rules of Niddah are most important, since they allow husband and wife to grow together in a manner that would not otherwise be possible. The relationship between man and wife thus grows into a bond that normally cannot exist between man and woman in humanity's imperfect state.

Man Against Nature

Another manifestation of man's fallen state is the basic conflict between man and the world around him. Unlike other species whose food is a natural part of their environment, man must toil and work in order to eat. Thus, after man sinned, God told him *(Genesis 3:19),* "by the sweat of your brow, you shall eat bread."

In many respects, metal represents man's ability to destroy nature.[47] Therefore, this too is a basic manifestation of man's lack of harmony with nature. Rather than being a sign of man's perfection, civilization is something that was necessitated by man's lack of natural harmony with nature. His use of metal utensils is therefore also a sign of his expulsion from Eden.

Because of man's fallen nature, he must eat his bread through "the sweat of his brow." He cannot use his intellectual faculties to elevate himself spiritually, but is compelled to use his mind to procure the most basic animal necessities of life. This is particularly evident when man makes use of metal utensils in order to eat and satisfy his animal appetites.

In essence then, just as Niddah represents humanity's basic conflict within its own reproductive process, man's use of metal utensils for eating also represents the conflict of his intellect with respect to another of his natural functions, namely, eating. The Torah therefore states that metal vessels must be *(Numbers 31:23),* "purged with water for a Niddah." Metal vessels must re-establish their harmony with nature through their association with the waters of Eden, just like a Niddah must do so with respect to her sexuality. Like a Niddah, such vessels must be immersed in the Mikvah.[48]

The context in which the law of immersion of vessels is derived is also very pertinent. The law was declared in the context of a war that Israel fought, which had its beginnings in sexual misconduct between the Jews and the Moabites that ultimately resulted in idolatry. The very fact that man could be tempted into a form of idolatry through sex, indicates that sex is a force that man finds difficult to control, and therefore is a sign of his imperfection. The fact that it can also lead man to wage war and kill, is another sign of his imperfection and inability to live in harmony. The premeditated nature of the battle on the part of the Moabites also underscored the difference between Jew and non-Jew, again a result of man's fall. This entire episode demonstrates that man is not in a perfected state, and that Israel must maintain eternal vigilance if it is ever to return to it.[49]

The spoil that the Israelites brought back from this battle were metal eating utensils — "gold, silver, copper, iron, tin, and lead." That they were obtained through harlotry, idolatry, and killing underscored the fact that these utensils were also indicative of man's fallen state. Therefore, before they could be used, they too, had to be re-elevated through the Mikvah.

We find a similar concept with respect to the giving of the Torah. Here, the Israelites were commanded to immerse in the Mikvah. The wording of the commandment, however, was (Exodus 19:10), "they shall wash their garments." As discussed earlier, this meant that they also had to immerse in the Mikvah, since in every instance where the Torah prescribes the washing of clothing, immersion must also be included .

As we have seen, clothing is another sign of man's sin. Before Adam sinned, humanity did not need clothing; people were naked and "not ashamed." Indeed, the very Hebrew word for clothing, Beged, comes from the root Bagad, meaning "to rebel." Clothing is a sign of man's rebellion against God.

Therefore, since the giving of the Torah represented man's path to his perfected state, it had to be preceded by a "washing of clothing," that is the immersion of the Israelites' clothing (as well as their bodies) in the Mikvah.[50] In this manner, their clothing, which was the very symbol of man's rebellion, was also elevated by the waters of Eden. Only then were the Israelites worthy of receiving the Torah, which is the ultimate instrument of man's return to his perfected state in the World to Come.

What Is A Mikvah?

Only a spring and a pit,
a gathering of water, shall be clean. . .

Leviticus 11:36

The Hebrew word Mikvah means a "pool" or "gathering" of water.[1] The one place where the Mikvah, as such, is specifically mentioned in the Torah is in the verse *(Leviticus 11:36)*, "Only a spring and a pit, a gathering *(Mikveh)* of water, shall be clean. . .." The Torah does not make a direct statement about what a Mikvah is, nor does it speak of its use. Nevertheless, as we shall see, all these things are ultimately included in this verse.

The place, however, where all the rules and laws associated with the Mikvah are enumerated, is in the unwritten or Oral Torah.[2]

It is important to realize that the Torah consists of two basic parts. One is the written Torah, the *Torah SheBeKesav*, with which we are all familiar. This is the Torah scroll that is kept and read in the synagogue and has been meticulously copied, generation by generation, from the first Torah written by Moses.

The second part of the Torah is equally important, even though it is not as well known. It is what we call the Oral or unwritten Torah, the *Torah SheBeal Peh*. This was by and large handed down orally, from master to disciple, for some 1500 years and served as the basis of the Mishnah which was finally put into writing by Rabbi Yehudah the Prince in the beginning of the third century C.E. Later this was elaborated upon with discussion and commentary, to form the Talmud. It is from this Oral Torah that all Jewish Law is derived.

The need for an Oral Torah is best illustrated by a simple

example. Suppose you want to be a tailor, and I wish to teach you the complexities of how to make men's jackets. There are two ways in which I could go about it. The difficult way would be for me to write a text on making jackets, and then let you try to unscramble a complex set of instructions. A much easier and more logical way would be for me to show you how to make a jacket, and guide you through the various steps. After several such lessons, it would be perfectly clear. A little personal contact can accomplish much more than many books.

The same is true of the Torah. A description of a Mikvah would take many pages, as we shall soon discover. Even then, there would be room for misunderstanding and error. The same would be true of the intricate laws involving such things as Tefillin, Tzitzis, Kashruth, or Sabbath observance. In all these cases, showing how it is done is much simpler and more accurate than trying to describe it. Thus, for example, any observant family knows the basics of how to keep Shabbos. Yet, it takes a keen scholar to master all the written material that tells us how to observe the Sabbath. Things that involve a way of life are taught much more easily by word of mouth and example than by the written word.

This is a possible explanation as to why some of our most common observances are mentioned only in the sparsest terms in the written Torah. There was simply no need for further elaborations, since these things could be best learned by word of mouth and were so commonplace that they could not be forgotten. The things put into writing were often those which were not commonplace and which involved circumstances that would occur only rarely. These had to be detailed in writing, since otherwise the particulars were likely to be forgotten.

A good example of commonplace laws that were not put into writing are those involving Mikvah. Every community had its Mikvah and it was in constant use. This being the case, the details were best preserved orally.

There are six necessary conditions that a body of water must fulfill before it can have the status of a Mikvah.

1. The Mikvah must consist of water. No other liquid can be used.[3]

2. The Mikvah must either be built into the ground, or be an integral part of a building attached to the ground. It cannot consist of any vessel that can be disconnected and carried away, such as a tub, vat, or barrel.[4]

3. The water of a Mikvah cannot be running or flowing. The only exception to this rule is a natural spring, or a river whose water is derived mainly from springs.[5]

4. The water of the Mikvah cannot be drawn, (Sha'uvim). That is, it cannot be brought to the Mikvah through direct human intervention.[6]

5. The water cannot be channeled to the Mikvah through anything that can become unclean, (Tomeh). For this reason, it cannot flow to the Mikvah through pipes or vessels made of metal, clay, or wood.[7]

6. The Mikvah must contain at least 40 Sa'ah (approximately 200 gallons).[8]

It is interesting to see how these laws are alluded to in the Torah. This example will provide us with considerable insight into how the Torah must he analyzed, and how, with proper analysis, it supports the Oral Tradition. (The following discussion is somewhat involved and the casual reader may wish to skip to the next section.)

Since some of the derivations depend on a precise understanding of the words in the verse, it would be useful to present it in the original Hebrew, together with a literal translation:

אַךְ	Ach	Only
מַעְיָן	Ma'yan	a spring
וּבוֹר	U'Bor	and a pit
מִקְוֵה	Mikveh	a gathering
מַיִם	Mayim	of water
יִהְיֶה	yihyeh	[it] shall be
טָהוֹר	tahor	clean . . .

(Leviticus 11:36)

The Torah was authored by God, and therefore its wording is as precise as an Infinite Intellect could make it. Therefore, there is no word, nuance, grammatical structure, or ambiguity that does not have some significance. Keeping this in mind, we shall see that this verse becomes quite puzzling when we try to analyze each word. We shall therefore introduce a number of questions within the context of these laws and this verse.

Looking at this verse, the first rule is fairly obvious. The Torah clearly states that "a gathering *(Mikveh)* of *water* shall be clean." This excludes all other liquids.[9]

Now let us begin to ask some questions.

Question 1. Why does the verse begin with the word *Ach* (only)? This would appear to be a superfluous word.

There is a tradition that wherever the word *Ach* (only) appears in the Torah, it is meant to be restrictive.[10] To see what it restricts, we must take the verse in context.

Going back two verses, we find that the Torah says *(Leviticus 11:34)*, "Any liquid that is drinkable, in any vessel, shall be unclean (if touched by something unclean)." Drinkable liquids, of course, include water, and the Torah states that if they are contained in *any vessel* they can become unclean. The Torah then says, "Only a spring and a pit, a gathering *(Mikveh)* of waters shall be clean. . .." From this, it is obvious that the Mikvah cannot consist of any sort of vessel.[11] We thus derive the second rule, that the Mikvah must be built into the ground.

Question 2. The main point of the verse is that a "gathering *(Mikveh)* of water" is clean. Why is it necessary to specify a spring and a pit?

Question 3. Why are a spring and pit both mentioned? What do we learn from one that we cannot know from the other?

The Torah begins by mentioning a spring. This refers to water that naturally comes from the ground. The word "spring" therefore comes to teach us that the water itself must be completely natural.

The next word, *Bor* or "pit" refers to a hole in the ground, whether or not it is filled with water. An empty hole is also called a *Bor,* as we find *(Genesis 37:24)*, "the pit *(Bor)* was empty, there was no water in it."

Furthermore, a *Bor* or "pit" does not have to be natural. It can also be man made, as we find *(Exodus 21:33)*, "when a man digs a pit *(Bor)."*

From the word "pit" we learn that the *receptacle* for the Mikvah can be man made. It is only the water that must come in a natural manner.

The first thing we derive from this is the fourth rule, namely, that the water cannot be drawn, or come to the Mikvah through any human intervention.

"Natural water" can consist of water flowing directly from a spring, or more commonly, rainwater. Lake or sea water can also be used. The main restriction is that it not be "drawn" or brought to the Mikvah through human effort.

The receptacle for the water, however, can be man made, the only condition being that it not be a vessel, as mentioned earlier. Included in the category of "receptacle" are any ducts and channels needed to bring the natural water to the Mikvah.[12] We shall explore some of the ramifications of this shortly.

> Question 4. Why is the word "gathering" included? The verse should have said, "a spring and a pit of water."

The next word, *Mikveh* or "gathering," indicates that the water must be standing still, "gathered" in one place and prevented from flowing or running. We thus find *(Genesis 1:10),* "the gathering *(Mikveh)* of waters [God] called seas." A "gathering of water" is therefore water than remains in one place, like a "sea."

A Mikvah must be a pool of water in which there is no flow whatsoever. In any case where the water drains from the Mikvah, it is unfit for use, for then it is "flowing" rather than "gathered" water. We thus derive the third rule, that the Mikvah cannot be running or flowing.

> Question 5. There is an obvious ambiguity in this verse. It is not clear whether the phrase "a gathering of water" refers just to the pit, or to both the spring and the pit. On one hand, the verse can be read, "a spring, and a pit [which is] a gathering of water." On the other hand, it can also be read, "a spring and a pit [which both are] a gathering of water." What is the reason for this ambiguity?

As we mentioned earlier, everything in the Torah, even ambiguities, must have a reason. The fact that this ambiguity exists indicates that both interpretations are correct.

In one interpretation, the verse reads, "a spring and a pit [which both are] a gathering of water." In this interpretation, the phrase "a spring and a pit" is the modifier, telling us something about "a gathering of water." What it is telling us is that the "gathering of water" must consist of natural water like a spring, but may be in a man made receptacle, like a pit. Thus, "gathering" is the word being modified.

In the other interpretation, the verse reads, "a spring, and a pit [which is] a gathering of water." In this case, the word "gathering" is the modifier, telling us something about the "pit." What it is telling us is that the water in the pit must be a "gathering" and not water that is flowing or leaking. In this interpretation, however, the word "gathering" only refers to "pit" and not to "spring."

From this, we see that the restriction against flowing water only applies to a "pit," but not to a spring.[13] A Mikvah made entirely of natural spring water can be flowing as well as "gathered." If the Mikvah is filled with rain water, however, it cannot be flowing at all. This completes the third rule.

This last rule has important implications with regard to rivers. If the major portion of a river's water comes from underground springs, then the entire river has the status of a spring, and can be used as a Mikvah. If, on the other hand, the river derives its flow primarily from rain water, then it no longer has the status of a spring, and since it is flowing, it is unfit as a Mikvah.[14] Therefore, even though rivers occasionally can be used as a Mikvah, each individual case must be checked by a competent rabbinical expert.

> Question 6. The verb of this sentence, "will be," in the Hebrew is in the singular. Since the sentence contains at least two subjects, "a spring and a pit," why is the plural verb not used?

The singular verb indicates that the "spring and pit" together form a *single* entity called a "gathering of water" or Mikvah. As seen earlier, "spring" refers to the natural water in the Mikvah, while "pit" refers to its man made receptacle. The singular verb teaches us that both of these make up a single entity that is the Mikvah.[15]

This, in turn, would indicate that in order for the Mikvah to be "clean," every element of the receptacle must also be "clean." Therefore, the verse says, "[it] will be clean," using the singular verb.

The only reason water can be brought to the Mikvah through man made ducts and channels is because they are all considered part of the receptacle, and are therefore included in the "pit," which may be man made. If these ducts, channels, or anything else that brings water to the Mikvah, are capable of becoming unclean, then the same will also be true of the pool — and it will no longer have the status of a Mikvah.

From this we learn the fifth rule, namely, that the water cannot be channeled into the Mikvah through anything that can become unclean. The Talmud thus says, " 'It shall be clean' all of its existence must come about through clean things."[16]

If we now look at the verse carefully, we see that each word teaches us a different law:

Only . . . . only this, but not a vessel
a spring . . . . .the water must be natural
and a pit . . . . .but the receptacle may be man made
a gathering . . . . the water cannot be flowing
of water . . . . .but not any other liquid
[it] shall be clean . . .the receptacle, including all its ducts, must be undefilable

All six rules are therefore included in this one basic verse. All that it takes to find them is some careful analysis.

There is one final law that we can derive from this verse. Once a pool has the status of a Mikvah, it does not lose this status, no matter what type or how much additional water is added to it.

The Torah says that a Mikvah "shall be clean," in the future tense. This indicates that once a body of water has the status of a Mikvah, there is no way it can become unclean. This is true no matter how much unclean water is poured into the Mikvah.

Therefore, once a pool has the status of a Mikvah, one can

add to it as much water as one desires, in any manner whatsoever.

In the Oral Torah, we find that an opening the size of the "neck of a leather bottle" *(Shefoferess HaNod) is* enough to unite two bodies of water into one. [17] According to tradition, this is a hole two finger-widths (approximately two inches) in diameter. If a wall separating two pools contains a hole this size, so that water flows freely from one pool into another, the two pools are considered as one pool.

There is, therefore, another way in which we can add water to a valid Mikvah. We can build a pool next to it, and leave an adequate hole connecting the two. As soon as the waters of the two pools intermingle, they are considered one, and the water in the second pool is considered to have been "added" to the Mikvah. The second pool, therefore, also becomes a Mikvah. This is the process known as *Hashakah,* which comes from the Hebrew word *(NaShak),* meaning "to kiss."

This is the manner in which most Mikvahs are made. The original Mikvah is a small pool, which is referred to as the *Bor* or "pit," alluding to the "pit" mentioned in the Torah. This is filled with natural rain water, fulfilling the six conditions mentioned earlier. Next to the *Bor is* a larger pool, connected to the *Bor* by an adequate sized hole. This larger pool is filled with ordinary tap water, but as soon as the water covers the hole, the two pools "kiss" and are considered as one. This larger pool than also becomes a Mikvah, and it is generally used for immersion.

One question still remains unresolved. The Torah says that "a spring and a pit, a gathering of water, shall be clean *(Tahor)."* All that the Torah is apparently saying is that the Mikvah itself is ritually clean, but not that it can purify a person. How do we know that it can?

In many places, when the Torah speaks of purification, it simply states, "he shall wash in the water, and he shall be clean.[18] Although no mention is made of Mikvah, we know from the Oral Torah that this washing refers to immersion in the Mikvah.

This can be understood from a relatively simple train of logic. Unless water is in a Mikvah, the water itself becomes unclean when it touches an unclean person. It would not seem logical that water which itself becomes unclean would render a person clean. Therefore, since the only water that cannot become unclean is Mikvah water, this must be the water purification.[19]

When the Torah speaks of ritual purification, the actual words it uses are *U'Rachatz BaMayim,* which literally translated means, "he shall wash in *the* water [and be clean.]" The Torah is not referring to *any* water, but to *the* water — special water. The only water that has a special status with regard to purity is that of the Mikvah.[20]

If there is still any question as to how one washes with the water of a Mikvah, the Torah specifies *(Leviticus 15:16),* "He shall wash *all his flesh* in the water." This clearly indicates that the entire body must come in contact with the water of the Mikvah.[21] It is from this that we also learn that there must be nothing intervening between one's body and the water. Any such intervention *(Chatzitzah)* renders the immersion invalid.[22]

The Torah furthermore states with regard to vessels (Leviticus 11:32), "Into the water it shall enter, and it shall be clean." We therefore see that the mode of purification is "entering the water," that is, immersion in a Mikvah. The same is true for a person.[23]

If we look carefully in the Torah, we find that the Hebrew word *RaChatz* — "to wash," — does not refer to a cleansing process, but rather to purification through water.[24] Therefore, a more accurate translation of *RacHatz* would be "to purify with water," rather than "to wash." Indeed, when we reverse the letters, we see that the word Rachatz is phonetically very closely related to the word TaHor, meaning "to purify." Thus, when the Torah says that one should *"RaChatz* in the water," it means that he should "purify himself in the water."

There is one place in the Bible where we clearly see that the meaning of the word *RacHatz* was generally accepted to mean immersion. When Naaman, an Aramanian captain, was struck with leprosy, he went to the prophet Elisha and asked for a cure. The prophet told him *(2 Kings 5:10),* "Go and wash *(RacHatz)* in the Jordan." He was just told to "wash" and nothing more. When Naaman finally took Elisha's advice, however, the Bible states that *(Ibid. 5:14),* "he went down and immersed *(taval)* himself in the Jordan." From this, we clearly see that *"washing"* was generally accepted to mean immersion.[25] These references from the written Torah reinforce the tradition of the Oral Torah, which is the source of all the laws involving Mikvah.

Next, we must discuss the size of a Mikvah. It obviously must be large enough for any person to immerse in it.

Like all other rules regarding Mikvah, the precise size is known from the Oral Torah, but at the same time, it is also alluded to in the written Torah. The Talmud derives it from a verse mentioned earlier *(Leviticus 15:16),* "He shall wash all his flesh in the water." The Talmud says that this is "water that takes in all his flesh . . . one *Amah* (cubit) by one *Amah* by three *Amos."* This, in turn, is said to be equal to 40 *Sa'ah,* (around 25 cubic feet or 200 gallons, as mentioned earlier.) [26]

One of the earlier authorities, Rabbi Yitzchok ben Sheshes (Rivash), explains this Talmudic statement in a most interesting manner.[27] There is a general rule that if something is mixed with twice its volume, it is considered to be nullified.[28] The largest normal human body has a volume of 20 *Sa'ah.* Therefore, the amount of water necessary to "nullify" this body is double this, or 40 *Sa'ah.* [29]

This fits very well with the concept that immersion in a Mikvah involves self nullification and rebirth. We see here, that this is true as a point of Jewish law, as well as from a philosophical viewpoint.

We stated earlier that the Hebrew word *Rachatz,* usually translated as "wash," is more accurately translated as "purify with water." Rabbi Samson Raphael Hirsch points out that it is also phonetically related to the word *Ra'atz,* which means to "overthrow" or "break down."[30] When the Torah speaks of "washing," it is essentially speaking of self-nullification and a "breaking down" of the ego, which is the essence of spiritual purification.

What we have outlined here is a general description of a Mikvah, and not a guide to making one. Those laws are extremely complex and only a rabbinical expert has the authority to supervise the design and building of a Mikvah.

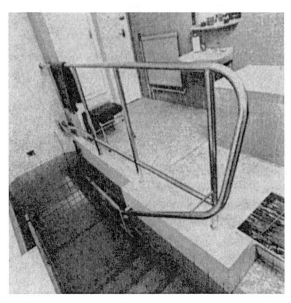

Steps leading down into the fresh, warm water of a Mikvah

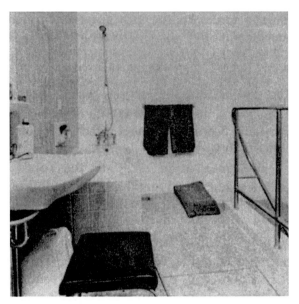

Modern bathroom facilities in the private Mikvah room

THE MYSTERY OF MIKVAH

Water

Up to this point, we have spoken mostly in symbolic terms. But we have a rule that the commandments, besides having symbolic value, also have profound spiritual effect on man.[1]

Closely linked to this idea is the teaching that everything in the physical world has a spiritual counterpart.[2] Every action in this world likewise has its counterpart in the spiritual realm. The spiritual counterpart of physical man is his divine soul. When man immerses in a physical Mikvah, his soul likewise becomes immersed in its spiritual counterpart. Before we can discuss this, however, let us first understand the spiritual nature of water.

One of the most obvious qualities of water is the fact that it is a liquid. Indeed, in a sense, water is the primary representation of the fluid state.[3] In many instances, when we speak of "water," we are actually speaking of the fluid state in general. Therefore, the spiritual counterpart of water is very closely related to its property of being a fluid.

But what is the main difference between a fluid and a solid? What special property does a fluid have that does not exist in the solid state?

The main difference between them involves change. If only solids were to exist, there would be no change at all. The world would be a dead, airless body in an unchanging frozen state.[4] For change to be possible, the fluid, as well as the solid state must exist.

If we only have fluids, however, we encounter another problem. Fluids are capable of change, but they do not have any permanence. A fluid will not hold any shape or configuration. If we had a world made only of fluids, there would be change, but no permanence.

Water, being the prototype fluid, is therefore the one substance that primarily represents change and instability. Indeed, when the Torah wants to speak of instability, it uses water as an example, as we find *(Genesis 49:4),* "Unstable as water."[5]

Life is a unique combination of change and permanence. A living thing is constantly changing, and yet, at the same time, it retains its identity. A person constantly undergoes change, and yet, he is still the same person.

Life is also a unique combination of solid and liquid; of course, the most important liquid in living things is water. Water dissolves the nutrients necessary for life, transports them to the various parts of the body, and then does the precise opposite with the body's wastes. Every movement that a living creature makes ultimately involves liquids. All creation contains these two essential spiritual opposites, permanence and change, represented physically by solid and liquid. The prototypes of these two states are earth and water respectively.

The Torah describes the world at the beginning of creation by saying, *(Genesis 1:2),* "The earth was formless and chaotic, with darkness on the face of the deep, and God's spirit causing motion on the face of the water." A few questions are immediately raised. Firstly, why is the idea of God's spirit and its connection to the water mentioned at all? Secondly, why is God's spirit primarily associated with water in this passage? Furthermore, the Hebrew word *MeRachefes,* which we translated as "causing motion," has the connotation of both causing motion and caring for something.[6] Why is this particular word used? Finally, why is this word used in the present tense, which seems to take it out of the context of the rest of the verse?

Before answering these questions, however, one thing must be made clear. In describing the six days of creation, the Torah is not attempting to provide us with a scientific description of how the world came into being. The Torah does not try to tell us those things that we can discover through our own intellect or through scientific observation. The Torah places man in perspective to the rest of creation and tells him how to relate to the rest of the universe. The Torah is concerned with the spiritual man and with teaching how the world relates to man with respect to God.

According to many authorities, the "water" mentioned in the first days of creation refers to the fluid state of the universe.[7] Before creation, change did not exist. God dwells in a realm above time, and the concept of change does not apply to Him in any way whatsoever. God thus told His prophet *(Malachi 3:6),* "*I* am God, I do not change."[8]

Therefore, one of the first ingredients of creation had to be the very concept of change. The newly created universe would be a dynamic, rather than a static entity. But change alone is not enough. Pure change can only result in chaos, and the Torah describes this initial state by saying, "the earth was formless and chaotic."[9]

Left alone, this chaotic fluid state could give rise to anything, good or evil. It was out of this chaotic state that the possibility of evil came into being, and this is alluded to in the next phrase, "and darkness on the face of the deep." This "darkness" is spiritual, rather than a physical,[10] and extended over the "deep," the depths of the "water" not influenced by "God's spirit."

In order for this concept of change to fit into God's general purpose of creation, and bring about spiritual enlightenment, it would first have to be brought under His constant control. The Torah describes this control by speaking of "God's spirit causing motion on the face of the water." The word, *MeRachefes,* used here also has the connotation of "caring for," since all of God's care for the universe is associated with His guidance of all change and development. This explains why the word *MeRachefes is* in the present tense, indicating that this guidance and providence is constant and continuous.[11]

In the very next verse, the Torah states *(Genesis 1:3),* "And God said, 'Let there be light,' and there was light." After God's providence was established, directing and guiding all change, spiritual enlightenment could be brought to the world.

The Midrash teaches us that this "spirit of God" which was over the waters refers to the "spirit of the Messiah."[12] The Messianic age represents the final fulfillment of God's purpose in creation. It is a time when evil will be vanquished, and good will reign over all mankind. Therefore, the "Spirit of God" that directs all change and movement is a positive force, moving the world toward its ultimate goal of perfection, which is the Messianic Age. (Incidentally, this is *not* in any way meant to identify God with the Messiah.)

On the second day, the Torah tells us that God divided the waters, separating them into the "upper waters" and the "lower waters." The Talmud teaches us that this division was sexual, with the "upper waters" representing the male element, and the "lower waters" representing the female.[13] This is the first place where we find the concept of male and female, representing the two elements of change, of the original "water."

This concept of male and female also alludes to the concept of conception, birth and growth. In giving the waters the attribute of being male and female, God gave them the ability to produce "children." The concept of change would not be haphazard, but would cause development in an organic manner.[14] Ultimately, every concept of "male" and "female" would develop from this.

On the third day of creation, the Torah tells us that God said *(Genesis 1:9),* "Let the waters under the heavens be gathered together to one place, and let the dry land appear." From the state of "water," that previously constituted the universe, a new concept appeared namely "dry land." In addition to fluidity and change, the concept of solidity and permanence also came into being.[15] This, in turn, would allow for the existence of life, and indeed, we find that the concept of plant life also came into existence on this same third day.

It is on this third day of creation that we see the source of the word Mikvah for the first time. The Torah speaks of the separated water and calls it a *Mikveh Mayim* — a "gathering of water." The Torah then says *(Genesis 1:10),* "to the gathering *(Mikveh)* of waters, He called seas."

The "gathering of water," consisted of the "water under the heavens," which are the "female waters" mentioned earlier. In order for the world to be able to produce life, these waters had to be "gathered to one place," which was called a Mikvah. Ultimately, this original "Mikvah of waters" represented the womb of all life. The scripture alludes to this when it says (*Job* 38:29,30), "Out of whose womb came the ice. . . the waters which congealed into stone."

We again see water as the concept of change and life in the account of Eden. The Torah says (*Genesis* 2:5-7), "All the bushes of the field had not yet come into being on the earth, and all the grass of the field had not yet grown, for God had not brought rain on the earth. . .. Then a mist rose from the earth, and watered the face of the ground. God then formed man out of the dust of the ground, and blew in his nostrils a soul of life."

Until God brought water to the earth, no life at all, not even plant life, was possible.[16] Man could be formed out of the "dust of the ground" only after water had entered the picture. As the Midrash teaches us, man is a combination of "dust and water," permanence and change. [17] As long as man is alive, this "water" is a most essential part of his being.

In contrast to this, when the Torah speaks of man's death, it says (*Genesis* 3:19), "you are dust, and to dust you shall return." "Earth" and "dust" refer to permanence, while "water" is change. When man is dead, all that is left is permanence — "dust" — since he can no longer grow and change.

The main spiritual concept of water is that of change and development. It represents the growth and development of the world toward fulfilling God's purpose, and, in this context, the Garden of Eden was "watered" spiritually as well as physically. As a result, it was an environment where man could grow and develop according to God's ultimate plan.

The waters of Eden therefore bring together a number of concepts. First of all, these waters represent the "womb" of humanity, since it was with this water that God "formed man of the dust of the earth." Secondly, these waters were the source of the "rivers" that left Eden, which gave man the ability to connect himself with his ultimate source, even in his fallen state, and thus grow toward God's goals.

Most important, we see that water itself represents the change and flow toward God's goal. When a person immerses himself in a Mikvah, he immerses himself spiritually in the basic concept of change itself. Man's ego represents the element of his permanence, and therefore, when he is totally immersed in the concept of change, his ego is nullified. Thus, when he emerges from the Mikvah, he is in a total state of renewal and rebirth.

Water represents two things at the same time. First, it represents change, impermanence and transience. But this very impermanence also means that no evil is ineradicable, and no sin unforgivable. One of the important teachings of Judaism is that repentance can wash away any sin, as the Jerusalem Talmud flatly states, "nothing can stand before repentance.[18] Water therefore also represents the concept of spiritual cleansing.

This is the meaning of the verse (2 *Samuel 14:14)*, "We must die, and as waters spilt on the ground, we cannot be gathered up. God does not respect any person, but He devises means so that no one should be banished from before Him." The concept of change is what makes our lives transient, so that we are like "waters spilt on the ground." But this same concept is what God uses to allow all evil to be expiated and forgiven. In essence, the Mikvah represents this spiritual cleansing and renewal.

Through water, everything is ultimately brought back to the fulfillment of God's goal. There may be "darkness on the face of the deep," but "God's spirit is causing motion on the face of the water" — in the present tense, indicating that this is a constant and continuous process. The main vehicle for this is the Torah, which, as our sages teach us, is also a spiritual counterpart of water.[19]

The Measure of Man

One of the laws of Mikvah is that it must hold at least forty Sa'ah, or approximately 200 gallons of water. In deriving this quantity of forty Sa'ah, we saw that in a sense, this was based upon a measure of man.

It is interesting to note that the concept of forty occurs a great many times in the Torah. The Flood of Noah lasted forty days,[20] Moses was on Mount Sinai for "forty days and forty nights" when he received the Torah,[21] and the Israelites similarly spent forty years in the desert.[22] There are many other places where we find the concept of forty in the Bible.[23]

Why is the number forty so important? Why do we come across this number as a duration of time so often in the Torah?

We find the beginnings of an answer in the laws of childbirth, as they applied in the time of the Holy Temple. The pain and infirmity associated with childbirth are an indication of the imperfection of human reproduction, and therefore, they bring about a state of "impurity" in a woman who has given birth. The Talmud states that one reason a woman had to bring a sacrifice after giving birth to a child was because she had so much pain that she would swear never again to bear a child.[24] Childbirth, and the pain associated with it, is related to man's imperfection and therefore requires "purification. "

In speaking of this purification, the Torah says (Leviticus 12:2,4), "When a woman conceives and bears a male child, she shall be unclean seven days, as the days of Niddah. . . And she shall continue. . . for thirty-three days. . .." Counting the days required for purification after childbirth, we find a total of forty.

Our sages teach us that these forty days represent the time

that an embryo takes to attain human form.[25] From a standpoint of Jewish Law, an embryo does not have any status as a human being until forty days after conception.[26] This concept is also sound from a scientific viewpoint, since it is well known that the human embryo begins to assume recognizable human form around the fortieth day after conception.

This helps explain why the flood described in the Torah lasted for forty days. According to the traditional interpretations, the main sin that brought about the flood was sexual immorality. The Midrash thus says that the flood lasted for forty days because the people of that generation "perverted the embryo that is formed in forty days."

It is interesting to note that the Zohar gives a similar reason for the fact that the punishment was through water. The division of the waters represent the original concept of sexuality in creation, with the "upper waters" as the male element, and the "lower waters" as the female. The generation of the flood perverted this basic concept of sexuality, and therefore, the "upper waters" and "lower waters" came together to punish them. The Torah thus says (Genesis 7:11), "The springs of the great deep were split open, and the windows of heaven were opened."[28] This same concept also applies to Mikvah, which can be made up of rain waters and spring waters.

The same concept also applies to the giving of the Torah. This also involves the idea of birth. The Jewish people were born anew under the covenant of the Torah, and the Torah itself, in being transmitted to man, had to undergo a birth process. As in the case of man, this was to take forty days.[29]

The same reasoning also explains why the Israelites spent forty years in the desert. When Moses sent spies to explore the Promised Land, the Torah tells us that (Numbers 13:25), "they returned from spying out the land at the end of forty days." The spies knew that the Israelites would undergo a spiritual rebirth when they entered the Promised Land. In order to experience this rebirth themselves and report on it, the spies spent forty days in the land. They were not worthy of the land, however, and therefore, they brought back a bad report.

As a result of this report, the Israelites rebelled against Moses, not trusting that God would give them the land. It was then decreed that they should spend forty years in the desert, as the Torah says *(Numbers 14:34)*, "Following the number of days in which you spied out the land — forty days — for every day, you shall bear your sins for a year — forty years." These forty years represent yet another kind of rebirth — the rebirth of an entire generation that would be worthy of eventually entering the Promised Land.

We see that the number forty represents the process of birth. As we have said, it is related to the measure of man. This also explains the forty *Sa'ah* of water that the Mikvah must contain. The Mikvah also represents the womb, and therefore, these forty *Sa'ah* parallel the forty days during which the embryo is formed.

In order to understand why birth and embryonic development always involve the number forty, we must introduce yet another concept. Creation consists of four stages, alluded to in the verse *(Isaiah 43:7)*, "All that is called by My Name, for My glory (1), I have created it (2), I have formed it (3), and I have made it (4)." These four stages are represented by the four letters of the Tetragrammaton, God's Name *Yud Kay Vav Kay.* [30] The first stage is "God's Glory," where things exist conceptually, but not in actuality.[31] The next stage is "creation," which represents creation *ex nihilo* — "something out of nothing." Then comes "formation" where the primeval substance attains the first semblance of form. Finally comes "making," where the process is completed and yields a finished product.[32]

Our sages also teach us that the world was created with ten sayings.[33] These are the ten times that the expression "and God said" appears in the account of creation.[34] Since these "ten sayings" enter into each of the four stages of creation, the total number of elements of creation is forty.[35] The number forty is therefore very intimately related to the concept of creation.

In enumerating the categories of "work" that are forbidden on the Sabbath, the Talmud teaches us that there are "forty less one."[36] As we know, these thirty-nine categories of "work" parallel the types of activity that went into creation, just as our own Sabbath rest parallels the Sabbath of creation. There is one type of "work," however, that we cannot duplicate, and that is creation *ex nihilo* — creating something out of nothing. This is the one category that is not included among the types of work forbidden on the Sabbath.

Otherwise, the categories of "work" represent the elements of creation — "forty less one."[37]

The four basic stages that we mentioned earlier are also alluded to in the "four branches" of the river from Eden. As we have discussed, this river is very intimately related to the concept of Mikvah.

The forty *Sa'ah* of the Mikvah represent the basic elements of creation. The primeval stage of creation was basically one of water. Therefore, when a person passes through the forty *Sa'ah* of water in the Mikvah, he is passing through the initial steps of creation.

The Letter of Transition

We have seen that Mikvah entails two basic concepts, namely, water and the number forty. Both of these concepts are contained in a single letter, namely, the Hebrew letter *Mem*.

The letter *Mem* derives its name from *Mayim*, the Hebrew word for water. Furthermore, the numerical value of the letter *Mem is* forty. Therefore, it is not very surprising to learn that the letter *Mem is* also said to represent the Mikvah.[38]

Another concept that we find associated with the letter *Mem is* that of the womb.[39] The closed (final) *Mem is* the womb closed during pregnancy, while the open *Mem is* the open womb giving birth.[40] The numerical value forty, associated with *Mem,* then also represents the forty days during which the embryo is formed.

In order to understand the meaning of this letter on a deeper level and see how it relates to Mikvah, we must delve into a most interesting Midrash. The Prophet says (Jeremiah 10:10,) "The Lord, God, is Truth *(Emes)."* The Midrash then gives the following explanation:[41]

What is God's seal? Our Rabbi said in the name of Rabbi Reuven, "God's seal is Truth."

Resh Lakish asked, "Why is Emes (אֱמֶת) the Hebrew word for truth?"

He replied, "Because it is spelled *Aleph Mem Tav* (אמת). *Aleph (א)* is the first letter of the Hebrew alphabet, *Mem (מ) is* the middle letter, and *Tav (ת)* is the last letter of the alphabet. God thus says *(Isaiah 44:6), "I* am first, and I am last."

From this, we see that the letter *Mem* has a most interesting property. *Aleph,* the first letter of the alphabet, represents the beginning. *Tav,* the last letter, represents the end. *Mem is* the letter that represents transition.

We see this most clearly in the word *Emes* (אֱמֶת) itself. The first two letters, *Aleph Mem* (אֵם), spell out *Em,* the Hebrew word for mother. This is the beginning of man. The last two letters, *Mem Tav* (מֵת), spell out *Mes* — the Hebrew word for death — the end of man.

Most important here, *Mem* represents the concept of transition and change. *Aleph is* the past, and *Tav* the future, so *Mem* represents the transition from past to future. As such, it is the instant that we call the present.

The past is history and cannot be changed. We have no way of even touching the future. Therefore, the arena of action, where all change takes place, is the present. Symbolic of water, the essence of change as well as the number forty, the essence of birth, the letter *Mem* also represents the present — the transition between past and future — which is the arena of all change. On a deeper level, the transition from past to future also represents an aspect of birth. Indeed, one word for "future" in Hebrew is *HaNolad,* which literally means, "that which is being born."[42] The womb in which the future is born is the present. This is the letter *Mem.*

Thus, when a person enters the Mikvah, he is actually entering the concept of the ultimate present. Past and future cease to exist for him. What he was in the past no longer counts. Even the forty days of formation are no longer an expanse of time, but a volume of water — forty *Sa'ah.*[43] Then, when he emerges from the Mikvah, he reenters the stream of time as if he were a new being.

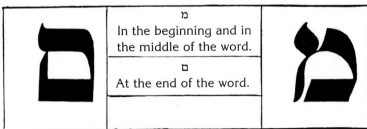

	מ	
	In the beginning and in the middle of the word.	
	ם	
	At the end of the word.	

The Ultimate Mikvah

Rabbi Akiba said: Happy are you, Israel. Before whom do you purify yourselves? Who purifies you? Your Father in heaven! It is thus written (Ezekiel 36:25), "I will sprinkle pure water upon you, and you shall be clean." And it is written (Jeremiah 14:8), "God (HaShem) is Israel's Mikvah." Just as the Mikvah purifies the unclean, so God purifies Israel.

Mishneh, Yoma 8:9 (85b)

Even though we have delved quite deeply into the concept of Mikvah, Rabbi Akiba's statement still seems quite puzzling. How are we to understand his declaration that "God is Israel's Mikvah?" Furthermore, in this verse, the word *Mikveh* actually means "hope,"and not a Mikvah filled with water, and therefore, the actual translation of the quoted passage is, "God is Israel's hope." What is Rabbi Akiba actually teaching us here?

In order to find the answer to this question, we must first understand the significance of God's name. In the Torah, we find that God is most usually called by two names. The first is *Elokim,* usually translated as "God." The second is the Tetragrammaton, which we read as *Ad-noy* or *HaShem,* and often translate as "the Lord" or "the Eternal." Each one of these Names has a very special significance.

The Name *Elokim* represents God as the Ruler of the universe. The same word — *Elokim* — is therefore also used for judges and angels.[44] We interpret *Elokim* to mean "master of all power," indicating God's relationship to the universe, constantly interacting with it and giving it existence.[45] When the Name *Elokim is* used to express God's relationship to man, it indicates that He is acting with strict justice.[46]

The Name *Hashem,* on the other hand, represents God as

the ultimate source of all existence, high above the universe and its laws.[47] We interpret this Name as indicating that God, "was, is, and will be."[48] It speaks of Him as existing completely beyond the realm of space and time. Past and future are exactly the same as the present for God, and indeed, He sees the entire expanse of time in a single glance "[49] Thus, when we make use of the Name *HaShem,* we are really saying that God, "was, is, and will be" all at once. Past and future are exactly the same as the present for Him.

The Name *HaShem is* also associated with God's attribute of mercy.[50] This, however, is closely related to the concept of His existence outside of time.

One of the most important teachings of Judaism is that of repentance. No matter how great a sin a person might have committed, his slate can be wiped completely clean if he sincerely repents before God. This, in essence, is also the concept of God's mercy.

There is, however, a very difficult question associated with the idea of repentance. Let us say that a person committed murder, or did some other irreparable harm. How can his repentance undo the damage that has already been done? We can see, perhaps, how the sin can be forgiven, but how can the slate be wiped completely clean?

The author of *Sefer Halkkarim* provides us with a very profound answer to this question.[51] The guilt for every wrongful deed is very dependent upon the motivation accompanying it. For example, there is a great difference between an individual who kills another person out of hate, and one who does so accidentally. Indeed, there are times when killing can be justified and virtuous, such as when it is necessary to stop a would be murderer.[52] There are many conceivable motivations that could mitigate acts which would otherwise be considered sinful.

Therefore, although the damage itself cannot be undone, the motive can be reappraised. When a person repents, he regrets his wrongdoing, and his repentance now is counted as his motive when he did this wrong. The Talmud thus teaches us that, "repentance is great, since it can make purposeful sins to be counted as accidental ones."[53]

Still, this answer does not remove the difficulty completely. How can my regret at this moment be transferred to a deed that I did a long time ago? How do we remove the barrier of time that separates the regret and the deed?

We, of course, cannot do this, since we are bound by time. But God can. God is completely outside of time, and, therefore, He can simply overlook the time barrier between the deed and the regret, and count the two together.

This is the concept of God's mercy. In erasing sin, God is above time, bringing past and present together. Both of these concepts — God's mercy and His existence outside of time — are contained in His Name *HaShem.* [54]

On a deeper level, the Name *Hashem* indicates that God is observing man from a perspective outside of time. He is judging the individual with respect to his future as well as his past, as well as in the context of the entire past and future of all creation.

We therefore see that when we use the Name *HaShem,* we are indicating that God is the ultimate present. Through this Name, which indicates "was, is, and will be" — all at once — both the past and future are also included in the present.

In this context, there is no difference between past, present and future. Just as the present can be altered and rectified, so can the past — and even the future. This represents the ultimate freedom. As long as a person is bound to the concept of *HaShem,* he is free of both the past and the future.

As we mentioned earlier, the Mikvah is connected to the concept of the letter *Mem,* which represents the present. The Name *HaShem,* however, draws everything into the present even the past and the future. It is a spiritual level where past, present and future are one, and where the evil of the past can be expiated by the regret of the present.

This is the meaning of Rabbi Akiba's declaration that *"HaShem is* Israel's Mikvah." Just as Mikvah represents the present, the Name *HaShem* represents a concept where the "present" even includes the past and future. Therefore, *HaShem is* the ultimate Mikvah. [55]

As we have pointed out, however, the word *Mikveh* in this context is actually more properly translated as "hope." How is this related to the Mikvah of water? The verse itself indicates this relationship, since it says (*Jeremiah* 17:13), "God (*HaShem*) is Israel's hope (*Mikvah*). All who forsake You shall be ashamed (dried up). . . because they have forsaken God, the Fountain of living waters."

Why does the Hebrew language use the same word for hope as for Mikvah?

But what is hope? It actually represents our feelings toward an event in the future. When we hope that some future event will happen, we are dealing with something that is beyond the barrier of time. We therefore say that our hope is *HaShem* — the Name that we use when we speak of God as existing outside of time. For *HaShem,* there is no barrier between present and future, and therefore, when we associate with Him, our hope can likewise pierce the barriers of time. Therefore, hope, like the concept of Mikvah, is that which places us outside the limitations of time. In both cases, we do so through the power of HaShem.

As we know, the word Mikvah actually means a *"gathering."* Taken in this context, it is also a gathering of time — a gathering of past and future into the present, making them both accessible to us.[56]

On a simpler level, as discussed earlier, the concept of Mikvah is related to that of self negation. When a person places all his hope in God, however, this in itself is a profound negation of one's ego.

Rabbi Samson Raphael Hirsch writes that the Hebrew word *Tumah,* which we usually translate as "unclean," belongs to a phonetic family of words relating to the lack of freedom and independence.[57] Thus, all things associated with ritual un-cleanness are things that indicate man's lack of freedom. Of all these, death is the ultimate, since it represents man's ultimate subjugation to the laws of nature.

The ability to transcend the bonds of time, on the other hand, is the ultimate freedom. Therefore, when a person enters the Mikvah, he enters a state where past, present and future are "gathered together," and is therefore ultimately free. He is no longer bound by either past or future, but exists in an absolute present, which is the one instant of time over which man has control. Therefore, the freedom of Mikvah overcomes the lack of freedom associated with *Tumah.*

Ultimately then, all purification comes from God's unity, which extends into time as well as every other aspect of existence. God's unity in time is precisely what we have been discussing, that He is one and the same in past, present and future, and therefore, conversely, past, present and future are all the same to Him.

This is the ultimate concept of the purification of the Mikvah. The scripture speaks of this when it says, (*Job* 14:4), "Who can bring the clean out of the unclean, if not the One?"[58]

NOTES

INTRODUCTION

1. Cf. *Turey Zahav (Taz)*, *Yoreh Deah* 268:8.
2. See *Biur Halachah, Orech Chaim* 468:4 *"VeChomrey."*
3. See Rashi, *Yoma* 67b *"Chok,"* Rashi, Ramban, on Numbers 19:1, *BaMidbar Rabbah* 19:1, *Pesikta* 4 (40b). The root of this word is *Chokek*, meaning "to rule" or "to decree," cf. Genesis 29:10, Numbers 21:18, Judges 5:9, Isaiah 33:22. For a general discussion of the three categories, see *Yoma*, 67b, *Sifra* on Leviticus 18:4, Rashi on Genesis 26:5, Leviticus 18:4, 20:26; Rambam, *Shemonah Parakim* #6, *Yad, Meilah* 8:8; Ramban on Leviticus 16:8, Deuteronomy 6:20; Radak on 1 Kings 2:3; *Emunos VeDeyos* 3:2 (54a), *Kuzari* 2:48 (55a), *Ikkarim* 1:17.
4. *Yad, Mikvaos* 11:2, *Chinuch* 159. See note 11.
5. *Yoma* 67b.
6. *Shabbos* 68a.
7. *Ibid.*
8. Rashi *ad loc.* Cf. *Sifra* on Leviticus 20:26, Rambam, *Shemonah Parakim* #6, *Chayay Adam* 68:18. Also see *Maharitz Chayos* on *Rosh HaShanah* 16a, Rambam on *Makkos* 3:16, *Chovos HaLevavos* 3:3.
9. *Yad, Tumas Ochlin* 16:8, *Moreh Nebuchim* 3:47, *Kuzari* 3:49 (55a). See Numbers 19:13,20.
10. *Yad, Mikvaos* 1:1-3. Also see *Pesachim* 16a, *Sefer HaMitzvos*, postive commandment 109.
11. *BaMidbar Rabbah* 19:8, *Tanchuma Chukas* 8, *Pesikta* 4 (40b). See *Megilas Esther* (on *Sefer HaMitzvos*) positive commandment 96.
12. *Yad, Temurah* 4:13, *Tshuvah* 3:14, *Mikvaos* 11:12; *Moreh Nebuchim* 327, 3:31; Ramban on Leviticus 19:19, Deuteronomy 22:6, *Chinuch* 545, Ibn Ezra on Exodus 20:1, *Tosefos Tom Tov* on *Berachos* 5:3, *Etz Yosef* on *VaYikra Rabbah* 27:10, *Devarim Rabbah* 6:1, *Maharitz Chayos* on *Sotah* 14a. Cf. *Tosefos, Sotah* 14a, *Chulin* 5a *"Kedey,"* *Gittin* 49b *"R. Shimon, "* Maharam *ad loc., Tosefos Yom Tov* on *Sanhedrin* 8:6,10:5. Also see *Baba Kama* 79b, *Baba Metzia* 3a, *Milchamos HaShem* (Ramban), *Rosh HaShanah* (Rif 11a) "VeOd."
13. *Yerushalmi Nazir* 7:2 (35a), *Maharam Di Lanzano, Shiurey Karban, ad loc., Shiltey Giborim, Avodah Zarah* (Rif 6a) #1, *Shnei Luchos HaBris, Torah SheBaal Peh, K'lal Drushim VeAgados* (Jerusalem 5720) 3:241a, *Terumos HaDeshen* 108, *Shiurey Berachah, Yoreh Deah* 183:1.
14. *Yad, Mikvaos*, 11:2, *Sefer HaChinuch* 175.
15. Exodus 29:4, *Targum J.*, Rashi, Hirsch *ad loc.* Cf. Exodus 40:12, Leviticus 8:6.
16. Leviticus 16:4, 24, *Targum J.*, Rashi *ad loc., Yoma* 3:3,4 (30a), 3:6 (34b), 7:3, 4 (70a). Cf. Rabbi Nathan of Nemerov, *Likutey Halachos (Yoreh Deah) Hechsher Kelim* 4:33.
17. Rashi, *Yebamos* 47b *"Sham Ger."* See, however, Rashba *Ibid.*
18. *Yebamos* 47b. Note that the basic act of purification is *emerging* from the Mikvah, see *Kesef Mishneh, Avos HaTumah* 6:16, *Makor Chesed* (on *Sefer Chasidim*) 394:3. Cf. Ran, *Nedarim* 76b (top) *"U'Mehadrin, "* Tosefos, *Shabbos* 35a *"VeYarad."*

19. *Yebamos* 22a, 48b, 62a, 97b, *Bechoros* 47a, *Tosefos, Sanhedrin* 71b "Ben", *Yad, Edos* 13:2, *Issurey Biah* 14:11.
20. *Reshis Chochmah, Shaar HaAhavah* 11 (New York, 5728) 92b. [From a Kabbalistic viewpoint, Mikvah is associated with the Name *Eheyeh (I Will Be)*, which, when "filled" with the letters *Heh,* adds up to 151, the numerical equivalent of Mikvah. *Shaar HaKavanos, Inyan Tevilah Erev Shabbos* (Ashlag, Tel Aviv 5722) p. 25, *Shaar Ruach HaKodesh* (Ashlag, Tel Aviv 5723) p. 36, *Shnei Luchos HaBris, Shaar HaOsios, Kedushah* 1:168a, *Shaarey Gan Eden, Shaar HaOsios, Mem* (95a), *Keser Shem Tov #2, Sefer Baal Shem Tov, Yisro* 11, *Pri HaAretz* (Menachem Mendel of Vitebsk) on *Lech Lecha;* HaGra on *Tikuney Zohar* 19 (37a) *"Inun," Likutey Halachos (Yoreh Deah) Melichah* 1:4. This Name, however, is associated with the womb of *Binah,* see *Etz Chaim, Shaar Huledes Abbah Velmah* 3(1:236), *Shaar HaYereach* 3(2:176), *Adir BaMarom* 90a. Mikvah is also associated with the Name *ELeD,* which literally means "I will be born." *Keser Shem Tov, loc. cit.]*
21. *Ohalos* 7:4, 5 *Chulin* 4 3 (71a), *Yad, Tumas Mes* 25:12.
22. *Sefer HaChinuch* 173, *Likutey Halachos (Yoreh Deah) Nedarim* 2:11, *Mikvah* 1:1, *Hechshar Kelim* 4:12; *Dover Tzedek* (R. Tzaduk of Lublin) p. 7b; Hirsch on Exodus 29:4, Leviticus 11:47. See *Berashis Rabbah* 4:1, 5 2, *Yerushalmi Chagigah* 2:1 (8b), *Zohar Chadash* 12a, Rashi on Genesis 1:1, Psalm 104:3.
23. *Yalkut Shimoni* 1:3 (on Genesis 1:8), *Keses HaSofer* (R. Aaron Marcus) on Genesis 1:2, *Likutey Halachos (Yoreh Deah) Mikvah 1.*
24. *Chulin* 89a.
25. *Likutey Halachos loc. cit.* 1:1, *Dover Tzedek loc. cit.*
26. *Yoma* 85a, *Bechoros* 46b, from Genesis 7 22.
27. *Likutey Halachos (Yoreh Deah) Hechshar Kelim* 4:20 (143c).
28. *Likutey Halachos, loc. cit.* 4:18,38. Cf. Proverbs 30:16.
29. *Shabbos* 129a, *Niddah* 21a, *Ohalos* 7:4.
30. *Sifra* on Leviticus 11:36.
31. *Terumos* 9:7, *Maasros* 5:2, *Pesachim* 34a, *Yerushalmi Maasros* 5:1 (22b), *Sifra* on Leviticus 11:38, *Yad, Tumas Ochlin* 2:19, *Kesef Mishneh ad loc.*

WHEN THE MIKVAH IS USED

1. Rashi on Leviticus 15:19, *Targum* on Leviticus 12:12, 15:19, Rashbam, Bachya, Hirsch, on Leviticus 12:12, Ibn Ezra on Numbers 19 9, Radak on Isaiah 30:22; Rashi, *Shabbos* 64b *"BeNidasa."*
2. *Sefer HaMitzvos,* negative commandment 348.
3. Leviticus 20:17, *Sefer HaMitzvos,* negative commandment 331.
4. Exodus 12:15, 19, Leviticus 23:29, 31, *Sefer HaMitzvos,* negative commandments 196, 197.
5. *Zohar* 2:142b, *Nefesh HaChaim* 1:18, *Likutey Amarim (Tanya)* 3:5 (95b), *Or HaChaim* on Leviticus 17:10. For further discussion, see *Emunos VeDeyos* 9:9 (8a), Ramban on Leviticus 15:31, 18 29, *Shaar HaGamul* 78a, from *Rosh HaShanah* 17a, Bachya on Genesis 18:25, Abarbanel on Numbers 15:23.
6. *Sanhedrin* 90b, *Makkos* 13b, Yad, *Tshuvah* 6:2, Rashi on Numbers 15:31, *Pri Megadim,* introduction to *Orech Chaim* 3:19.

7. *Targum J. ad loc., Torah Temimah* on Leviticus 15:33. Cf. *Yad, Issurey Biah* 4 3,11:16, from Leviticus 15:18, cf. *Sifra ad loc.* A Niddah is in the same category as a Zav, and therefore, her purification is the same, cf. Ramban on Leviticus 15:23. The *Gaonim* derive this immersion logically from the fact that even the things that a Niddah touches must be immersed, see *Tosefos, Yebamos* 47b *"BaMakom,"* *Chagigah* 11a *"Lo Nitzracha,"* *Yoma* 78 *"MiKan,"* *Sefer Mitzvos Gadol (Smag),* positive commandment 248, *Hagahos Maimoni* on *Yad, Issurey Biah* 4 3, Bachya on Leviticus 15:19.

8. Rashi, *Yebamos* 47b *"Chotzetz."* Cf. *Kuzari* 3:49 (55a).

9. *Avodah Zarah* 75b, *Tosefos loc. cit.*

10. Radak ad loc., Yoma 78, *Yerushalmi Shekalim* 6:2 (6a), Hirsch on Numbers 31 23.

11. *Niddah* 31b. This, however, is not the only reason, and therefore, the laws of Niddah apply equally well to an *unmarried* girl. See *Sefer HaChinuch* 95, *Toras HaShelamim (on Yoreh Deah)* 183:4, *Tiferes Yisroel (Keresei U'Plesei)* 183 3, *Darkey Tshuvah (on Yoreh Deah)* 183:13.

12. *Yoreh Deah* 183:1 in *Hagah*.

13. *Shaarey Tshuvah* (R. Yonah) 3 95.

14. *Tshuvos Rivash* 425.

15. *Targum 1.*, Rashi, Ramban, *ad loc., Sotah* 37b, *Shavuos* 37a. See Joshua 8:33,34.

16. *Shavuos* 29a, Maharsha *ad loc. "KeSheHishbia, "* Rashash *ibid., Nedarim* 25a. Also see *Nedarim* 8a, *Nazir* 4a, *Yad, Nedarim* 3:7, *Shavuos* 113, *Shach, Yoreh Deah* 119:22, HaGra, *Yoreh Deah* 228:99, Maharitz Chayos on *Nedarim* 8a, *Nazir* 4a.

17. *Kerisus* 9a, *Yad, Issurey Biah* 13:1.

18. See Exodus 12:48, Joshua 5:5, *Yebamos* 71b. Also see Radal (on *Pirkey DeRabbi Eliezer*) 29:1, 49; Ramban, Rashba on *Yebamos* 46a *"SheKen."*

19. *Mechilta,* Ramban *ad loc., Yebamos* 46b, *Yad, loc. cit.*

20. Radak, Abarbanel *ad loc.*

21. *Kerisus* 9a, *Yad, Issurey Biah* 13:4.

22. *Yebamos* 46b, *Tosefos ad loc. "Mishpat," Yad, Issurey Biah* 13:6, *Yoreh Deah* 268:3, *Shach ad loc.* 268:8,9.

23. *Sifri* (32) on Deuteronomy 6:5, *Avos DeRabbi Nathan* 12:8, *Berashis Rabbah* 39:14, *BaMidbar Rabbah* 14:1, Rashi on Genesis 12:5.

24. *Berashis Rabbah* 84:4, Bachya on Genesis 12 5.

25. *Zohar* 1:102b. Cf. *Sifra,* Rashi, on Leviticus 15:11, *Yad, Mikvaos* 1:2. Also see *Shaar Ruach HaKodesh p.* 36.

26. Rashi on Genesis 18:4, *Baba Metzia* 86b.

27. *Avodah Zarah* 5:12 (75b), *Yad, Maachalos Issuros* 17 3, *Yoreh Deah* 120.

28. *Yerushalmi, Avodah Zarah* 5:15 (37b). Cf. *Torah Temimah* on Numbers 31:23 #32.

29. *Yoreh Deah* 121:1.

30. *Yoreh Deah* 120:3, Meiri, *Avodah Zarah* 75b, Rosh, *Pesachim* 1:10, Mordecai, *Pesachim* 538, *Avodah Zarah* 849 (note).

31. In *Yad, Maachalos Issuros* 17:5, this is called a law from *Divrey Sofrim*. In general, the Rambam uses this expression to denote any law that is derived from the Oral Torah, see *Sefer HaMitzvos, Shoresh* 2 (26b), *Kesef*

Mishneh on *Ishus* 1:2. Therefore, we find that *Tshuvos Rashba* 3:255, quoted in *Bais Yosef, Yoreh Deah* 120 (191b), maintains that the Rambam takes it to be a Torah law, *cf. Lechem Mishneh ad loc.* However, see Ran, *Avodah Zarah* (Rif 39b) *"Mishkanta"* who writes that the Rambam takes it to be a rabbinical law, see Meiri, *Avodah Zarah* 75b, Radbaz, *Kesef Mishneh,* on *Yad, loc. cit. Terumas HaDeshen 156 (quoted in Bais Yosef, loc. cit.)* and Raavad (quoted in Ran, *loc. cit.* and *Toras HaBayis* 4:4) maintain that it is a Torah law, *cf. Chidushey Hagahos* on *Tur, Yoreh Deah* 120:6, Meiri, *Avodah Zarah* 75b. Ramban on Numbers 31:23, writes that it is a rabbinical law, *cf.* Hirsch on Leviticus 11:32. *Tosefos,* quoted in notes 7 and 9, however, clearly must hold it to be a Torah law.

32. *Sifri ad loc., Avodah Zarah* 75b, *Orech Chaim* 451.4.
33. *Targum J.,* Rashi, Ibn Ezra, Ramban, *ad loc., Avodah Zarah* 75b.
34. *Berachos* 55a, *Chagigah* 27a, *Minachos* 97a, *Orech Chaim* 167:5 in *Hagah, Magen Avraham* 180:4. See Ezekiel 41:22.
35. Hirsch on Numbers 31:23.
36. *Cf. Zebachim* 9:7 (86a), 87a, from Exodus 30:29, *Yad, Pesuley HaMik-dashin* 3:18.
37. *Yoreh Deah* 268:12 in *Hagah,* 267:8 in *Hagah, Taz* 267:5, *Magen Avraham* 326:8, *Machatzis HaShekel ad loc.; Nimukey Yosef Yebamos* (Rif. 16b) *"Kidushav,"* Maharil, *Erev Yom Kippur* (44a), *Avos DeRabbi Nathan* 8:8. Also see *Tshuvos HaGaonim (Shaarey Tzedek)* 3:6:8 (24b), *Tshuvos Rashba* 5:6, *Makor Chesed* (on *Sefer Chasidim*) 203:1.
38. Mordecai, *Yoma* 723, Rosh 8:24, *Rokeach* 214, *Sefer Chasidim* 394, *Abudraham, Erev Yom Kippur* (p. 279), *Maharil loc cit., Menoras HaMaor* 5:2:2:1 (295), from *Pirkey DeRabbi Eliezer* 46; *Orech Chaim* 606:4, *Taz* 606:5, *Beer Hetiv* 606:68, *Tshuvos Chavas Yair* 181.
39. *Orech Chaim* 581:4 in *Hagah; Kol Bo* 64 (p. 27a).
40. *Zohar* 2:204a, *Yesod VeShoresh HaAvodah* 8 (Yerusalem 5725) p. 213, *Shaar HaKavanos* 2:25, *Shnei Luchos HaBris* 1:167a.
41. *Sefer Chasidim* 394, *Rokeach* 214 (p. 103), *Shnei Luchos HaBris* 1:167a, *Maharil loc. cit., Magen Avraham* 606:8, *Taz* 606:5. The three times are Genesis 1:10, Exodus 7:10, and Leviticus 11:36. God is also called the "Mikvah" of Israel in three places, Jeremiah 14:8, 17:13, 50:7.

A DEEPER LOOK

1. *Emunos Ve Deyos* 1:4 (end), 3:0, *Sefer HaYashar 1, Pardes Rimonim* 2:6, *Etz Chaim, Shaar HaKelalim 1, Reshis Chochmah, Shaar HaTshuvah 1, Shnei Luchos HaBris, Bais Yisroel* 1:21b, *Shomrei Emunim (HaKadmon)* 2:13, *Derech Ha Shem* 12:1. See *God, Man and Tefillin, p.* 35.
2. This entire discussion is taken from *Derech HaShem* 1:2.
3. *Cf. Mechilta* on Exodus 14 29, *Berashis Rabbah* 21:5, *Shir HaShirim Rabbah* 1:46, *Yad, Tshuvah 5:1.*
4. *Derech HaShem* 1:2 2. *Cf. Midrash Tehillim* 26:3, 36:4, *Reshis Chochmah, Shaar HaYirah* 7 (22bk *Sanhedrin* 39b, *Berashis Rabbah* 9:12-14. See Isaiah 45:7, *Derech HaShem* 1:5:8; *Bahir* 13, *Moreh Nebuchim* 3:10, *KaLaCh Pischey Chochmah* 39 (24b). Also see *Akedas Yitzchok* 70 (3:145b), *Etz Chaim, Shaar HaMelachim 5, Sefer Baal Shem Tov, Sh'mos* 9.
5. *Chulin* 60b. *Cf. Shefa Tal* (Brooklyn 5720) 2c.

6. *Targum J.* on Genesis 2:15, *Yalkut ad loc.* 22, *Sifri* on Deuteronomy 11:33, Alshich, Bachya, *ad loc.*
7. *Kiddushin 4:14* (82a).
8. *Nefesh HaChaim 1:5* (6a), note: *"VeHaInyan."* Cf. *Zohar* 1:35b.
9. *Ibid.*
10. *Ibid.* 7a. Cf. Abarbanel *ad loc., Berashis Rabbah* 16:6. Also see *Avodah Zarah* 5a, *Avodas HaKodesh 2:21* (41d).
11. *Berachos* 5a, *Succah* 52a, *Kiddushin* 30a, *Zohar* 1:190a, 3:268a.
12. See *Adir BaMarom* 11a.
13. *Kiddushin* 30b, *Sifri* on Deuteronomy 11:18; *Baba Basra* 16a.
14. *BaMidbar Rabbah* 13.2, *Shir HaShirim Rabbah* 5:1, *Pesikta Rabosai* 5 (18b).
15. *Yad, Tumas Ochlin* 16.8, *Moreh Nebuchim* 3:47, *Kuzari* 3:49 (55a).
16. Rashi on Numbers 19:13, *Shavuos* 16b; *Sifra,* Rashi, on Leviticus 17:16, *Yad, Biyas HaMikdash* 3:12.
17. Cf. *Yad, Mikvaos* 11:12, *Shnei Luchos HaBris, Shaar HaOsios, Taharah* (1 :108a).
18. *Derech HaShem* 1:5:9, 4:6:2, *Kav HaYashar* 17. See Leviticus 16:30, Jeremiah 33:8, Ezekiel 14:11, 20:43, 36:7, Psalm 51:4, Proverbs 20:9, Job 4:17. In particular, Tumah is associated with sexual immorality, and indeed this is the first context in which we find the word in the Torah in Genesis 34:5. Also see Leviticus 18 24, Numbers 5:13, 14, 27, 28, Ezekiel 18:6, 22:11, Hoseah 5:3, 6:10.
19. Cf. Numbers 19:13 ff., Leviticus 11:8, 24, 31, 39, 21:1. See Alshich on Leviticus 21:1.
20. Alshich, *loc. cit., Likutey Halachos (Yoreh Deah) Mikvaos* 1:1.
21. *Alshich loc. cit.* Cf. *Zohar* 3:47a, 3:79a.
22. *Bechoros* 55a. See Malbim on Genesis 2:10.
23. *Pirkey DeRabbi Eliezer* 20 (47b).
24. Midrash, quoted in *Yalkut Reuveni* on Genesis 2:10 (31b); *Likutey Halachos (Yoreh Deah) Giluach* 4:16, *Hechshar Kelim* 1:2. Cf. *Shaarey Orah* 8 (83b), that this river is *Binah,* which is also associated with Mikvah. See Jeremiah 31:8, *Tikuney Zohar* 12a. See *BaMidbar Rabbah* 18:21, *where the* Midrash derives *the fact that a* Mikvah must contain 40 Sa'ah from (Isaiah 8:6), "The waters *of* Shiloach, that go slowly *(L'at)."* The numerical value *of* the word *L'at is* 40. Shiloach, however, is identified with Gichon, one *of* the rivers from Eden, cf. Targum 1. on 1 Kings 1:33, 38, 45, Rashi, *Berachos* 10b, *"Sasam,"* Radal on *Pirkey DeRabbi Eliezer* 20:30.
25. *Tikuney Zohar 19* (39a), *Kisey Mlech* (61b #2). HaGra, *ad loc., Shnei Luchos HaBris, Shaar HaOsios, Kedushah* 1:166b, *Sefer Baal Shem Tov, Yisro* 11.
26. *Derech HaShem* 1:3:5,1:3:8, 2.4 2, 2:4:6, *Adir BaMarom* 11a.
27. *Avos* 5:2.
28. *Sh'mos Rabbah* 30:13, Maharzav on *Berashis Rabbah* 32:5.
29. Cf. *Berachos* 7b, *Sotah* 10b, *Berashis Rabbah* 31:21, Rashi on Genesis 12:5, Maharitz Chayos on *Chagigah* 3a. Also see *Yalkut* 1:766, *Yoma* 28b, *Yad, Avodas Kochavim* 1:3.
30. *Zohar* 1:75a, Alshich on Genesis 11:1.

31. *Derech HaShem* 2:4:3.
32. Sifri, Bachya, Alshich, *Or HaChaim, ad loc.*
33. *Avodah Zarah* 2b, *Mechilta* on Exodus 20:2, Sifri, *Targum J.* Rashi, Ramban, on Deuteronomy 33:2, *Sh'mos Rabbah* 27:8, *BaMidbar Rabbah 14:22, Eichah Rabbah* 3:3, *Tanchuma, Yisro 14, Shoftim 9, Zos HaBeracha 4; Pirkey DeRabbi Eliezer 41* (95b), *Pesikta* 29 (186a), *Zohar* 2:3a, 3:192b.
34. See "When Mikvah is used," note 20.
35. Cf. *Likutey Halachos (Yoreh Deah) Avadim* 2:9.
36. *Likutey Halachos (Yoreh Deah) Niddah* 1:3, *Giluach* 4:16, *Mikvah* 1:1. See Zechariah 14:8, Bachya on Numbers 19:16.
37. Bantam Books, New York 1970, p. 25.
38. Abarbanel *ad loc.*, Rashi Sforno, Alshich, on Genesis 2:25, *Moreh Nebuchim* 1:2, *Reshis Chochmah, Shaar HarKedushah* 16 (196b).
39. *Shabbos* 32a, *Eruvin* 100b, *Yerushalmi, Shabbos* 2:6 (20a), *Berashis Rabbah* 17:8, *Tanchuma, Metzorah 9.*
40. *Kiddushin* 2b. Cf. *Tosefos ad loc. "deAssar."*
41. Rashi, *Sanhedrin* 82a *"Kodesh,"* Rashi, Rashbam, on Genesis 38:21, Rashi, Ibn Ezra, Hirsch, on Deuteronomy 23:18. Cf. 1 Kings 14:24,15:12, 22:47, 2 Kings 23:7, Hoseah 4:14, Job 36:14.
42. *Tiferes Yisroel* (Maharal) #2. Cf. *VaYikra Rabbah* 27:10, *Derech Mitzvosecha* (Chabad) p. 9b.
43. *Likutey Halachos (Yoreh Deah) Niddah* 2:7.
44. Genesis 17:14, *Kerisos* 1:1 (2a), *Yad, Milha* 1:1.
45. Cf. Leviticus 18:29, *Kerisos* 2b, *Yad, Issurey Biah* 1:1, *Sefer HaMitzvos* negative commandment 352.
46. *THE ROAD TO RESPONSIBLE JEWISH ADULTHOOD,* by Rabbi Pinchas Stolper, page 12.
47. Cf. *Sanhedrin* 7tb, *Midol;* 3:4, *Berashis Rabbah* 5:10, *Mechilta,* Rashi, Ramban, on Exodus 20 22. Metal also represents the concept of money and commerce, cf. *Baba Metzia* 4:1, *Likutey Halachos (Yoreah) Hechshar Kelim* 3:3.
48. *Likutey Halachos, loc. cit.* 1:2.
49. *Ibid.* 4:13.
50. Cf. Alshich on Leviticus 14:8. The main concept of clothing is wool and linen *(Shabbos* 26b, *Yebamos* 4b, *Minachos* 39b). Since these have no place in water, everything in the sea is clean. Cf. *Sifra* on Leviticus 13:48, Bertenoro *on Negaim* 11:1, *"Oros HaYam,"* Kelim 17:13.

WHAT IS A MIKVAH

1. The word Mikvah alone occurs only once in the Bible, in Isaiah 22:11. Otherwise, it is usually called a "gathering *(Mikveh)* of water." Cf. Genesis 1:10, Exodus 7:10.
2. *Yerushalmi, Chagigah* 18 (7a).
3. *Yoreh Deah* 201:23. See note 9.
4. *Yoreh Deah* 201:6. See *Pesachim* 16b, *Sifra* on Leviticus 11:36 (#143), Tosefos, *Pesachim* 17b *"Eleh,"* Baba Basra 66b *"MiKlal,"* HaGra on *Yoreh Deah* 198:29, 201:29.

5. *Yoreh Deah* 20:12, *Sifra* on Leviticus 11:36 (#145), *Yad, Mikvaos* 10:16, Rashi, *Shabbos* 65b *"VeSavar," Tosefos, ibid'. "Shema,"* Rashi, *Niddah* 67a *"Mikvaos," Tosefos, Bechoros* 55a *"Shema."* Cf. *Mikvaos* 1:7, 5:4, 5, *Tosefos, Chagigah 11a"BaMey."*

6. *Yoreh Deah* 201:3, *Sifra* on Leviticus 1136 (#143). There is a question as to whether the fact that drawn water renders a Mikvah unfit is a rabbinical law *(DeRabanan)* or a Torah law *(DeOraisa)*. The accepted opinion is that if the majority of the water is drawn, then the Mikvah is unfit from Torah law, while if only a minority is drawn, it is unfit by rabbinical law; *Yoreh Deah* 2013 in *Hagah, Shach* 201:141, *Taz* 201:81. See *Tosefos, Baba Basra* 66b *"MiKlal,"* R. Gershom *ibid.,* R. Yaakov, quoted in *Sefer Mitzvos Gadol (Smag)*, positive commandment 248, R. Shimon, quoted in *Shiltey Giborim, Shavuos* (Rif 5a) #1, Rosh, *Baba Kama* 7:3, *Mikva'os* 1 (after *Niddah*), *Tshuvos HaRosh* 31:11, Ritva, *Pesachim* 17b. Also see Rashi, *Baba Kama* 67a, Rashbam, *Baba Basra* 66b *"LeOlam."* Another opinion, however, maintains that the entire rule forbidding drawn water is only rabbinical, see *Yad, Mikvaos* 4:1, 2, R. Yitzchok, quoted in *Tosefos, Pesachim* 17b *"Eleh," Baba Basra, loc. cit.,* Ran, *Shavuos* (Rif 5a), Bertenoro on *Mikvaos* 2:3. A third opinion is that of R. Shimshon, who concludes that drawn water is only unfit by Torah law if it also violates rule 6, and is drawn with vessels that can become unclean, R. Shimshon (Rash) on *Mikvaos* 2:3, *Tosefos Yom Tov ibid.,* Ran *loc. cit.* A final opinion is that of the Raavad, who maintains that if water is drawn by vessels alone, it is only unfit by rabbinical law, but if drawn by man, then it is unfit by Torah law. Raavad, quoted in *Shitah MeKubetzes, Baba Kama* 67a, Ran, *loc. cit.* For a general discussion, see *Bais Yosef, Yoreh Deah* 201 (p. 97b).

7. *Yoreh Deah* 201:34, *Shach* 201:76, *Taz* 201:43. See *Zevachim* 25b, R. Shimshon, Bertenoro, on *Para 6:4, Mikvaos 5:5;* Rosh, *Mikvaos 5:12, Tshuvos HaRosh 31:7.* R. Shimshon on *Mikvaos* 2:3 writes that this is a Torah law. Raavad, however, quoted in *Shitah MeKubetzes,* Ran, *loc. cit.,* maintains that this is merely a rabbinical law. There is an opinion that this requirement only applies to "living water." *(Mayim Chayim),* see Mordecai, *Shabuos 746,* Rambam on *Eduyos 7:4, Parah 6:4, Mikvaos 5:5, Yad, Parah Adumah 6:8, Mishneh Acharonah* on *Parah loc. cit., Bais Yosef, Yoreh Deah* 201 (p. 109b) *"VeHaRambam,"* Chidushey R. Chaim HaLevi on *Yad, Mikvaos* 9:9 (end). Raavad on *Eduyos 7:4* seems to concur with this opinion, but maintains that in the case of Mikvah, this is a rabbinical law, as mentioned earlier. For a complete discussion, see *Tshuvos Chasam Sofer, Yoreh Deah 199.*

8. *Yoreh Deah* 201:1. This is equivalent to three cubic *Amos,* see note 26. According to *Taharos Mayim* 20a, quoted in *Shaarim Metzuyanim KeHalacha* (on *Kitzur Shulchan Aruch)* 37:14 (#2), this is equivalent to 191 gallons. This is based on an *Amah* of 24.5 inches. Estimates of the *Amah,* however, usually vary between 18 and 24 inches. An 18 inch *Amah* yields 61.4 gallons, while a 24 inch *Amah* yields 177 gallons for the capacity of a Mikvah. Except in an emergency, however, the measure of 191 gallons should be abided by. This would mean that the volume of the *Bor* should be at least 25 cubic feet.

9. *Chulin* 84a, *Sifra* on Leviticus 11:36 (#146).
10. *Yerushalmi, Berachos* 9:5 (67b). Cf. Rashi, *Baba Basra* 14a "*Ain Miut,*" Maharshal *ad loc.*
11. Rashbam, Ramban, Malbim, Hirsch *ad loc., Pnai Yehoshua, Pesachim* 16a "*Chad DeTelushin.*" Cf. *Sifra* on Leviticus 11:34 (#136), Hirsch *ibid.*
12. Cf. *Sifra ad loc.* #143.
13. *Sifra ad loc.* See note 5.
14. *Yoreh Deah* 201:2. See *Shabbos* 65b, *Nedarim* 40a, *Bechoros* 55b, *Niddah* 87a.
15. We see that *Mikveh Mayim* refers to the container as well from Genesis 1:10. See Bachya *ad loc.,* from Isaiah 119, where we find that the water "covers the sea."
16. *Zevachim* 25b. See note 7.
17. *Parah* 5:8, *Mikvaos* 6:7, *Yebamos* 15a, *Chagigah* 21b; *Yad, Mikvaos* 8:5, 6, *Yoreh Deah* 201:40, 52.
18. Exodus 29:4, 40:12, Leviticus 8:6,11:32,14:8, 9:15:5,6,7,8,10,11,12, 13, 16,17, 18, 27;16:4, 24, 26, 28;17:15, 22:6, Numbers 19:7, 8, 19; 31:23, Deuteronomy 23:12. In three places, however, we find that "washing" does not refer to Mikvah, see Leviticus 19, 1:13, 621, but these are specifically excluded, see *Sifra ad loc.*
19. Malbim *ad loc.* #143. Cf. Hirsch *ad loc.* See *Sifra* (#145), Rashi, *ad loc.,* Rashi, *Pesachim* 16a "*Yihyeh,*" R. Chananel *ibid.,* Rashi, *Chulin* 84a "*Ach Mayin.* "
20. Rashi, *Chagigah* 11a "*BaMayim,*" Rashbam, *Pesachim* 109a "*KeDe-Tanya,*" Mizrachi, *Sifsey Chachamim,* on Exodus 24:9. Cf. *Sifra* on Leviticus 14:8. Also see *Tosefos, Chagigah* 11a "*BaMey.*"
21. This cannot refer to water taken from the Mikvah, since as soon as it is removed, it can become unclean. See *Eruvin* 4b, Rashbam, *Pesachim* 109b "*Kal Basaro,*" Hirsch on Exodus 29:4, *Yad, Mikvaos* 1:7.
22. *Eruvin* 4b, *Yad, Mikvaos* 1:12. Cf. *Sifra,* Rashi, on Leviticus 15:11.
23. *Yoreh Deah* 201:1, *Sifra* (#122) on Leviticus 1132, Hirsch *ibid., Sefer Mitzvos Gadol (Smag)* positive commandment 248. Cf. *Sifra* on Leviticus 22:6, Rashi, *Eruvin* 4b "*Kal Basaro.*" If any part of the body is not covered by the water, it remains unclean, and in turn makes the rest of the body unclean, *Reshis Chochmah, Shaar HaAhavah* 11 (92a); *Chesed LeAvraham,* quoted in *Taamey HaMinhagim* B26 (p. 501).
24. Cf. Isaiah 1:16. Even the "washing of the feet" in Genesis 18:4 refers to immersion in a Mikvah, see *Zohar* 1:102b. Likewise, the washing of Joseph's face in Genesis 43:31 refers to the washing away of a mood, see Targum J. *ad loc.* The same is also true of the washing of Pharoah's daughter in Exodus 2:5, see *Sotah 12b, Sh'mos Rabbah* 1-.23, *Tanchuma, Sh'mos* 7.
25. Indeed, Targum on 5:10 and 5:13 renders *Rachatz* (wash) as *Taval* (immerse). See *Torah Temimah* on Leviticus 15:33.
26. *Eruvin* 4b, 14b, *Yoma 31a, Chagigah 11a, Pesachim* 109a.
27. *Tshuvos Rivash* 292-295, quoted in *Tshuvos Chasam Sofer, Yoreh Deah* 209. See *Mikvaos* 6:3.
28. *Gittin* 58b. Cf. *Yoreh Deah* 109:1.

29. The *Gemorah* thus says that the human body is "elevated" *(Olah)* in 40 *Sa'ah*. The expression *Olah,* however, also refers to nullification *(Bitul),* as we find in *Terumos* 4:7 and other places.

30. Hirsch on Exodus 30:18. Cf. Exodus 15:6, Judges 10:8. It is also related to the word *Lachatz* (to crush), see Targum on Judges 10:8.

THE MYSTERY OF MIKVAH

1. *Zohar* 1:24a, 3:86b, 3:99b, *Likutey* Amarim *(Tanya) 1:4* (8a), *Nefesh HaChaim* 1:6 (note *"VeYadua"),* 2:6, Anaf Yosef on *Yoma* 8a (in *Eyin Yaakov* #23). Cf. *Sh'mos Rabbah* 20:18, *Tanchuma, Mishpatim 3; Koheles Rabbah* 2:26, 3:16, 5:24, 8:16. Also see Isaiah 3:10, *Zohar* 3:29b, 3:227a (end), 3:224 (end).

2. *Derech HaShem* 1:5:2, *Etz Chaim, Shaar MaN U'MaD* 3 (229a). With relation to Mikvah in particular, see *Reshis Chochmah,* Shaar *HaAhavah* 11.

3. See Hirsch on Genesis 1:9, *Jeshurun* 7:118, 436, 474. Also see *Moreh Nebuchim* 2:30, Abarbanel, introduction, on Genesis 12, *Likutey Halachso (Yoreh Deah) Hechshar Kelim* 4:12.

4. Motion may exist, as in a planetary system or clockwork, but this motion is cyclic and cannot result in change.

5. Cf. Rashi, Malbim, *Torah Temimah, ad loc., Shabbos* 55b. In *Berashis Rabbah* 98:4, we see that this refers to Mikvah in particular.

6. Rashi, Abarbanel (introduction), *ad loc.,* Rashi on Deuteronomy 32:11, *Targum J.,* Rashi, Radak, *Metzudos, on* Jeremiah 23:9. See *Chagigah* 15a; *Etz Chayim, Shaar RaPaCh Nitzutzin* 1 (255a).

7. *Yerushalmi, Chagigah* 2:1 (8b), *Mechilta* to Exodus 15:11, *Berashis Rabbah* 4:1, 5 2, *Sh'mos Rabbah* 15 22, *Midrash Tehillim* 104:7, from Psalm 104:3. Cf. Job 28:20.

8. *Yad, Yesodey HaTorah* 1:11, *Moreh Nebuchim* 1:11.

9. Ramban,Likutey *Torah* (HaAri), *Shaar HaPesukim, ad loc., Berashis Rabbah* 2:5, *Bahir* 2, *Zohar* 1:16a, 3:305b, *Etz Chaim, loc. cit., Likutey Halachos (Yoreh Deah) Hechsher Kelim* 4 38.

10. Ibid. See *Tanchuma, VaYeshev* 4.

11. See Maharzav on *Berashis Rabbah* 2:4, *"Bris Kerusah."* With regard to how this is related to Mikvah, see *Sefer HaChinuch 173, Likutey Halachos, loc.* cit. 4:12, 4:38.

12. *Berashis Rabbah* 2:4, *Zohar* 1 :192b. Cf. *Tosefos,* Avodah *Zarah* 5a *"Ki Ruach. "* 13. *Yerushalmi, Berachos 9:2* (65b), *Taanis* 1:3 (4b); from Psalm 42:8; *Berashis Rabbah* 13:13, *Pirkey DeRabbi Eliezer* 23 (43a), *Etz Chaim, Shaar MaN U'MaD* 1 (p. 221). See note 28.

14. Cf. Isaiah 48:1, Targum, Radak, *ad loc.* Also see Zohar 1:30a, from Job 38:20.

15. Hirsch on Genesis 19, Radal on *Berashis Rabbah* 5:10 #7. Cf. *Moreh Nebuchim* 2:30.

16. Thus, the final formation of plant life actually took place on the sixth day, see *Chulin* 60b, *Berashis Rabbah* 13:1, Rashi, Ramban, on Genesis 2:5; *Zohar* 1:46b, 1:97a, 2:128. Cf. *Sifra* on Leviticus 26:4.

17. *Yerushalmi Shabbos* 2:6 (20a), *Berashis Rabbah* 14:1, *Sh'mos Rabbah* 30:13. Man was created from male and female elements, see *Berashis Rabbah* 14:7. Also see Rashi on Genesis 6:7.

18. *Yerushalmi, Peah* 1:1 (5a), *Sanhedrin* 10:1 (49a).

19. *Baba Kama* 17a, Rashi on Isaiah 41:17. See *Zohar* 1 25a, that water is the Torah, and its vessel is Israel. Also see Ezekiel 43 2, Amos 8:11, Proverbs 17:14, Job 14:19. For how this relates to Mikvah, see *Berachos* 16a, *Tanna DeBei Eliahu Rabba* 18 (90a), Alshich on Leviticus 14:8, *Nefesh HaChaim* 121, *Likutey Halachos (Yoreh Deah) Mikvaos* 1:2, 4: 24.

20. Genesis 7:4,12,17, 8:6.

21. Exodus 23:18, 24 28, Deuteronomy 9:9,11,18, 25,10:10. We also find that the Tablets weighed forty *Sa'ah, Yerushalmi* Taanis 4:5 (23a), Tanchuma, *Ki* Tisa 26.

22. Exodus 16:35, Deuteronomy 2:7, 8:2, 4, 29:4, Joshua 5:6.

23. Thus, Isaac was forty years old when he married Rebecca (Genesis 25:20), Esau was forty when he married (Genesis 26:34), Jacob was embalmed for forty days (Genesis 50:3), the land was quiet for forty years in the time of the Judges (Judges 3:11, 5:31, 8:28), Elijah fasted for forty days (1 Kings 19:8, *Tanchuma, Sh'mos* 14), during the Babylonian exile, the land was desolate for forty years (Ezekiel 4:6, 29:11,12). For other important cases, see *Zohar* 1:136b.

24. *Niddah* 31b.

25. *Kerisus* 10a, *Niddah* 30a.

26. *Niddah* 3:7 (30a), 15b; *Mishneh LaMelech* on Yad, *Tumas Mes* 2:1, *Shach, Choshen Mishpat* 210:1, *Tshuvas Toras Chesed, Even HaEzer* 42:33, *Tshuvos Bais Shlomo, Choshen Mishpat* 132. Also see *Ohalos* 18:7, Bertenoro, R. Shimshon, *ad loc.,* Rashi, *Pesachim* 9a "Arbayim Yom." The Talmud also euphemistically speaks of conception as being "forty days before the formation of the fetus," *Berachos 60a, Sotah 2a.*

27. *Berashis Rabbah* 32:5, Rashi on Genesis 7:4. Cf. *VaYikra Rabbah* 23:12.

28. *Zohar* 1:61b.

29. *Bereshis Rabbah* 32:5, *Likutey Halachos (Yoreh Deah) Nedarim* 2:11. See *Zohar* 1:136b.

30. *Pardes Rimonim* 16:1, 19:*2, Shaarey Kedushah* 3:6, *Derech HaSheim* 4:6:13. These are the four universes, Atzilus (Emanation), *Beriah* (creation), Yetzira (formation) and Asiyah (making or action). *31. Derech HaShem,* ibid. This is the world of *Sefiros* (Emanations).

32. Radak on Isaiah 43:7, *Nefesh HaChaim* 1:13 (note *"U'Lefi").*

33. *Avos* 5:1.

34. These are Genesis 1:3,1:6,1:9,1:11,1:14,1:20,1:24,1:26,1:28, and 1:29.

35. *Reshis Chochmah,* Shaar *HaAhavah* 11, *Shnei Luchos HaBris,* Shaar *HaOsios, Taharah* (1:108a). In Kabbalah, this refers to the four Yud's in the Name adding up to 72 (Ab). See sources quoted in part 1, note 20. This is closely related to the fact that Adam, Eve, the Serpent, and the earth, each received ten punishments, making a total of forty. See *Pirkey DeRabbi Eliezer* 14, *BaMidbar Rabbah 5:5,* Tanchuma, *BaMidbar* 23, *Zohar* 3 280b.

36. *Shabbos* 7:2 (73a).

37. Cf. HaGra *ad loc.* The forty categories of work parallel the forty times that the word *Malachah* (work) appears in the Torah, *Shabbos* 49b, *Yerushalmi Shabbos* 72 (42a). One of these forty, however, is not counted.

38. *Tikuney Zohar* 19 (39a), according to reading of *Kisey Melech*, HaGra *ad loc.*, *Adir BaMarom* 89b, *Reshis Chochmah, Shaar HaAhavah* 11 (92a), *Shnei Luchos HaBris, Shaar HaOsios, Kedushah* 1:168a. For the relationship of *Mem to* water, see *Sefer Yetzira* 3:4, *Zohar* 2:159b, *Likutey Moharan* 51, *Likutey Halachos (Yoreh Deah) Gerim* 3:4. Gramatically, the Hebrew word *Mayim is* literally the plural of the plain letter *Mem.*

39. *Sefer Yetzira* 3:4, *Bahir* 85, *Etz Chaim, Shaar HaYereach* 3 (p. 176).

40. *Bahir* 84.

41. *Berashis Rabbah* 81:2. Cf. *Shabbos* 55a.

42. *Avos* 2:9, *Tamid* 32a. See *Adir BaMarom* 37b.

43. Note that the word *Sa'ah is* phonetically related to *Sha'ah,* meaning "hour." Actually, it is the surface of the Mikvah that is involved in the purification, and this surface represents the interface between past and future. This surface is represented by the Name *Eheyeh,* which literally means "I will become." See *Keser Shem Tov* 2, and other references in part 1, notes 18 and 20.

44. *Moreh Nebuchim* 1:2, 2:6, *Kuzari* 4:1 (2b), Ibn Ezra on Genesis 1:1, Exodus 3:15, 33:21, Ramban on Exodus 3:13.

45. *Orech Chaim* 5:1, Cf. *Likutey Amarim (Tanya)* 2:6 (80a), *Nefesh HaChaim* 12.

46. *Mechilta* on Exodus 15:2, *Sifra* on Leviticus 18:2; *Berashis Rabbah* 33:3, 73:3, *Midrash Tehillim* 47:2, *Pesikta* 22 (151b), Rashi on Genesis 1:1, Hoseah 14:2, *Rokeach* 200.

47. *Likutey Amarim (Tanya)* 2:4 (79a), *Nefesh HaChaim* 2:2 (end). Cf. *Moreh Nebuchim* 1:61.

48. *Orech Chaim* 5:1, HaGra *ad loc.*, *Shnei Luchos HaBris, Bais HaShem* 1:40b, *Mesechta Shavuos* 2:100a.

49. *Rosh HaShanah* 18a. Cf. Rambam, *Tosefos Yom Tov, Rosh HaShanah* 12.

50. See note 46. Also see *Taz, Orech Chaim* 6212, *Pri Megadim ad loc.*

51. *Ikkarim* 4.27. Cf. *Nesivos Olam, Tshuvah* 5.

52. *Sanhedrin* 8:7 (73a).

53. *Yoma* 86b. Cf. *Etz Yosef* (in *Eyin Yaakov* # 76) *ad loc.*

54. See Rashi on Exodus 34:6, *Rosh HaShanah* 17b, that the doubling of God's name in this verse, "HaShem, HaShem," means that God is the same before and after the sin. The idea that the Name *HaShem* relates to mercy is derived from this verse, see *Berashis Rabbah 33:3, 73:3.*

55. *Likutey Halachos (Yoreh Deah) Milah* 4:23. See Ezekiel 36:29, *Yalkut* 2:627, *Tikuney Zohar* 19 (39a), *Keser Shem Tov* 2, *Baal Shem Tov, Yisro* 11. The water of the Mikvah therefore alludes to the letters in God's Name, see references in part 1, note *20*.

56. See Hirsch on Genesis 19.

57. Hirsch on Leviticus 5:13, 7:20,11:43.

58. *Targum ad loc.*, Rashi, *Niddah* 9a *"Lo Echad, " Likutey Moharan* 51. Cf. *Zohar* 1:12a, Ezekiel 37:23.

Typical structure of a modern Mikvah